General David S. Stanley, USA

ALSO BY DENNIS W. BELCHER
AND FROM MCFARLAND

*The 11th Missouri Volunteer Infantry in the Civil War:
A History and Roster* (2011)

*The 10th Kentucky Volunteer Infantry in the Civil War:
A History and Roster* (2009)

EDITED BY DENNIS W. BELCHER
AND FROM MCFARLAND

*"This Terrible Struggle for Life": The Civil War Letters of a
Union Regimental Surgeon* by Thomas S. Hawley, M.D. (2012)

General David S. Stanley, USA
A Civil War Biography

Dennis W. Belcher

Foreword by Michael R. Bradley

McFarland & Company, Inc., Publishers
Jefferson, North Carolina

LIBRARY OF CONGRESS CATALOGUING-IN-PUBLICATION DATA

Belcher, Dennis W., 1950–
General David S. Stanley, USA : a Civil War biography / Dennis W. Belcher ; foreword by Michael R. Bradley.
    p. cm.
Includes bibliographical references and index

ISBN 978-0-7864-7645-9 (softcover : acid free paper) ∞
ISBN 978-1-4766-1624-7 (ebook)

1. Stanley, David Sloane, 1828–1902. 2. United States—History—Civil War, 1861–1865—Campaigns. 3. Generals—United States—Biography. 4. United States. Army—Biography. I. Title.
E467.1.S79B45 2014
355.0092—dc23   [B]   2014015175

BRITISH LIBRARY CATALOGUING DATA ARE AVAILABLE

© 2014 Dennis W. Belcher. All rights reserved

No part of this book may be reproduced or transmitted in any form or by any means, electronic or mechanical, including photocopying or recording, or by any information storage and retrieval system, without permission in writing from the publisher.

Union General David Stanley, engraving by J.C. Buttre (U.S. Army Heritage and Education Center); *Battle of Franklin. November 30, 1864*, Kurz & Allison, Art Publishers, 1891 (Library of Congress, LC-USZC4-1732)

Printed in the United States of America

*McFarland & Company, Inc., Publishers
Box 611, Jefferson, North Carolina 28640
www.mcfarlandpub.com*

To the
Stanley family—
soldiers and wives of soldiers
and
to Helen Johnson,
who taught me
there is no kindness
too small

Table of Contents

Acknowledgments   ix
Foreword by Michael R. Bradley   1
Preface   5

1. Early Life and the Wilson's Creek Campaign   7
2. New Madrid and Island No. 10   30
3. The Siege of Corinth   45
4. The Battle of Iuka   62
5. The Battle of Corinth   75
6. The Battle of Stones River   92
7. Middle Tennessee and Tullahoma   124
8. The Advance on Chattanooga and the Battle of Chickamauga   142
9. The Atlanta Campaign   169
10. Spring Hill and Franklin   196
11. Post–Civil War   217

Conclusion   243
Chapter Notes   251
Bibliography   262
Index   267

Acknowledgments

It is truly an honor to write about the life of David Stanley. In doing so, I have wanted to acknowledge the legacy of military service of his family. I am particularly thankful to Joanne Holbrook Patton and Marni Roberson for their comments and insights regarding their famous ancestor and for reviewing the final chapter of this book.

There were many people who contributed to the completion of this project. I want to thank Jonathan Webb Deiss for his assistance with materials from the National Archives. I also want to thank Paul Kurazawa and Donald Fair for their contributions with the David Stanley materials in the West-Stanley-Wright Papers at the United States Army Heritage Center in Carlisle, Pennsylvania. I am very grateful to Cynthia Zippo for her assistance with the Holbrook, Stanley and Rumbough papers at the United States Military Academy at West Point, New York. In addition, Nan Card, Curator of Manuscripts at the Rutherford Hayes Presidential Library, was especially helpful in searching and locating materials regarding David Stanley.

The Special Collections and Archives Department at West Point provided remarkable and valuable support in locating materials regarding David Stanley's life. David Stanley loved the United States Military Academy and it seems fitting that so much material was preserved there. I am deeply indebted for the efforts of Susan Lintelmann, Manuscripts Curator, and Suzanne Christoff, Associate Director for Special Collections and Archives, at West Point.

Megan Mitchell, Oberlin College, was also very helpful in locating materials which were very important to this work. Steve Nielsen, Minnesota Historical Society, provided valuable information about the David Stanley materials located in that collection. I also want to thank Olivia Nagel—who has authored material about Anna Stanley's art—for her insight into the life of the Stanley family. Nancy Miller, Assistant Director of Development, Buffalo Seminary, was very helpful in locating information about the education of the Stanley family. Martin Callahan, Fort Sam Houston Museum, also provided important information about David Stanley's time as commander of the Department of Texas. I also want to thank Molly Kodner, Associate Archivist, Missouri History Museum and Research Library, for her efforts in finding materials for this book.

I am very fortunate to have had the advice of Jim Lewis, Tom Parson and Connie Langum of the National Park Service; all are experts on the Civil War events summarized in this book. These are knowledgeable individuals whose contributions were invaluable.

They graciously reviewed the chapters of this book relating to their areas of expertise. In addition, Charlie Crawford, president of the Georgia Battlefields Association, knows more about the Atlanta Campaign than anyone I know and reviewed the section on that topic. Eric Jacobson, author, historian and expert on the Battle of Franklin, reviewed the section relating to that battle and also the actions at Spring Hill. Jeff Patrick and Connie Langum, Wilson's Creek National Battlefield, continue to support the history of the Civil War and have always been on hand to offer their support and assistance to me. Connie Langum and Missouri historian and author Robert Schultz reviewed and offered their insights on the chapters relating to the actions at Wilson's Creek and the Island Number 10 Campaign. For the efforts of all these individuals, I am forever grateful.

I also want to thank Keith Beason, historian, for his advice regarding the section on the Battle of Resaca, and I thank Ashley Adair, archivist at the Austin History Center, for her hard work in obtaining information about David Stanley in Texas. Deborah Wood, Museum Curator, Wilson's Creek National Battlefield, was of great help in locating and sharing photos used in this book.

This is my third collaboration with George Skoch, mapmaker extraordinaire. I cannot say enough good things about his maps, which are an invaluable component to any Civil War history, and I am always grateful to have the benefit of his skill and dedication.

Finally, I want to thank Michael Bradley, professor emeritus and author of numerous books on the Civil War, for contributing the foreword to this book.

Foreword

by Michael R. Bradley

If one were to ask the proverbial man on the street to identify David S. Stanley there is little doubt the response would be a blank stare. If the question were asked of those identified as Civil War buffs the response would not be much better. David S. Stanley is one of the almost-forgotten men of United States history. But he should not be. During the Civil War, and afterward as well, David Stanley played an important role in securing the Union victory and in opening the western frontier to settlement and development. Too much of the study of the history of our nation has been allowed to revolve around well-known figures while the contributions of hundreds of competent, dedicated patriots have been allowed to languish. Dennis Belcher takes a step in rectifying this situation in his biography of David S. Stanley.

The death of Stanley's mother and the remarriage of his father made Stanley's childhood something of a search for love, security, and identity, especially when the economic condition of the family forced him to live with a neighbor at an early age. While these circumstances were not uncommon on the frontier, they were still events which affected the developing character of the young man. When the opportunity to attend West Point Military Academy came his way it should not be a surprise that Stanley found in the United States Army the stable home he desired.

Even stable homes have moments when relationships are less than smooth, and the long career of Stanley in the armed forces is no exception. Since political alliances can affect military careers, it is no surprise that Stanley found himself disgusted when men of lesser ability were given command of troops as a reward for political service. As, even in the most loving family, the members of the family sometimes squabble, it is not surprising that Stanley spent his share of time and ink engaging in disagreements with other members of the officer corps. The presence of such rough patches do not lessen the love Stanley displayed for his country or for his chosen profession.

Professional military men, by long-standing honorable tradition, serve the nation and hold their personal political opinions in abeyance in public. As we look back one hundred fifty years to the events leading up to the Civil War it is a cause for wonder that army officers were so often silent on issues we consider full of moral import, especially the issue of slavery.

It is tempting to allow our moral concerns to be exported backward in time to become the template by which the people of the past are measured; yet this would be a false and misleading way to attempt to understand the past. History is rather like swimming in muddy water: things are seldom as clear as we would like for them to be.

Stanley's attitude toward slavery is a good example of this point. There is no question that David Stanley disliked much of what he observed in the practice of slavery. He spoke of slaveowners "bullying" slaves and commented that the ownership of slaves gave the owners an arrogant attitude in their relations with those who were of the same race as the owners. There is no question that Stanley supported the policies of the United States government as those policies evolved toward making emancipation and abolition goals of the war effort. Yet, it is a historical fact that David Stanley hired three slaves from their owner and purchased two to help care for his own family. Stanley continued to own these two slaves until late 1862 when his wife took them with her on a trip to Detroit. While there the two made their way into Canada. While recognizing the incompatibility of the ideas of human rights and the ownership of slaves, Stanley could not resist the temptation of making life easier for himself and his wife by owning slaves. Like us all, David S. Stanley was a man whose life exhibited contradictions.

Stanley was also a man on a spiritual pilgrimage, a search for personal meaning which transcends the present. Born into a family which, by tradition, followed the Reformed Protestant ideas of Calvinistic theology and worshiped in the Presbyterian church, Stanley became a practicing Roman Catholic. This change in religious affiliation was made in 1862 when Stanley was a general officer with a solid combat record and was done in a very public fashion. This change was also made at a time when Catholics faced a great deal of discrimination in political and social life in the United States. The fact that Stanley followed his conscience and his convictions, regardless of the cost, speaks highly of his character.

In the prewar army, Stanley served in the cavalry on the western frontier. When the Civil War began he found himself called on to command infantry, units whose men were volunteers. Stanley rose to the challenge of imparting a professional attitude and a professional appreciation for discipline to volunteer troops. In the process of teaching his men the skills and attitudes they needed for survival, Stanley won the admiration and even the love of his command. This made him a rare officer and is a testimony to his ability as a soldier as well as his character as a man.

But the demands of the service did not allow Stanley to remain an infantry officer. In late 1862, when William S. Rosecrans took command of the Army of the Cumberland, an efficient, competent officer was needed to create an effective cavalry for service in Tennessee. Stanley made the transition from commander of infantry to commander of cavalry smoothly and successfully. In less than six months he had reorganized the structure of Rosecrans' cavalry from scattered regiments to an effective corps. He also showed his grasp of the importance of developing technology by arming the cavalry with revolving pistols and breech-loading carbines even as the army developed a mobile strike force of mounted infantry which carried Spencer repeating rifles. This reorganized cavalry force would begin to make the Union cavalry in the west a force which could counter the Confederate riders led by Wheeler and Forrest.

At the beginning of the Atlanta Campaign, Stanley was again assigned to an infantry command, in which role he behaved with his usual efficiency and ability. At the Battle of

Jonesboro, however, Stanley found himself assigned to envelop the Confederate corps of William J. Hardee only to find his route blocked by three brigades which had strongly entrenched their position. Stanley recognized that the position was too strong to be taken by direct assault and sought another route to follow to his objective. That route was not to be found. William Sherman decided that the fault was not that Stanley confronted stout defenses but that Stanley was "slow," perhaps because of a reluctance to fight. Such an assessment was far off the mark. At no time during the war was there ever any legitimate question as to Stanley's personal bravery or his willingness to lead his men into fierce combat. He had always put himself in exposed positions to supervise and to encourage his men. He had led from the front in hand-to-hand fighting at Stones River, and he had been in the thick of the fight at numerous locations in the Atlanta Campaign. During the Nashville Campaign of 1864 Stanley put up a tremendously brave defense at Spring Hill, using a single division to hold open the Franklin Pike and to protect the army's train of 800 supply wagons. Without the stand made by Stanley at Spring Hill there would have been no battle at Franklin, Tennessee, on November 30, 1864, and there may well have been a major Confederate success at Nashville. As it turned out, not only did Stanley allow the U.S. forces to make a withdrawal to Franklin, he made a major contribution to their victory there, riding to the front to lead an attack which restored the lines near the Carter cotton gin on the Columbia Pike. Though it was not bestowed until 1893, Stanley was awarded the Medal of Honor for his actions at Franklin.

In the following chapters readers will be led through a careful description of the life of David S. Stanley, including minutely constructed battle accounts of the numerous conflicts in which Stanley fought. The description of his postwar career gives insights into the settling and development of the American West and depicts the routine of military garrison life. The life of David Stanley does not provide a record of a spectacular rise to national prominence but it does tell the story of an honorable and dedicated patriot who served his country for over four decades. Too often history tells us only of the very good or of the very bad. Most people are neither of these, but are sincere folk who do the best they can under the circumstances they face. Stanley was such a one. His is a story well worth telling.

Michael R. Bradley, a professor emeritus of the Tennessee Board of Regents Colleges, received a Ph.D. from Vanderbilt in 1971. He is the author of *The Tullahoma Campaign*; *With Blood and Fire: Behind U.S. Lines in Middle Tennessee*; *The Escort and Staff of Nathan Bedford Forrest*; *David Campbell Kelley: Forrest's Fighting Preacher*; *They Rode with Forrest*; *The Raiding Winter*; and *Murfreesboro in the Civil War*.

Preface

The personal memoirs of David Stanley, written in 1896, were posthumously published in 1917 and since that time little has been written about him. While the memoirs are well written, some people felt Stanley was overly critical of many of his contemporaries and the bitterness of his later life was reflected in this work. This caused many to ignore the contributions of his long military career. Because the memoirs were written in such a manner, Stanley's own story has not been tested by historical facts. Certain very important areas of his Civil War career were incomplete in his memoirs and needed further development and correction. Overall, he offered valuable firsthand accounts of the events of his long, fruitful career from his point of view. It is also important to note that a person changes over time and who David Stanley was in the Civil War is very much different from the David Stanley who penned his memoirs thirty years later. This is aptly emphasized by the fact Stanley wrote in disparaging terms in his memoirs of James A. Garfield, who served as chief of staff of the Army of the Cumberland, but there is little evidence which would suggest animosity between the two individuals in 1863. However, personal problems developed after the Civil War when Garfield aligned with Stanley's opponents, which could have jaundiced his opinion of Garfield. So his comments about events which occurred many years before his memoirs were published need to be considered from an impersonal and historically accurate point of view. One who has made so many contributions to his country should be measured in the light of historical facts.

While researching the life of David Stanley, I found various accounts of his life from many sources. In addition to his own autobiography, the National Archives contained "Union Generals Papers" and his own personnel record, which contained valuable information about his life. Because his life was so long and he served in various locations, Stanley collections also are found at the University of Wyoming, the Minnesota Historical Society, and the University of Texas. The United States Army Education and Heritage Center and the United States Military Academy Special Collections were sources of much of the information contained in this book. Numerous accounts of events were collected from regimental histories and papers from soldiers who served under him. Stanley worked closely with prominent individuals, such as James A. Garfield and William S. Rosecrans, and accounts of his life were found in other biographies, autobiographies, letters and historical papers of various sources. The controversies and successes involving him were often found in local and national newspapers and are recorded in this work. Finally, many of the accounts of the Civil War are firsthand reports contained in the Official Records of the War of the Rebellion.

In 1895, General Richard W. Johnson wrote of the man: "Few officers did more faithful service than Gen. David S. Stanley. When he commanded the cavalry, he was the 'eyes and ears of the army.' When in command of the infantry he was always in the forefront of battle, and no troops did more faithful service than those under his leadership. I knew him at West Point, and he was the same popular, clever fellow that he has always been since he entered the service."[1] The bitterness of years of service, living in poor conditions, and observing the politics of the military caused Stanley great unhappiness. Of Stanley's memoirs, historian M. John Lubetkin wrote, "A bitterness permeates his posthumous memoirs, and his last years were likely unhappy. If one person on the surveys truly needed to rest in peace it was the able but self-tortured Stanley."[2]

Stanley was always very private about his family and a true biography cannot be presented because of the limited information about his personal life. It cannot be denied, however, that he made important contributions to the United States and left a legacy for future generations. He had a large family, daughters who would marry soldiers, and a son who would also serve in the army. Stanley's friendship with many of those with whom he served contradicts allegations that he was an unhappy and bitter man during his life. This work presents an exploration of the general's Civil War career in light of official records, personal accounts, and accounts of others who served with him.

Hero of Franklin

No power on earth can save us, and Hood will gain the day.
But to one man the peril brings purpose stern and high,
And, seizing on the moment, with fury in his eye,
He dashes 'mid the conflict, his only conscious thought,
"The patriot dead must be avenged, the battle lost refought."
Around the name of Stanley a glory shall be cast.[3]

1

Early Life and the Wilson's Creek Campaign

This is the real thing, the real sure-enough war.

Lieutenant David S. Stanley watched the conflict in eastern portions of the United States intensify from Fort Washita in the Indian Territory during the spring of 1861. The fort was located near the confluence of the Washita River and the Red River and just north of the Texas state border.

The Indian Territory was a long way away from Lieutenant Stanley's birthplace of Cedar Valley in Wayne County, Ohio; but the 1852 West Point graduate was used to the western areas of the United States. After graduation from the United States Army Military Academy, he accompanied a survey expedition in the unexplored West. Stanley's time in the West was not idle and like many men of this period, he was experienced in fighting Indians. Only 120 miles from Fort Washita to Fort Worth, Texas, Stanley was no doubt troubled on February 1, 1861, when the state of Texas seceded from the Union, first announcing its intention to become an independent republic before agreeing to join the Confederate States of America.

While at Fort Washita Lieutenant David Stanley served in the 1st U.S. Cavalry and was promoted to the rank of captain of Company C in March 1861. The tall, dark-haired, steely-eyed man had no idea of the extent of the conflict that was to come, but he had served in the cavalry for nine years and was at home in the saddle. Born on June 1, 1828, he was 32 years old when the cannons fired on Fort Sumter. While the Indian Territory was far removed from the flames of secession, he was relatively close to the Kansas and Missouri border, which served as an example of the bitter partisan dissention sweeping the country. Violence had erupted and "Bleeding Kansas" fought for self-determination. Stanley's proximity to these events made him keenly aware of the emotions at work in the hearts of his fellow Americans. As he gazed across the plains, he wondered how this union of states had become so divided.

Stanley's Early Life

David Stanley lived his early life in Chester Township, in Wayne County, Ohio, about fifty miles south of Cleveland. He was born on a farm in Ohio and his earliest recollections included his log home, which had only one large living room that also served as the bedroom, dining room and kitchen. He lived in the midst of friends and family who had moved to Ohio from Pennsylvania and was educated in a small, local school which had no regular teacher.

David Stanley was the son of John Bratton Stanley, born in 1799 and a native of Pennsylvania, and Sarah Peterson, born in 1807 in Virginia. David Stanley had one older brother, William Clinton, who was born in 1825, and three younger brothers, Jonathan, born in 1830; John Calvin, born in 1832; James Bartholomew, born in 1837. A younger sister, Mary Ann, was born in 1834.[1]

David was clothed in buckskins in his early life, and his youth was that of a farmer's son. He cleared the forest for cornfields, and logging became part of his everyday life. The Stanleys depended on the craftsmanship of all in the extended family—grandfather, grandmother and the immediate family. In addition to corn, timothy and flax, the Stanley farm products included sheep, which provided for homespun and home-dyed fabric for the family to wear. When Stanley was not helping on the farm, he was attending school, which he began at five years of age. His classrooms were divided, boys on one side and girls on the other. The schoolteachers were of a variety of types—a farmer, a schoolmistress (which Stanley and all the other children fell in love with), and later, more professionally, prepared instructors.

In addition to the schoolhouse, the church was the other center of the community in Stanley's early life. When he was very young, there were only two churches nearby—the Presbyterian and the Methodist churches. The Stanley family was Presbyterian, and religion was always an important part of David Stanley's life.

While Stanley lived on a farm, he was very poor, but subsistence farming was common in this geographic area. The Stanley family did not have glass for windows, but used oiled paper as a source of light in some of the rooms. Even the plow used on the farm was made mostly with wood. Hunting was a source of food for the family and it was also a part of family and community life.

David Stanley's mother died when he was 11 years old, and after a year and a half his father remarried. The loss of his mother was tragic and hurtful to Stanley. She suffered from a long and protracted illness that was misdiagnosed, in Stanley's opinion. She finally died of what appeared to be consumption, but the doctors had treated her for a liver ailment. There was much bitterness associated with this loss, which ultimately resulted in the breakup of the family.

David Stanley's stepmother was Elsie Ann Lowry. After the marriage, David was sent to live with Dr. Leander Firestone, a young physician, in Congress, Ohio, a few miles north of Wooster. Although Stanley never explained why he was sent to live with Firestone, he noted his new stepmother was a good and kind woman to his siblings. Stanley had a very close attachment to his mother and he recalled the home was never the same after his mother died. He lived with the Firestone family for four years, during which time he was taught grammar, philosophy and chemistry; and with the aid of Dr. Firestone, he began to prepare for the study of medicine. During Stanley's second year with the Firestone family, he attended the Canaan Academy. After Stanley had lived with Dr. Firestone for two years, his family sold their farm and moved to Roann, Indiana, because the Ohio farm could no longer support the family. This had a severe impact on Stanley, as he observed, "This home which I ... still found so beautiful, the home of my happy childhood, the home made by my mother, was sold to strangers .... The final breaking up of our beautiful home was one of the sad periods of my life."[2] At the age of 16, Stanley agreed to "keep" a country school just east of his old home, but when he turned 17, he began studying medicine in earnest. Stanley recalled Dr. Firestone was a "demonstrator of anatomy in Cleveland and I used to drive with him in a buggy forty miles and stay for lectures at the Medical College. He also procured cadavers to dissect at home and I learned a great deal of anatomy."[3]

Grandparents were very important to Stanley. Stories told by his grandfather and grandmother recalled battles of the Revolutionary War and, in particular, his grandmother described the Battle of Brandywine, which she had witnessed personally. He grew up in an area where the Ohio militia was present, though not actively engaged on a day-to-day basis. The militia was organized under state law, but in Stanley's youth the duty was primarily ceremonial. The local militia was called the cornstalk militia and every able-bodied male was required to serve, but only the general officers had uniforms. A muster was generally held at least once a year, usually after harvest, and the company was marched, drilled and paraded. The influence of the military presence in his family and community no doubt influenced David Stanley as he decided his life's work; but the military was not his first choice. Only fate allowed Stanley to embark on a career in the military.

It was the Mexican-American War that redirected David Stanley's life from medicine to a career in the military. David's Uncle Homer and cousins, Robert and James Lowry, enlisted and served in this war. David Stanley's assessment of the cause of the war was "our ruthless invasion of territory in dispute, lying between the Nueces and the Rio Grande, without any toleration or discussion or any thought of arbitration, brought on a war which a fair sense of morality could not justify."[4] Despite his assessment of the war made later in life after serving several years in Texas, Stanley was caught up in the excitement of the mobilization of the country. Many of the men in the community were involved in preparation of the war and the 3rd Ohio Infantry was organized from this part of Ohio. David Stanley, no exception, wanted to join the army and go to war with the Mexicans, but he was not accepted into military service due to his age. He remained in Ohio and continued with his studies in medicine in 1847, studying the theory and practice of medicine while accompanying Dr. Firestone on his house calls. In the winter of 1847, Stanley again taught school, for a salary of $30 per month, because his personal funds were so low.

Life is full of surprises, and for David Stanley an opportunity arose in January 1848 when the West Point Military Academy appointee from Ohio was found to be deficient. By coincidence, the new appointment to the military academy was to be decided by Dr. Firestone, through the influence of Congressman Samuel Lahm, also a brigadier general in the Ohio militia, and he offered this opportunity to young David Stanley. Stanley later wrote, "It was a time of great importance to me. I was at the turning point of my life. I rather liked the study of medicine and never doubted my success as a doctor. Of the Military I knew little although I had drilled as a private in our local Congress Guards. But the picture of a cadet and the fine stately bearing of Colonel Samuel Curtis, the only graduate I had ever seen, now returned from the wars and following the profession of the law in Wooster, decided me."[5] (Samuel Curtis commanded the local Ohio militia and served as the colonel for the 2nd Ohio Volunteers in the Mexican-American War.)

In early May 1848, David Stanley set off by stagecoach on the beginning of his new career in the military. As he traveled to Cleveland he rode with a lovely young woman and a "little dapper, rather dandified young man." By coincidence, the young man was Philip Sheridan, "small and red faced, long black wavy hair, bright eyes, very animated and neatly dressed in a brown broadcloth sack suit."[6] Stanley recorded that once Sheridan reached West Point, his suit was replaced with a brown linen jacket and his locks were removed, revealing a rather "insignificant" looking person. For Stanley, this new appearance meant nothing because Sheridan was a "good fellow and he and I remained friends until his death."[7] Phil Sheridan also remembered his first encounter with David Stanley and recalled that their friendship increased while on the steamship crossing Lake Erie. Sheridan said, "I found out that he had no 'Monroe shoes,' so I deemed myself just that much ahead of my companion, although my shoes might not conform exactly to regulations in Eastern style and finish."[8]

Sheridan was only one of the cadets Stanley was soon to meet. The most efficient route to West Point from Cleveland was by steamer, which traveled to Buffalo. On the steamer, Stanley met other West Point cadets—George Crook, Milo S. Hascall, Lyman Kellogg and Henry B. Davidson. The steamer took four days to reach Schenectady and the final part of the journey was a short rail trip to West Point.

Stanley's poverty was noted as he entered the military academy and was required to pay $90 for his uniform but had less than $25. Next, he went through several weeks of miserable homesickness, but he persevered and had an enjoyable experience during his four years there. He loved his time at the academy and spent his free hours exploring the countryside. He exclaimed that he had never seen any place more beautiful than the area around West Point.

While at West Point, from his second year until he graduated, he roomed with Southerners Mathew L. Davis of North Carolina, George B. Anderson of North Carolina, and George B. Cosby of Kentucky. All of his roommates would ultimately offer their talents to the Confederacy, and only Cosby survived the war. Stanley's class enrolled 120 members but only 43 graduated, and David Stanley graduated 9th in his class of 1852. Thomas Casey graduated first in the class, which included such individuals as Henry Slocum, George Hartstuff, Alexander McCook, George Crook, and Hezekiah H. Garber, of Illinois, who graduated in 43rd place in the class of 43.[9]

It was also at West Point that Stanley met his future wife, Anna Maria Wright, through an introduction by the wife of Captain G.W. Smith. Miss Wright was the daughter of an army surgeon who had been stationed at West Point for six months. Stanley visited Captain Smith often and became well acquainted with Anna Wright, who was five years younger than he was. When her father was transferred from West Point, David Stanley gave her his class ring. She returned it to him, but the connection was made. Stanley described her as "a small, well formed and very pretty girl, very modest and almost bashful."[10] Anna Maria was the daughter of a prominent surgeon in the U.S. Army, John Jefferson Burr Wright, and Eliza Jones, and was one of five children. Anna's father had been a surgeon in the U.S. Army since 1843 and had served in the Mexican War. Being the daughter of a regular army surgeon, Anna was aware of life in the army, having lived in various locations; but Wilkes-Barre, Pennsylvania, was the family home.

After graduation, Stanley had time to return to Ohio and Indiana to visit family and friends; but he also made a stop at Carlisle Barracks where Dr. John Wright and his family were posted. Stanley spent a week there before continuing his visits, but by the end of the week, it was all settled, at least on Stanley's part, that Anna was the woman for him.

Stanley Heads West

After graduation, David Stanley's first assignment was at Carlisle Barracks, Pennsylvania, which served as a training ground for new cavalry officers. He reported to Major Philip St. George Cooke, 2nd U.S. Dragoons, and later his commander was Captain Charles F. Ruff of the Mounted Rifles.

Dr. Joseph J.B. Wright, Stanley's future father-in-law (National Library of Medicine).

The relationship between David Stanley and Anna Wright blossomed during his training at Carlisle Barracks. The couple loved to ride together and explored the landscape of central Pennsylvania. Soon, David proposed marriage and Anna accepted.

He trained at Carlisle Barracks through the winter of 1852–1853, and in the spring of 1853 he volunteered to join an expedition to survey routes for railroads connecting to the Pacific Ocean. He traveled by riverboat to Fort Smith, Arkansas, and became part of Lieutenant A.W. Whipple's Topographical Engineers expedition consisting of about 20 men. From Fort Smith they traveled west by horse and wagon, the detachment being escorted by a group of 30 soldiers of the 7th U.S. Infantry. The engineers' task was to survey a route from Fort Smith, Arkansas, to San Diego, California.

A skin infection was the cause of Stanley's inclusion on the expedition. Dr. J.J.B. Wright, army surgeon at Carlisle Barracks and David Stanley's future father-in-law, wrote a letter in support of Stanley's participation on the surveying expedition. Wright wrote that Stanley had an "obstinate cutaneous and subcutaneous infection which has proved intractable under several plans of treatments"[11] Wright believed the outdoor conditions would help improve Stanley's infection. The skin condition was quite serious and would continue to be troublesome into 1855.[12]

While Stanley was on the surveying expedition through the West, he wrote an extensive diary of his experiences. The diary recounted deserts, mountains, storms, excessive heat, frigid temperatures, buffalo herds, numerous animals, and the geography of the route surveyed. Stanley also wrote about the various Native American tribes encountered and the guides who were used to lead the expedition. The expedition was not necessarily the adventure he had hoped and mostly consisted of the tedium of traveling on the frontier. During this expedition, Stanley revealed a deeply religious nature: "Ah! that God may forgive me the wickedness I have and am constantly guilty of on this expedition, owing to the constant crosses and consequent fits of bad temper I fall into."[13] He later chastised himself: "Mr. Jones remarked, looking at some Indians, that they were spending Sunday evening in elegant leisure, which recalled to my mind and the self reproach of having spent the Lord's Day in perfect thoughtlessness."[14]

Departing Fort Smith on July 24, 1853, the group moved westward and David Stanley encountered the Plains Indians for the first time. The management of the details of the expedition fell on the shoulders of Lieutenant Stanley, and he lamented more than once that he wished he had never agreed to come on the trip. As he settled into his role, he had a very valuable and enjoyable experience. Few people had the experience to traveling such distances in the untamed West. As the journey progressed westward, several prominent men were encountered, including John Pope, John Tidball and Samuel Sturgis. The expedition finally reached San Bernardino on March 14, 1854, the last four months totally without communication with the outside world.

Stanley returned to New York via ship, reached the East Coast in June, and found his next assignment was at Fort Chadbourne, Texas, as part of William Hardee's Second Dragoons. The fort was primarily manned by the 8th U.S. Infantry, and was located about halfway between Abilene and San Angelo, Texas. Stanley again encountered numerous individuals who would be prominent in the Civil War, including Dick Anderson, George "Tige" Anderson, Alfred Pleasanton, Charles Field and Albert Sydney Johnston. His immediate commander was Captain Patrick Calhoun, son the famous secessionist John C. Calhoun of South Carolina.

In 1854 on his way to Texas, Stanley stopped at Jefferson Barracks in St. Louis to pay his respect to Dr. J.J.B. Wright, surgeon for the military installation. He intentionally planned the stop in St. Louis to visit Anna M. Wright, but, while the visit was very pleasant, the family was in mourning. Eliza Wright, Anna's mother, had just died of cholera while residing at Jefferson Barracks.

The Indians were a force to be respected in Texas and Stanley noted when he went out of his quarters at night that he always lowered the light and carried a cocked and loaded shotgun. Stanley transferred from the 2nd Dragoons to the 1st U.S. Cavalry in 1855 because the army had increased in size. He had an opportunity to find a place in the cavalry and he seized it, preferring the cavalry over service as a dragoon. It was during this time that Stanley was on sick leave, from May through October, due to the unidentified skin disease which had troubled him since 1853. He moved from Texas to Newport Barracks on the Ohio River for the winter. On October 18, 1855, Leander Firestone also tried to treat the skin condition and his opinion was that it would take at least another three months for the condition to improve.[15] Finally, on March 19, 1856, the skin condition had improved so much that Stanley was able to report for duty. Soon afterward, he traveled up the Missouri River as a member of the 1st U.S. Cavalry to deal with the Sioux Indians. He was given a detachment of men by General William Selby Harney north of Sioux City and Harney told him he would have to make his own laws in this wilderness. No longer a novice, the leadership and command styles of Stanley were evident as he dealt with "some New York City toughs, who constantly stole the cut loaf sugar, until one morning I caught one of them with some of it in his pocket. I had him tied up and gave him thirty-nine lashes with a rope's end and the stealing ceased."[16]

Soon afterward, Stanley completed his duty in Sioux country and was ordered to Kansas. He traveled 600 miles down the Missouri River to Omaha and then took a stage to Saint Joseph, Missouri. From there, he traveled to Fort Leavenworth and joined the 1st U.S. Cavalry commanded by Colonel E.V. "Bull" Sumner. Upon reaching his new assignment, he found the regiment was ordered to return to assist Harney in his actions against the Sioux. In the winter of 1856, they returned to Kansas and were involved in dealing with the political situation between the Pro Slavery Party and the abolitionist Free Soil Party. Stanley recorded, "With this disagreeable duty I was kept busy until late in the winter of '56 and '57. The Kansas troubles were the prelude to the Civil war. Freedom and slavery were the bones of contention."[17] It was during this time period that Lieutenant Stanley served under the command of another prominent military figure, Captain George B. McClellan.

While stationed in Kansas, Stanley's regiment was called twice to defend the town of Lawrence. During one of the incidents, in August 1856, the regiment joined a U.S. military force made up of the 1st Cavalry, 2nd Dragoons, 6th Infantry, and part of the 4th Artillery and formed a line on the east side of Lawrence. Facing them was, reportedly, 12,000 men under the command of former senator David Atchison of Missouri. Colonel Philip St. George Cooke commanded the U.S. troops and met with Atchison and convinced him to return to Missouri. Though no blood was shed, this incident demonstrated the level of intensity of emotions and actions citizens were willing to take to support their cause. Stanley knew Lawrence had no armed men present, but Atchison was intent on burning the town to the ground. Finally, the last major partisan clashes ended in 1858 and Kansas entered the union as a Free State in 1861. With the border conflict abated in Kansas, the cavalry tended to more military issues, including dealing with the Cheyenne Indians.

One such assignment almost cost Stanley his life but he was saved by future Confederate cavalry legend J.E.B. Stuart. In 1857, Stanley's command was ordered to search for a group of marauding Cheyenne Indians near Solomon Fork, Kansas. While being pursued, the Indians dispersed and, as luck would have it, Lieutenant Stanley and Lieutenant Stuart rode stirrup to stirrup after one of them. The chase covered four miles and the horses were winded when the Indian the troopers was chasing stopped. He then fired at Stuart. Stanley recorded, "I turned my horse and rode in on the Indian, firing one shot, but as I fired near my horse's ear, it scared him, and immediately jumping off my horse, tried to get a good aim at the Indian, but to my horror, my pistol stood firmly cocked and refused to fire. The Indian saw my fix in a flash and ran towards me, presenting his pistol."[18] Stanley dropped his pistol, drew his sword and waited for the shot, but Stuart rode ahead and swung his sabre at the Indian. Stuart hit his target, but, at the same time, the Indian's pistol went off, wounding Stuart in the chest. Second Lieutenant Eli Long recorded the incident in his diary: "Lts. McIntyre, Lomax and Stanly [sic] were after about 50 but could not catch but one, he had an old fashioned self-cocking 6 shooter, he stopped doubtless to save the rest.... Stewart attacked him when he shot Stewart in the breast. McIntyre ran up in time to run him through with the sabre. Stewart was not wounded very badly the ball not penetrating deep."[19]

Stanley's experiences with the Plains Indians were not over. He narrowly escaped injury in a skirmish with a Comanche who had raided a rancher, making off with a horse. Stanley's cavalry troop set off in pursuit and located their quarry in a rocky canyon. Stanley attacked the Indians, and five were killed during the battle. Another two broke away, and Stanley rode after them. Unfortunately, his horse fell during the pursuit, causing Stanley to bruise his leg. While Stanley was recovering from the fall, two Indians turned toward him and moved to attack. Stanley was saved when two of his troopers rode to his assistance and the two Indians resumed their retreat. After the harrowing experiences of the day, Stanley's troop camped for the night, but the next morning Stanley again rode in pursuit of the Indians. His scouts noticed movement about 200 yards ahead of Stanley's advance. The movement was thought to be an animal, but the movement revealed the two Indians who had escaped the previous day. The troop pursued the first Indian and Stanley and Private Dempsey pursued the second. "They spotted their quarry ducking under a cutback above a water hole. When they got there, the two dismounted, and the lieutenant ordered Dempsey to fire under the overhang. Moments later the Indian emerged, clutching a bow and loosing a string of arrows, one of which whistled between Stanley's legs." Both Stanley and Dempsey fired, killing the Indian.[20]

David S. Stanley, sometime between 1860 and 1870 (Library of Congress).

Another important event occurred in Stanley's life in 1857, when he married Anna M. Wright at Carlisle Barracks, Pennsylvania. Anna Wright's father was again posted as surgeon at Carlisle Barracks. Surgeon Wright graduated from Jefferson Medical College in 1836. He would have the honor of serving on the staffs of General George McClellan and General Henry Halleck. Dr. Joseph J.B. Wright was later assigned to duty in Texas until the beginning of the war. After Stanley's marriage on April 2, 1857, Stanley was on duty for four months and then was assigned duty at Fort Leavenworth, where he lived with his wife. Fort Leavenworth was overcrowded and the Stanleys soon found themselves in Fort Riley, Kansas. The time with Anna was short and duty again called. This time the issue was with Mormons. The relationship between the United States government and Mormons was contentious at various times in history, and in 1857–1858, President James Buchanan sent a military force to Utah. The Mormons, fearing this force was sent to annihilate them, resisted, although the confrontation was largely bloodless.

Stanley was sent from Kansas to Fort Kearney and was under the command of Colonel E.V. Sumner. Utilizing some of Stanley's medical training he had received prior to attending West Point, he was the acting surgeon of Sumner's command. The irascible Sumner disapproved of "sick call," which he felt only encouraged the troopers to report as sick, and as a result Stanley discontinued the practice during this expedition, which spent most of the time in present-day Nebraska until a peace was negotiated before the return to Fort Riley.

In 1858, Stanley returned to Kansas and was ordered to Fort Arbuckle in the Indian Territory under command of Captain James McIntosh. Stanley served with 2nd Lieutenant Lunsford Lindsay Lomax. Again, the task of the 1st U.S. Cavalry was maintaining the peace with the Indians. The list of prominent military figures of Stanley's acquaintance was numerous at this location, including Earl Van Dorn, Fitzhugh Lee, Eugene Carr, and Alfred Iverson.

It was also in June 1858 that Stanley became the proud father of his first child, a daughter, Florence Elizabeth Stanley. Unfortunately, the child died shortly afterward in 1859. Stanley's wife, Anna, suffered through a long and dangerous illness during the winter of 1858. There are no existing records of Stanley's feeling upon the death of his first child, but the loss had to be severe for him. Stanley's second child, Josephine Huntington Stanley, was born on June 24, 1860, in the Indian Territory and brought brightness back into his life.

In 1860, Stanley's troops were moved to Fort Cobb located on the Washita River. Next, Stanley was ordered to move from Fort Cobb to Fort Smith, Arkansas, in the fall of 1860. He felt the events in the fall of 1860 signaled the end of the Union, and he wrote, "This fall of 1860, we moved to Fort Smith and our dream was passed. Mr. Lincoln was elected and already the alarm bells had rung."[21] While at Fort Smith, Stanley observed the sentiment of the country, particularly Southern sentiment. As he had been disgusted by the partisan conflict in Kansas, the situation in Arkansas was equally unpleasant. He noted it was obvious that Arkansas would support secession and those who supported slavery were very aggressive in their position. He observed the pro-secession population which dominated the political arena in Arkansas were "the idle trifling, unprincipled class prevailing over people of property, principle and good sense, simply because this latter class were not prepared to fight for their love of the Union. At any rate the secession sentiment grew every day. The young Southerner at that time was a very absurd character, perhaps because brought up as masters of slaves. He had imbibed the idea that he was a superior being and the white man of the North was as easy to chastise or to kill as the black slave he bullied."[22]

Interestingly, the pro–Union and antislavery David Stanley sent his wife and "three slaves" to St. Louis. Anna Stanley did not want to leave her husband, but the situation in Arkansas and the call of duty for David Stanley required her to leave the area. While in the Indian Territory in the late 1850s, Stanley had looked for servants to help with daily chores and hired Mily, a black cook, and then later hired two Indian-black women to assist around his home. He later bought Sarah Cobbert and her twelve-year-old daughter as slaves. Stanley recorded he bought the slaves as a way of finding reliable domestic help, as well as his thoughts on slavery: "I never could see, nor can I now, why a white man should own a negro rather than a negro own a white man. I found the institution already established and had no compunctions in buying a slave to save my wife from work unsuited to her state. I did, however, promise the woman that she would never be sold and that when she had earned her cost at a fair rate of wages, I would free her."[23]

An awkward condition developed in the army after Lincoln's inauguration and the country drifted toward civil war. As the sentiment favoring secession grew stronger, decisions had to be made within the ranks of the military regarding the allegiance of the various officers. Stanley's superior, Captain James McIntosh, from New Jersey, decided to join the

Confederate army and was subsequently killed in the Battle of Pea Ridge. Stanley, too, was offered a commission in the Southern army.

As the resignations mounted in the U.S. Army due to officers returning to their home states, opportunities for promotion increased. David Stanley was promoted to the rank of captain of Company C, 1st U.S. Cavalry, and assigned to Fort Washita, Indian Territory. As the firing on Fort Sumter reverberated across the country, the emotion which wrenched the country apart finally reached Fort Smith, Arkansas. Three days after Stanley left Fort Smith for Fort Washita, Arkansas state troops advanced on Fort Smith intent on capturing the troops and supplies stored there. However, Captain Samuel Sturgis had moved the U.S. troops, along with a quartermaster train containing the ammunition and weapons, ten miles away from the Confederate force.

The Beginning of the Civil War

Once Stanley reached Fort Washita, there were six troops of cavalry and a regiment of infantry concentrated under the command of Colonel William Emory, a very conflicted commander. While Emory had overall command of the Union detachment, Captain Samuel Sturgis commanded the cavalry. Sturgis, Stanley's immediate commanding officer, was a Pennsylvania native and a graduate of the United States Military Academy in 1846. Sturgis had fought during the Mexican War and after the war he had served in the western United States.

After concentrating the U.S. military forces at Fort Washita, Emory was asked to surrender to Confederate authorities, which he promptly declined to do. Afterwards a group of Texans advanced on Fort Washita but were captured by the cavalry before they could do any harm. They were subsequently paroled and returned to their homes. The conflicted Colonel William Emory was a native of Maryland and was absolutely loyal to his home state, which had some Southern allegiance. He was not trusted by the officers of the cavalry, who had agreed among themselves to arrest him should he try to surrender to Confederate authorities. Emory received orders from Assistant Adjutant-General E.D. Townsend on April 17, 1861: "On receipt of this communication, you will, by order of the General-in-Chief, with all the troops in the Indian country west of Arkansas, march to Fort Leavenworth, Kans., taking such useful public property as your means of transportation will permit."[24]

Emory complied with the orders and moved his force from Fort Washita to Kansas. Upon entering Kansas, he noticed a group of escaped slaves was following. Emory was concerned it would be perceived the cavalry was aiding in the escape of slaves from their masters and he ordered Lieutenant Fish to capture the four ex-slaves and bring them into camp. Next, Emory told a group of gamblers accompanying the expedition he would release the ex-slaves and advised the gamblers to capture them and return them south for the reward. Lieutenant Fish released the ex-slaves the next morning, as ordered; but when the gamblers tried to capture them, the ex-slaves successfully resisted, although one was killed in the process. Some of Emory's command were not pleased with his tactics. Later in the day, in what started as a joke over a horse, Stanley threatened to have Emory brought up on charges of murder for his involvement in the death of one of the ex-slaves, which occurred on the free soil of Kansas. Emory had already submitted a letter of resignation from the army and, coincidentally, he received notification his resignation had been accepted the next day at Emporia, Kansas. William

Emory's decision to resign from the U.S. Army was prompted by his belief his home state of Maryland would also secede from the Union. When Maryland voted not to secede, Emory realized he had made a mistake and appealed to be reinstated. Through some difficulty, his request was granted and he later rose to the rank of major general in the Union army.

The Union column arrived in Fort Leavenworth amid a flurry of activity. The same secession sentiment Stanley had observed in Arkansas was occurring across the river in Missouri, and pro–Southern forces were capturing steamboats and threatening Fort Leavenworth. In June, Captain Stanley moved his troopers into Missouri from Fort Leavenworth as part of newly brevetted Major W.E. Prince's Union force. Prince was concerned the pro–Southern forces in Missouri were concentrating to attack Union forces in Kansas and also in various locations in Missouri. Likewise, one of the major reasons the pro–Southern state guard was created in Missouri was to prevent an invasion from troops outside the state, particularly those from Kansas, where so much animosity still existed from the border conflicts of the 1850s.

As Prince's force crossed into Missouri at Kansas City in June 1861, he encountered about 600 Southern troops camped 12 miles east in Independence. Prince ordered David Stanley and Company C to carry a flag of truce to the secessionist camp. As Stanley advanced toward the camp, he encountered a Mr. Reed, a congressman, who begged Stanley not to go any farther because the Southern-sympathizing Missouri State Guard troops were holding a barbeque and he was concerned some of the soldiers would be drunk. Despite this warning, the cavalrymen continued on to the camp. Fortunately, Edmunds B. Holloway, a captain in the 8th U.S. Infantry, has just been elected colonel of the Southern regiment.

Stanley and Holloway conferred, Stanley's objective being to ascertain Holloway's intention in regard to the Union force which was advancing into Missouri. Holloway was uneasy during the meeting and Stanley noticed a column of men advancing with the intent of capturing Stanley's men.[25] When Stanley objected to this action, Holloway rode a short distance toward the advancing Missouri State Guard column intending to stop the advance. He waved to stop the column and when he did so, Stanley, his men and Holloway received a volley from the column: "Some one had accidentally shot his gun off, which the rank and file of Holloway's men thought was a signal to fire, when there was a general fusillade from the State Guard mortally wounding the commanding officer."[26] Stanley's cavalry formed a line and returned fire and a general exchange of volleys occurred. Holloway was mortally wounded and died later in the night. Before he died, he urged his troops to return home until they were properly trained and blamed Stanley for coming too close to his men without forewarning. Stanley wrote it was "a thing I never reproached myself for, although I was sorry for Holloway. He was shot by his own men while encouraging rebellion."[27] Afterwards, Stanley returned to the Union column and reported to Major Prince. The Union column advanced on the Southern camp the next day but found it vacated. Stanley recorded one man wounded and two horses shot. In addition to Holloway, three of his companions were killed and another six were wounded. Missouri was a border state and the state was being torn apart by the divisions of the country.

The Situation in Missouri

Abraham Lincoln was not the popular choice for president by the citizens of Missouri in the 1860 election. In fact, Lincoln carried only St. Louis and Gasconade County in the election. He finished in a weak fourth position in Missouri, and John C. Breckenridge, a Southern Democrat, was third. Stephen Douglas won Missouri's electoral votes and John Bell finished second. Because Lincoln lost so decidedly, many in the state questioned the direction the country was heading. Missouri was a slaveholding state but was not tied to the values of the states of the Deep South. It was divided on the issue of secession, and blood had already been shed over it, citizens of the state being involved in Kansas for several years regarding the slavery issues in that state. Missouri's fourteenth governor, Claiborne Fox Jackson, had been elected from the Democratic Party in August 1860, and he wanted Missouri to align with slave-holding southern states. Jackson made clear his intentions when he placed the "current crisis squarely as the feet of Northern abolitionists who threatened millions of dollars of Southern slave property."[28] He felt the Southern states were not being represented by the increasingly industrialized North and he felt the Union had already been abandoned.

Both pro–Union and pro–Southern paramilitary organizations had been assembled prior to the Ft. Sumter incident, particularly in the St. Louis area where pro–Southern minute men and pro–Northern home guards were being trained in response to the deteriorating state and national situation. Governor Jackson's refusal to furnish the 4,000 recruits requested by Lincoln offered an opportunity for the pro–Union home guards to be mustered into service. The commander of the Union military forces in St. Louis was William Selby Harney and his subordinate, Nathaniel Lyon. Captain Nathaniel Lyon, a hard-line, pro–Union military officer whose experience in Kansas during the time when Missourians attempted to force Kansas to become a slave-holding state hardened his resolve against the South.[29]

As the pro–Southern state guards were mustered into service, the importance of protecting and controlling the St. Louis military arsenal was clear. The nonessential military supplies were moved to Illinois. Authority was also given to enlist 10,000 men into the Union army to protect St. Louis and other parts of Missouri. The best laid plans of Governor Jackson seemed to be slipping away, but he began a plan to muster the state militia to better protect the rest of the state and counter the increased number of pro–Union troops being recruited. In addition, Jackson was "confident that Missouri would furnish 100,000 to the Southern cause."[30]

The inflexibility of Governor Jackson and the equally aggressive and inflexible Nathaniel Lyon polarized an already difficult situation. By mid–May 1861, Governor Jackson pushed through bills in the state legislature funding and authorizing the enrollment of men to become part of the Missouri State Guard, which was commanded by ex-governor Sterling Price, who had committed himself to the secessionist camp after the Camp Jackson affair. In the meantime, the pro–Union forces in St. Louis were given authority to capture all illegal arms and contraband.

As the state continued to divide, the Harney-Price Agreement was reached while the state guard and the Union soldiers were being mustered into service. It was agreed the state guard would maintain order within the state and the Union troops would be given authority to maintain order in the St. Louis area. This temporary solution initially calmed the situation, but the extremists on both sides were not happy with the compromise. Governor Jackson used this time to strengthen his efforts to guide Missouri toward the Confederacy, and General Nathaniel Lyon continued to push for greater enlistments for the Union side. Finally a meeting was held on June 11, 1861, between Nathaniel Lyon, Frank Blair, Sterling Price and Governor Jackson. After four hours it became apparent that no agreement could be reached. Lyon was quoted as stating that, rather than give up any part of Missouri to non–Union control, "I would see you, and you, and you, and every man, woman, and child in the state dead and buried."[31]

At that point, any hope of peace within Missouri was lost. By the next morning, General Sterling Price communicated to the Missouri State Guard there would be open hostility with the Union army. The Missouri executive government in Jefferson City fled the capital on June 13 and on June 15 General Lyon, promoted to the rank of brigadier general on May 17, arrived there with 2,000 troops. The pro–Southern troops of Governor Jackson and Price moved to Cowskin Prairie in southwestern Missouri in July, and Union troops from Kansas, Iowa, and Illinois joined Captain Nathaniel Lyon's Union troops in Missouri.

In July 1861, Major General John C. Frémont was placed in command of the Union forces in Missouri and was informed Brigadier General Nathaniel Lyon was in the countryside seeking out the Confederate forces under the command of general and ex-governor Sterling Price. In the meantime, "Governor Jackson issued a call for a special session of the legislature to meet at Neosho, Mo., on October 21, 1861. Only a few members met. They passed an act of secession declaring Missouri's withdrawal from the Union. The United States government never regarded Missouri as out of the Union, but the Confederacy accepted this secession act as legal."[32]

During June and July 1861, the opposing forces were garnering their strength and began to identify their respective military objectives. The Southern-sympathizing Missouri State Guard under the command of Colonel John S. Marmaduke met the advancing Federal forces under command of General Nathaniel Lyon near Boonville, Missouri, in early July 1861. The result of this battle was the removal of Sterling Price's state guard from central Missouri to the southwestern part of the state. The battle shed the blood of Missourians, further dividing the state and nation. Soon after the skirmish at Boonville, another skirmish occurred at Carthage, Missouri, on July 5, 1861, as Colonel Franz Sigel attempted to prevent Governor Jackson and John Marmaduke from reaching southwest Missouri to join with Brigadier General Benjamin McCulloch's Confederate troops.

The Wilson's Creek Campaign

As tempers flared and men began dying, it was apparent the American Civil War was to be a fighting war. With commanders and leaders like Nathaniel Lyon and Claiborne Fox Jackson, the outcome was to be one without compromise. Lyon, in command of the Union forces in Missouri, seized the initiative. His plan included the unified movement of three columns marching toward southwestern Missouri. The first two columns marched from St. Louis and the third marched from Fort Leavenworth, Kansas. The first column, commanded by Lyon, was to march from St. Louis along the Missouri River and captured the state capital, Jefferson City, which was a key transportation (due to its location on the Missouri River) and governmental center. The second column, under Franz Sigel, planned to travel by the Pacific Railroad from St. Louis to Rolla and march to Springfield in southwest Missouri. The third column involved David Stanley's cavalry under the command of Samuel Sturgis and marched from Fort Leavenworth, Kansas, toward Clinton, Missouri, where it was to be united with the first column. Together these columns were to march to Springfield.[33]

Lyon, upon his arrival in Springfield, Missouri, about 100 miles south of Clinton—his

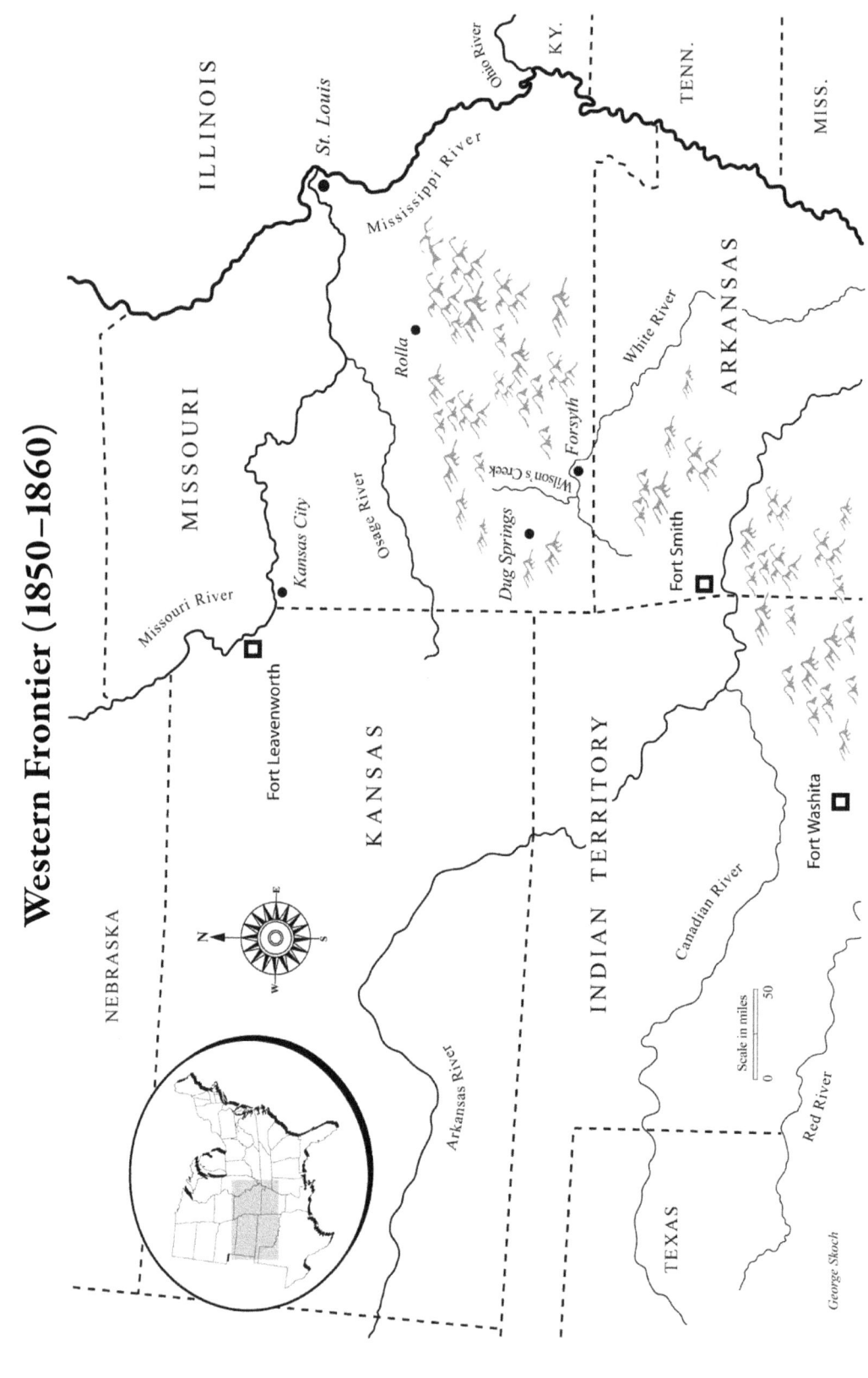

intended rendezvous point—positioned his troops in an arc from Little York, about 10 miles west of Springfield, to Springfield. On July 3, Brigadier General Nathaniel Lyon was placed under the command of Major General John C. Frémont, although Frémont did not physically arrive in St. Louis until July 25. Frémont's command consisted of about 7,000 men, mostly concentrated in southwest Missouri in the field and under direct command of the ever-aggressive Nathaniel Lyon. Lyon was facing the combined forces of Texan and brigadier general Ben McCulloch, commanding the Confederate Western Army, and Major General Sterling Price, commanding the Missouri State Guard.

David Stanley and Company C of the 1st U.S. Cavalry moved southward from Leavenworth, Kansas, as part of Major Samuel Sturgis' column. Sturgis commanded about 2,200 men and his column included the 1st and 2nd Kansas Volunteers and a contingent of U.S. Regulars—four companies of cavalry, one company of dragoons and a six-gun battery commanded by Lieutenant George Sokalski and Lieutenant John Van Deusen. As Sturgis' column moved southward, Stanley was concerned about the volunteer troops as they marched deeper into Missouri.

Samuel Sturgis. Stanley's cavalry traveled to Springfield as part of Sturgis's column (Library of Congress).

Discipline was one of the most basic principles Stanley maintained for a good soldier and he was right to be concerned about these troops. The march was a disgrace in his eyes due to the total lack of discipline by the Union troops. Within a week, the local population was being abused by the advancing soldiers. Stanley was most concerned about the two Kansas regiments, which entered houses and pillaged without regard for any other consideration. Finally Major Samuel Sturgis took matters in hand when a group of soldiers were caught in the act of robbing a house. Sturgis ordered them to be flogged with 39 lashes with a bull whip, at which time the Kansas soldiers, without regard for their officers, grabbed their weapons and threatened to open fire on the whipping party. Sturgis, not to be diverted, ordered the artillery batteries to fire on the mutineers if they resisted the flogging. At that point, the soldiers allowed the discipline to continue and this stopped further pillaging by Sturgis' troops.[34]

Forsyth Expedition

In mid–July, Lyon planned to continue his offensive against the Missouri State Guard but was concerned about a Southern concentration of troops near Forsyth, Missouri, a small community of five hundred citizens located on the navigable portion of the White River. Lyon's concern was that the town was a center of Confederate forces only 35 miles from Springfield. Historian William Garrett Piston noted, "Lyon's scouts and local Unionists reported that Forsyth served as a rallying point and supply depot for men of McBride's Division who had not yet reached the encampment at Cowskin Prairie. As Lyon faced the main enemy to the southwest, the Forsyth post potentially threatened his left flank."[35] Lyon sent a detachment of more than 1,200 men under the command of one-armed, 41-year-old Brigadier General Thomas Sweeny, who had recently been appointed to the rank of general of the Union Volunteers. The column included a battalion of infantry, and Captain David Stanley's Company C and Company D of the 1st U.S. Cavalry. The 2nd Kansas Infantry under command of Colonel Robert Mitchell and Lieutenant George Sokalski's section of Totten's Battery completed the Union expedition. Part of the Kansas Infantry was mounted and served under the command of Captain Samuel Wood. Wood's mounted Kansans often rode in combined cavalry actions with the 1st U.S. Cavalry during the Wilson's Creek Campaign.

On July 20, the first day of the expedition, Sweeny's force was able to cover only 7 miles and temperatures were so hot men began suffering heatstroke. To make matters worse, the first night brought a deluge of rain which continued into the next day. Fortunately, men from the Missouri Home Guard, the Union counterpart to the Southern-sympathizing state guard, joined the expedition and served as guides as Sweeny advanced toward Forsyth. The rain continued through the second day and turned into a severe thunderstorm during the night. After a long march on July 22, the expedition approached Forsyth. Sweeny was able to capture a few enemy pickets. The Confederate pickets had seen only a small number of Sweeny's entire force and reported only 150 members of state guard were present in the town. Based on this information, Sweeny sent Stanley's cavalry and Wood's mounted Kansans to surround the town to prevent the small enemy force from escaping. "No sooner had the riders passed than one of the captured Missourians bragged to Sweeny there were actually 1,000 State Guardsmen in Forsyth. Alarmed, Sweeny sent an orderly after Stanley, urging him to use caution, then rushed his infantry and artillery forward as quickly as possible."[36] Fortunately for Stanley and Sweeny, there really were only 150 Missouri State Guard soldiers in Forsyth and twenty-five of these were unarmed; but when they heard the Union force

Thomas Sweeny. The one-armed, Irish-born Sweeney led the expedition to Forsyth, Missouri (courtesy Wilson's Creek National Battlefield; WICR 31495).

was advancing the "entire civilian population began to flee, apparently fearing the vengeance of Kansans for past atrocities committed by Missouri 'border ruffians.'"[37]

Forsyth was located at the fork of Swan Creek and the White River, which bordered the town on the northwest and southwest. A large, heavily wooded bluff was located on the east.[38] "Stanley veered to the right of the road and led his horsemen through a small grove of oaks, emerging in a field of corn which was tall enough to conceal them completely from the Rebels. The cavalry then dashed down the muddy corn rows to the swollen stream and crossed to the other side, where they rapidly formed in line and readied their Sharp's rifles and revolvers for action."[39] Stanley's cavalry rode toward the town along the main road and the mounted Kansans circled to the right, intending to attack from the other side of the town. Because of Sweeny's message, the 1st U.S. Cavalry approached the town cautiously and on foot. Aware of the Union advance, Major Franklin, commanding the Missouri State Guard in Forsyth, ordered the men to take positions just outside of the town with one group on the bluffs south of the town and the second group occupying a hill east of the town. After reconnoitering, Forsyth, the Union cavalry, 250 men strong, advanced against the remaining state guard. "With a shout the U.S. troops charged headlong into town along the main road, while the Kansans swung to the side to enter it from the right. The Rebels greeted the charge with a blast of musket fire that dropped Stanley's horse and wounded two or three other horses and men. The Union men weathered the storm without breaking stride, however; and the cavalry pushed hard after the retreating Rebels, while the Kansans, to Stanley's disgust, stopped to loot a large store of supplies found in the courthouse. The secessionists for their part dashed to safety."[40]

The group of Southerners came close to ending David Stanley's career. Although firing from long range, they wounded two Union troopers and killed Stanley's horse under him. Stanley recalled, "As I made a rush into the town across the River, they made a stand and greeted us with volleys. One miserable bullet from one of these volleys, killed my fine horse, Prince, passing through his lungs and barely missing my leg. He was a beautiful bay, left me by [Lunsford] Lomax, who went into the Confederacy .... He was the finest horse I ever owned."[41] (Lunsford Lomax, who had joined the Confederate army, and David Stanley served together at Fort Washita and attended West Point together. It would take some years before Stanley was compensated for the loss of this special horse. He was still working on the paperwork with the army in March 1863 trying to recover the cost of the horse.)[42]

"Unruffled, Stanley had his bugler give the signal to charge."[43] Stanley's cavalry rode through the town and moved against the pockets of state guards located in the bluffs around Forsyth. The volleys from the advancing Union force drove the remaining men away. The training and the firepower of Stanley's men was immediately felt, "but a hundred shots or so from the Sharpe's rifles of the Dragoons sent them flying towards the Arkansas border," recorded a local journalist.[44] Lieutenant George Sokalski was ordered to fire his artillery on the town and a ball was sent into the upper story of the courthouse. Only then did the Union looters realize it was time to reengage in the task at hand. Stanley observed, "Never did rats desert a burning brush pile as did these plunderers. They did not run out, they tumbled out, and ran, each man for his horse, mounted and spurred out of town. This afforded me both fun and satisfaction, as these fellows had quit the fight for plunder."[45] Stanley led his troopers back to Forsyth but the advancing infantry came under fire again, this time by a group soldiers which had regrouped in the bluffs around the town. The combatants exchanged fire for half an hour before the State Guard, clearly outnumbered, withdrew.

General Thomas Sweeny recorded this in his official report of the expedition: "Under cover of the trees and bushes, they collected in considerable numbers upon the hills to the left of the town, from which they were dislodged by a well-directed fire of shell and canister from the artillery. The infantry meanwhile had been deployed as skirmishers through the woods and in the rear of the city, and but a short time elapsed before we were in complete possession of the place."[46] Unfortunately, the anger of Sweeny's Union soldiers was unleashed on Forsyth, which was looted and those civilians identified as disloyal placed under arrest. Sweeny returned to Springfield, arriving on July 25.

Dug Springs

At the beginning of August, the hot weather in southwest Missouri began to take its toll on some of Lyon's troops unaccustomed to the climate and marching in woolen uniforms. Not only was the temperature sweltering, supplies were getting short and the enemy was near. Lyon's scouts reported Brigadier General James Rains' division of Missouri State Guard was located near Dug Springs a few miles southwest of his camp. The Southern Coalition of forces of Confederate Brigadier General Benjamin McCulloch and Major General Price were advancing on Lyon at Springfield, and Brigadier General James S. Rains was chosen to lead the advance, which included six mounted companies of the 8th Division of the Missouri State Guard. Accompanying the State Guard was one company of Arkansas troops under the command of Captain Americus Reiff. Because Rains was familiar with the geography, he was chosen to lead the Southern advance. The entire force of 400 men was about ten miles in advance of Rains' full command.

Lyon, believing McCulloch and Price had yet to combine their forces, hoped to defeat them in detail. Lyon decided to take on the state guard force to his front. Rains' troops, also advancing, encountered Lyon's force about 9:00 a.m. on August 2. In an effort to determine the size of the force in his

Frederick Steele led the Union troops in the engagement at Dug Springs (courtesy Wilson's Creek National Battlefield; WICR 11511).

front, Lyon formed a battalion "from his Regulars, sending it ahead as an advance guard. Commanded by Captain Frederick Steele, a balding forty-two-year-old West Pointer from Connecticut who had distinguished himself in the Mexican War, this consisted of four companies of infantry, a section of guns from Totten's Battery, Captain Stanley's cavalry, and a company of unassigned recruits commanded by a sergeant."[47]

Dug Springs is located about 10 miles southwest of Springfield. The advance units of Rains' Missouri State Guard found Steele's force at Hayden's Farm about 9:00 a.m. and were chased off by two rounds of artillery fired by Totten's battery. Both Steele and Rains moved their forces forward and were stalemated as they probed each other's line. As the line remained stationary, Lyon received reinforcements of two companies from the 1st Iowa Infantry. Later in the afternoon, Confederate colonel James McIntosh reconnoitered Steele's position but was unable to determine the number of troops Rains faced. McIntosh, serving as McCulloch's adjutant, returned during the afternoon to report his findings to the commanding general.

About 5:00 p.m. due to adjustments in the respective Union and Southern Coalition lines, Steele, who was concerned about being outflanked by Rains, ordered his men forward. When Rains saw the Union troops starting to move forward, he assumed Steele had waited long enough and sought to advance on his troops. To prevent the attack, Rains launched an attack with most of his force. Rains marched directly into Steele's waiting infantry supported by Totten's artillery, which poured canister into the advance State Guards. As Rains' soldiers were recoiling from their first combat situation, they were charged by David Stanley's cavalry, much to the surprise of Stanley. As Rains' troops were beginning to break under the fire of the artillery, the retreating troops appeared an opportune target for the cavalry. A correspondent from Curran, Missouri, reported on Stanley's cavalry charge:

> Presently we could see a column of infantry approaching from the woods with the design of cutting off our infantry. Capt. Stanley immediately drew up his men, and, as soon as within range, they opened fire from their Sharp's carbines, when several volleys were exchanged. The number of the enemy's infantry was seemingly about five hundred; our cavalry not quite a hundred and fifty. The infantry kept up the firing for some minutes, when some enthusiastic lieutenant giving the order to "charge," some twenty-five of the gallant regulars rushed forward upon the enemy's lines, and, dashing aside the threatening bayonets of the sturdy rebels, hewed down the ranks with fearful slaughter. Capt. Stanley, who was amazed at the temerity of the little band, was obliged to sustain the order, but before he could reach his little company they had broken the ranks of the cowards, who outnumbered them, twenty to one. Some of the wounded asked, in utter astonishment, "whether these were men or devils—they fight so?"[48]

Frederick Steele recorded the cavalry charge: "The enemy was now in complete rout, a part of Captain Stanley's troop having gallantly charged and cut through his line."[49] Rains' retreat left 200 horses tied in a ravine which were a tempting target for Steele, but he received orders from Lyon to return to Springfield. Steele, fearing Lyon's orders signified he was being cut off by an enemy column in his rear, hastened back toward the main Union line, leaving the horses.

General Rains was embarrassed as his troops turned and ran. Historian William Garrett Piston noted, "Nevertheless, Rains' entire command fled back down the Wire Road in abject panic. Many soldiers did not halt even when they encountered McIntosh's men, who were still riding back toward the Western Army's camp at Crane Creek."[50] In his official report Rains recorded he sent 150 men to stop a Union flanking movement, pushing Steele's troops back in confusion. He had expected reinforcement to support his actions but receiving none

"Splendid Charge of the U.S. Cavalry at Dug Spring, Missouri," *Harpers Weekly*, August 24, 1861 (courtesy Wilson's Creek National Battlefield).

he retired "in accordance with instructions."[51] It was unclear where Rains expected to find the reinforcements since he was some distance in advance of the main Confederate force.

Colonel James McIntosh, who had just visited Rains and understood Rains had no orders to engage the enemy, had to be amazed, when, as he was returning to General McCulloch, he was overtaken by Rains' retreating troops. McIntosh wrote the following in his report to McCulloch: "When about 3 miles from your camp, the command of General Rains, as I expected, came down upon us in full flight and in the greatest confusion. I drew up my men across the road, and rallied the greater portion of them and sent them on in regular order. General Rains had engaged the enemy unadvisedly, and had sent for my small command to re-enforce him, which I respectfully declined, having no disposition to sacrifice it in such company."[52]

Stanley's cavalry certainly spooked Rains' State Guard, as did the Union artillery during the engagement. A journalist traveling with the Federal forces reported:

> The praise of all tongues was upon the magnificent charge of our cavalry. The men, actuated by a supreme disdain for the novices who had but recently left the plough for the musket, determined to give them a real taste of war at the onset, and they must have given the poor deluded fools a bitter foretaste, with their navy revolvers and carbines. Two of the lieutenants returned with their swords stained with the blood of men they had run through and through, up to the hilt. One horse which was led home was pierced by nine balls; another with sides so covered with gore as to conceal the wounds. Four of their wounded men were afterward picked up on the ground, some of them fatally. Unfortunately our loss, as might be expected, was severe. Four of our gallant regulars were brought in dead, and five wounded, one of which has since died.[53]

Stanley's command gained the attention of the army, but the charge had not been ordered by him and he was as surprised as anyone at its audacity.

An account by one of the soldiers of the 1st Iowa Infantry recorded the following "I remember one of the cavalrymen having his sword out and shaking the blood from the tip of it. He said he was going to dry it on. Some of his comrades told him to wipe it off, but he said 'no.' They halted near us for a few minutes; this man said he had run the saber through a man and pulled him off his horse with it.... This, I said, is war, this is the way it looks in books, this is the real thing, the real, sure-enough war."[54]

The official estimates of casualties were 20 Southerners killed and 50 wounded, while the Union lost 4 men killed and another 37 wounded. Among the losses reported by David Stanley from his charge into the Missouri State Guard were "four of his 42 troopers ... killed and six wounded. One of the dead was Lt. M.J. Kelly, who had led a cavalry charge at Forsyth on July 22."[55] While this was not a significant victory, the retreat alleviated the more serious potential of a pitched battle between the opposing forces. The real significance of the battle was the loss of confidence by General Ben McCulloch toward Price's Missouri State Guard. When informed of Rains' retreat, McCulloch verbally denounced the Missouri troops, which "boded ill for future cooperation between McCulloch and Price."[56] Lyon's account of the incident was succinct: "My advance guards of infantry opened fire upon them, and without orders from me, by a spontaneous emotion, the advance guard of my cavalry charged and drove back the rebels."[57]

The Battle of Wilson's Creek

Lyon skirmished with the Southern Coalition on August 3 and began his return to Springfield on August 4, marching in temperatures of 105°. Lyon's army was in terrible physical condition due to lack of supplies, lack of reinforcements, lack of rest, and the sweltering heat of August. Lyon was a single-minded and narrowly focused commander, but his experience in the field was limited. After the skirmish at Dug Springs, Lyon was criticized for losing contact with his opponent by under-utilizing his cavalry. McCulloch and Price's Southern Coalition was in little better condition as it slowly followed Lyon toward Springfield and suffered through the hot summer days and nights on August 5 and 6. The Southern troops rested from August 7–9.

On the afternoon of August 9 Price's State Guard cavalry clashed with David Stanley's command and Captain Samuel Wood's mounted 2nd Kansas on Grand Prairie. The Union cavalry got the best of Price's troopers. Again, on August 9, "Lyon received a message from Captain David S. Stanley, reporting yet another skirmish on Grand Prairie which had significant consequences. Captain Samuel N. Wood's Kansas Rangers killed two Southerners and captured six, who identified themselves as members of a foraging party from the Missouri State Guard."[58] Through Stanley's and Wood's success in capturing some of the Southern cavalry, it is likely Lyon was aware he was not facing two separate columns, but instead faced the combined troops of McCulloch and Price.

Ironically, Lyon was pleased the Missouri State Guard troops had been successful in cutting his supply line to Rolla, because he was now committed to bringing the battle to Price and McCulloch, even though he faced twice his numbers. Despite being outnumbered, Franz Sigel proposed splitting the Union force, and Lyon agreed with the plan. Sigel planned to lead 1,200 men in a flanking movement while Lyon attacked from the north. Lyon decided to march toward his enemy on the evening of August 9 and attack on August 10. Captain David Stanley's 1st U.S. Cavalry, the 1,200 man Greene and Christian County Home Guard, and a section of Backof's Missouri Light Artillery did not participate in the ill-fated attack on McCulloch and Price. This detachment was ordered to remain and protect supplies and the town of Springfield. Lyon needed a backdoor if the day's battle was unsuccessful, and these men were ordered to be the route of escape, if needed.

David Stanley's part in the Battle of Wilson's Creek was over when he was ordered to escort a wagon train as Lyon marched his 5,431 men to face McCulloch and Price with 12,125 men. The Union army suffered a major defeat during the battle, which included the death of Lyon. The Union force lost 1,317 men including 258 killed, 873 wounded, and 186 missing compared to 1,230 casualties for the Southern Coalition forces with 279 dead and 951 wounded. The Union army began a return march to Rolla and the Southern forces were unable to pursue. General Ben McCulloch was concerned about his supply line and still lacked confidence in the Missouri State Guard. He returned south and Price began a push northward into the heart of Missouri that resulted in the First Battle of Lexington on September 20.[59]

Stanley's analysis of the Battle of Wilson's Creek was that the Union defeat should have been a victory. He felt Lyon had failed to bring another 2,000 troops stationed in Rolla to assist in the action, that Lyon should not have divided his forces. He also felt Lyon's German soldiers stopped their pursuit of the enemy during the battle prematurely. And he blamed Frémont's lack of physical and material support of Lyon's actions in southwest Missouri. Frémont's communication after the battle was one of concern: "Their loss reported heavy, including Generals McCulloch and Price. Their tents and wagons destroyed in the action. Sigel left one gun on the field, and returned to Springfield, whence, at 3 o'clock in the morning of the 11th, continued his retreat upon Rolla, bringing off his baggage trains and $250,000 in specie from Springfield Bank. I am doing what is possible to support him, but need aid of some organized force to repel the enemy, reported advancing on other points in considerable strength."[60]

Certainly Nathaniel Lyon was one of the Civil War's most interesting characters, and the examination of how his actions impacted the early part of the Civil War in Missouri makes him a controversial person to this day. David Stanley reflected on Lyon after his death at Wilson's Creek:

> A man of great resolution, he had traits that made him unpopular. He was a radical abolitionist and an aggressive atheist. He continually thrust his doctrines upon people who despised them. Lyon liked to argue, especially with women, and he would insist that religion was only superstition. Of course such a man could not be popular, but he was an unflinching patriot; firm, brave. Prompt in detecting humbug and hypocrisy, as the rebels soon found when Lyon's keen policy succeeded the baleful vacillating stupidity of General Harney. Lyon's was a great loss to the Union cause, but I doubt if he could ever have become a great general.[61]

Franz Sigel assumed command of the Union army in the field during the retreat to Rolla, much to the dismay of the other commanders. A group of officers who participated in the retreat from Springfield also wrote of the poor command abilities of Sigel after the battle:

> It might easily be shown that while Sigel was in command our forces more nearly resembled a crowd of refugees than an army of organized troops. Sigel put his brigade in advance, and the rear was brought up by the regulars. This arrangement was the only evidence of skill manifested

by him during his memorable retreat. The column was broken by crowds of refugees, wagons, horses, mules, cows, etc., which were mixed up with the troops in such a manner that it would have been very difficult to have made any disposition for battle. The command moved before sunrise during the three days that Sigel commanded, and was halted on the second day, and remained exposed to the rays of a burning sun for several hours. The reason given for the halt was that Sigel's men were cooking breakfast. During the halt on the third day, the officers, having become disgusted with the manner in which Sigel conducted the retreat, insisted that Major Sturgis should assume command. Sigel yielded, on the ground that he had no commission.[62]

Summary

The medical-student-turned-U.S. Cavalry officer had a firsthand view of the worst that was possible as the United States entered the Civil War. David Stanley had cast his lot with the United States Army when he decided to attend the United States Military Academy. For nine years afterward the farm boy from Ohio served in the far western regions of the United States and loved what he did. He also found Anna Wright and married her, an event whose importance is reflected in his own words, written in true military terms: "I had truly found my messmate, my heart's joy for the years to come, my loving model wife."[63]

While serving on the frontier, Stanley met many men destined to be key figures in the upcoming Civil War. These experiences and acquaintances were invaluable to his wartime career. What he didn't like were the conflicts between the pro-slavery and antislavery factions in Kansas and Arkansas. Americans fighting Americans was decidedly distasteful for him. His unhappiness continued as he lost good friends who left the army and returned to their home states to take up arms against the country he had sworn to defend. His outlook on the war had its own sadness, as his youngest brother, James Stanley, decided to enlist in the Confederate army.

He also saw the type of people who wanted to influence others about the rights of slaveholders in the South. He barely escaped capture at Fort Smith and even after returning to Fort Washita he was asked to surrender to the Confederate authorities. He was forced to battle a group of Texans seeking his capture and watched with disgust as his commanding officer tried to send a group of ex-slaves back to their masters. Next, he had watched a West Point graduate like himself shot by his own men in an emotion-laden encounter in Independence, Missouri. He knew the country he loved so much had much pain to suffer.

Although David Stanley was involved in three minor skirmishes in the Wilson's Creek Campaign, his leadership and other skills were evident. He even received recognition for an unplanned cavalry attack at the skirmish at Dug Springs. He was efficient and had found a way to get the necessary job done even when dealing with undisciplined volunteer troops. He, in return, was well liked by the volunteers and was referred to as "our friend, Captain David Stanley" by the 1st Iowa Volunteers. He did not know what would follow, but he had seen the aftermath of the fury of two armies of the United States and he understood that professional soldiers like himself would play an important role in this Civil War.

2

New Madrid and Island No. 10

*The division of General Stanley ... displayed coolness,
courage, and fortitude worthy of all praise.*

Frémont's Command

One of the principle Confederate strategies in Tennessee in late 1861 was to prevent the Federal forces from descending the Mississippi River. The Mississippi River north of Memphis was heavily fortified at Fort Pillow and Fort Taylor where Confederate guns commanded the river while the Union forces fortified the city of Cairo, Illinois, at the confluence of the Ohio River and the Mississippi River. Both armies recognized the value of the Mississippi River in 1861 as a source of transportation and supply. The offensive value of the river for the North was the rapid deployment of troops and supplies; and from a defensive standpoint, it was important the enemy did not show up unexpectedly at an important geographic location or at a key city such as Memphis or New Orleans. As the war advanced, the importance of the Mississippi River served to protect the Union flank when operations were near the river.

Kentucky was neutral until September 1861 and had resisted construction of fortifications by either Union or Confederate troops in the state, but Missouri had active warfare. By no means were the Confederate activities in Missouri during the first months of the war confined to the southwestern part of the state. While David Stanley was still in southwestern Missouri, Major General Leonidas Polk dispatched Brigadier General Gideon Pillow's force upriver to occupy New Madrid, Missouri: "On July 28, 1861, eight Confederate steamers splashed up to the New Madrid levee, and amid the cheers of the local citizenry General Pillow's Army of Liberation tramped down the gang plank onto Missouri soil."[1]

After the Confederate victory at Wilson's Creek in August, the Southern forces sought to strike further into the Union-held territory of Missouri. A two-pronged attack was planned which called for General Sterling Price to flank the Union camps in Rolla and Jefferson City, Missouri, while General Gideon Pillow advanced overland and captured Cape Girardeau, further strengthening Confederate control on the Mississippi River.

Brigadier General William Hardee and the Missouri State Guard commanded by Brigadier General M. Jeff Thompson were to operate in concert with Brigadier General

Gideon Pillow in pressing northward toward Cape Girardeau and St. Louis. Hardee marched to Greenville, Missouri, about fifty miles south of the southern terminus of the St. Louis and Iron Mountain Railroad while Thompson advanced to Commerce, Missouri, on the banks of the Mississippi River. They waited for Pillow to arrive with his troops, but were soon disappointed: "In New Madrid, Pillow was nursing a carbuncle on his buttock that made riding anything but pleasant. And his offensive fervor was displaced by thoughts of defense."[2] Pillow concluded that rather than advancing northward, just the 'threat' of an attack on Cape Girardeau was sufficient to hold the Union troops in place while Price advanced into the heart of the state. Pillow, a Tennessee native, also concluded it was more important to protect the Mississippi Valley than to liberate Missouri from the numerous Union troops flocking into the state.

After the Battle of Wilson's Creek, St. Louis was alive with activity. "In St. Louis the excitement was still greater than it had been three months before," recorded John Buegel, a member of the 3rd Missouri Infantry. "From all sides came Union soldiers—artillery, infantry, and cavalry. All agitated, recruited and drilled."[3] David Stanley moved to Rolla after the Battle of Wilson's Creek and the Union forces in Missouri remained under the direct command of Major General John C. Frémont.

The fact the defeat at Wilson's Creek occurred under his command seemed to gain Frémont's attention, which had been previously focused on establishing his extravagant headquarters in St. Louis. He called upon governors from the surrounding Union states to send as many troops as possible to meet the Southern menace and he also ordered $300,000 from the United States Treasury to be used as "the exigency requires."[4] Although, Frémont worked diligently, he was not successful in his command in St. Louis. Almost immediately his mistakes seemed to multiply and the optimism which accompanied Frémont's appointment soon began to fade.

One of the most controversial actions which occurred under Frémont's command was the declaration of martial law and issuance of the first emancipation declaration. On August 30, 1861, amid concerns that Confederate forces were amassing to attack in Missouri, Frémont announced he would assume the administrative powers of the state. He did this without consulting the new governor of Missouri, senior officers or the president. He also stated he would confiscate the property of anyone taking arms against the United States, and he planned to liberate slaves of those supporting the Confederacy. Lincoln received an official version of the text of Frémont's declaration on September 2 and asked Frémont to modify his proclamation to be in compliance with a more moderate stance agreed upon on August 6 by the U.S. Congress. Lincoln sought to guide Frémont from the action he had taken and wrote, "This letter is written in a spirit of caution, and not of censure."[5] "'I did it without consultation or advice of anyone' [Frémont wrote]. He still believed it a first-rate piece of work as proclamations go, and he wouldn't change it or shade it," wrote Carl Sanburg.[6]

While the issues of Frémont's command mounted, the Battle of Lexington, or the Battle of the Hemp Bales, occurred from September 13 to September 20, 1861. After the Confederate success at Wilson's Creek in August, General Sterling Price's forces marched on Lexington, Missouri, and forced the garrison of 3,500 Union soldiers to seek protection behind fortifications. On September 20, Price's men advanced behind mobile fortifications—hemp bales—until they were close enough for the final assault. Price forced the entire Union garrison of 3,500 men to surrender.

Within two weeks of Price's victory at Lexington, Frémont reorganized his grand "Army of the West," consisting of five divisions. Brigadier General Samuel Sturgis and Brigadier General James H. Lane were stationed in Kansas City and along the Kansas-Missouri state line with 5,500 troops. Frémont had about 39,000 troops in Missouri and, in combination with the Union troops on the Kansas border, commanded an active force of 45,000 men.[7]

Despite Frémont's military challenges, it was charges of scandal and corruption which contributed significantly to his final removal as commander of the Western Department. Since taking command in St. Louis, Frémont's lifestyle, home and headquarters were extravagant and were referred to as a regal court. He was also alleged to have misused government funds, purchased rotted and damaged supplies, and purchased defective weapons. This was in addition to a long list of inefficiencies and incompetence.

On November 2, Frémont was relieved of command and his one hundred days of command were over in the West. For David Stanley, Frémont's one hundred days were very important and significant. Stanley recorded of Frémont, "[He] had inaugurated a system of wasteful administration, which if it had not been checked would have bankrupted the United States in one year."[8] Stanley also noted Frémont, who had recently traveled to Europe, tried to model his military style after the Europeans, including surrounding himself with many foreign advisors. In true, humorous and sarcastic David Stanley style, he spoke of these advisors' names: "mostly spelled with constants—no English tongue could ever pronounce them."[9] Among the criticism of Frémont recorded by Stanley was the fact that many of Frémont's friends received large government contracts for the immense fortifications at St. Louis, Cape Girardeau, Ironton, Rolla and Jefferson City, the latter of which Frémont was so fond. Also noted was one of Frémont's friends who had fraudulently shipped brass fittings in place of gold dust.

Stanley was involved in one final incident of the doomed Frémont command when he was approached by a paymaster, Major Cheney. Cheney had been ordered to give $175,000 to J.K. Wood, the Frémont subordinate who had shipped the brass fittings instead of gold dust to California. Cheney had refused to do so, but he was concerned he would be coerced into complying with orders. Stanley agreed to support Cheney's decision and told him that he had command over the local troops and he would use them to protect the money. Stanley felt "one hundred seventy-five thousand dollars was saved to the government."[10]

Despite Stanley's unhappiness with the extravagance of Frémont's administration, Stanley received an excellent promotion to the rank of brigadier general

David Stanley was promoted to the rank of brigadier general in the fall of 1861 (Library of Congress).

of volunteers on September 28, 1861. He was one of many experienced West Point graduates needed to convert the new volunteer army into an effective fighting force. In accepting the new rank, Stanley wrote, "I accept with gratitude this favor from the President who has rewarded me far beyond my deserts. Through applications and attention to duty, I will try to fit myself for the responsibilities this new rank devolves on me."[11]

Also, it was during the fall of 1861 that David Stanley broke his ankle. As he was mounting his horse, a spirited animal, the horse jumped and he landed on his ankle, resulting in a Pott's fracture which took six weeks to heal, although Stanley suffered the effects of this injury in later life. While he was recovering from his fracture, he served as the president of a military tribunal charged with determining the guilt or innocence of Colonel Ebenezer Magoffin of the pro–Southern Missouri State Guard. Magoffin, the brother of Governor Beriah Magoffin of Kentucky, was charged with murder and violation of parole. Stanley's tribunal found Magoffin not guilty of murder but guilty of violating a parole and sentenced him to death. Luckily for Magoffin he was reprieved by President Lincoln, despite the fact Magoffin temporarily escaped from prison.[12]

With Frémont's departure, Stanley's new commanding officer was Major General Henry Halleck, who was an effective administrator and an overly cautious fighting general; but clearly Halleck was an improvement for the Union army over John Frémont. Halleck had graduated from the U.S. Military Academy in 1839 and served as an engineer in the U.S. Army. He resigned from the army in 1854, but remained active in the militia in California. He had been recommended for command rank by Winfield Scott and was given the rank of major general in August 1861. Given command of the Department of Missouri on November 9, 1861, he carried the nickname "Old Brains."

The New Madrid and Island No. 10 Campaign

Stanley recuperated from his ankle injury during the winter of 1861–1862 and was able to enjoy the company of his wife in St. Louis. While he was recuperating in St. Louis he was greeted with the joyous news that his third daughter was born and was doing well. Sarah Eliza Stanley was born in November 1861 in St. Louis, Missouri.

In 1862 duty again called him away, and with his new rank he was given command of the First Division in Major General John Pope's Army of the Mississippi in March 1862. Pope's army consisted initially of three divisions, each commanded by a brigadier general, but in reality, each of the divisions was of brigade strength. Stanley, much to his delight, was given command of four Ohio regiments. The First Brigade was commanded by Colonel John Groesbeck, and the Second Brigade was commanded by Colonel J.L. Kirby Smith. Each brigade contained two regiments each, but command at any level at this point in the Civil War was a new experience. The four regiments contained in the First Division were 27th Ohio, 39th Ohio, 43rd Ohio, and 63rd Ohio infantries.[13] The other two divisional commanders were Charles Schuyler Hamilton of the Second Division and John Palmer of the Third Division. In addition, Colonel Gordon Granger was given command of the army's cavalry.

David Stanley, John Palmer and Charles Schuyler Hamilton were assigned to division command under John Pope, who was a rising star. Pope was promoted and given command of the Army of the Mississippi by Henry Halleck on February 23, 1862, and was charged with the clear objective to remove Confederate control of the Mississippi River. Pope, a graduate of the U.S. Military Academy in 1842, served under John C. Frémont from July through November 1861 and had a strained relationship with his commander. Halleck saw promise in Pope and gave him the opportunity to demonstrate his abilities. David Stanley agreed and wrote, "This army was really formed to give General Pope a command."[14] John Pope was a 39-year-old son of a judge from Illinois with political connections directly linking him to the president. His experience was somewhat limited, but he had served in the Mexican War as part of Zachary Taylor's staff.

The structure of Pope's Army of the Mississippi was soon changed to include five divisions, an artillery division, and a cavalry division. The Fourth Division was commanded by Brigadier General Eleazer Arthur Paine, the Fifth Division was commanded by Brigadier General Joseph Plummer, and the Artillery Division was commanded by Major W.L. Lothrop.

John Pope commanded the Army of the Mississippi during the siege of New Madrid and Island No. 10 (Library of Congress).

After serving under Frémont in 1861, the group of officers John Pope had assembled found a comfortable and welcome change. Stanley had much in common with this group of commanders, many of them West Point graduates, most serving in the regular army, and many serving on the western frontier before the war. He was also very pleased with Pope, whom he described as "very agreeable and ... a very witty man and often turned the laugh on his staff officers and others."[15] One example of Pope's wit was directed at Louis Marshall, who had been the colonel of the Benton Cadets, a short-lived independent infantry regiment. Marshall had been elected colonel in the first regimental elections, and in subsequent elections he had been demoted first to lieutenant colonel and then to major. Stanley recorded Pope's conversation with Marshall when he humorously said, "Why Lou, if those fellows had given you another promotion, they would have landed you in the penitentiary."[16]

Gone was the pomp and circumstance of the Frémont era and this band of professional soldiers worked to turn the volunteers into an effective fighting force. Pope tried to insure his commanders had a common objective and that they worked together to achieve success on the battlefield. David Stanley had to be struck with the irony of being an experienced

2. New Madrid and Island No. 10

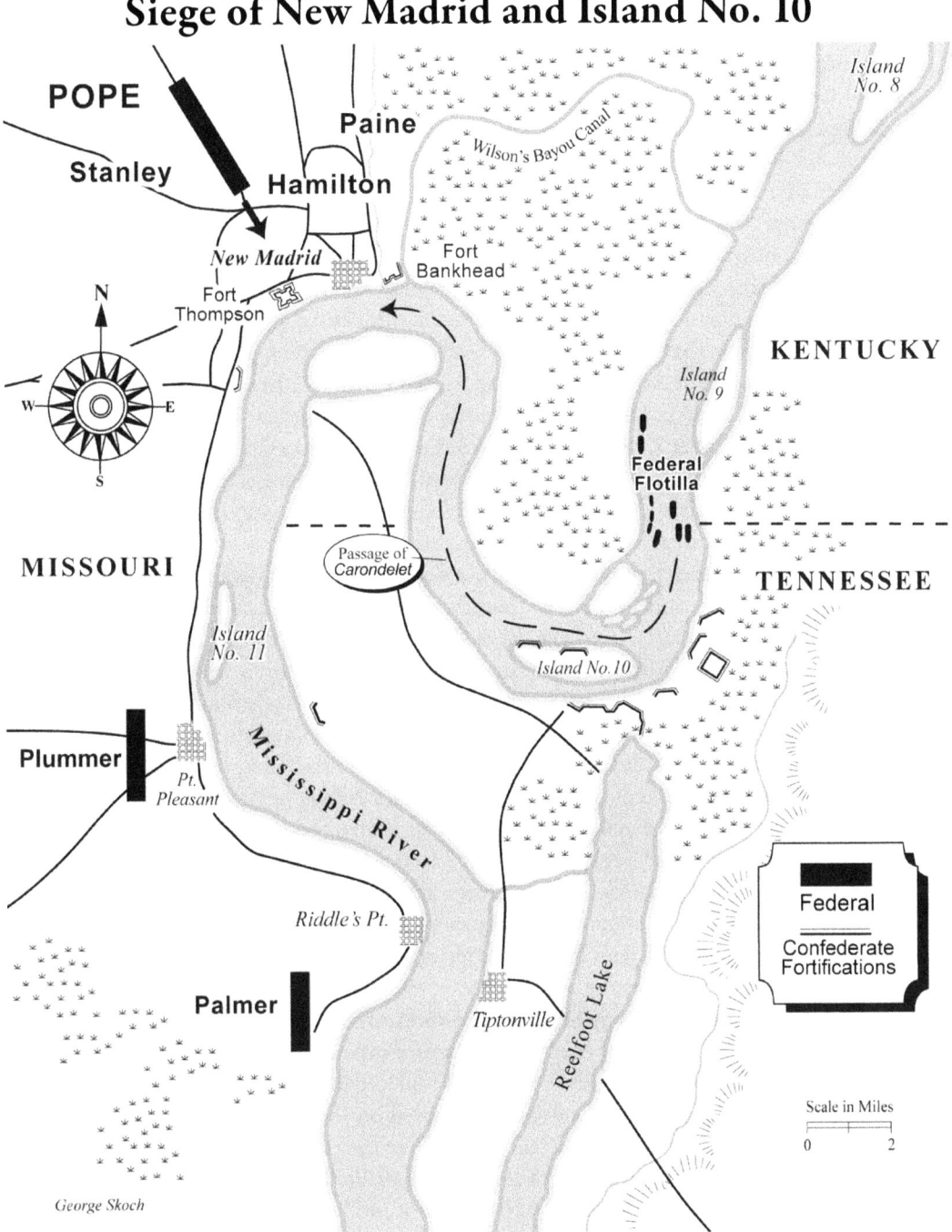

cavalry officer now in charge of infantry. But Pope allowed Stanley, and his other generals, to command relatively small divisions as they familiarized themselves with their new duties serving as generals in the field.

In March 1862, Stanley, commanding an infantry division, was part of a cohesive Union army intent on removing the Confederate obstacle at New Madrid, Missouri, and the formidable Island No. 10. Captain Asa B. Gray of the Confederate army and the engineer supervising the construction of fortifications on Island No. 10, wrote, "Since I have seen Columbus, I have not lessened my opinion, previously given to the commanding general, of its strong natural facilities for defense; but further examinations have strengthened my belief of the great importance of Island No. 10 in connection with a line of defense including New Madrid and Union City, as a powerful base of operations against the enemy."[17] Island No. 10 was so named because it was the tenth island in the Mississippi River south of the Ohio River. The combination of New Madrid—which strategically protected northeast Arkansas and was a potential center to launch an advance into Missouri—and Island No. 10—an obstacle to all traffic on the Mississippi—made a formidable defense for the Confederacy. However, the Confederate command had deemed Columbus, Kentucky, to be the principle Southern defensive position on the Confederate-held section of the Mississippi River. The next Confederate defense south of New Madrid, Missouri, and Island No. 10 was Fort Pillow, located downriver on the Chickasaw Bluffs in Lauderdale County, Tennessee. The Battle of Belmont was fought on November 7, 1861, and this battle between Ulysses Grant and Gideon Pillow convinced the Confederate command even more of the importance of fortifying Columbus, Kentucky, rather than Island No. 10. Although Kentucky had tried to remain neutral, both Federal and Confederate armies moved into the state.

Columbus, Kentucky, proved an effective defense on the Mississippi River as long as the Confederate Army could protect the countryside and prevent Union forces from isolating and besieging the fortification from a land-based assault. However, the isolation of Columbus came true when General Ulysses Grant marched upon and captured Fort Henry and Fort Donelson in February 1862. General Leonidas Polk, realizing his position in Columbus was no longer defensible, evacuated the Confederate defenses at Columbus, and the importance of Island No. 10 became evident. After evacuating Columbus, Polk split his corps, sending one division to New Madrid and the remainder to Fort Pillow.

Confederate brigadier general John McCown arrived to assume command at New Madrid in late February and began to fortify the Confederate position. When the Confederate defenses had been enhanced, the armament in the Madrid Bend was impressive. There were 24 artillery pieces mounted on the shore and another 19 cannon on the island. In addition, nine cannon were placed on floating batteries, and another 12 heavy guns were placed in New Madrid, creating a strong defense. McCown's chief of artillery, Brigadier General James Trudeau, arrived on March 1 to assume command of the artillery. The ground forces at New Madrid were also strengthened with additional infantry regiments and artillery companies. Brigadier General Alexander P. Stewart was placed in command of New Madrid and he immediately ordered a new fort to be constructed on the eastern edge of town. Island No.10 and five shore batteries on the Tennessee side of the river were reinforced with additional infantry regiments, cavalry, and a regiment of artillery.

General Pope wrote after the fall of Fort Henry and Fort Donelson: "This result had been for some time foreseen by the rebel generals, and General Beauregard, who had been assigned to command, selected Island No. 10, 60 miles below Columbus, as the strong place where the possession of the Mississippi River was first to be contested. The place was strongly fortified, mounted with 150 pieces of heavy artillery, and garrisoned by about 9,000 men."[18] Pope correctly noted the artillery and infantry were not only positioned on the island, but also on the north and south banks of the Mississippi River. The surrounding defenses made a direct assault on the island very difficult. Within two days of the fall of Fort Henry and Fort Donelson, Pope was ordered by General Henry Halleck to march on New Madrid and Island No. 10.

The Advance on New Madrid and Island No. 10

Pope landed in Commerce, Missouri, on February 21, 1862, and within a week he was able to organize his army and was ready to march. He gave credit to his divisional commanders for quickly organizing the army. Within a week the advance on New Madrid was ready to begin. Pope wrote that the Army of the Mississippi was "widely known and greatly distinguished in the West for its discipline, its gallantry, and its effectiveness, and for the soldierly and cordial good feeling which characterized both officers and men."[19] Pope continued: "It is not only proper, but it is my duty, to say here that during my whole experience in this war I have never seen troops which would compare with this little army. Of the mobility and *esprit de corps,* of courage in battle and patience and fortitude under exposure, labor, and privation, and of the cordial harmony which existed among the officers and men, from the highest to the lowest, the services and the reputation of this little army, from the beginning to the end of the war, whether acting together or separated and serving in other organizations, are sufficient evidence."[20]

Pope began his march toward New Madrid through some of the most adversely wet and muddy conditions imaginable: "The weather was cold and wet [Pope wrote]. A drizzling snow and rain was falling upon us, and adding to our almost insuperable difficulties from the time we marched from Commerce until we reached New Madrid."[21] Pope opined the reason the enemy did not resist his advance was because they thought an advance at this time of the season was impossible, or at least impractical.

While David Stanley was well satisfied with his assignment with the First Division, General John Palmer, who had been assigned the Third Division, was decidedly unhappy: "My situation here is rather disagreeable. Generals Stanley, Hamilton and myself each command divisions. Pope has given all the choice regiments to these army chums of his and I command the reserve poorest."[22] Stanley's initial appearance at Pope's army seems to have caused much consternation among the divisional commanders, including Schuyler Hamilton, who was much more gracious about the loss of the Ohio regiments which would make up Stanley's First Division: "Brigadier-General Stanley arrived in camp on the evening of the 3d. On the 4th a reorganization of division, &c., was made. General Stanley being from Ohio, the Ohio regiments passed from under my command. Having had evidence of their gallantry and coolness under fire, and feeling grateful for the cheerfulness with which both officers and men had responded to my efforts to enforce discipline and excite their ardor, I parted with them with regret."[23]

Stanley's First Division contained a total 3,697 troops in the two brigades, but only 3,330 men were present for duty during the Island No. 10 Campaign. This was a great many more men than Stanley had ever commanded and this really was his first major command challenge in the Civil War. He was fortunate to be serving under a commander whose style was to appreciate and recognize the assets his subordinates possessed.

The advance guard of Pope's army arrived at New Madrid on March 2 and the entire army arrived on March 3, 1862. When Pope arrived, he appraised the fortifications around New Madrid and, observing the fortifications did not extend to the swamp on the eastern side of the town, enveloped the town. Confederate brigadier general M. Jeff Thompson, observing the envelopment, tried to trick Pope by sending twenty of his men with three one-pound cannons to Pope's rear near Sikeston. He was unsuccessful because, when the Union cavalry was fired upon, rather than retreating "a bugle sounded and the blue-coated cavalrymen charged.... Thompson ordered an immediate retreat. Then, according to an Illinois cavalryman who took part in the pursuit, 'the fun commenced.'"[24] Chastened, Thompson returned to the friendly confines of the Confederate lines.

The town of New Madrid, while actually north of Island No. 10, was downstream and had two forts on the river near New Madrid. Fort Thompson lay to the west of the town and Fort Bankhead was to the south and east of the town. Fort Thompson was composed of four earth walls about 400 feet long and was protected by fourteen heavy cannon. Fort Bankhead consisted of a long parapet ditch which was dug in an irregular line. In front of the fort was a line of abatis of brush and felled trees. The works were about 300 to 400 yards long and extended from the river to the north side of town. A series of trenches connected Fort Bankhead, also a four-sided fortification, to Fort Thompson. It was the most recently constructed of the two forts and was more poorly fortified. Fort Bankhead boasted a battery of six cannon and four 32-pound heavy cannon. The two forts were manned by five regiments of infantry, in addition to the artillerymen. Also, sitting in the Mississippi River were six Confederate gunboats searching for opportunities to shell Union troops.[25]

The Siege of New Madrid

David Stanley, upon being given command of the First Division on March 4, wrote, "On the same night a detachment of 500 men, commanded by Col. J.L. Kirby Smith, Forty-third Ohio Volunteers, made a reconnaissance in force, and after cannonading the town and forts for half an hour retired to their camp without loss."[26] Stanley had a new command and the siege had begun.

Stanley's next major action occurred on March 6. He moved his division into New Madrid to within 700 yards of Fort Bankhead, pushing the Confederate infantry back into the fort as he advanced. Once his division approached the fort, it was subjected to a devastating artillery barrage from the gunboats in the river and from both forts. Stanley noted, "I deemed it proper to withdraw my troops. We were for half an hour under a fierce cannonade, and, strange to say, suffered only in 3 wounded."[27] His division was selected by Pope to probe the Confederate defenses and ascertain their strength. Colonel Gordon Granger's cavalry also probed the Confederate left on March 6 and returned after a two-hour exchange with the defenders.

Colonel William H. Worthington, commanding the First Brigade of Brigadier General Schuyler Hamilton's Second Division, recorded the engagement. Worthington noted his brigade was ordered to the northeastern part of New Madrid and out of sight of the Confederate defenders. He was ordered to wait for Stanley's division to attack the lower part of the town. It was planned that Stanley's attack would divert troops and artillery from Worthington's front. Worthington recorded he waited until the attack was initiated by Stanley's division before moving his brigade in support of the attack. Worthington's brigade received much of the initial artillery fire because the Confederate defenders had observed his men in formation and anticipated he would begin the assault. Stanley's attack soon resulted in the artillery's being directed at his division moving toward the fort. The cannons from both forts and the riverboats began firing. As Worthington's men joined in the assault, the attack was halted. Worthington wrote, "General Stanley himself soon appeared, to whom I reported. He, deeming it utterly impracticable to make a successful assault with the gunboats in the position then occupied, ordered the entire command to take position under cover of the woods, and sent to headquarters for further instructions. Whilst waiting for these the enemy continued to throw shell over us. Upon the return of the messenger I was ordered by General Stanley to return to camp. This was done in perfect order by the troops comprising the brigade, the enemy in the mean time continuing to fire upon us."[28]

With the siege in place, Pope was unable to dislodge the Confederate defenders until large siege guns were transported to him. On March 11, four 128-pound siege guns arrived and were entrenched 800 yards from the Confederate works. Stanley's First Division was ordered to support the new siege guns as they were positioned to begin firing on the Confederate forts. Captain Joseph Mower, 1st U.S. Infantry, was given command of the siege guns. The Union infantry pushed the Confederate pickets from the location selected for the siege guns. Pope noted, "The work was prosecuted in silence and with the utmost rapidity, until at 3 a.m. two small redoubts, connected by a curtain and mounting the four heavy guns which had been sent me, were completed, together with rifle pits in front and on the flanks for two regiments of infantry."[29] On March 13, the Confederates were surprised by the four large cannon as they began to pound away at the fortifications. During the day the Union soldiers busily worked moving the entrenchments ever closer to the Southern defenses. The artillery duel continued through the day, and one of the Union siege guns was hit. But the Union army prepared to move the remaining three closer during the night.

On March 13 Stanley's division entered the trenches to support the Unions siege guns at 3:00 a.m. and was ordered to protect the siege batteries and prevent a Confederate infantry attack on the guns. Stanley noted the excellent work of the engineers who had mounted the large siege guns and recognized Joseph Mower's command of the large cannon. Stanley observed, "As day broke our batteries opened and were immediately replied to by the enemy's batteries and gunboats, they firing at least two guns to our one."[30] Once the large guns began the cannonade, Stanley was able to remove his smaller batteries to a more safe location, and his infantry regiments dug in relative safety as the return fire from the Confederate artillery whizzed overhead. The low, wet ground around New Madrid helped diminish the impact of the cannonading because the cannonballs simply hit the mud and stuck rather than causing additional damage. Stanley also heard the Confederate gunboats steaming along the river during the stormy night. He wondered if the enemy were preparing an attack of their own along his left flank and he positioned his troops to prepare for an assault.

Stanley rode among his division on the morning of March 13 encouraging his men to find safety from the shelling that was yet to come, and as soon as the shelling started his men were glad for his advice. Stanley also found that not everyone was command material. As he repositioned his troops for greater safety from the Confederate artillery, a cannonade was directed at his troops. Stanley wrote of John Groesbeck, commander of the First Brigade: "The ranking Colonel was perfectly unnerved by this fire. I never saw a man in such a crazy fright. He was mounted but could not sit in his saddle; he laid down on his frightened horse, his hat came off and he could not tell one to pick it up. Seeing his bad plight and knowing that he was a very good fellow, I quietly made to the head of his regiment, and took command and soon got the regiment to a place of safety. The Colonel went to the rear, and immediately resigned. He was a man of wealth and influence and really wanted to be a soldier. He was not fitted for it."[31]

Stanley's report of Colonel John Groesbeck was unfortunate for a man who wanted so much to serve his country. Groesbeck's report of the action on March 13 was one of thorough calm: "I take pleasure in mentioning the good conduct of my command. It behaved with great coolness, although exposed to heavy fire the whole day. Considering the closeness and rapidity of the firing, the casualties were remarkably few."[32] The loss in the brigade was one killed and four wounded in the engagement. Groesbeck did not officially resign and leave the brigade until May 1862. There were various other reasons given for Groesbeck's resignation. One was that it was to make room for his replacement, Colonel Edward F. Noyes, and another was his dissatisfaction with General Henry Halleck. The unfortunate Groesbeck's troubles continued after the war, and finally his body was found floating in a river in New York City, where he is believed to have committed suicide in 1879.

The Confederate commanders met at New Madrid during the night of March 13 and realized they could not hold their position without reinforcements. With little hope of more troops, it was decided to abandon New Madrid during the night. Historian Jay Mullen wrote of the events of the evening: "During the night while Union troops were eagerly advancing trenches and moving cannons, sullen Confederates were haphazardly attending to a confused evacuation. A thunderstorm created chaos and the surly Confederates refused to load the cannons, ammunition, and other supplies aboard the boats. With a complete breakdown in discipline, the officers joined the men aboard the boats and the town was evacuated with most of its armament and supplies left behind."[33] David Stanley's First Division had held the Union position in the trenches opposite the Confederate defenses on March 13. Just before daybreak on March 14, his troops were relieved by General Charles Schuyler Hamilton's division.

The Union advance and ultimate capture of New Madrid had a significant impact on the defensive position of Island No. 10, and Major General John P. McCown knew it. McCown, the commander of the Confederate forces at New Madrid and Island No. 10, requested reinforcements from General Pierre G.T. Beauregard. Beauregard, with limited resources at his disposal, concluded to concentrate on the Union army of the Tennessee before sending reinforcements to McCown. McCown was on his own. General Pope was highly complimentary of his subordinates for their actions in securing New Madrid, and no small praise was offered to David Stanley and his division:

> The division of General Stanley, consisting of the Twenty-seventh, Thirty-ninth, Forty-third, and Sixty-third Ohio Regiments, supported the battery from 2 o'clock a.m. on the 13th to daylight on the 14th, exposed to the full fury of the cannonade, without being able to return a shot, and the severe storm of that night, and displayed coolness, courage, and fortitude worthy of all praise.... To General Stanley, who commanded in the trenches on the 13th, and to General Hamilton, who relieved him on the morning of the 14th, I am specially indebted, not only for their efficient aid on the last days of the operations here, but for their uniform zeal and co-operation during the whole of the operations near this place.[34]

With the capture of the northern bank of the Mississippi River and the movement of Brigadier General Joseph's Plummer's Fifth Division five miles south on the Mississippi River, the vulnerability of Island No. 10 had increased, although it remained a highly fortified position. Plummer's 3,000-man division was in place at Point Pleasant on March 7 with orders to prevent Confederate reinforcements, naval or ground, from advancing on New Madrid from the south.

Stanley recorded 2 men killed and 10 wounded through March 14 from his division. From March 14 until April 7, the siege of Island No. 10 continued, but for David Stanley's division the action was limited. Stanley noted, "The time elapsing between the 13th of March and the 7th of April was occupied in instructing the division in the duties of outposts and the drill of the battalion and brigade. In all these I am happy to report decided progress."[35]

The Union navy began the initial assault on Island No.10 on March 15 and intensified its efforts on March 16, including utilizing 10 mortars. Late in the afternoon, the 27th Illinois Infantry landed on the Missouri shore opposite Island No.10 with the 2nd Illinois Artillery, Battery I, and by 6:00 p.m. the land-based artillery began shelling Island No.10. On March 17, the Union gunboats attacked with the USS *Benton*, USS *Cincinnati*, USS *St. Louis*, USS *Mound City*, and USS *Carondelet*. On March 18, shelling from the Union gunboats continued along with the mortar barrages, but the island was not taken and the siege continued through the end of March.[36]

Because of the formidable defenses on Island No. 10, Pope had to consider another way around this obstacle, and he decided a canal could be dug through the peninsula east of New Madrid. Over a nineteen-day period the canal was dug and a six-mile corridor was cleared. The canal entered the Mississippi River west of Island No. 10 and east of New Madrid. On April 2, after weeks of construction, four transports and five barges emerged from St John's Bayou moving much needed reinforcements and supplies west of Island No. 10. Although the canal was not deep or large enough for gunboats, transports and supply vessels were able to avoid the island and move safely to New Madrid. On April 4, the ironclad USS *Carondelet* made a night run past Island No.10 and on April 6 the gunboat USS *Pittsburg* also ran past the island. Two Union warships docked at New Madrid made sure that no Confederate naval reinforcements would threaten the Union siege. On the morning of April 7, the Union warships began shelling the Confederate batteries from the west.[37]

The Confederate Retreat and Surrender

As the Union batteries and gunboats pounded the Confederate defenses on Island No. 10, it became apparent to the Confederate commanders the island would fall. Even more concerning was the realization the Confederate infantry on the Tennessee bank of the Mississippi River was located on a peninsula and if the Union army crossed the Mississippi at a more southern location, the Confederate troops could be trapped. This fact was not lost on Pope and his commanders. Suddenly the Confederate troops raced to the south followed closely by General Eleazer Paine's Fourth Division which had crossed the Mississippi River, with Stanley's First Division close behind.

On April 7, Stanley's First Division crossed the Mississippi River from Fort Bankhead just after Eleazer Paine's division. Schuyler Hamilton's division was third in line to cross the river. His march was directly toward Tiptonville. Along his march Stanley noticed "deserted camps and abandoned artillery indicated a flying enemy. Night coming on very dark and our guide being uncertain of the route, the command was bivouacked until morning, when a contraband informed me the enemy had surrendered to General Paine. Subsequently the same day we crossed the New Madrid Bend to Island No. 10. Covering the country for 7 miles perpendicular to the main road with skirmishers, we picked up about 40 prisoners. All the houses were found full of the enemy's sick, and cannon, ammunition, tents, wagons, and various material of war were found scattered through the bend."[38] A member of the 43rd Ohio recounted the march after the retreating Confederates:

> After the Ohio Brigade crossed the Mississippi River below New Madrid, April 7th, 1862, we were pressing the Rebels so hard near Tiptonville, that they abandoned their camp equipage, left their camp kettles on the fire, and did not have time to relieve their picket guards. The 43rd Ohio were halted near the Rebel camp, when General Stanley rode in front of the Regiment, and called for a detail to go down in the rebel camp. Captain Marshman, of Co. B, called for volunteers, and with a boy's spirit of adventure, I volunteered with a number of others from the Regiment. On the way we came across a Rebel Captain who had been the officer of the day, who was so disgusted at not being relieved from guard duty on their retreat, that he had drowned his sorrows from the contents of a demijohn of peach brandy at his side, and was leaning up against a log. Our boys were very anxious to sample the brandy, but were afraid that it might have been poisoned, and as a test one of them poured some out in his tin cup and offered it to the captain, who drank it. This gave us courage, and one of them poured out his cup heaping full. The captain seeing this, exclaimed, "Boys, don't act the hog." At this time General Stanley came up, saw the red sash, and accosted him as follows: "Are you an officer, sir?" to which the captain replied, "I'm a prisoner, by__!"[39]

Communications from Pope's Army of the Mississippi on April 7 were a series of exchanges that showed excited anticipation. Pope's message to General Henry Halleck on April 7 stated, "Paine's, Stanley's, and Hamilton's divisions are across, together with three batteries of light artillery and a battalion of cavalry. Everything will be over by 12 tonight. The divisions of Paine and Stanley are on the march to Tiptonville. Rebel force in the bend rapidly retreating on that place. Hamilton's division and the cavalry move forward at once. Do not believe there will be more than a skirmish. Am just embarking myself. You will not hear from me before tomorrow. All goes well and everybody in fine spirits. No. 10 will be ours before to-morrow night."[40] At 7:00 p.m. on April 7, Pope wrote again to Halleck: "Enemy in rapid retreat, leaving artillery, baggage, supplies, and sick. Paine is near Tiptonville; Stanley within mile of him; Hamilton 3 miles in rear of Stanley; Plummer now at landing on this side; our gunboats below Tiptonville on the bank. Think we shall bag whole force, though not certain. No escape for them below Tiptonville, except by wading shoulder-deep in swamp. Whole command well in hand and will move forward at daylight."[41] Pope again wrote, on April 8, the final tally: "Everything is ours. Few, if any, of the enemy escaped. Three generals, 6,000 prisoners, an immense quantity of ammunition and supplies, 100 pieces of siege and several batteries of field artillery, great numbers of small-arms, tents, wagons, horses, &c., have fallen into our hands. Our success has been complete and overwhelming."[42] The elation continued from assistant secretary of war Thomas Scott, who had been traveling with the Army of the Mississippi, in a message to the secretary of war, Edwin Stanton, on April 8, including an overly optimistic promise to capture Memphis in ten days: "Just returned from Tennessee. General Pope's movement has been a glorious success."[43]

When New Madrid was evacuated, General John McCown had been replaced with Brigadier General William Mackall. The Confederate forces under command of Mackall were, in fact, trapped as they feared on a peninsula of land and had no exit. They moved south to Tiptonville to try to escape the noose that was being tightened. However, the Union forces had landed at Tiptonville and blocked this last hope to escape. On April 8, Mackall surrendered. Also, Island No. 10, finding their shore support gone, formally surrendered on April 8.[44]

A key to the Union victory was the action taken by the USS *Carondelet* and Commander Henry Walke. The USS *Carondelet* successfully aided in silencing the Confederate shore batteries and also served to prevent any interference from Confederate gunboats, thereby assuring the ability of the Union ground and naval forces to move against the Confederates. After the Confederate surrender, David Stanley congratulated Commander Walke for his action and was rewarded

Brigadier General John Palmer commanded the Third Division during the Island No. 10 Campaign (courtesy Wilson's Creek National Battlefield; WICR 31474).

with an invitation to join him in a drink to celebrate the victory. The commander of the other Union gunboat involved in the same action, presumably the USS *Pittsburgh,* was verbally challenged by Walke, who shouted, "'D__you, I don't congratulate you, you stayed behind, my boat and fired shells over my deck' and then added, 'D__you, if you ever do such a thing again I will turn my batteries on you and blow you out of the water.'"[45] Stanley enjoyed his drink and the tirade of the salty Commander Walke.

The only official report by a brigade commander of the First Division was by Colonel Groesbeck: "On the morning of the 7th I embarked the brigade on board transports *Trio* and *Fanny Gilmore.* After crossing the Mississippi we marched 6 miles toward Tiptonville and bivouacked. Next morning marched 8 miles to Tiptonville. On our arrival there found that the whole rebel force had surrendered to Brigadier-General Paine."[46]

The camaraderie of Pope's army was evident in his report of siege of Island No. 10: "Generals Paine, Stanley, Hamilton, and Plummer crossed the river, together with a portion of General Granger's cavalry division, under Col. W.L. Elliott, Second Iowa Cavalry. To all these officers I am deeply indebted for their efficient and cordial aid in every portion of our operations. They conducted their divisions with eminent skill and vigor, and to them I am largely indebted for the discipline and efficiency of this command."[47]

The siege of Island No. 10 was by no means an equal contest. By March 31, 1862, the Union army totaled greater than 25,000 combatants and the Confederates had approximately

7,400 men in the Island No.10 conflict. Reports of the number of men captured at Madrid Bend varied, with General Pope reporting greater than 7,000 (but more likely 4,500) men captured.

The amiable David Stanley found an old classmate among those who surrendered at Tiptonville, Captain Henry B. Davidson. This was a day for Stanley to enjoy drinks with friends, even Confederate friends. He invited some of the officers to share in a drink of brandy. General Mackall declined, but Brigadier General Edward W. Gantt, who had commanded Fort Thompson at New Madrid, and Henry B. Davidson enjoyed the hospitality of General Stanley. Although on the opposite sides of the war, these men remained cordial to one another.

Stanley genuinely loved his Ohio division, but he was disappointed and learned a valuable lesson from an unnamed lieutenant of the 39th Ohio Infantry after the Confederate surrender at Tiptonville. The spring was cool and the past thirty days had been rainy and muddy. Finally, a lieutenant from the 39th Ohio Infantry complained during another of the many rainstorms and Stanley, a veteran regular army soldier and somewhat salty on his own, stung the lieutenant when he said, "You have enlisted for soldiers and the sooner you make up your minds to endure the rain when it comes, the better for you."[48] Stanley's remarks were printed in the *Cincinnati Times* and were used to show the harshness of regular army officers toward the new volunteers.

Summary

The Island No. 10 campaign was David Stanley's first test as a general in the Union army. Previously he had limited command in the 1st U.S. Cavalry, rising only to the rank of captain as other officers resigned and returned to serve in their home states. In addition, Stanley, a cavalry officer, was commanding infantry for the first time, and volunteer infantry at that. A West Point graduate, he had a decided bias in favor of professional soldiers who were well trained and well disciplined.

Stanley's first campaign as brigadier general was very successful. Despite the somewhat tarnished reputation of Pope resulting from action taken later in the war, Pope provided excellent leadership during this campaign. He commanded green troops and green commanders, but he molded the new Army of the Mississippi into a cohesive fighting unit with an inclusive and patient command style. Not only did Stanley excel under the command of Pope, he commanded two brigades of Ohio troops, which he clearly enjoyed. He was social and collaborative with other commanders and he thrived within the command structure of Pope, not only with the West Point trained soldiers, but the new volunteers also.

Stanley's style of leadership was clearly seen when Colonel John Groesbeck lost his nerve during a bombardment. Stanley calmly rode to the head of the regiment and took command in a professional manner. There were no exclamations about Groesbeck's performance and Stanley showed a great deal of empathy for the man. Ever aware of the men who served under his command, he quietly moved Groesbeck's men to safety, demonstrating a sound ability to lead men in battle.

3

The Siege of Corinth

*Stanley sometimes seemed almost savage in battle,
and would fight the devil himself if he got in the way.*

David Stanley commanded the Second Division during the Siege of Corinth (courtesy Wilson's Creek National Battlefield; WICR 31760).

With the success at New Madrid and Island No. 10, the next major Confederate obstacle on the Mississippi River lay about 100 miles downstream at Fort Pillow, which was named after Brigadier General Gideon Pillow of Tennessee. The fort was built on Chickasaw Bluff Number One overlooking the Mississippi River and it was located about 40 miles north of Memphis. Batteries of cannon were directed toward the river and offered a formidable deterrent to any vessels trying to slip past the fort. An impressive series of breastworks were built to protect the fort. The fort was originally built by slaves in 1861 under the watchful eye of General Pillow, who designed the fort to include three stages of semicircular earthworks to further protect the fort. The entire perimeter of the fort was 13 miles long and, while the construction of the fort was impressive, it was estimated that to fully defend the fort 15,000 troops were needed.

Within a week of the capture of Island No. 10, General John Pope sent thirty steamboats carrying his army toward Fort Pillow. Pope wrote, "It was a grand sight, this great fleet descending the great river and loaded with men and munitions of war. The health of the command was excellent and their spirits were bordering on the boisterous."[1] Captain William Stewart of the 11th Missouri Infantry echoed Pope's sentiments after the fall Island No. 10: "We are all in high glee and fine spirits."[2] The Union commanders in the west and in Washington had to be very pleased with the progress made in March and April. Not only were New Madrid and Island No. 10 captured, the Confederates had been beaten in the Battle of Pea Ridge, and the Union victory at the Battle of Shiloh had raised the morale to a very high level. On April 9, secretary of war Edwin Stanton wrote to Henry Halleck: "That the thanks and congratulations of the War Department are rendered to Major-General Halleck for the signal ability and success that have distinguished the military operations of his department and for the spirit and courage manifested by the army under his command .... The daring courage, diligent prosecution, persistent valor, and military result of these achievements are unsurpassed. That there shall this day be a salute of one hundred guns from the United States Arsenal at Washington in honor of these great victories."[3]

On April 14, the Union cannons fired on Fort Pillow, but this fort was reminiscent of the Confederate fortifications at New Madrid that bogged down Pope's Army for five weeks. Meanwhile in southwestern Tennessee on April 6–7, the Battle of Shiloh was fought, resulting in the Confederate Army's withdrawal toward Corinth, Mississippi. During the Battle of Shiloh General Albert Sidney Johnston was killed, and command of Johnston's Army of Mississippi fell to Pierre Beauregard. Rather than tie up Pope's Army of the Mississippi in another two-month siege, the Union army moved eastward to capitalize on the situation in west-central Tennessee. The Confederate defeat at Shiloh resulted in a strong Union force advancing toward Corinth, Mississippi. Pope's army was called to add to this Union strategic initiative. The Confederates were clearly on the defensive and the Union plan was to drive the recently defeated Confederate army deeper into Mississippi.

The Advance on Corinth

The commander of the Union armies in the west was Major General Henry Halleck, who until this point had wisely allowed his field commanders to direct the recent campaigns. However, Halleck decided to assume direct command of the Union actions after the Battle of Shiloh. The Confederates had returned to Corinth, Mississippi, which served as the junction of two of the South's most important and longest railroads, and begun to enhance the defenses of the town. Corinth was the junction of the Memphis and Charleston Railroad (east-west) and the Mobile and Ohio Railroad (north-south). These railroads were critical to the movement of supplies in the mid-south. The Memphis and Charleston Railroad was the direct line between the Mississippi River and the Atlantic seaboard. Corinth, with a population of 1,200 people, was located in Tishomingo County in the northeastern part of Mississippi in 1861.

The Battle of Shiloh had united Major General Don Carlos Buell's Army of the Ohio and Major General Ulysses S. Grant's Army of the Tennessee, and soon General Pope's Army of the Mississippi would be joining these armies. By the end of April the Army of the Tennessee was commanded by Major General George Thomas, and Ulysses Grant was appointed second-in-command of Halleck's combined armies. But Grant was underutilized because he had no defined duties. The Confederates retreated to Corinth and enhanced the fortifications through the sweat of slave labor gangs. By April 9, General P.G.T. Beauregard was urging the citizens of Corinth to leave the town in anticipation of the Union advance. Beauregard's Army of Mississippi was joined by Major General Earl Van Dorn's Army of the West in preparation for repelling the Union movement on Corinth. While Van Dorn was urged to hurry to Beauregard's aid, the Confederate commander was unaware Halleck had assumed control of the three Union armies totaling 120,000 men facing the combined Confederate forces of about 65,000. There was no need for Van Dorn to hurry anywhere due to Halleck's "Little-Loss-as-Possible Art of War" strategy utilized in the advance on Corinth. Although Halleck initially marched his army quickly, he became overcautious and managed to move only twenty-eight miles in thirty days during the advance on Corinth.[4]

Henry Halleck, "Old Brains," commanded the slow advance on Corinth in May 1862 (Library of Congress).

David Stanley, as part Pope's Army of the Mississippi, reached Pittsburg Landing on April 21. His troops were allowed to disembark from the steamboats at Hamburg Landing about three miles south of Pittsburg Landing. Stanley and his division were in high spirits, but soon the slow, muddy march to Corinth added reality to their current situation. Pope's army marched on the left flank, Buell's Army of the Ohio held the center and Thomas's Army of the Tennessee marched on the right flank as the Union troops approached Corinth from the northeast. There were numerous complaints about the conditions of the roads as the Union armies advanced on Corinth, slogging through the mud encountered along the way. Assistant secretary of war Thomas Scott, who accompanied Pope's army in New Madrid, Missouri, continued his journey and recorded, "All quiet here tonight. Roads in terrible condition."[5] An addendum was added to the message from the telegraph operator that the rain had continued for the past four days.

General Order 38 issued on April 24 gave the new organization of the Army of the Mississippi, which now included three infantry divisions and one cavalry division. The First Division was commanded by Brigadier General Eleazer Paine, the Second Division was commanded by Brigadier General David Stanley and the final infantry division was commanded by Brigadier General Schuyler Hamilton.[6] The first two divisions were designated as the "battle corps" and the Third Division was the reserve. Brigadier General Gordon Granger continued to command Pope's cavalry. Brigadier General John Palmer, who was unhappy with the command structure in the Island No. 10 campaign, must have been more unhappy now because he was relegated to brigade command. Brigadier General Joseph Plummer, who also had command of a division at New Madrid, Missouri, was assigned brigade command.

Stanley's Second Division consisted of two brigades and eight infantry regiments, which effectively doubled his command responsibility. He not only had his "Ohio Brigade," he had also gained the "Eagle Brigade" commanded by Brigadier General Joseph Plummer, an excellent commander who had been a regular army officer before the war. The Eagle Brigade was nicknamed after the mascot, "Old Abe," of the 8th Wisconsin Infantry. Old Abe was a bald eagle and it is unclear whether it was male or female, but the mascot was part of the regiment and soon the entire brigade was designated as the Eagle Brigade. The eagle had been captured by a Chippewa Indian in Price County, Wisconsin, and traded to Mrs. Margaret McCann, but it became too large for the McCann family. Next Old Abe was sold to Lieutenant James McGuire of the Eighth Wisconsin, and the regiment and Old Abe joined the brigade permanently. Old Abe rode on a standard "consisting of a pole and copy of the shield from the Great Seal of the United States."[7] These brigade designations were encouraged by Stanley and built a sense of camaraderie among the various regiments:

SECOND DIVISION
BRIGADIER GENERAL DAVID S. STANLEY

First Brigade—The Ohio Brigade
COLONEL JOHN GROESBECK

27th	Ohio Infantry	Colonel J.W. Fuller
39th	Ohio Infantry	Colonel J. Groesbeck
43rd	Ohio Infantry	Colonel J.L.K. Smith
63rd	Ohio Infantry	Colonel J.W. Sprague
1st	Michigan Light Artillery, Battery C	Captain A.W. Dees.
2nd	U.S. Artillery, Battery F	Captain T.D. Maurice.

Second Brigade—The Eagle Brigade
BRIGADIER GENERAL JOSEPH B. PLUMMER

26th	Illinois Infantry	Colonel J.M. Loomis
47th	Illinois Infantry	Colonel J. Bryner
11th	Missouri InfantryLieut.	Colonel W.E. Panabaker
8th	Wisconsin Infantry	Colonel R.C. Murphy
2nd	Iowa Battery	Captain N.T. Spoor

Stanley effectively doubled the total number of his command, to over 7,000 men with over 6,000 present for duty.

The March Toward Corinth

Immediately after the march began Stanley took action against the Confederates at Monterey, Tennessee, a few miles from the Mississippi state line. Stanley recorded the following

> [O]n the morning of the 29th of April I marched to attempt the surprise of the rebel force at Monterey and make a reconnaissance of the country. My force consisted of the First Brigade of my division, Col. John Groesbeck commanding; sixteen companies of cavalry, Col. W.L. Elliott commanding, with Dees' and Spoor's batteries. We met the first of the enemy's pickets 2 miles north of Monterey, and soon after learned that the enemy was probably retreating. In accordance with Colonel Elliott's desire, I directed him to follow with the entire cavalry force at speed, passing through their deserted camp and the village of Monterey.[8]

The cavalry quickly pursued and caught the retreating enemy, and twenty prisoners were collected. Major Hiram Love commanding the 2nd Iowa Cavalry pushed ahead until he came upon a small bridge covered by four cannons that opened fire upon the 2nd Iowa with canister at close range. Love lost one trooper killed and four wounded in the shelling. He tried to find a way across the creek to attack the artillery but he found the creek impassable. Love asked Stanley for orders and Stanley pulled the cavalry back in compliance with Halleck's orders not to bring on a general engagement. Love, commanding the Second Brigade of the Cavalry Division, reported: "About 18 prisoners were taken from them. I learned that the Fourth, Thirteenth, Seventeenth, Twentieth, and Twenty-fifth Louisiana Regiments, from 200 to 250 cavalry, and four pieces of artillery, composed the force of the enemy near Monterey."[9]

Pope ordered David Stanley's Second Division to march to the left of the advance and Paine's Division would march to the right and Hamilton would march in the rear of the other divisions. Stanley's division marched with two days rations from Hamburg, Tennessee, on April 24 in what was destined to be a very slow advance. By April 30, Stanley's Division and the Army of the Mississippi had approached to within 2 miles of Farmington, Mississippi, four miles east of Corinth. When some Confederate pickets were captured they revealed a fairly accurate estimate of about 50,000–60,000 Confederate troops defended Corinth, many of whom were sick.[10]

The Army of the Mississippi held the left flank of Halleck's armies as Stanley marched forward and his division continued to march on the extreme left flank. As the march continued, Hamilton's Third Division marched to the left and rear of Stanley, effectively extending his flank. Stanley's division was in the most vulnerable position should the Confederate army take action to turn Halleck's flank. Of particular concern to Beauregard was the possession and operation of the railroads. Stanley's division was the closest and the one most likely to strike this vital resource.

The town of Farmington stood directly in the path of Pope's approach to Corinth. Farmington was a small village about four miles due east of Corinth, and as Stanley searched for Confederate defenders on May 3, he found that about 4,500 Confederates held the town. The Southern forces in Farmington protected the town with 4 cannon, infantry, and cavalry. Paine's First Division marched against the Confederates in Farmington and was able to push them back toward the defenses at Corinth. Paine recorded 30 of the enemy were killed while reporting his casualties of 2 killed and 12 wounded. The remainder of Pope's Army of the Mississippi was still two miles from Farmington and these troops occupied the town the next day. Pope's strategic position in Farmington allowed him to be able to advance against Corinth, but as the extreme left of the army, he was also the most vulnerable to attack.

On May 1, John Groesbeck was officially relieved of duty commanding the First Brigade of David Stanley's division and was replaced by Brigadier General Daniel Tyler. Tyler was born in 1799 and was a graduate of the U.S. Military Academy in 1819. He had served with the Union army in the first Battle of Bull Run. Soon, Tyler, a spit and polish regular army officer, made the men of the brigade lament Groesbeck's resignation. Oscar Jackson, 63rd Ohio Infantry, wrote, "We pitched our camp and as we were getting pretty weak in numbers, our Brigadier-general Tyler, began criticizing everything concerning us, such as ordering our sick on guard and picket duty, making us drill, etc. General Tyler took command of our brigade on May 1st. I have a private opinion of him. In his introductory speech, he said he was glad we resembled the New Englanders, etc. He is from New England and that kind of talk does not please Western soldiers."[11]

On May 4, Pope's reconnaissance of the railroad south of Farmington revealed a considerable defensive presence. Rumors from deserters caused the Union army to fear their quarry was evacuating Corinth and Pope pushed Halleck to allow him to advance to determine the strength and defenses of the Confederates. Halleck approved his request on May 7 and, even given the snail pace of Halleck's army, Pope questioned Buell's ability to stay connected with his right flank. Buell agreed to allow Brigadier General William Nelson to move to protect Pope's right flank but lamented a three-mile march and the conditions of the roads. Fortunately, Pope's reconnaissance was accomplished with little loss.

David Stanley recalled an abortive attempt by Confederates to attack his division as related by the Dr. W.R. Thrall, surgeon of the 27th Ohio Infantry who had been captured. As Stanley's troops reconnoitered toward Corinth they heard an explosive exchange of musket fire, but no one could determine the cause of the firing. Thrall, who was with the Confederate units involved in the exchange, recounted to Stanley: "The rebels deceived by our movement, sent detached forces to attack us. Marching blindly through the woods, they furiously attacked each other about a mile from our flank, pouring several volleys into the ranks of the supposed enemy. At this time we were marching quietly back to our camp and we were very puzzled by the uproar as we felt certain that none of our troops had marched in that direction.... [Dr. Thrall] witnessed the fratricidal fight between the Confederates, whose volleys had puzzled us so much. Dr. Thrall had given his services to the wounded and in consideration of his doing so, he was paroled and allowed to return to his regiment."[12]

Assistant secretary of war Thomas Scott wrote on May 8: "Slight skirmishing all afternoon. Our forces have pressed forward, and are now within 1 mile of enemy's works. Heavy cavalry and infantry force on the left, beyond the railroad. The woods appear to be full of rebels; they will not fight much outside of their works. A steady artillery fire in front for the past twenty minutes and still continues."[13] Pope's reconnaissance was less than revealing, and the enemy allowed him to advance without much resistance.[14] Few Confederate troops impeded his advance and very few enemy soldiers were even seen. Pope was able to move close enough to observe the Confederate army within their entrenchments.

Pope correctly realized that even though he faced little resistance, he was too far from the support of Buell to make an attack on what was perceived to be a weak defense. If Beauregard had intended to confuse Pope, he was successful, as Pope communicated to Halleck he was somewhat confused by what he observed. Halleck's return message was a reminder to Pope to avoid a general engagement. Whether this was Halleck's "Little-Loss-as-Possible" war or his concern about Buell's inability to march faster was unclear because Halleck indicated Buell had not responded to him about protecting Pope's right flank. Pope was pushing forward, in any way possible, regardless of Buell's ability to stay connected to his right flank.

By the end of the day on May 8, Pope ordered David Stanley to move his second brigade under command of John Loomis forward, and the Second Division advanced to within range of the Confederate cannon at Corinth the same day.

The Engagement at Farmington, Mississippi

Beauregard's Confederates were not idle as the Union army slowly advanced on Corinth. Being outnumbered, Beauregard utilized the terrain to his advantage and had to wait for Pope to make a mistake. Realizing he was exposed and vulnerable to a Confederate attack by being so far in front of his support and heeding Halleck's concern about lack of communication from Buell, Pope withdrew to the relative position of Buell's line on the evening of May 8. As Stanley withdrew his division, he was ordered by Pope to leave part of Colonel John Loomis's Eagle Brigade in the town of Farmington and Stanley was promised his brigade would be relieved the next morning.

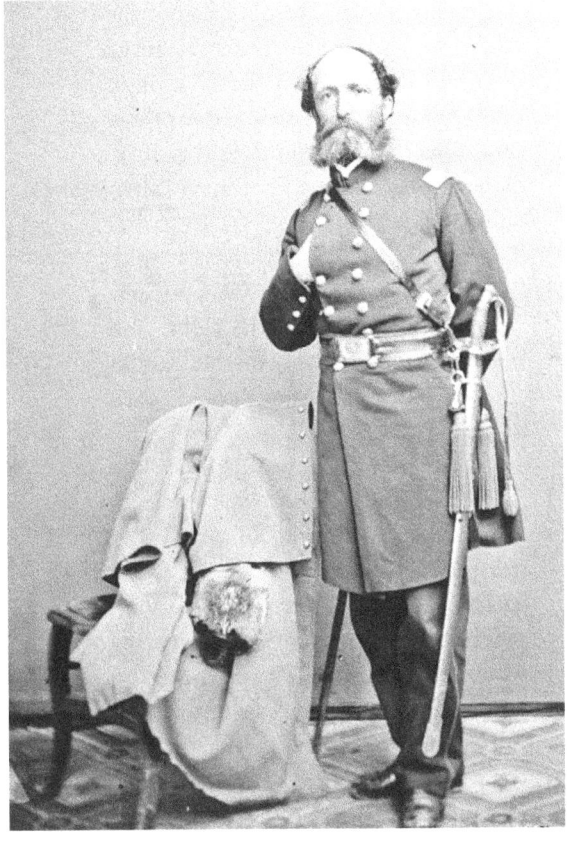

Colonel John Loomis's brigade was attacked at Farmington on May 9, 1862 (Library of Congress).

Colonel Loomis was commanding Stanley's Second Brigade, 26th Illinois, 47th Illinois, 11th Missouri, and 8th Wisconsin, which was usually commanded by General Joseph Plummer but he was sick and absent. The exposure to the elements that occurred during the March and April expedition to Point Pleasant had taken its toll on General Plummer. Therefore, the command of the Second Brigade fell to Colonel J.M. Loomis of the 26th Illinois Infantry. Loomis had been a businessman before the war. He wrote:

> On the return of General Stanley was ordered by him to leave four companies, with a field officer, in Farmington, as an advance guard and bivouac the brigade in front of the creek in rear of Farmington. These orders were executed, and Major Jefferson, Eighth Wisconsin Volunteers, left in command of the advance guard, and the brigade bivouacked on a ridge about half a mile in rear of the building called the cotton-gin, the right and left resting on the swamps on either side, with skirmishers thrown out in front and on each flank; Spoor's battery in front of center. The brigade was out of rations, but I was informed by General Stanley that the brigade would be relieved next morning.[15]

Pope's probing of the Confederate defenses had attracted the attention of the Confederate command. Loomis's occupation of Farmington posed a threat to Beauregard's supply line and Loomis's isolated position provided the impetus for a Confederate attack. Major

General Earl Van Dorn's Army of the West was ordered northeast to strike Stanley's division. On the evening of May 8, Van Dorn positioned his three divisions to strike Stanley with Brigadier General James H. Trapier's division forming on the left, Brigadier General Daniel Ruggles' division holding the center and Major General Sterling Price forming to the right. Van Dorn shifted his forces further east on the morning of May 9 and then attacked.

On the morning of May 9, the Confederates attacked Stanley's Second Division, hoping to envelop at least a brigade; the brigade receiving the blow was the Second Brigade. Colonel Loomis reported: "Skirmish firing commenced in front of Farmington and continued at intervals until about 9 o'clock, when Major Jefferson [8th Wisconsin Infantry], commanding advance guard, reported that without reinforcements he could not hold the ground."[16] General John Palmer's rein-

Colonel Joseph Mower's 11th Missouri Infantry held Loomis's flank during the May 9 engagement (Library of Congress).

forcements arrived as promised and none too soon, then rushed to the front to relieve the 8th Wisconsin. Loomis recorded, "I had made preparations to withdraw the brigade, considering myself relieved, when General Stanley, having arrived, ordered one regiment across the swamp on our left to occupy the high, clear ground, to hold it, and prevent the planting of batteries there. I ordered Colonel Mower, Eleventh Missouri Volunteers, to that point, and they performed the duty well, held the position, and thus prevented the possibility of a flank movement against our left."[17] Confederate Brigadier General Daniel Ruggles commanding a division of Braxton Bragg's Corps reported finding the enemy ahead of him. He quickly deployed the batteries of Hodgson's Battery (Louisiana), Ducatel's Orleans Guards and Hoxton's Tennessee artillery to begin shelling the Union forces and awaited the attack of Major General Earl Van Dorn's other troops scheduled to join the fight on his right. Robertson's Battery also joined in the artillery barrage.[18]

On the previous day, General Pope prophetically reported from Farmington, Mississippi: "Judging from the very feeble resistance offered to our advance on any of the roads leading to Corinth and the ease with which close reconnaissance was made, I am inclined to think either the enemy is evacuating or that he desires to draw us in on this road."[19] Now Stanley was aware the enemy was not evacuating and he had a fight on his hands.

In Loomis's report of the action at Farmington, he stated a Confederate battery, located about a mile away on the brigade's left, began shelling the most forward units of the brigade.

Soon thereafter, another Confederate battery opened up on the brigade's right. Union Battery G, 1st Missouri Light Artillery (Hescock's), located the Confederate batteries and began to return fire. "The skirmishers and battle line of General Palmer's brigade covered our front from right to left, and considerable fighting occurred."[20] Under fire from the enemy's artillery, Loomis ordered the 47th Illinois, 8th Wisconsin, and 26th Illinois infantries to lie down behind a ridge because, with Generals Palmer's troops advancing, these regiments could not fire without hitting their own troops. Spoor's 2nd Iowa Light Artillery battery was ordered to a position to counter-fire the enemy's batteries. The battle began to intensify and Loomis stated, "We suffered considerably from the fire of the enemy."[21] After relieving the advanced Union troops, General Palmer's brigade began to withdraw, resulting in the 47th Illinois and 8th Wisconsin infantries again becoming the front line. These regiments were ordered to open fire on the advancing enemy, "which order they promptly and with effect obeyed."[22]

The 26th Illinois was directed to change their front to face the oncoming Confederates and open fire. As the withdrawing Union forces flowed through the Second Brigade's lines, Loomis's men unleashed a volley into the Confederates. "The fire of these three regiments checked the advance of the enemy and compelled a portion of their line to retire under cover."[23] Confusion occurred within the Union forces when the 26th Illinois, which had moved to face the enemy, was surprised by a cavalry charge coming from their rear. Loomis was incredulous that he had not had any indication that this was happening. This was the charge of the 2nd Iowa Cavalry, which was thrown forward by the order of Brigadier General Eleazer Paine to stop the advance of the rebels. The cavalry charged from the rear of Loomis's infantry without any warning and spooked the troops. The 2nd Iowa Cavalry recorded 51 casualties for May 9 as a result of their charge on the attacking Confederates, which represented the largest number of casualties of any unit for the engagement at Farmington. Loomis gave the order for his infantry to cease fire while the cavalry charged. The 26th Illinois Infantry quickly re-formed after their surprise from the rear and along with the 8th Wisconsin again began firing at their gray-clad foes. Confusion continued as Loomis began searching for Spoor's battery, which was supposed to fire at the Confederate artillery, but he could not find them. Loomis likely was lamenting the role of brigade commander as he watched his own regiment begin to withdraw to the right of the original line, much to his chagrin. He asked the 26th Illinois' Lieutenant Colonel Tinkham why he was moving, and "he answered, 'By order of General Paine' and that he was further ordered by him to retire by right of companies to the rear into the swamp, which movement was executed."[24] Meanwhile, the remaining two regiments, the 47th Illinois and 8th Wisconsin, were still in line firing forward.

Forces engaged at Farmington, Mississippi on May 9, 1862, are as follows:

CONFEDERATE
Commanding Officer: Brigadier General Daniel Ruggles

1ST BRIGADE

Brigadier General James Patton Anderson—25th Louisiana Infantry Regiment, 36th Mississippi Infantry Regiment, Florida Confederate Guards Infantry Battalion, Hodgson's (Louisiana) Battery

2ND BRIGADE

Major Daniel Gober—11th Louisiana Infantry Regiment, 16th Louisiana Infantry Regiment, 18th Louisiana Infantry Regiment, 19th Louisiana Infantry Regiment (Not engaged), Orleans Guard Artillery.

3RD BRIGADE

Brigadier General Lucius Walker—13th Louisiana Infantry Regiment, 20th Louisiana Infantry Regiment, 37th Mississippi Infantry Regiment.

4TH BRIGADE

Colonel James Fagan—1st Arkansas Infantry Regiment, 2nd Texas Infantry Regiment, 38th Tennessee Infantry Regiment, Ketchum's Alabama Battery, Hoxton's Tennessee Battery

UNION

Commanding Officer: Major General John Pope

PLUMMER'S BRIGADE

(Stanley's Division): Colonel John Loomis—26th Illinois Infantry Regiment, 11th Missouri Infantry Regiment, 8th Wisconsin Infantry Regiment, 47th Illinois Infantry Regiment

PALMER'S BRIGADE

(Paine's Division)—22nd Illinois Infantry Regiment, 27th Illinois Infantry Regiment, 42nd Illinois Infantry Regiment, 51st Illinois Infantry Regiment

Artillery

2nd Iowa Battery, 1st Missouri Light Artillery, Battery G

Other Units

14th Michigan Infantry Regiment, 4th U.S. Cavalry Regiment, Dismounted, 2nd Iowa Cavalry Regiment

As the battle intensified, General Pope reported, "the enemy has advanced in such heavy force that the infantry command on opposite side of creek could not retain their position,"[25] To Loomis's relief General John Palmer arrived and directed him to form a new line at the edge of a swamp and under cover. Loomis was able to withdraw the 47th Illinois and 8th Wisconsin and he united his three regiments when he ordered the 26th Illinois to reform with the other two regiments.

But the Second Brigade had four regiments. The 11th Missouri Infantry was obediently holding the high ground preventing any Confederate attempt to turn the Union flank under the command of Colonel Joseph Mower in his first combat command of the regiment. He was ordered to hold this ground, and hold it he would, even though his brigade was withdrawing. Luckily for the 11th Missouri, Captain Temple Clark, assistant adjutant-general, gave the order for the regiment to withdraw, finally uniting the regiments of the brigade. A third defensive battle line was being formed under the order of General Palmer, but General Stanley wanted the brigade to form in front of its own camp about a mile to the rear of Farmington. Once the Union line was re-formed, the Confederate attack stopped.[26]

Colonel Loomis's brigade recorded 64 killed and wounded in the engagement at Farmington. The bridge across Seven Mile Creek was burned by the enemy. The Confederate loss was reported as 8 killed, 2 missing and 89 wounded, while the Federal forces lost more heavily, the total casualties being 16 killed, 148 wounded and 14 captured or missing.[27]

General Pope's final message came May 9: "All is quiet. Our pickets occupy the bridge across Seven Mile Creek, which is half a mile in the swamp and near the farther side. My impression is that the enemy has retired, but he may possibly be massing forces on our left, as the cars have been very busy last night and to-day as far as Glendale. I shall have early notice if it is so."[28] But the action at Farmington was over, and at least for Colonel Loomis it was a day of confusion and conflicting orders. General Stanley, in his official report, stated, "As Brigadier-General Palmer has made a full report and commanded, it not deemed necessary to repeat any of the incidents of the fight."[29] It is important to observe Stanley's reports, and as much can be learned by what is not written as what is written. Certainly, this single sentence carried more weight than it first appeared, but if Stanley had more to say on this engagement it is not recorded.

Interestingly, an account by Colonel Richard Hinton, serving with the 51st Illinois, recorded Stanley being in the heat of the battle in which he faced a Confederate officer. Hinton noted, "The tall cavalry commander held my eyes as he arose in his stirrups, executed the left molinet, and brought his flashing saber down on the officer opposite him, who fell cloven from shoulder to the waist." When Stanley was questioned about the incident, he simply replied, "One doesn't like to think of those things!" Hinton exclaimed, "It was one of the most terrible blows I ever saw in my life!" Perhaps the ferocity of the battle was the cause for Stanley's silence, or perhaps there were just too many generals on the field to suit him.[30]

It was fortunate for the Union army and David Stanley's Second Brigade that the full plan of the Confederate attack did not take place. Colonel Loomis and General John Palmer found themselves in a precarious situation in the Confederate attack facing Ruggles' Division with two additional divisions prepared to strike. "Van Dorn, alerted that Buell had moved a division forward to reinforce Pope, did not attempt to force his way across the stream, but led his troops back to their camps."[31] After the clash with Confederates at Farmington on May 9, better coordination of the three Union armies was needed. Pope's flank proved an attractive target for the Confederate army.

On the evening of May 9, Halleck tried to coordinate the Army of the Ohio, which was lagging, and the Army of the Mississippi, which was straining at the bit. Halleck sent word to Buell to reestablish a link with Pope and he also wrote to Thomas Scott, assistant secretary of war: "Don't let Pope go too far ahead; it is dangerous and effects no good."[32]

After the engagement on May 9, Pope repeatedly sent messages to Halleck about lack of opposition to his front. Pope wrote, "My whole command is on the road to Farmington. I trust I need not say that I am always ready to move, and only delayed this morning because I understood yesterday that my movement depended upon General Buell."[33] Pope noted as his army advanced on Farmington that alarm drums could be heard from within the Confederate defenses at Corinth.

The Siege of Corinth

By May 13, the Army of the Mississippi pressed to the outskirts of Corinth without opposition. A little surprisingly, Halleck ordered the troops of the Army of the Mississippi to mass behind Seven Mile Creek in the rear of Farmington, only to be informed they were in advance of that location. On May 15, Pope again stressed to Halleck there was no "serious opposition" to his front. As Pope pulled the Union line forward, Halleck tried to push it forward by encouraging the other army commanders to advance. Halleck, in particular, was trying to encourage Don Carlos Buell's army to keep up with Pope's advance. On May 17, Halleck wrote to Buell: "You were ordered to move at 8 o'clock this morning. The movements of the right wing were based upon that. I do not understand the reason for the delay."[34]

On May 22, Van Dorn again ventured out of the defensive works of Corinth with the intent of striking Brigadier General Schuyler Hamilton's Third Division, which was positioned on the left flank of Stanley's Division. Little did Pope realize his flank was the target of a major attack by Beauregard that was to include Van Dorn's Army of the West supported by Hardee's Corps and Bragg's Corps. Pope soon detected the infantry movement on his flank on May 22; however, the attack never occurred. Van Dorn was unable to get his troops into position and the attack was called off. This was another bit of luck for Stanley, who was also in a position to be struck hard by the mass of the Confederate forces at Corinth.

By May 24, the Army of the Mississippi began positioning 20- and 30-pound Parrott Rifles and 24-pound siege guns to initiate a bombardment of the defenses in Corinth. Ever encouraging his commanders toward victory, President Lincoln sent a message on May 24: "I believe you and the brave officers and men with you can and will get the victory at Corinth."[35]

Also on May 24, the 11th Missouri and the 39th Ohio of Stanley's division got into action. Under orders from Pope, Stanley decided to drive the Confederates to Corinth and he selected five companies of the 11th Missouri, commanded by Colonel Joseph Mower, five companies of the 39th Ohio under Major Edward Noyes, and Dees' 3rd Michigan Battery to accomplish the task. The companies charged the Confederate defenders, only to find them gone. As the companies pushed ahead, they emerged from some dense timber, where they were seen by the Confederate defenders, who sent a volley of musket fire into the advancing Union skirmishers as the Confederate artillery opened fire. The Union infantry returned fire and the Confederates continued their withdrawal.

As the enemy began firing on the advancing Union troops, General David Stanley recorded the fire was becoming "exceedingly annoying and insolent." Stanley ordered the 3rd Michigan to begin firing into the main Confederate line while the Union infantry pushed the Confederate skirmishers in their front. Stanley estimated they faced three infantry regiments supported by cavalry. The Confederates moved to the rear and formed a line in an open field and Stanley's troops advanced. Stanley was riding ahead of his infantry to determine the movement of the enemy and to his surprise emerged in a clearing only a few hundred yards away from the Confederate battle line. Stanley quickly rode back into the trees, realizing he had just had a close call, and concluded the Confederates probably thought they had seen some of their own officers. Stanley returned to Mower's infantry and ordered them forward. Mower, knowing the location of the Confederate line, moved his infantry silently forward. When he was in position, he ordered a volley into the unsuspecting Confederates, sending them "scampering in all directions for the cover of the woods." The Confederate infantry quickly moved back to the defenses of Corinth, and Stanley moved Dees' artillery forward and threw a few shells into the town. Stanley seemed particularly happy about his efforts and wrote, "Considering the disparity of numbers this was a very pretty little exploit for the numbers engaged, and did great credit to Colonel Mower and his troops."[36]

May 28—The Engagement at Bridge Creek

On May 28, Halleck reported that Pope's army on the Union left flank had received the greatest resistance that day and had lost 25 killed or wounded, while their enemy had left 30 dead on the field after a skirmish. This fairly routine report failed to show the seriousness of the exchange between the soldiers of Stanley's division and three columns of attacking Confederates. It was during this attack Stanley would have his most severe challenge of the war so far. Only Stanley's leadership and clear thinking prevented a great loss to his division and perhaps Pope's entire army.

Stanley marched his division about a mile and stopped near the White House on Bridge Creek. His division formed a forward line and secondary line diagonally toward Corinth with his right flank placed nearest to the Confederate lines. He faced a large battery behind an earthwork located south of the Memphis and Charleston Railroad. Throughout the morning, the battery remained quiet.[37] At noon, Stanley ordered his artillery batteries to begin firing on the Confederate position, which resulted in an artillery duel between the respective batteries. Stanley recorded that "as soon as our infantry was in position I directed Dees' and Maurice's Batteries to open upon them."[38] The Confederates immediately returned fire on Stanley's batteries, and a Union battery of 20-pound Parrotts joined the artillery duel. The Union and Confederate batteries hammered away at one another while Stanley's troops entrenched themselves. The cannons hammering away, the Union soldiers continued entrenching until about 3:00 p.m. At that time, three Confederate columns, among which were Cleburne's brigade of Arkansas and Tennessee regiments, attacked Stanley's division at Bridge Creek near the Shelton House while Stanley was still under artillery fire. Stanley was hard pressed by the Confederate attack, and he described the fight:

> Maurice's battery fired one round, but the men and horses being rapidly shot down, one section was limbered up by Capt. Maurice and carried off, two pieces and one caisson being left on the field. Capt. Dees of the 3rd Mich. Battery had fallen from sunstroke, and his second in command, Lieut. Lamberg limbered up and fled with the battery from the field. This left me Capt. Spore's [sic] Iowa battery. The 5th Minnesota, a new regiment, broke and ran, but most of them rallied by the exertions and example of their Colonel Von Borgenstrode. Other regiments near the point of attack fell into confusion. I repaired in person to Capt. Spore's battery (2nd Iowa) and directed him to ply [?] the advancing enemy, rushing to the abandoned guns of Maurice's battery, with canister and case shot. This was coolly and faithfully done; the officers and men of this Battery deserve great credit for their part in this affair. Capt. Williams's battalion of the 1st Infantry were immediately under the enemy's fire, and they laid down their artillery equipments, and resorted to their Springfield muskets, their old weapon—they did effective service. The enemy still pressing his attack, matters began to look critical, and I sent an order to Gen'l Tyler to move up his Brigade but before this movement could be effected, the 8th Wis., a sturdy regiment, had advanced under cover of the crest of the ridge, within fifty yards of the enemy, and poured upon them such a volley of ball and buck shot, as covered the ground with their killed and wounded, and sent the survivors flying for cover.[39]

In addition to the service performed by the 8th Wisconsin, Stanley recognized the actions of General Daniel Tyler, commanding the Ohio Brigade; Spoor's Battery; and the 11th Missouri Infantry for their actions in stopping this potentially dangerous situation. The preceding report was never submitted but was held by Stanley until his memoirs were published in 1917. While this engagement is a small footnote in the Civil War, this was a "close run thing" for Stanley and his career. Stanley calmly wrote about the action on May 28, but this affair had all the potentially of a collapse of a Union division and a very bloody fight. As it developed, the Confederate assault was repulsed and the day ended as it had begun. This engagement, while somewhat embarrassing for Stanley as he tried to get his volunteers prepared for the war, demonstrated his leadership. He was always in the fight when he was needed and what could have been a rout was averted because of his calm manner, his control, and his ability to utilize his resources. This was a defining moment for Stanley.

Stanley reported over 50 Confederate soldiers were buried after the attack. Patrick Cleburne recorded "eighty to ninety casualties, blamed his problems on Colonel Robert D. Allison of the 24th Tennessee. Cleburne said that Allison had not moved forward as ordered, thus throwing off the rest of the advance," noted historian, Timothy Smith.[40] After Stanley handled this attack, the Confederates did not bother his division for two days, and he was able to move very close to the Confederate defenses at Corinth. By May 29 he had securely entrenched his division as the advanced salient of the Union line.

The organization of the Army of the Mississippi changed on May 29 when Pope divided his command into two wings: the right wing was to be commanded by Brigadier General William S. Rosecrans. Stanley's and Paine's divisions composed the right wing of the army. The left wing of the army was to be commanded by Schuyler Hamilton and this wing was to be composed of Hamilton's Third Division which was now commanded by General Joseph Plummer, and a new Fourth Division commanded by Brigadier General Jefferson C. Davis. Davis's division consisted of two brigades of Thomas A. Davies and Alexander Asboth. In addition, Colonel William Carlin commanded the 21st and 38th Illinois Volunteers. Carlin's command was ordered to be held in reserve and reported directly to Pope.

The Union armies again pressed forward and by May 29 had pushed within a 1,000 yards of the Confederate fortifications and began to establish positions for large siege cannon. By May 29, Pope's artillery began shelling the Confederates. Stanley's Second Division spent May 29 in the rifle pits and Paine's First Division was ordered to be prepared to support Stanley should he come under attack. Orders were sent for a general assault on Corinth to begin on May 30, and according to Corporal Duncan McCall in Stanley's Division, "everything being ready, the ball was to open on the morrow."[41] The men had prepared and were ready to charge the Confederate defenses. However, having already lost the ability to protect the railroads, Beauregard ordered a withdrawal from Corinth on the evening of May 29.

The Confederate Retreat

The Confederate retreat from Corinth was no easy task, as 120,000 Union soldiers were preparing to attack. Beauregard knew that, not only was he outnumbered, outgunned, short of food and water, he also had many soldiers too sick to fight. Prior to his withdrawal he called a meeting of his generals and it was decided to withdraw to Tupelo, but this action had to be done in absolute secrecy to prevent precipitating a Union attack. The sick and supplies were moved by rail southward and the Confederates went through an elaborate set of activities to convince Halleck the army was still defending Corinth. On the morning of May 30, Beauregard had accomplished a masterful deception and had extricated his army from the tightening grip of three Union armies.

The Confederates retreated south toward Baldwyn and finally about 50 miles south to Tupelo. Two regiments led Pope's advance into the works at Corinth, the 42nd Illinois Infantry of Paine's Division and the 39th Ohio Infantry of Stanley's Division. Finding the defenses abandoned on May 30, John Pope's Army of the Mississippi pressed forward to pursue the retreating Confederates. Union General Henry Halleck reported, "For miles out of the town the roads are filled with arms, haversacks, etc., thrown away by his flying troops."[42]

The cavalry of the Army of the Mississippi caught the rear guard of Beauregard's retreating army eight miles south of Corinth and the chase was on. David Stanley was ordered on June 1 to move his division to Booneville, Mississippi, about 20 miles south of Corinth, there to wait for further orders. Also on June 1, a center wing was added to the Army of the Mississippi which was commanded by Brigadier General Thomas W. Sherman; serving under him was Brigadier General Thomas Davies, who was assigned to divisional command. These two divisions composed the center wing of Pope's army. While Pope pursued Beauregard's army, he insisted his force be within range of support should the Confederates launch a counterattack. Stanley's and Paine's divisions advanced on Baldwyn, Mississippi, about 10 miles south of Booneville, but no further action was taken by either side and the Army of the Mississippi returned to Corinth on June 12.

David Stanley wrote of his actions during the Siege of Corinth: "I have thus endeavored to trace out the service of this division for fifty days. Of course it is a mere outline. The labor of road-making, of camp labor, of marches through heat and dust, of privations in short rations, in bad clothing, in bare feet, all I am happy to report borne with patience and cheerfulness, have shown that our young soldiers already begin to appreciate Napoleon's maxim, that 'the first quality of a soldier is constancy in enduring fatigue; that poverty and privation are the soldier's school.' Neither have they ever shown that their courage may be classed as secondary to these qualities."[43]

In late June 1862, John Pope was promoted and given command of the Army of Virginia. Pope had the dubious honor of facing General Robert E. Lee in the Second Battle of Bull Run. On June 26, the command of the Army of the Mississippi was ably filled by Major General William Rosecrans. Ohioan William Starke Rosecrans was born in 1819 and graduated fifth in his class at West Point in 1842. He was an engineer in the army until his resignation in 1854. Prior to the Civil War he ran a kerosene factory in Cincinnati, then received a commission as a colonel serving as General George McClellan's aide early in the war. He was soon promoted to the rank of brigadier general and distinguished himself in action at Rich Mountain, Virginia. Serving under McClellan was revealing to Rosecrans when McClellan failed to acknowledge that much of the success at Rich Mountain was due to Rosecrans' efforts. As a result, Rosecrans requested a transfer to the western theater of the Civil War rather than serve under McClelland in the East.

Major General Henry Halleck was also given a promotion after the siege of Corinth. On July 23, 1862, President Lincoln summoned Halleck to Washington to become general-in-chief of all the Union armies. Also, during the summer of 1862, General Ulysses Grant was restored to the command of the District of West Tennessee, including command of the Army of the Mississippi with its 25,000 men and the Army of the Tennessee with over 38,000 men. David Stanley recorded Brigadier General Gordon Granger's conversation with John Pope before he assumed command of the Army of Virginia: "'Good bye, Pope, your grave is made.'"[44] Stanley also was impressed with Grant: "He was very modest and quiet and was surely the last man ... one would select to become the great man of the war."[45]

Stanley was recognized as a commander who respected and valued the men who served under him. During the summer, the health of Colonel Joseph L. Kirby Smith, commanding the 43rd Ohio Infantry, was seriously affected by a disease which threatened to become chronic. Colonel John Fuller recalled David Stanley's counsel:

> After repeated warnings from his surgeon, and at the earnest instance of some comrades who were alarmed about him, he applied for a leave. Rosecrans said he would find some duty for Colonel Smith, temporarily, at the North, and would order him there. But he forgot it, and so the next month, when I also was ill, we each requested a leave of absence. When these requests reached Rosecrans, he said: "What! grant a leave to two colonels at once, and of the same brigade! Can't think of it!" "All right," said General Stanley, who happened to be at General Rosecrans' head-quarters at the time—"all right, General; but if you don't give them a leave, God Almighty will, pretty soon." "Is it so bad as that?" responded Rosecrans; "well, then, Mr. Adjutant, send these leaves at once." I remember that little kindness of General Stanley with deep gratitude to this day, and I know that Colonel Smith appreciated it keenly. Stanley sometimes seemed almost savage in battle, and would fight the devil himself if he got in the way; and yet he was as gentle and considerate as a woman when his sympathies were touched.[46]

Summary

John Pope wrote of the commanders in the Army of the Mississippi: "There were many officers in that army who became men of fame and station, whose association and friendship I am always glad to remember. Stanley, Hamilton, Palmer, McCook and T.J. Wood were among them and it seems amazing that with such an army and such wealth of commanders we did not accomplish more in that campaign."[47] Many have criticized Halleck for his handling of the siege of Corinth, but many also applaud what was accomplished during this campaign. Brigadier General Henry Cist wrote, "Brilliant campaigns, however, without battles, do not accomplish the destruction of an army."[48] Perhaps a more aggressive commander, such as Grant, with three fresh Union armies could have drawn Beauregard into such a battle.

Stanley agreed the Confederate Army still needed to be defeated, but there were many positive results of the campaign. Portions of two key railroads were lost to the Confederacy, and the loss of Corinth resulted in the abandonment of Fort Pillow on the Mississippi River. With the inability to prevent a land-based attack on Fort Pillow, the fort was abandoned. Soon thereafter, Memphis fell and Vicksburg was opened as a target by General Grant. Stanley continued to enjoy his interaction with the many officers he knew from his regular service. He wrote, "The number of new acquaintances made was immense. I knew almost all the general officers. How many of these have risen to eminence in history; how many have dropped into obscurity, leaving scarcely a name even in the War Records."[49]

Stanley's ever improving ability to command was demonstrated in the advance on Corinth, and he flourished under Pope. Stanley had been faced with combat challenges during May 1862. The first was the engagement at Farmington on May 9 and the second was the repulse of Hardee on May 28. The ability of Stanley to be ever present on the field of battle was one of his greatest strengths and was evident on May 28 when his leadership prevented disaster on the Union left flank. Perhaps more commendable, and an even greater measure of his leadership ability, was how he handled reporting the battle in which some of his regiments did not perform well. Rather than embarrass the troops involved and grab the glory for himself, he simply reported about the repulse of the Confederate attack: "Of how this was met and repulsed a full report has been made to the general commanding the army. Suffice to say that the result was satisfactory to the Second Division."[50] This report also showed Stanley did not minimize what had occurred within his division, nor did he claim the glory of the victory. Likewise, he did not tarnish one's reputation lightly.

However, those in command during this campaign did not all get along. David Stanley recalled an encounter between Pope and Brigadier General William "Bull" Nelson as Halleck's armies advanced. Nelson commanded Major General Don Carlos Buell's Fourth Division, and before the troops the two generals began cursing each other. Pope threatened to arrest Nelson, who said he would not honor the arrest. Nelson's volatile personality would be his downfall. It certainly was a poor career move to curse a superior officer and even a more severe mistake to dishonor a fellow officer. Nelson humiliated Brigadier General Jefferson C. Davis in the lobby of the Galt House Hotel in Louisville by confronting him about how he led his troops in September 1862. Obscenities were exchanged and Nelson slapped Davis. Davis lost control, pulled a gun, and shot and killed the unarmed Nelson. Davis was never prosecuted for this action.

4

The Battle of Iuka

*The heavy pall of sulphurous smoke
that hung like a breath from Hell ....*

In July 1862 General David Stanley had served under the command of William S. Rosecrans since the siege of Corinth, and Rosecrans reported to Ulysses Grant, who commanded the District of West Tennessee. The chain of command worked well. In June and July 1862 the railroads, now carrying Union men and supplies, had to be reconstructed. The impressive defensive works at Corinth also needed to be enhanced and redesigned, not to stop troops from the north but from the south.

One significant event occurred during the summer of 1862 which explained much in regard to the relationship of David Stanley and his immediate commander, William Rosecrans. David Stanley had been baptized in Mississippi in 1862 and Rosecrans was his godfather. Rosecrans was a devout Roman Catholic, and his brother was a priest, later a bishop, in the church. Rosecrans wrote his wife about the baptism: "I had also the great joy to be God father to Genl. David S. Stanley who was baptized this morning at seven o'clock this morning previous to the Holy Sacrifice which was offered by the Rev. Father Tracy of Tuscumbia or rather of Huntsville in whose mission the region lies and who has come here to administer the sacraments to those he finds willing ...."[1]

Before Stanley entered the United States Military Academy he was a Presbyterian, but the war caused him to search the core of his personal convictions. John Ireland, chaplain of the 5th Minnesota Infantry and, after the war, archbishop of St. Paul, Minnesota, recalled that Stanley's public conversion occurred during a mass held in a public square at Iuka with a very large congregation. Before this group Stanley publicly read his profession of faith and was conditionally baptized. Word of the event swept through the army. Ireland stated, "Not many weeks later I met General Stanley, and he told me that he was most happy in realizing that he had obeyed the calling of his conscience; and that by so doing he was nearer to his God, and ready to meet Him, if death came to him in the performance of his duty on the battle field." Afterward, it was common to see Stanley kneeling on the ground with the common soldiers with his prayer book in his hand. Ireland noted, "Catholics and non–Catholics expressed their respect for him on account of his open profession."[2]

The first part of the summer found the heat oppressive and marching almost intolerable, but conditions improved as the months passed. Stanley worked diligently to make his volunteers into professional fighting men, and drill was an essential part of the training. Stanley repeatedly stressed the importance of discipline in the military, but life was not all drill and exercises for him. Once Grant resumed command upon Halleck's departure, Stanley had lunch and dinner with the Grant family on several occasions. Also, he had an opportunity to leave the front for a much needed furlough. He went to Cleveland, Ohio, to see his wife, who had moved there after leaving St. Louis. Stanley's wife had taken a slave woman, Sarah Cobbert, and her two children, Dinah and Philip, with her to Detroit after she left Fort Smith, Arkansas, in 1861. Stanley harshly recorded the events after they arrived in Cleveland: "By taking these slaves into a free state, they became free, yet while my wife was in Detroit, employing Sarah as a nurse and boarding her children at cost and trouble, Sarah deliberately walked off one day and crossed into Canada. She was very ignorant and the meddlesome negroes in Detroit had persuaded her that she was still a slave and that the thing to do was to run away. My wife was much grieved at the woman's ingratitude, but being relieved of the responsibility of caring for a negro family was some compensation. I was absent ten days and returned to camp."[3]

When Stanley returned, he had the grievous experience of losing his Second Brigade commander, General Joseph Plummer. Plummer was wounded in the Battle of Wilson's Creek in August 1861 and he had suffered ill health since that time, despite the fact his performance was excellent. He was a regular service officer and had been very valuable to Stanley as he led his division. In May, while Stanley's Division marched toward Corinth, Plummer was sick and later consulted a Baltimore physician to try to combat his debility. However, on August 9, almost twelve months to the day of his wounding at Wilson's Creek, Plummer died, from "congestion of the brain secondary to his wounds, hepatic derangement and the fatigues and exposures to active campaigning."[4] Plummer's loss was severe news to Stanley and the Union army. Upon Plummer's death, Colonel Robert Murphy, 8th Wisconsin Infantry, was temporarily promoted to brigade command.

Plummer, who began his volunteer service as colonel of the 11th Missouri Infantry in September 1861, was permanently replaced with "Fightin" Joseph Mower, who was also referred to as "the Wolf" because of his predilection for riding up and down the battle line and also for his inherent ability in battle. Mower, colonel of the 11th Missouri, was to prove to be a valuable asset for Stanley.

Since the beginning of the Civil War, Stanley had performed well and received accolades from his commanders, but another measure of his ability to lead was how the common soldiers felt about him. In August, Lieutenant Jacob Cohen, 27th Ohio Infantry, wrote a letter which was published in the *Jewish Messenger* showing his assessment of the commander of his division: "Stanley is a regular army officer, and from his untiring energies and assiduous attention to the wants of his command, justly receives the commendation and love of all."[5]

Stanley was soon to be tested by the Confederate soldiers of a Missourian, Major General Sterling Price. Price, a native Virginian, was active in the Missouri legislature and had served in the U.S. House of Representatives. He was elected governor of Missouri and served from 1853 to 1857. Price committed his talents to the Confederacy and by the summer and fall of 1861 he had fought at Wilson's Creek and captured 3,500 Union soldiers in Lexington, Missouri, which added to his growing reputation within the Confederate army. On March 7–8, 1862, Sterling Price, under the command of Major General Earl Van Dorn, led Con-

Sterling Price led the Confederates at the Battle of Iuka (courtesy Wilson's Creek National Battlefield; WICR 31402).

federate troops in the Battle of Pea Ridge in Arkansas. By April 1862, Price had been rewarded for his service in the Confederacy by being commissioned a major general.

General Pierre Beauregard's health began to decline in the fall of 1861, and during the summer of 1862 his health continued to worsen after his withdrawal from Corinth. He left the army without authorization and traveled to Bladon Springs, Alabama, to convalesce. With Beauregard's exit, General Braxton Bragg assumed control of the Confederate army in the West. Since June, Henry Halleck's three Union armies had pushed Beauregard out of Corinth and gained control of Memphis; then the armies separated to carry the war to different areas of the South. By the first week in June, Don Carlos Buell's Army of the Ohio had pressed toward Chattanooga, Sherman's forces were sent to repair and guard the railroad west toward Memphis, and General John McClernand was sent to Bolivar, Tennessee. At Corinth, Rosecrans' army was given the job of improving the "Halleck Line" of defenses including the earthworks which were intended to connect Batteries A-F. Rosecrans' primary building efforts were directed toward the creation of the "Rosecrans Line" to meet the Union objectives of keeping the railroads functioning. Rosecrans and Grant decided to enhance the defenses at Corinth, including the fortification of the six earthen lunettes or forts. "Each had high parapets, ten-foot-wide ditches in front, and embrasures for cannons."[6] Controlling the railroads gave the Union forces an opportunity to rapidly move troops and supplies where they were needed.

The Union troops fortified their position in the Corinth area and drilled their troops. The cavalry from both sides skirmished throughout the summer, but no large battles were fought. The military stalemate did not last long, and in late July Bragg decided to take the offensive. He intended to move the bulk of his army toward Chattanooga to stabilize the situation where pro–Union sentiment was high. Next, he decided to take the war out of Mississippi and strike Buell's Army of the Ohio. He planned to leave Mississippi in the hands of General Earl Van Dorn to protect Vicksburg with 16,000 men and Sterling Price with his Army of the West commanding the District of Tennessee. As Bragg moved to face Buell, he ultimately decided to strike northward into Kentucky and confronted Buell at Perryville, Kentucky, in October 1862.

Responsible for the Confederate activities in northern Mississippi and western Tennessee, Price had several problems which concerned him. Some of his Missouri troops wanted to return to their home state and not fight in Mississippi, but Price knew he had to deal with the task at hand. He convinced his troops that their need was in Mississippi and they would later return to Missouri. The Missouri troops had not had a pleasant experience since they had left their home state, but these troops were welcome in Mississippi. Price's major problem was that he had the responsibility for northern Mississippi and western Tennessee but had too few soldiers for this vast territory. Also, Bragg was "exhorting him to hold the line of the Mobile and Ohio Railroad and keep Grant and Rosecrans from reinforcing Buell."[7] Given this task, Price was left to his own devices without specific orders. Hoping to garner support from Van Dorn, he wrote that the success of General Bragg's movements into Tennessee and Kentucky "depends on the promptness and boldness of our movements and the ability which we shall manifest to avail ourselves of our present advantages."[8]

Price tried to develop a plan to engage Rosecrans' troops but he felt he needed additional manpower. He requested that Earl Van Dorn's troops join in his advance and suggested the best strategy would be the concentration of their forces to overwhelm the remaining Union defenders in northern Mississippi, but Van Dorn denied any assistance. Van Dorn felt his forces were needed to deal with the Union threat near Vicksburg where the Union army had begun digging a canal opposite the city. He himself stretched thin, he was concerned about the Union actions in Louisiana where the Federal forces had increased their activity and threatened Port Hudson. He had ordered his other division, under Major General John Breckenridge, to Baton Rouge.

In August, Price's commanding officer, Van Dorn, was again urged to "press the enemy closely in West Tennessee,"[9] but he was given no clear direction of how he was expected to proceed without assistance from other Confederate forces. Price felt an attack on Rosecrans' Army of the Mississippi was rash; however, he did order Brigadier General Frank Armstrong's cavalry to conduct a reconnaissance into Union-held western Tennessee to determine the strength and location of Federal troops. Without permission, Armstrong's reconnaissance became a raid. Even though he was able to capture over 200 prisoners, he was stymied at Britton's Lane, Tennessee. Although the engagement at Britton's Lane had little importance, it did result in Grant's moving a division to Bolivar, which in turn resulted in the Federals having troops in place for the fight at Davis Bridge on October 5.

Meanwhile in early September, Bragg was moving toward Kentucky and was continuing to challenge the Army of the Ohio. As predicted, Union forces from the west were beginning to be shifted to Buell, leaving Rosecrans with only two divisions (commanded by Brigadier General David Stanley and Brigadier General Charles Schuyler Hamilton) to defend the Corinth area of Mississippi. There were also three additional divisions from the Army of the Tennessee near Corinth. The Union vulnerability was becoming evident as the troops left this area and Frank Armstrong's cavalry penetrated into Tennessee. To correct this situation, Union troops were redeployed to adjust for these weaknesses.

Finally, on September 1, Braxton Bragg informed Price he was successful in drawing Buell toward Nashville. Then, Bragg formally ordered Price to take actions to prevent the unification of Rosecrans and Buell. Although Price hoped that Van Dorn would send troops to his assistance, when this yielded no positive outcome he could wait no longer. Bragg and Major General Kirby Smith were striking into Kentucky and they needed Price to strike Rosecrans as part of the Confederate "grand offensive."[10] Bragg erroneously believed Rosecrans was about to cross into Tennessee to reinforce Buell, when in reality Rosecrans had no plans of moving from the Corinth area of Mississippi. Price finally decided to march his force of 12,000 men, divided into two divisions, to Iuka. The first division was commanded by Brigadier General Henry Little and consisted of four brigades of infantry.

Price's Second Division, which trailed behind Little's, was commanded by Brigadier General Dabney Maury. By September 5, Little's division had advanced to Saltillo, Mississippi, about 5 miles north of Tupelo, and Maury moved into Baldwyn, Mississippi, which had just been vacated by Little. The commander of Price's First Division was Henry Little, a native of Maryland. Little was the son of a member of the U.S. House of Representatives, Peter Little, and at the age of 45 Henry Little had Price's full confidence. Little was an experienced soldier, having served in U.S. Infantry after he graduated from West Point in 1839.

Despite the loss of combat troops from northern Mississippi and western Tennessee, it was critical for the Union to hold on to the gains won earlier in the year. Corinth was won in the action in May 1862 and was a vital junction of two major railroads. Rosecrans believed, in addition to Corinth, a strategic location that needed to be defended was Eastport, Mississippi, which was the best river port on that section of the Tennessee River. Eastport was just a few miles north of Iuka, and to protect Eastport it was essential Iuka be held.

By September 11 Price's Army of the West was advancing closer to Iuka, but his movements did not go unnoticed by Union scouts and cavalry that remained in northeastern Mississippi. So Grant and Rosecrans became aware an engagement with Price was likely, but they were unsure if Price intended to attack Corinth or Iuka. Rosecrans began to concentrate his forces at Jacinto, Mississippi, and he ordered Colonel Robert Murphy, who had previously commanded the Second Brigade of David Stanley's Second Division, to remain at Iuka with orders to protect the railroad and large Union stores there.

In a letter, Captain William Stewart, 11th Missouri, described the activities of some of the Union troops during this time at Iuka: "The 6th we came out of Iuka 7 miles into a nest of Guerrillas and have been skirmishing with them ever since. We have pitched our camp with orders to clean out the country around here which you may be sure we will do. Gen. Price with a large Army is not far off, but we are watching him."[11] Clearly, Rosecrans and Price were closing in on one another.

In northeastern Mississippi, Iuka was a small town with a population of about 300 people and for the most part, its importance was as a Union supply depot. In September, Colonel Robert Murphy commanded the garrison at Iuka with orders from Rosecrans to defend the depot. In war, Robert Murphy was not lucky, and luck is important. At 8:00 a.m. on September 13, Murphy's pickets were attacked by General Frank Armstrong's Confederate cavalry. There were skirmishes throughout the morning. Murphy determined from prisoners that Price's main force of infantry was following behind Armstrong's cavalry. To give Murphy credit, he tried to contact Rosecrans for orders, but the telegraph was down and all the couriers he dispatched failed to return. Murphy was alone in Iuka and he did not know for how long or the extent of the force he was facing. His garrison held its ground throughout the day of September 13, and at 2:00 a.m. on September 14, he sent a wagon train westward toward Corinth, with the infantry following at day break.

Receiving dispatches from Armstrong about the Union garrison defending Iuka, Price planned an infantry attack on the morning of September 14 but he was surprised to find his prey gone. Price force-marched his men as he approached Iuka, desiring to overwhelm the

Union garrison and nearly exhausting his men in the process. Murphy had marched from Iuka; however, he had not fulfilled orders to destroy the Union supplies and Price's men enjoyed their bounty.

Price's intent was to follow what he thought was Rosecrans' advance to Nashville, but Rosecrans was still in Corinth and, likewise, Rosecrans was confused about Price's purpose for attacking Iuka. Regardless of this, Colonel Robert Murphy was in trouble because of his decision to leave Iuka. The ire of the Union commanders focused on Murphy and they were greatly disappointed in his decision to abandon Iuka. There is no record of Stanley's assessment of Murphy's actions at Iuka but Rosecrans was clearly angry about Murphy's decision to leave. David Stanley was ordered by Rosecrans to arrest Murphy, who was immediately relieved of command and brought up on charges, but he was ultimately acquitted.

With Price in Iuka, Grant felt he needed to attack Price before he could unite with Van Dorn's command. Grant and Rosecrans maneuvered to cut off and destroy Price's isolated divisions. By September 16, Stanley ordered his Second Brigade to advance toward Iuka, traveling by rail from Corinth to Burnsville, about halfway between the two towns. Colonel Joe Mower's Union soldiers detrained and began a march eastward to gather information about Price for Rosecrans and Grant. His march was hard and swift and earned his Second Brigade the nickname of "Joe Mower's Jack Ass Cavalry."[12] Mower was making a meteoric rise in command. In April, he was a captain in the 1st U.S. Infantry; now, five months later, he had advanced from regimental commander to brigade command. Mower was a "scrappy, hard-drinking Vermonter, he had entered the army during the Mexican War as a private.... Already Mower made an enviable record for himself as one of the most reliable regimental commanders in Rosecrans' army."[13] When he was given command of the brigade, command of the 11th Missouri Infantry was passed to Major Andrew J. Weber.

By 4:00 p.m. on the 16th Mower discovered the Confederate pickets from Frank Armstrong's cavalry about six miles west of Iuka. The Union skirmishers were deployed forward to find the enemy. Private William Gilliard of Mower's brigade described the reconnaissance of Iuka: "We moved out in the open with our entire force .... When we got nearly across the enemy's skirmishers opened fire on us, but we went forward with a rush until we reached the top of a hill, where we could see Iuka."[14] Armstrong raised the alarm within Price's camp and the Confederates fell into a defensive line. Mower ended the day about a mile from Price's defenses near Iuka and sent word back to Stanley that 12,000 Confederate soldiers occupied Iuka.

After determining the size of the Confederate force he faced and anticipating Van Dorn would move to combine his forces with Price, Grant decided to attack Price before this could happen. Grant decided to send 15,000 men—6,000 with Brigadier General Edward Ord and 9,000 with Rosecrans—to battle Price's 12,000 Confederates. If Van Dorn and Price combined, Grant felt he be would outnumbered 2 to1.

Rosecrans was ordered to lead his remaining two divisions, under the command of Charles Schuyler Hamilton and Stanley, as a unified force in a flanking movement against Price by sending them toward Iuka along the Fulton Road while Major General Edward Ord advanced from the northwest. General Hamilton was ordered to send his troops to the east of Iuka. Price would be boxed in on three sides with the Tennessee River blocking his north. This was accepted as the best plan and the Union troops began their march on Iuka beginning on September 17. Often coordinated attacks in the Civil War went awry because communication was slow and proper timing was so difficult to accomplish: the plan was good; the implementation was the challenge. This was to be the case at Iuka in September 1862.

Brigadier General David S. Stanley's Second Divison at Iuka

First Brigade, Colonel John W. Fuller
27th Ohio, 39th Ohio, 43rd Ohio, 63rd Ohio, Battery M 1st Missouri Artillery, 8th Wisconsin Battery, 2nd U.S. Artillery

Second Brigade, Colonel Joseph A. Mower
26th Illinois, 47th Illinois, 11th Missouri, 8th Wisconsin, 2nd Iowa Battery, 3rd Michigan Light Artillery

Price knew the Union infantry was near and expected a fight at any time. On the morning of September 19, General Earl Van Dorn finally sent a communication stating that Price should move from Iuka to combine his forces with Van Dorn, with Corinth as his target. After weeks of being on his own, Price was relieved to be given any kind of direction at all. But before he could implement this order, he had to deal with Grant's army, which was converging on his troops.

On September 18, General David Stanley's Second Division was to have marched and to be approaching Iuka, but Stanley's guide led him in the wrong direction and Stanley was already behind schedule. He started toward Barnett's Crossroad at 4:30 a.m. on September 19 trying to make up time. The plan called for the attack to begin at dawn but that was no longer practical. The delay in Stanley's march was recorded by Charles Smith, historian of the Ohio Brigade. Smith recounted the delay in Stanley's march was due to being misled by a "stupid guide, whom Rosecrans himself had sent to show the road." However, Smith recorded on the evening of the September 18, Rosecrans rode into the camp of Stanley's First Brigade indignant about the route of the march. Rosecrans, who had quite a reputation for his tirades, unleashed his anger on Stanley. Smith recorded of Rosecrans, "He spoke his mind with greater freedom than was pleasant for his subordinates to hear."[15]

On the morning of September 19, Hamilton and Stanley's divisions were marching swiftly toward Price. Ord understood his orders from Grant to move in coordination with Rosecrans. When Rosecrans' divisions were reported to be delayed, Grant eventually ordered Ord to commence his attack when he heard Rosecrans initiate the battle. As previously stated, communication was very difficult during the Civil War. Grant anticipated an attack by Ord in the early afternoon when the firing began, thereby, relieving pressure on Hamilton and Stanley. Due to further problems in coordinating the attacks, the stage was set for a difficult afternoon for Ord's comrades in Stanley's and Hamilton's two divisions.

The first exchange of fire between Rosecrans and Price occurred at noon when the 2nd Iowa Cavalry commanded by Colonel Edward Hatch pushed some of Falkner's 1st Mississippi Partisan Rangers back from Peyton's Mill. The clash between the two cavalry regiments was coincidental. Falkner was detached and acting independently of Price while Hatch was patrolling the extreme right flank of the Union line when he came upon the Rangers.

Meanwhile, Hamilton's First Brigade commanded by Colonel John Sanborn had advanced to Cartersville, boxing Price on three sides. At noon, Rosecrans discovered an error

4. The Battle of Iuka

The Union Advance to Iuka, September 1862

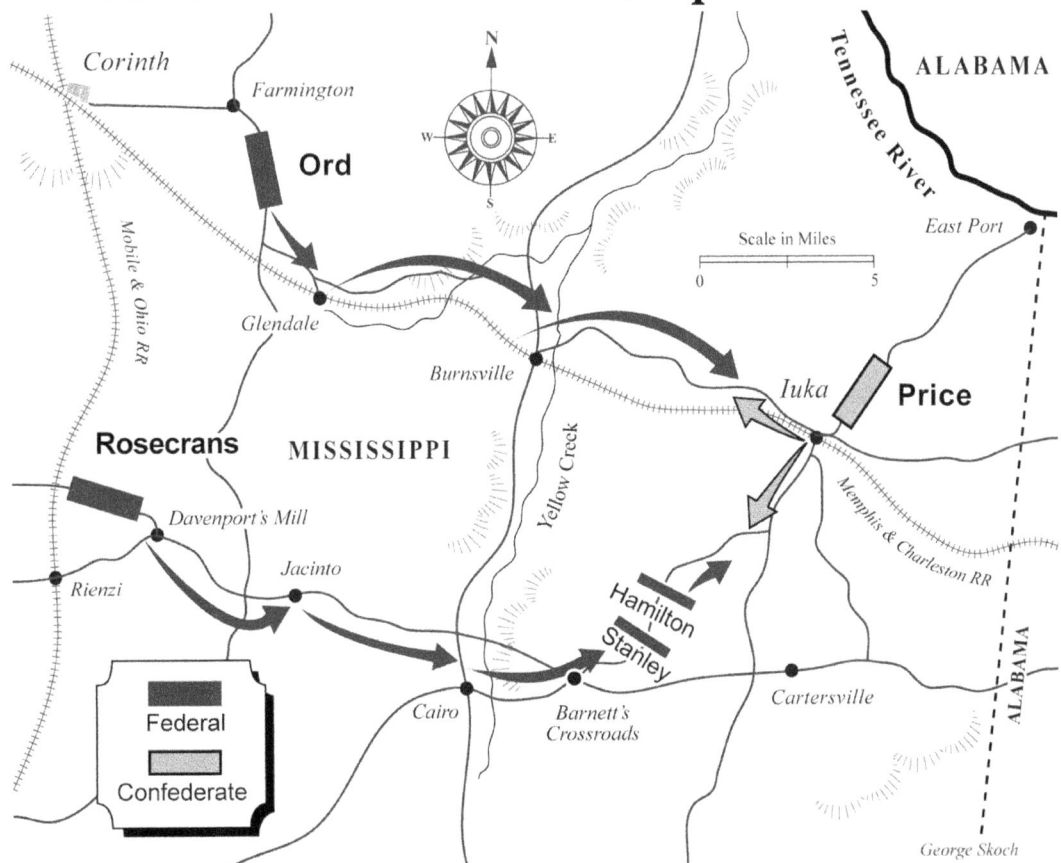

because he had thought Hamilton and Stanley's divisions would be within supporting distance while traveling down the Jacinto and Fulton roads, but they were five miles apart. Rosecrans feared Price would defeat each division in detail, and he quickly made efforts to remedy this situation when he ordered the divisions to proceed up Jacinto Road together. However, the action left the Fulton Road unprotected should Price attempt to retreat. Also, Rosecrans still thought Ord would engage Price after the battle started, allowing his divisions to take advantage of their position. So a great plan was not proceeding smoothly.

The conflict at Iuka began to develop in earnest at 1:30 p.m. when the 3rd Michigan Cavalry screening Sanborn's brigade ran into Confederate Cavalry, 1st Mississippi Partisan Rangers, along the Jacinto Road about four miles west of Iuka. The Union cavalry fell into line and was positioned to move the defenders out of the way near the Moore House. As the Confederate cavalry gave way, General Hamilton ordered the Moore house to be set afire.

By 3:00 p.m. Sanborn had pushed another mile closer to Iuka and traveled northward along the Jacinto Road until he reached the Ricks Farm, about 2 miles west of Iuka. The Union infantry marched to a meeting house at the fork in the road, and being unsure of where Price's main force was located, they probed forward with skirmishers. Rosecrans' arrival from the southwest came as a surprise to Price and he quickly ordered Little to respond to the advance with his First Division. Until Rosecrans made his appearance Price thought the threat lay to the northwest, where he knew Ord was preparing for an attack. Price's infantry quickly marched to meet this threat.

At 4:00 p.m. the 26th Missouri Infantry found Price's infantry about ¾ miles west of Iuka. The 26th Missouri Infantry discovered Brigadier General Louis Hébert's Second Brigade, which was supported by artillery. Hébert's infantry was forming a battle line on a high knoll and the 26th Missouri, located on a low ridge, faced them across a ravine. Faris' Confederate Missouri artillery quickly began shelling Sanborn's men and came under fire in return from the Missourians as the Union artillery was unlimbered. Hébert's men fell into line and began to cross a ravine to meet the Union infantry.

More Federal and Southern regiments began falling into line and the result was a bloody seesaw across the battlefield. Both of Hamilton's brigades, Sullivan and Sanborn, were roughly handled by Price's Confederates and were involved in severe struggle. One of the greatest losses was to the 11th Ohio Artillery and it was terrible. The gunners "stood by the cannon to the last" but soon the 11th Ohio Artillery fell to the Confederate onslaught: "Of the 54 cannoneers, 46 were hit."[16]

Hamilton needed Stanley's fresh division and he needed it quickly. Rosecrans' biographer William Lamers, wrote, "As the fight opened, Rosecrans was riding with Stanley a mile to the rear of the head of Hamilton's column."[17] Rosecrans' earlier fear his divisions would be defeated in detail seemed close to becoming a reality. Finally, David Stanley's division was emerging on the scene. Stanley hurriedly rode forward to meet with Sanborn and assess the situation. Sanborn's response to Stanley, when asked where he needed help, was that he should send reinforcements as soon as possible or the day would be lost. Stanley sent word to Mower to hurry forward. Joseph Mower's "Jack Ass Cavalry" was leading the way and at the head of the column was the 11th Missouri Infantry hustling forward to the sound of battle; They wanted to get into the fight and it looked like they were going to get the chance. As the 11th Missouri moved forward they moved to the extreme right of the Union line in an effort to reach the field as soon as possible, and Joseph Mower accompanied the regiment to the front. The 47th Illinois, 26th Illinois, and the 8th Wisconsin advanced to the left of the 11th Missouri and supported the existing Union line.

As the 11th Missouri prepared to move forward and to the right of the 5th Iowa they moved in four columns, loaded their muskets and marched forward at double quick time. The regiment advanced and they shifted their formation from column to battle line as they crossed a field on the extreme right of the Union line. They passed through a wooded area and as soon as they emerged from the woods, they came "face to face with an enemy line of battle, thirty yards away."[18] The 11th Missouri fired the first volley but there was no return fire. Major Andrew Weber, commanding the Missouri regiment, recorded that all became clear when a soldier ran forward from the regiment to their front: "For God's sake, stop firing into your own men, you are firing into the Thirty-seventh Mississippi."[19] With that the Missourians cheered and sent a second volley into the Confederate line.

The two battle lines set about firing volleys into one another. Major Weber reported the smoke was so thick "an object could not be seen five paces distant."[20] The 37th Alabama and 36th Mississippi regiments ran forward in a bayonet charge with hopes of pushing the 11th Missouri back, but this regiment did not give. The 11th Missouri, fighting for its life, "repelled three charges in brutal, close quarter fighting."[21] Major Weber reported that the enemy was received on the point of the bayonet and shot off. In many cases the officers placed their pistols directly in the faces of the Confederate attackers and fired. "The rebels approached so close that they used their revolvers; but as the smoke had darkened where we were, they fortunately did no damage, except scorch some of the boys' faces with powder."[22] The chaplain of the 11th Missouri, Reverend Samuel Baldridge, described the battle: "But no words can describe the scene. O the awful roar of musketry, sharp and wicked, murderous. overwhelming—now & then the hollow horrible crash of a cannon loaded with canister & the heavy pall of sulphurous smoke that hung like a breath from Hell ...."[23] The 11th Missouri and their Confederate foes fought for nearly an hour before the Alabamians and Mississippians stopped their attacks and withdrew. The 11th Missouri, with no ammunition remaining, slowly pulled back. The day was over.

General Stanley's appraisal of the 11th Missouri actions was this: "The only regiment that became heavily engaged was the 11th Missouri. This regiment stood its ground under a storm of musketry, which they repaid with double interest."[24] His report hinted at a little reproach of Mower advancing the 11th Missouri and not his entire brigade. After dark, all of Stanley's regiments moved to the forward position of the Union line and then rested after a twenty-mile long, arduous march. His regiments had no blankets and the soldiers huddled together to keep off the cold; all had a restless night, expecting to renew the battle in the morning. The wounded were moved away from the battlefield and suffered through the night. The wounded from both sides were taken to respective field hospitals, "where every major building had been converted into a hospital. Federal surgeons performed amputations by candlelight, operating without anesthetics."[25]

After the battle, Sterling Price met with his divisional commanders, Dabney Maury and Louis Hébert, and decided to move southwest to Baldwyn the next morning. They needed to meet up with Van Dorn, but Maury and Price had expected an attack from Ord and they were puzzled about Ord, who had failed to attack at all during the day.

During the evening, as Stanley's division moved into the front of the Union line, he was given orders to attack in the morning. About midnight General Rosecrans called a meeting of his brigade commanders. He addressed the meeting:

> Generals, we move at daylight. The infantry will go in on the bayonet; the cavalry with the saber; not a shot is to be fired"; Gen. Stanly [sic] was not at this meeting. He was next in command under Rosecrans, and a favorite of that General. He was sleeping in a fence corner when Rosecrans came up and thus addressed him: "Stanly, Stanly"; He awoke and replied, "What do you want, Rosie?"; "You will go in at sunrise on the bayonet; not a shot is to be fired." "Our loss has been fearful," said Stanly. "They are five to our one; they have butchered my men like sheep." Rosecrans wrung his hands in agony, as he said, "Where, in the name of God, is Grant? But go in on the bayonet don't fire a shot." "I feel," said Stanly, "that I shall be killed tomorrow, but your order shall be obeyed," and folding his blanket about him he again fell asleep.[26]

By the next morning Price had withdrawn from Iuka down the unguarded Fulton Road, and as Stanley's men moved forward they found the carnage from the previous day's battle. They marched past bodies, dead horses and destruction.

While Rosecrans had battled Little's Confederates, Dabney Maury positioned his division north of Corinth and waited for Edward Ord's attack, which never came. Rosecrans questioned Ord about his failure to attack and Ord pulled a copy of the orders he received from Grant directing him to postpone the attack until he heard the sound of battle. Ord recorded his responses to Grant about his actions on the afternoon of October 4: "At the same time you directed me to move my whole force forward to within 4 miles of Iuka, and there await sounds of an engagement between Rosecrans and the enemy before engaging the latter."[27] The order was also supposed to have been given to Rosecrans but he never received it.

Certainly Ord's failure to act at Iuka was questionable despite his order, but Ord also claimed he was in an acoustical shadow that prevented him from hearing the battle. Acoustical shadows are areas sound waves fail to reach due to topographical or other obstructions. In other words, the battle was raging but Ord could not hear it. Grant had expected Ord to start his attack when he heard the battle commence. Regardless of this situation, there was a great deal of anger within the Army of the Mississippi towards Ord and Grant. Captain William Stewart, 11th Missouri Infantry, stated, "If Grant had come up the whole rebel Army would have been captured or killed. But Gen. Grant was dead drunk and couldn't bring up his Army."[28] This claim was without foundation, but the comment showed the anger of the soldiers of Stanley's and Hamilton's divisions facing Price alone on September 19. Ord advanced on the morning of September 20 to Iuka and also found that Price had marched south.

Many in the Confederate army felt that they had won the day, and some of the officers were unhappy Price intended not to resume the battle the next day. Price ordered his army to move southward by way of the Fulton Road, which was unoccupied due to Rosecrans' decision to move Hamilton's and Stanley's divisions along the Jacinto Road in their advance the afternoon before. Price was forced to leave his seriously wounded men in Iuka and some of his supplies, but he was packed and gone by daylight. He had accomplished a tricky maneuver by extricating his men from Rosecrans and Ord and he did this by beginning his march at 3:00 a.m. By 2:00 p.m. Price was more than eight miles from Iuka.

The exact losses of either side for the Battle of Iuka may never be known, but the medical director for the Army of the Mississippi placed the Confederate casualties at 520 killed, 1300 wounded and 181 captured. Price reported his casualties at 535: killed, 85; wounded, 410; captured or missing, 40. Rosecrans estimated Confederate losses at 385 killed, 692 wounded and 361 captured. Rosecrans reported the Union losses as 141 killed, 613 wounded, and 36 captured.

Some authorities claim a Union victory at Iuka because Price was forced to retreat southward, but clearly Price's Confederates man-handled the Union infantry in battle. Price was able to escape to combine his forces with Van Dorn, but Grant was able to force Price out of Iuka. If it was a Union victory, it was not worthy of many accolades. David Stanley wrote, "Although the enemy was defeated and compelled to retreat very precipitately, our victory did not count for much."[29] Historically, the Battle of Iuka was of great importance. The battle was one of missed opportunity, perhaps on both side of the battlefield; but it is generally considered to have been more so for Grant. The failure of Ord to attack and the ease of withdrawal of Price's army would allow the Confederate forces to unite and within two weeks another, more severe, battle would result. It should also be noted a long-term animosity between Rosecrans and Grant resulted from the battles in northern Mississippi in September and October 1862.

Summary

It is remarkable David Stanley included less than two paragraphs in his entire memoirs on the Battle of Iuka, and it is difficult to know what he really thought about the preparation and outcome of the battle. Iuka was a difficult battle for Stanley, and Rosecrans censured him for his late arrival on the battlefield.

The question of Stanley's delay in marching to Iuka is one without a clear answer. The responsibility of Stanley's late arrival fell privately on him, but publicly Rosecrans praised the efforts of Stanley and Hamilton. Rosecrans defended Stanley's actions in his communications with Grant, writing on the evening of September 18 that Stanley was trailing Hamilton due to no fault of his own but "through fault of guide." Rosecrans continued writing that Stanley's division would have to march 20 miles the next day to reach Iuka.[30] Next, Rosecrans subsequently wrote of Stanley's actions, "the general commanding bears cheerful testimony to the fiery alacrity with which the troops of Stanley's division moved up cheering to support, when called for, the Third Division and took their places to give them an opportunity to replenish their ammunition, and to the magnificent fighting of the Eleventh Missouri, under the gallant Mower. To all the regiments who participated in the fight he presents congratulations on their bravery and good conduct."[31]

Rosecrans again wrote: "Brig. Gen. D.S. Stanley, indefatigable soldier, ably aiding the advance division; to their staff officers, as well as to the regiments which have been mentioned in this order, the general commanding tenders individually his heartfelt thanks and congratulations."[32] Finally Hamilton, who, of anyone, had a right to be angry with Stanley, wrote, "While these events were transpiring along the road the brave General Stanley had come to the front, and joining his personal exertions to mine the regiments that had fallen into disorder were rallied and held in position to the close of the battle. One of Stanley's regiments, the Eleventh Missouri, coming up fresh and eager for action, was pushed in to the right, where, uniting its efforts with the Fifth Iowa and Twenty-sixth Missouri, it made a most gallant fight and aided much in first holding our ground against the enemy and afterwards in driving him back in confusion to the cover of the ravine from which the attack was begun."[33]

Stanley did not make a record of his approach to Iuka in his official after action report, but later he wrote, "The inner and shorter road assigned to me, was effectively blocked by fallen trees. I was therefore compelled to march along a longer road.... Rosecrans was disposed to censure me for not taking the interior road, which was so heavily blocked with fallen timber. I cut the obstructions out of this road subsequently and it took a large force of pioneers all day to do it."[34] Stanley never mentioned being misdirected by a guide; however, the misdirection by the guide is also chronicled in the history of the 47th Illinois Infantry. In addition, all accounts record the guide was selected by Rosecrans and sent with specific directions for Stanley to follow.[35]

Certainly there was enough blame for the poor performance of the Union forces. Mower, marching to the battlefield appears to have forgotten he commanded a brigade rather than a regiment, or communication was so poor he was told only one regiment was needed. Hamilton was fighting for his life and only one of Mower's regiments advanced. Stanley recorded, "Colonel Mower, commanding the Second Brigade, was ordered into immediate action by General Rosecrans, and by some mistake carried in only his own regiment, the Eleventh Missouri."[36] At this point in the war, this was as strong a rebuke as Stanley would make in writing. He was very sensitive of the impact of words in reports and he strongly protected the actions of his subordinates. In addition, Hamilton marched forward into the fight in a piecemeal fashion, and some of his regiments gave less than stellar performance. Hamilton threw his brigades into the battle one at a time and nearly paid the ultimate price for this action.

Ultimately, the actions of those serving under Rosecrans became his responsibility and historically the focus of bad generalship has been shifted to the question of whether Ord should have attacked on the afternoon of September 19. In the context of the Civil War, where communication was so poor and any engagement could result in catastrophic surprises, those soldiers on the Union and Confederate sides during the Battle of Iuka performed well under the circumstances they faced.

It is important to make note of Stanley's conversion to Catholicism on September 12, because this reveals much about the close relationship with his commanding officer. Rosecrans most certainly was influential in this decision, but the presence of a remarkable Roman Catholic priest coincidentally entering Stanley's life changed him forever. The priest was Father Jeremiah F. Trecy, a native of Ireland, who was noted for ministering to troops on both sides during the Civil War. Trecy's involvement in the Union army began after the Battle of Shiloh, when he asked to tend to the religious needs of the Southern wounded and prisoners. Permission was granted by Major General Ormsby Mitchell and soon the good father was providing spiritual care for both sides.[37]

Trecy moved from place to place providing much needed spiritual support and he was often accused of being a spy. In northern Mississippi in late summer 1862, he was detained and taken to Colonel Robert Murphy's headquarters of the 8th Wisconsin Infantry. Trecy noted Murphy hastened to point out that his Irish name did not mean he was Roman Catholic and Murphy proceeded to do his best to "hurt his feelings" during the interrogation.[38]

While Murphy was questioning Father Trecy, David Stanley entered the room. Stanley spoke with the priest about the activity he had seen and telegraphed the information to Rosecrans. As Stanley spoke with Father Trecy, he formed such a favorable impression that the priest was invited to spend the night at Stanley's headquarters before being sent to Rosecrans. Trecy noted, "This invitation stung Col. Murphy and he endeavored though unsuccessfully to persuade the general to allow the priest to remain with him, which he refused to do that night." Stanley learned Murphy had confiscated Trecy's vestments, horses and buggy, and he ordered Murphy to return them. "General Stanley ordered Murphy to send sufficient forage for the horses for that night, which order the infidel colonel did not do."[39]

The connection had been made and Trecy recorded Stanley's baptism on September 12: "On that day he received General Stanley into the church and on the following day five others." Trecy remained near Stanley throughout the rest of the war, first as chaplain for the 4th U.S. Cavalry. He also remained with Stanley's headquarters through the last battle of the war.[40]

5

The Battle of Corinth

Should God spare me to see many battles I never expect to see a more grand sight than the battlefield presented at this moment.

Sterling Price's army slipped from the trap William Rosecrans and Ulysses Grant has set for him on September 19 after introducing the Union troops in Rosecrans' army to a new level of ferocity in battle. Price's Confederates withdrew from Iuka to Baldwyn, Mississippi, with the intent of meeting General Earl Van Dorn's main force.

General Earl Van Dorn was a colorful and inconsistent military commander who was born in Mississippi in 1820. He attended West Point, graduating in 1842, and finishing 52nd in a class of 56. Van Dorn served in both the Mexican War and also in the conflict with the Seminoles in Florida. He was promoted to the rank of captain in the 2nd U.S. Cavalry in 1855, where he served with Albert Sidney Johnston, Robert E. Lee, William Hardee and John Bell Hood. Van Dorn offered his military skills to his home state and to the Confederacy at the beginning of the Civil War. He began his service with the state of Mississippi and was commissioned a colonel in the new Confederate army in 1861. In 1862 Van Dorn was promoted to the rank of major general and was given command of the Trans-Mississippi District of the Confederate army. His forces were defeated at the Battle of Pea Ridge, but in October 1862 Van Dorn was determined to deal with the Union forces located near Corinth, Mississippi.

Van Dorn's stated plan was to drive Grant's forces out of Mississippi and West Tennessee all the way to the Ohio River. Then he intended to reinforce Bragg in Kentucky, but the first step in completing this plan was to destroy the Union garrison at Corinth. Even if he couldn't drive the Union army to the Ohio River, he could distract Grant to such an extent he would not be able to reinforce Buell's Army of the Ohio. Van Dorn planned to unite his forces with those of General Sterling Price at Ripley, Mississippi, and then, believing the Federal remnants near Corinth to be vulnerable from a concentrated attack, he intended to strike Corinth before Union reinforcements could concentrate there. This plan was exactly what Ulysses Grant feared and which had precipitated the Union attack on Price at Iuka. Van Dorn felt "swiftness and surprise were critical."[1]

The combined Confederate force marched northward and entered Tennessee. Because

Earl Van Dorn commanded the Confederates forces in the Battle of Corinth (courtesy Wilson's Creek National Battlefield; WICR 31608).

the Union forces were scattered at various locations, including Memphis, Bolivar, Jackson and other minor outposts, Van Dorn's march into Tennessee served as a feint, his objective being to strike Corinth before the Federals could react. Although Van Dorn was unfamiliar with the new Union defenses, he felt he could exploit their weaknesses. General Rosecrans continued the work of improving the fortifications immediately after the Battle of Iuka utilizing what troops he had on hand to complete the task. He used "colored engineer troops organized into squads of twenty-five each, headed by a man detailed from the line or the quartermaster's department."[2] The actual design and oversight was conducted by Captain Frederick Prime.

Van Dorn was adamant that for success he needed to attack Corinth immediately, and he planned to strike Rosecrans with three divisions. Van Dorn wrote, "The troops were in fine spirits, and the whole Army of West Tennessee seemed eager to emulate the armies of the Potomac and of Kentucky. No army ever marched to battle with prouder steps, more hopeful countenance, or with more courage than marched the Army of West Tennessee."[3] With the Confederate advances of Bragg in Kentucky and Lee in Virginia, it was important Van Dorn and Price play their part in the Confederate grand offensive occurring across the country. Van Dorn's command included Price's Army of the West: General Louis Hébert's First Division, General Dabney Maury's Division, and General Mansfield Lovell's Division of the District of Mississippi. Also, General Frank Armstrong's cavalry was attached to Maury. Mansfield Lovell's division was the first to begin their march on September 29 and Price's two divisions began their march on September 30. So within two weeks of the Battle of Iuka, the Confederates were marching again. This time the Confederate force was larger by one division—Price with 14,363 men and Lovell with 7,000, for a total of more than 21,000 men.

Despite Van Dorn's confidence, not all of his brigade or divisional commanders were so sure about attacking the heavily fortified Corinth. Facing Van Dorn in this fortified town were two Union divisions totaling 10,000 men: General Thomas Davies' Second Division and General Thomas McKean's Sixth Division. Van Dorn faced two lines of earthworks. The defensive line included the original Confederate defenses of the "Beauregard Line" and the inner "Rosecrans Line" made up of forts. Breastworks and abatis served as the primary defenses, but the anchors in the defenses were heavily constructed forts containing cannon. Rosecrans had two remaining divisions, one of which was Stanley's, positioned around Corinth in a defensive screen attempting to keep Van Dorn at bay.[4]

5. The Battle of Corinth

Van Dorn's plan was to march north into Tennessee and turn east and attack Corinth from the northwest. This meant Van Dorn would face both lines of Union defenses, but he hoped speed and concentration of force would allow him to win the day. By the end of September Rosecrans was relatively sure Van Dorn planned to attack, but his exact target was unknown. In addition to Corinth, Van Dorn's possible targets were Jackson, 50 miles north, and Bolivar, Tennessee, 35 miles northwest. On September 30, David Stanley reported to Rosecrans: "Gen Rust, Price, Vellipgue & Rust are all together & camped on the Pocahontas Road. Villepigue & Rust brought up 15,000 men.... Prisoners don't know where they are going."[5] Pocahontas, Tennessee, is about twenty miles northwest of Corinth; and although Stanley was not clear of the exact location, Van Dorn's movements were being watched by the Federal scouts.

On October 1, Van Dorn's cavalry began to destroy the railroads leading to Corinth, thus preventing the rapid reinforcement of the Union troops. By October 1, Rosecrans ordered Hamilton's division to move closer to Corinth. Stanley's division, located just southwest of Corinth close to the Hatchie River near Kossuth, was also ordered to Corinth. The presence of the enemy had been detected near Chewalla, Tennessee, and Rosecrans was trying to place his men where they could be moved to support wherever the blow would fall. Facing Van Dorn were four Union infantry divisions, but the risk was ever present that Van Dorn could strike single divisions and defeat each in detail.

The terrain around Corinth consisted of low rolling hills with oak trees and often swampy bottoms near the streams which flowed through the region. Corinth itself was located on low and flat terrain. The strategic importance of the town was as a crossroads of the Mobile and Ohio Railroad and also the Memphis and Charleston Railroad. In addition, it was only 90 miles east of Memphis and to control Corinth was to control supplies and transportation for the region.

On October 2, the Union cavalry detected Van Dorn's advancing infantry near the junction of the Chewalla and Kossuth roads, about 6 miles northwest of Corinth. Later on October 2 the Confederates pushed the Union advance pickets from Colonel John Oliver's Second Brigade, McKean's Division, to within four miles north and west of Corinth. General Rosecrans, becoming more concerned about the proximity of Van Dorn, was still unsure whether the attack would be in Tennessee or at Corinth; but of one thing he was sure, it was imperative to concentrate his scattered command. McKean's Sixth Division (5,300 men) was located northwest of Corinth and was the closest to Van Dorn. General Thomas Davies' division (3,200 men) was already located south of Corinth. General Hamilton's division (3,700 men) was camped two miles south of Corinth, and Stanley's Division (3,500 men) was about 10 miles west of Corinth. After midnight on October 2, General Rosecrans sent the message for his troops to begin their movement to concentrate at Corinth, but, unfortunately, General Van Dorn was already poised to attack the next morning.[6]

Stanley knew he needed to move his division quickly to Corinth. Cloyd Bryner, 47th Illinois Infantry, recorded, "At one o'clock in the morning, the brigade was aroused; two days rations hastily prepared—easily enough when you have only to choose between pickled pork raw and pickled pork fried with your 'hard tack.' The 'hard tack' [army bread] was not unlike water wafers and when fresh, good; when mouldy, intolerable; when only wormy, if hungry enough, you are not fastidious."[7]

General David Stanley, being the greatest distance away from Corinth, began marching at 3:00 a.m. General Hamilton's division began marching at daybreak, and General Davies was moving at 7:00 a.m. On the Confederate side of the battle, Van Dorn had his men marching toward Corinth at 4:00 a.m., and he had to cover ten miles before he could sweep over Corinth before McKean's reinforcements could arrive. All were converging on Corinth.

The Battle Begins

The first clash of these two forces occurred northwest of Corinth, at Alexander's Crossroads about three miles from Corinth, when Lovell's advance units ran into Colonel John Oliver's Second Brigade of McKean's Division. Oliver's job, although he was greatly outnumbered, was to hold the enemy until the Union forces could prepare a proper defense. Lovell's attack began at 7:00 a.m. and Oliver fell back across Cane Creek and attempted to destroy the bridge, thus slowing Lovell. Lovell pressed Oliver backward until he came to the old Confederate earthworks, which he established as his next defensive position. At 8:00 a.m. General John McArthur of McKean's division, seeing Oliver's situation unfold, ordered his First Brigade forward to support him.

As the conflict started to develop near Oliver, Rosecrans rushed General Thomas Davies' Second Division to join Oliver and McArthur. Other Federal divisions were moving toward the battle. "General Charles Hamilton had his division a mile and half northeast of Corinth, watching the Monterey and Purdy Roads. The head of Stanley's column was still at least two hours away and Davies division was only then entering town," remarked historian Peter Cozzens.[8]

Van Dorn's Confederates continued the battle near Cane Creek, while Rosecrans frantically tried to pull his scattered troops together. Van Dorn opened the battle in splendid and terrible fashion as he marched his entire army toward McArthur and Davies in line of battle. By 9:00 a.m., the battle began in earnest as a section of Battery D, a section of Battery I of the 1st Missouri Light Artillery, and a section of the 1st Minnesota Light Artillery began shelling the advancing Confederates. General McArthur marched the 21st Missouri Infantry and the 16th Wisconsin Infantry to aid Oliver in his defense. Oliver and McArthur were hastily arranging their regiments into a defensive line when they observed General Thomas Davies' division marching to their right with about 3,000 men.

At 10:00 a.m. the Confederate infantry slammed into McArthur's defenders and they were "irresistible."[9] The attack on McArthur and Oliver came from three sides, and although the Union defenders tried to hold their ground, they were propelled backward from the sheer force of the Confederate assault. By 1:00 p.m. the entire Union line was retreating toward Corinth. While the main body of the Confederate line pressed forward, General John Moore's brigade took advantage of a gap in the Union line between McArthur and Davies. After Moore's success in penetrating the Union line, McArthur rallied his men beyond the tracks of the Memphis & Charleston Railroad, just to the northeast of Battery F, and counterattacked. Moore's brigade was halted and repelled, but by 3:00 p.m. McArthur was again retreating towards Corinth as the full force of Van Dorn's attack proceeded.

Rosecrans was steadily being pushed back and he called on Stanley's Division to assist in stopping the Confederate attack. Stanley, realizing the seriousness of the attack, whipped his troops toward Corinth. "Utterly worn from thirty-four miles' march of the preceding, twenty-four hours, the brigade moved forward with alacrity but not sufficiently rapid for the impatient Stanley, who constantly urged them to greater speed," remarked Cloyd Bryner, 47th Illinois Infantry.[10] Rosecrans had confidence Mower's brigade would fight and called on him to slow the Confederate attack. Rosecrans sent a message to Stanley stating, "The general commanding directs you to send a brigade across on to the Chewalla road, through the woods by shortest cut; re-enforce Davies from your left, close in, in conformity with that movement. You had better send Mower."[11] Mower had marched hard from Kossuth and his men were tired and suffering from lack of water. In Mower's battle report, he stated that he had reached the Corinth earthworks around noon and was resting. Although the men of Mower's brigade were tired, the men of Davies' division were exhausted from fighting their relentless Confederate adversary. Finally at 4:30 p.m. Colonel Joseph Mower's brigade emerged onto the battlefield, coming to the assistance of General Thomas Davies' division. General Stanley reported, "These troops moved off promptly and with loud cheers, although sadly distressed for the want of water."[12]

Mower's regiments entered the battle and immediately were under fire. Mower's brigade had been marching throughout the day and Mower had to be shocked at the situation he faced as he took up the defensive line. Ever present, David Stanley accompanied the advance of Mower's brigade to the front. Duncan McCall, 11th Missouri Infantry, remarked as his regiment was preparing to enter the battle that there was a momentarily halt and stillness. "'What was it that made us so still?' All at once everything seemed quiet. It was a calm before an approaching storm."[13]

As the Union regiments withdrew from the fighting where they had been engaged since 3:30 p.m. the 11th Missouri, 8th Wisconsin, 26th Illinois and 47th Illinois infantries held their ground but were four regiments being flanked by Van Dorn's advancing infantry. Missourian fought Missourian in this battle as the Confederate 3rd Missouri Infantry began an enfilading fire on the Union 11th Missouri. The 11th Missouri adjusted their line to meet this threat as the 47th Illinois moved to meet the threat of General C.W. Phifer's brigade. The 47th Illinois made a gallant bayonet charge, temporarily pushing Phifer's Confederates backward before the reinforcing Confederate troops forced them to give way. The 47th Illinois recorded over 100 casualties and the regiment lost their colonel in this courageous charge.[14]

Relieving Davies, the 47th Illinois' flank was exposed. "A moment more the regiment would be surrounded and prisoners, but [Colonel] Thrush and Stanley were there. 'Fix Bayonets,' rang the command from Thrush, 'Charge bayonets ....'"[15] After the charge and death of Thrush, Stanley rallied the regiment into line and slowly withdrew. Stanley later wrote of the loss of the colonel of the 47th Illinois: "Among the first to fall in the battle of the 3d was Colonel Thrush, of the Forty-seventh Illinois, gallantly cheering on his men."[16]

As the situation deteriorated around the 47th Illinois and 8th Wisconsin, Stanley and Mower left the 11th Missouri to handle the Confederates the regiment faced to the best of its ability. After fighting for 30 minutes with the enemy on three sides, the regiment fell back toward Corinth. Next the 8th Wisconsin gave way and retired to Corinth. But certainly Mower's regiments, which after marching throughout the day were thrown into battle facing Phifer's and Green's brigades, could not be expected to stem the Confederate assault. As the day ended, Rosecrans had been roughly shoved backwards into Corinth, but he finally had his troops in one place and he did have the advantage of the defenses of Corinth as he looked for renewed fighting the next morning.

David Stanley recorded the following: "[I]f our lines were hard, the enemy's were by no means easy. They marched ten miles in the morning, fought all day and had only the water they carried in their canteens."[17] It has been rumored that one cause for the collapse of the 8th Wisconsin Infantry was the dispensing of whiskey by the quartermaster to the regiment before they entered the engagement. Even the 8th Wisconsin's mascot, "Old Abe," the bald eagle, was nearly lost when a Confederate bullet cut the rope that bound him to his perch.[18]

At 11:30 p.m. on October 3, General Rosecrans sent an optimistic message to General Grant referring to the actions of the day and described his defensive line and his attitude about the inevitable battle on the 4th. Rosecrans explained that McKean and Stanley's divisions faced Price's Confederates on his left while Hamilton and Davies' divisions were on the right. Hamilton and Davies occupied the north of the town and Stanley occupied a lower elevation near Henry Halleck's old headquarters.

William Rosecrans, Stanley's commander and godfather. The two men developed a close relationship in 1862 and 1863 (courtesy Wilson's Creek National Battlefield; WICR 941).

Van Dorn's Confederates, he noted, were stretched to his front bracketed by the two railroads running out of town. Rosecrans wrote, "If they fight us tomorrow I think we shall whip them."[19] He was overly optimistic in his message to Grant and was probably trying to reassure his commander after a tough day facing Van Dorn. Rosecrans' troops had yet to effectively deal with the Southerners in Mississippi. His troops at Iuka on September 19 and at Corinth on October 3 had been badly handled by their enemy on both occasions.

Stanley positioned his division in an arc connecting the redoubts of Phillips and Robinett, but there were no connecting entrenchments or rifle pits between the forts. Rosecrans wrote in regard to the placement of Stanley's division: "The plan was to rest our left on the batteries, extending from Battery Robinett, our center on the slight ridge north of the houses, and our right on the high ground covering both the Pittsburg and Purdy roads, while it also covered the ridge road between them, leading to their old camps. McKean held the extreme left, and Stanley, with his well-tried division, Batteries Williams and Robinett, the Memphis Railroad and the Chewalla road, extending nearly to the Columbus road. Davies' tried division was placed in the center, which was retired, reaching to Battery Powell."[20]

David Stanley recorded at 4 a.m. that "an enterprising captain had quietly brought his guns—it was a four gun battery—close to our picket line and then suddenly fired a volley over our heads and into the town. The battery continued to fire until one of the twenty-four pounders in Battery Robinette was trained on it, when they limbered up and hurried away, but not until the pickets of the Ohio brigade made a rush on it and captured one of the guns."[21] Stanley was unsure what the purpose of a 4:00 a.m. cannon volley near the Union pickets was to accomplish, but Sterling Price recorded his batteries were moved forward to begin a general barrage on the Union line at that time. Moving in the dark, the Confederate artillerymen had inadvertently moved too close to the Union line.

Major Andrew Weber, 11th Missouri Infantry, recorded, "About 4:30 a.m. we were awakened by a shell from a 12-pounder howitzer, which the enemy had during the night succeeded in placing within 400 or 500 yards of us."[22] Stanley remembered, "After this rude reveille we anxiously awaited daylight; it came and not the crack of a gun disturbed us. We had our coffee."[23]

Battle of Corinth—October 4

On the morning of October 4, Van Dorn had high hopes of finishing the job he had started the day before. The attacking Confederate army was positioned with Price's troops formed north of Corinth across the angle of the Memphis & Charleston Railroad and the Mobile & Ohio Railroad. Lovell was to the west of Corinth with his left flank on the Memphis & Charleston Railroad. On the left of the Union line was the entrenched battery—Phillips, the western most entrenched battery of the Union line. Battery Robinett was at the salient of the Union defenses on that part of the line just west of the town. Davies' division held the center of the Union line and the town center, supported by Battery Powell; and Hamilton held the right of the Union line. Batteries Tanrath and Lothrop, located on the western-most part of the Union line, were directed away from the attackers and were not significant in the upcoming battle. During the night Van Dorn had not been idle, establishing his own artillery within 600 yards of Battery Robinett. Stanley's Second Division was left of the center of the Union line with Mower's Eagle Brigade (47th Illinois, 26th Illinois, and 8th Wisconsin) positioned to the left of Battery Robinett and Fuller's Ohio Brigade (27th Ohio, 39th Ohio, 63rd Ohio, 43rd Ohio) protecting Battery Robinett on the left and right. The 11th Missouri Infantry had been detached from Mower's brigade and was positioned behind Battery Robinett during the night to support Fuller's brigade. Positioned slightly behind Battery Robinett was Battery Williams, in excellent position to support Stanley's division. Also, Stanley's 5th Minnesota Infantry was held in reserve near the center of the town.

On October 4 the Confederate artillery began firing on Corinth with a significant cannonade beginning at daylight and the Union artillery returned fire. Stanley's division suffered through the artillery barrage. "Nearly all the shells passed over us and went crashing through the town," Duncan McCall recalled. The Union artillery "soon silenced the rebel guns, killing most of their horses."[24]

The artillery duel lasted about a half an hour. By 9:00 a.m. the artillery action was diminished as lines of gray-clad soldiers emerged from the woods intent on pushing Rosecrans' army out of Corinth. The initial Confederate attack consisted of four brigades advancing *en echelon* from Van Dorn's left to right, first striking Davies. Next Van Dorn attacked

The Battle of Corinth, October 4, 1862

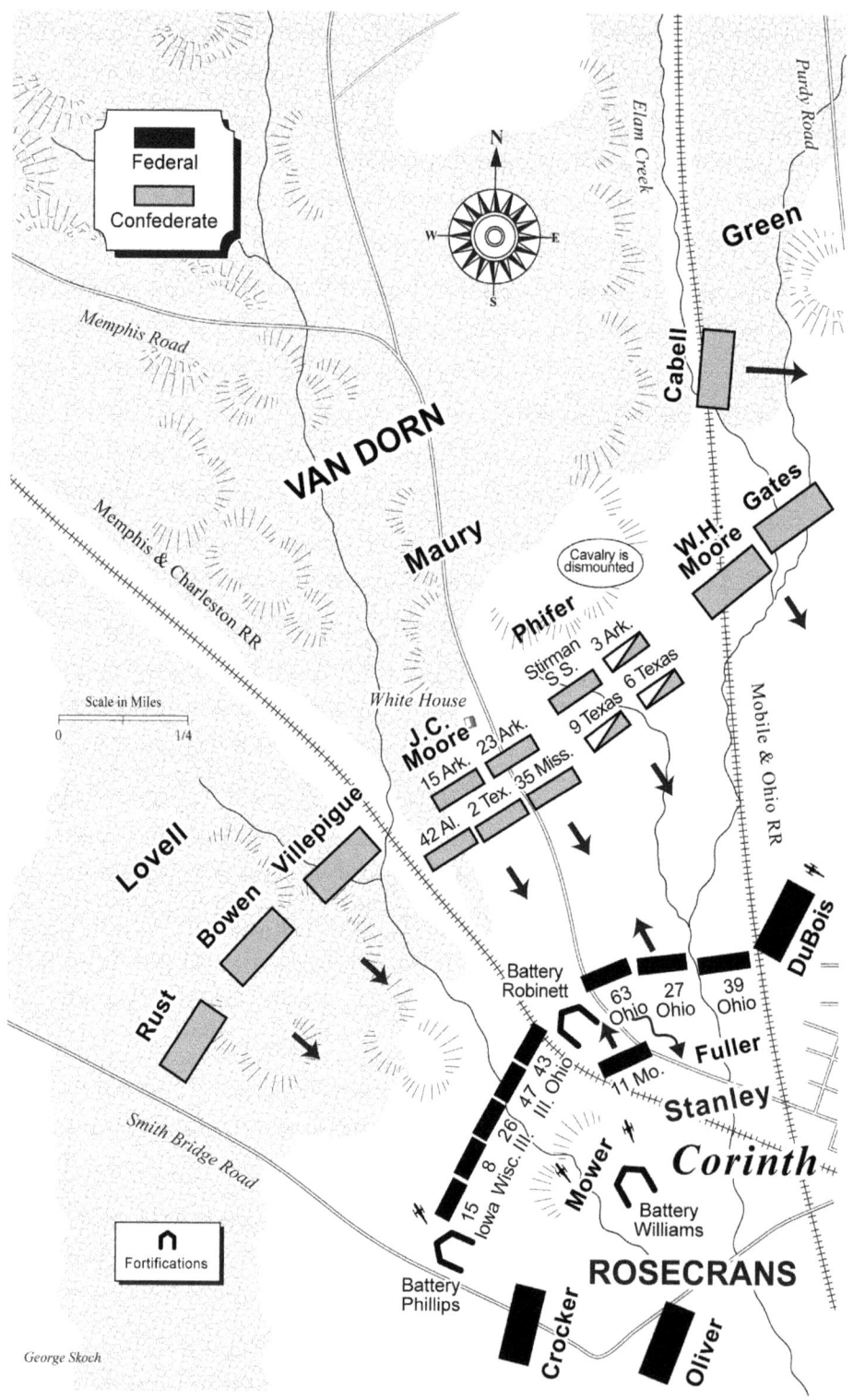

Stanley's division and then Hamilton's division. General Price's divisions (Maury and Green) drove forward and the Union line yielded as they were pushed to the north side of the town. As Brigadier General Dabney Maury's and Brigadier General Martin E. Green's soldiers drove forward, much of Brigadier General Thomas Davies' division was pushed back to the Memphis & Charleston Railroad tracks. The remainder of the division retired to the eastern part of town, where they rallied.

Having penetrated the Union line, but before Maury and Green could take advantage of their success, Davies' troops and the reserve, 5th Minnesota Infantry, counterattacked, converging on the Confederate attackers from all sides. Stanley's first contribution to the success of the Battle of Corinth resulted when his 5th Minnesota Infantry plugged the gap in the Union line. Rosecrans exclaimed, "Stanley's Indians of the 5th Minnesota sprinted northeast through the town to rescue Davies."[25] Unable to stand the counterattack, the Confederates were repulsed and thrown back. "Caught in a counterattack converging on the crossover from the south, east, and west, the Confederates who remained in town were soon driven back in disorder," remarked historian Stacy Allen.[26] The Union line proved too much and the battle along the Union right flank was over. Stanley observed, "Should God spare me to see many battles I never expect to see a more grand sight than the battlefield presented at this moment. The enemy had commenced falling back from the town and batteries before our advancing infantry."[27]

"Stanley was everywhere during this battle," said Colonel John Fuller of the fighting at Corinth (courtesy Wilson's Creek National Battlefield; WICR 31846).

Colonel John Fuller's Ohio Brigade and the 11th Missouri Infantry from Mower's Brigade waited for their appointment with Price's Confederates. Prior to the Confederate attack on Stanley's division, Confederate sharpshooters began picking off targets within the Union line and in return Union artillery and soldiers attempted to reduce their effectiveness. "Many a rebel paid the penalty of climbing a tree, being picked off by our sharpshooters," recalled Duncan McCall.[28]

As the battle raged on the Union right, Mansfield Lovell's division attacked the Union left about 20 minutes after Hébert's Division, commanded by Brigadier Martin Green due to Hébert's illness early that day, attacked the right. At 10:30 a.m. Dabney Maury's division began its attack on the Union line near Battery Robinett, where Fuller's Ohio Brigade was positioned. The Union artillery blasted away at the advancing lines of Confederate soldiers shelling them with canister until they had advanced to within 50 yards of Battery

Robinett. The Confederate line had to advance 300 yards under the fire of the three 20-pound Parrot rifles in Battery Robinett while also being exposed to the fire of Battery Williams, which contained five 30-pound Parrott rifles and an 8" Siege Howitzer. Colonel John Fuller's Ohio Brigade defended the right and left of Battery Robinett with four regiments: 43rd Ohio to the left of Battery Robinett and the 63rd Ohio, 27th Ohio and 39th Ohio, from left to right of the battery. "Presupposing that the Sixty-third would collapse, Fuller placed the Eleventh Missouri twenty-five yards behind them. General Stanley shared Fuller's concern, and he placed himself and his staff behind the Sixty-third," noted Peter Cozzens.[29] Maury's soldiers "advanced in solid column from the north. When I saw them coming I changed my front and laid down, with bayonets fixed, about 40 paces in rear of the Sixty-third Ohio," Major Andrew Weber reported.[30]

Captain Oscar Jackson of the 63rd Ohio Infantry watched as Confederates marched toward them and reported "not a sound was heard but they looked as if they intended to walk over us. I afterwards stood a bayonet charge when the enemy came at us on the double-quick with a yell and it was not as trying on the nerves as that steady, solemn advance."[31] David Stanley recalled the Confederate attack on his division near Battery Robinett: "Scarcely had the big column broken up when another column from Price's corps emerged from the shelter of the woods and came straight toward the center of my division. The key of the position was Battery Robinnette."[32]

Fuller stated at 11:00 a.m. he observed Maury's division emerge from the woods to their front in four columns. General C.W. Phifer's Texas and Arkansas brigade were the first troops onto the battlefield, and General John C. Moore's brigade consisting of the 42nd Alabama, 15th Arkansas, 23rd Arkansas, 35th Mississippi and 2nd Texas infantries formed to the right. The Ohio regiments (63rd, 39th and 27th) waited on the right of Battery Robinett until the columns reached to within 100 yards of their lines and opened with a volley. "In a few minutes the fusillade became general along the whole line of the Army of the West," noted Brigadier General Dabney Maury.[33]

The 42nd Alabama attacked the 43rd Ohio and the 6th and 9th Texas Cavalry (Dismounted) attacked the 27th and 39th Ohio infantry regiments. It was during this attack Stanley lost the colonel of the 43rd Ohio, J.L. Kirby Smith. Colonel Smith was an exemplary officer and had graduated from the U.S. Military Academy at West Point in 1857. Smith was the son of Major E. Kirby Smith, who was killed in the U.S.-Mexican War. Smith was one of the first causalities of the regiment and he was killed as the regiment was moving to face the Confederate line. "'Those fellows are firing at you, Colonel,' said one of the Forty-third's men. 'Well, give it to them,' answered the Colonel, and immediately thereafter fell from his horse."[34] Not only was Colonel J.L. Kirby Smith, commanding the 43rd Ohio, mortally wounded in the attack but his adjutant, Charles Heyl, was also killed. Smith's mortal wound came as he was moving the regiment in a complicated right wheel maneuver. He was replaced by Lieutenant Colonel Wager Swayne, whose actions over the next half hour resulted in the award of the Medal of Honor.

Next, the 35th Mississippi and 2nd Texas concentrated their attack on the 63rd Ohio and Battery Robinett. Once it was clear the focus of battle would be at Battery Robinett, Stanley rode to the area of the battle to support the Ohio regiments. The battle raged with heavy losses on both sides, but none as fierce as the battle near the 63rd Ohio and Battery Robinett. The 63rd Ohio's first volley struck the line of attackers, but the Confederates relentlessly advanced toward the Union defenders. The 63rd Ohio held on until they were nearly wiped out, losing nearly half their men. Colonel John Sprague, commander of the 63rd Ohio, recorded, "Every officer and man of my command seemed to put forth superhuman exertions to hold our position, but no troops could long stand against such unequal odds pouring a fire upon front and flank. Out of 13 line officers 9 were killed or wounded and 45 per cent of my whole force had shared the same fate, to say nothing of the number necessarily detailed to carry off the wounded."[35] David Stanley was present with the Ohio Brigade as the Confederates marched to within thirty yards exchanging volleys with the defenders. The 43rd Ohio and 63rd Ohio bore the brunt of the attack.

A soldier of Hamilton's Division recalled, "About nine o'clock on the morning of October 4th, there was suddenly heard something like a distant whirlwind. My regiment rose to its feet and was amazed to see a great column of the enemy like a mighty storm-cloud moving out of the woods and attacking the troops on our left. It was the storming of Battery Robinett defended by Fuller's Ohio Brigade. Twenty thousand rebel troops in the greatest assault made by them during the war, covered the ridge opposite, and commenced to pour a destructive fire upon the Twenty-seventh, Forty-third, and Sixty-third Ohio Regiments, and then advanced in three columns, climbing over fallen trees, bending their heads against the awful storm of grape and musketry. I saw the Ohio Brigade rise en masse and pour in a perfect blaze of musket fire, mowing them down like grass. I never expect to see a grander sight than this battle field presented."[36]

Stanley observed the position held by the Ohio Brigade was less than favorable: "The position I was obliged to occupy was one of great disadvantage, as the enemy had it in his power to deploy a long line of battle upon the crest opposite, having a concentric fire upon the very key of my position. Yet I could not form upon and occupy the ridge, since by so doing I would have been in the way of my own artillery fire, and if pushed back must have passed through a single defile. My men needed respite. For two days they had but a very scant allowance of water, and when the excitement of battle was over they lay down exhausted on the ground."[37]

Fuller observed the battle, noting, "Stanley was everywhere during this battle. To go back a few minutes, when Colonel Smith, his Adjutant, and others of the Forty-third were shot; but Lieutenant-Colonel Wager Swayne immediately began to steady the ranks, and General Stanley galloped up just in time to help. Stanley was a host in battle, and always seemed to be where the strife was fiercest. Just as our boys were moving for the charge, which broke the Rebel column in the road, I was astonished to see Stanley rushing in between the file closers and the line of battle of the Eleventh Missouri, his arms outstretched, to touch as many men as he could reach, pushing them forward to strike the head of the Rebel column. I wondered how he got there; for, only a minute or two before he was with the Forty-third, making it hot for the Rebels to the left of the Battery."[38]

The importance of David Stanley's presence among the troops cannot be overstated, as recorded by Lieutenant Colonel Wager Swayne, 43rd Ohio Infantry: "Fire was kept up upon the enemy during and after the execution of the movement until the head of his column had gained the parapet and opened fire on our rear from the opposite side of the earthwork on our right. The regiment was then moved slightly to the left and the right thrown back, so as to fire into the battery and meet the enemy in the new direction. This movement was attended with confusion, which was promptly checked on the appearance and by the efforts of General Stanley."[39] A member of the 63rd Ohio also recalled Stanley's presence during the battle: "When the Confederates came out of the woods to make their first assault on Battery Robinett, there was quite an excitement on our line of battle, getting the lines well closed up and orders to lie down until we could see the whites of their eyes, then rise and pour a volley into them. I heard General Stanley give this order to all the officers as he was riding along the line of the Ohio Brigade and encouraging them to hold the line and never let them drive us back.[40] Colonel John Sprague wrote of the proximity of Fuller and Stanley during the heaviest fighting of the day: "I need not attempt to describe the fierce assault and murderous fire to which my command was exposed, either to General Stanley, commanding the division, or to Colonel Fuller, commanding the brigade, for the fighting of my regiment was in their immediate presence and many of my men fell fighting bravely within an arm's length of them."[41]

John Fuller commanded the Ohio Brigade, which held the line during the Battle of Corinth (Library of Congress).

The Confederate infantry made two charges into the ranks of the defenders but were repulsed. The Confederate attack was an impressive sight as rows of soldiers advanced intending to silence the battery and break the Union line. The artillerymen at Battery Robinett fought with the same intensity as the rest of the Union line, and the advancing Confederate soldiers fell under the barrage of the shell and canister from the Union artillery. The third attack was spearheaded by Colonel William P. Rogers' 2nd Texas, which pushed forward. The 63rd Ohio had been victims of Confederate sharpshooters and received the brunt of the previous attacks. The third Confederate assault on the Union line near Battery Robinett caused the 63rd Ohio to give way, and Colonel John Fuller, on the scene, watched as the 11th Missouri rose, joined by the 27th Ohio, and charged into Rogers' Texans.[42] As the left-hand companies of the 63rd Ohio fell back the "Missourians opened their files to let the Ohioans by, then fired. They reloaded and fired again. The enemy kept coming. When the rebels were thirty yards away, the Missourians raised a yell and charged."[43] David Stanley was also with the men of his brigade. Captain Frank T. Gilmore of the 63rd Ohio regiment described Stanley rushing to the front line and clapping his hands together as he told the men of the 11th Missouri and the 27th Ohio, "Go in boys. They are running. Go in—Go in!!"[44] Gilmore also noted when Stanley gave the order the Confederates were not ten feet from Stanley's position.

Colonel Rogers was reported to be the fifth color bearer of the Texans, so determined was he to achieve his objective. Even the Union soldiers who participated in the defense near Battery Robinett had praise for the dedication, skill and sacrifice of those soldiers who attacked over and over again. For the 11th Missouri, the Color Guard suffered severely during the charge on Battery Robinett when the color sergeant, James Fyffe, was wounded and another "seven guards were also killed or wounded."[45] The counterattack stopped the Confederate advance. Van Dorn's attack had been repulsed all along the Union line and his troops began to withdraw.

It was later discovered that another commander of Stanley's division was wounded during this battle—Colonel Joseph Mower. While the Eagle Brigade waited for the Confederate attack, their beloved colonel, Joseph Mower, was having problems of his own. At 8:00 a.m. on October 4, he received orders from General Stanley to take a group of skirmishers to determine the position of the Confederate forces that faced Stanley's division. Colonel Mower took some men from each regiment along the Memphis Railroad to dislodge the enemy's sharpshooters, which "were at that time causing considerable annoyance."[46] He was successful in driving the sharpshooters about three-quarters of a mile when the skirmishing party ran into the main lines of the Confederates. Mower reported, "My men received several volleys from them, some shots reaching us from the rear of our left."[47] He assumed the fire was from friendly troops and rode away to stop the firing when he found himself surrounded by butternut-clad soldiers. While trying to escape, he was wounded with a gunshot wound to the neck and was captured.

The initial reports made to General Stanley and General Rosecrans indicated that Mower had been shot and killed. Wounded, he was taken to the Confederate camp, but the battle was turning into a defeat for his captors, and during some confusion which occurred in the camp he was able to escape as the Confederate retreat began. When Colonel Mower went into battle, he had removed his designation of rank and wore only a common blouse; because of this he was not closely guarded. He received cheers as he rode into the Union camp on a Confederate horse he had stolen. The rumor of Mower's brigade being intoxicated on the previous day rankled Mower and when he approached Rosecrans, he said "Yes, General, but if they had reported me for being 'shot in the neck' today instead of yesterday, it would have been correct."[48] Rosecrans reported that Mower had been unjustly accused of allowing his brigade to be intoxicated the day before.

In defeat, General Sterling Price described the gallantry and glory of the battle which had been so bravely fought: "They have won to their sisters and daughters the distinguished honor, set before them by a general of their love and admiration upon the event of an impending battle upon the same field, of the proud exclamation, 'My brother, father, was at the great battle of Corinth.'"[49]

At the end of the battle on October 4, the Union army had lost 355 men killed, 1841 men wounded and 324 missing in action. Another 570 men were killed or wounded at the action at Davis Bridge as a result of Major General Stephen Hurlbut's attempt to block Van Dorn's Confederate army retreat across the Hatchie River. The Southern losses were estimated at 505 men killed, 2150 wounded and 2183 missing during the battle, and an additional 400–500 men killed or wounded at Davis Bridge. The victory by Rosecrans at Corinth, while not destroying Van Dorn's army, did open the door for the actions that would take place in 1863. General Grant, sensing that the Confederate forces in Mississippi were weakened, seized the strategic initiative and targeted the fortress at Vicksburg as his goal in the new year.

As Stanley walked the Union defensive line after the battle, he recalled, "I was passing amongst the men stretched upon the ground after the fight, when a young Lieutenant, named McFadden, who had received his promotion only a few days before, called to me and said, 'General, come here, I want to say good bye, I am mortally wounded.' He spoke so naturally that I could not believe it and tried to encourage him, but he died in half an hour. He was born within two miles of my old home." Stanley's conclusion was that "the battle of Corinth was not a great battle as compared to those of first magnitude in the war, yet it was bloody enough."[50]

Rosecrans wrote, in General Orders, "I congratulate you on the decisive results. In the name of the Government and the people I thank you. I beg you to unite with me in giving thanks to the Great Master of all for our victory. It would be to me a great pleasure to signalize in this general order those whose gallant deeds are recorded in the various reports, but their number forbids. I will only say that to Generals Hamilton, Stanley, McArthur, and Davies, to General Oglesby and Colonel Mizner, and the brigade and regimental commanders under them, I offer my thanks for the gallant and able manner in which they have performed their several duties."[51] The losses within Stanley's division were significant, and the Ohio Brigade was hit hard at Corinth. Private Newton Preston also lamented the losses the 11th Missouri had suffered in the battles at Iuka and Corinth. He stated the regiment was so reduced in numbers that there were only 180 men left in it.[52]

That night Stanley and Fuller went to the hospital to visit Colonel Kirby Smith of the 43rd Ohio. Fuller recalled, "That evening I went with General Stanley to the hospital. It will be readily understood that the nature of Kirby's wound prevented speech; but as soon as he saw us he indicated a desire to write. I took out a memorandum book and pencil, when he immediately wrote: 'How did my regiment behave?' General Stanley commenced to write a reply, when a quizzical look of the Colonel's reminded us he could hear well enough, and Stanley answered 'Most gallantly.' This seemed to please Smith greatly, and he at once acknowledged it with one of his graceful salutes."[53] Stanley wrote of Smith: "Colonel Kirby Smith was a model soldier, an engineer officer of rare talent, and the son of a brave captain killed in the Mexican War. He had taken this 43rd Ohio regiment and had made it a well disciplined and drilled body. He had been under fire before but only a few days previous to this battle, said to me, 'I want to go into one fight where there is a storm of bullets, just to see how I can behave.' Also, his wish was gratified but it was his last storm."[54]

At the end of the day on October 4, William Rosecrans decided his bloodied army had endured enough for the day; he began his pursuit of Van Dorn the next day. While the battle was over for the troops of the Union army in Corinth, more bloodshed was in store for Van Dorn's retreating army. As Van Dorn retreated on the morning of October 5, a detachment of Union troops commanded by Major General Edward Ord was able to stop the retreat. Major General Stephen Hurlbut's Fourth Brigade was positioned on the west of Burr's Branch and the Hatchie River and was able to push Van Dorn's troops back about five miles and across Davis Bridge over the Hatchie River. With Hurlbut in Van Dorn's front and Rosecrans in his rear, Van Dorn was perilously close to annihilation, but fortunately for him his scouts found another crossing of the Hatchie River and the Confederate army escaped.

The feeble pursuit of Van Dorn caused a significant, and lasting, rift in the relations between Rosecrans and Grant, who felt the pursuit was not aggressive enough. Grant was disappointed with Rosecrans because he allowed Price to escape along the Fulton Road after the Battle of Iuka, and his displeasure with Rosecrans increased after the Battle of Corinth.

Stanley agreed with this assessment, but he wrote in defense of Rosecrans' decision: "The test is put yourself in his place. Rosecrans' troops had marched for two and three days, had fought for two days, had scarcely a supply of even drinking water, the heat was immense and the men were worn out; they had narrowly escaped a most terrible defeat and no one was anxious to crowd their late antagonists."[55]

McPherson's brigade was designated to lead the pursuit, followed by Stanley's division, and in the rear Davies' division. When McPherson began his march on the morning of October 5, Stanley was not ready because he had not finished distributing ammunition and rations. Because Stanley was late beginning his march, Davies was also late. Stanley was so late he lost contact with McPherson and soon his guide led him down the correct fork at a crossroads. After marching a few miles Stanley collided with Hamilton's column, not McPherson. Although being reassured the road was the right one, due to congestion along the road he decided to march in Van Dorn's retreat trail.

Stanley made the adjustment in his march and within a mile collided with McKean's division, which was also lost. Stanley wrote to Rosecrans: "Things do not look right here. McKean's train is a mile long. His command covers two good miles. The Divisions are not in supporting distance of each other.... Come up or send word if you can."[56] So Stanley, Hamilton, McKean and Davies were all bogged down on the same road; but by the evening the divisions were sorted out, having marched only 14 miles and missed the Battle of Davis Bridge. Stanley's explanation for the slowness of the pursuit was this: "As to the want of progress, I regret it but have no excuse to offer. Genl. McKean had the road and poked along ... all day."[57] The next day Stanley was again pleading with Rosecrans for better orders to aid in the pursuit. Stanley sent a message to Rosecrans explaining his situation. Rosecrans responded: "You should have taken the road to the right, this side of Cane Creek, which keeps north of the railroad. If you are too far advanced it would be better for you to face by the rear and do it now as you will reach Chewalla sooner."[58] Having separated his divisions from McKean's, Stanley was soon hindered by the movements of John McArthur's troops. Stanley wrote, "Cannot you send a new and distinctly defined order of march. The passing of Divisions on the road leads to great confusion."[59] David Stanley was finally able to advance and his division marched with the Army of the Mississippi to Ripley, Mississippi, in pursuit of Van Dorn. On October 13, the chase was over. Stanley's division returned to Corinth, where the soldiers rested and regiments were reorganized and refitted for the subsequent few weeks.

Based on the victories at Iuka and Corinth, Major General William S. Rosecrans was given command of the Army of the Cumberland and the Department of the Cumberland on October 30, 1862. The Army of the Cumberland was formed from the old Army of the Ohio; after the Battle of Perryville, the commanding general of that army, Major General Don Carlos Buell, was relieved of command. Rosecrans was given command of the new army and the department. And with the new army, Rosecrans took a fighting general he had grown to admire during his command of the Army of the Mississippi, David Stanley.

Allegations of Drunkenness

On October 3 and 4, parts of Stanley's Second Brigade were alleged to suffer from excessive alcohol consumption. Historian Peter Cozzens noted the 8th Wisconsin Infantry advanced to battle on the afternoon of October 3 and a quartermaster opened a barrel of whiskey and the alcohol was passed out to the marching soldiers: "The effect of liquor on hot, tired, and thirsty men can be imagined."[60] On October 22, Stanley responded to allegations he had also been drunk during the Battle of Corinth. A Confederate doctor, Joseph Scott, was captured by the Union army in northern Mississippi and reported there were rumors Stanley had been drunk then. The details of the accusation are not known; however, Stanley wrote to Brigadier General John W. Davidson, commanding the Military District in St. Louis:

> General—Doctor Joseph Scott, a surgeon in the rebel service ... informs me that in a conversation with a Mr. Churchill of your staff, the latter made use of the following expression with regard to the late battle of Corinth viz. 'Why Stanly (meaning me) was drunk.' Now as I never know, indeed never before heard of Mr. Churchill and I presume he is equally a stranger to me. I cannot for a moment believe that this caluming originated with him. You General, as a man of honor ... will appreciate my feelings when I say I cannot let the matter pass, without an endeavor, to find out, the author of a slander so cruel, so untruthful, and ungenerous. I therefore appeal to you General ... to find out for me whether this report can be traced to any responsible person, or if a rumor, if any person I can hold to account has engaged in circulating it.... And it is with feelings of distress that I learn I have back bitings at home .... I hope I may never have occasion to do you a like favor.[61]

Stanley's response to these allegations is important to note. This was not the reaction of one who had been caught, but he quickly responded, writing directly to the source of the rumor's commanding officer. He stated the rumor was false and asked the situation be corrected.

Summary

The Battle of Corinth demonstrated the leadership and fighting ability of Stanley's excellent division. Stanley's Second Division was being recognized as an extension of their commander—efficient and fighters. His Ohio Brigade and Eagle Brigade provided excellent fighting abilities during the battle, and Stanley was remarkable. He drove his regiments hard to reach Corinth on October 3 and reached the battle in time to allow Rosecrans to assemble his defensive line. He was with the 47th Illinois as they made a near suicidal charge into a brigade of angry Confederates. He was everywhere in the battle on October 4 and was absolutely fearless. He was in the ranks with the Ohio regiments as they withstood the attacks throughout the morning and he joined the 11th Missouri and 27th Ohio in the charge which saved Battery Robinett.

The historical accounts of the Battle of Corinth describe Stanley as being ever present on the field of battle and as being a haste unto himself, driving his soldiers to march faster and fight harder. Stories began to take form around Stanley's courage. It was recorded, "The colonel [of an Ohio regiment] was in advance on the skirmish line with his regiment, and as the bullets were flying very thick, the colonel and his command were behind trees and such other objects as would afford them protection. Stanley, who was in the front line near him, asked him for a drink from his canteen, which was handed him, and in plain view of the enemy. As he started to raise it to his lips, a bullet struck the canteen and tore off part of it. Stanley deliberately turned it up and drank from the opening thus made, and handed it back to the owner as unconcernedly as if he were taking a drink in his own dining room."[62]

It is unfortunate Stanley had to deal with allegations about drunkenness during the campaign; however, he immediately set about correcting the charges. There are no indications or historical evidence to assume the charges had any basis. Allegations were made about Mower and also the men of the 8th Wisconsin; perhaps these claims were somehow extended to Stanley. The claims of excessive alcohol use were to plague Stanley throughout 1863 and after the war.

6

The Battle of Stones River

Here's to gay old Stanley.
Pass him round, Pass him round.

Jacob C. Cohen, a lieutenant in the 27th Ohio Infantry in the Army of the Mississippi, wrote this on November 19, 1862: "The smoke of the late battles of Iuka and Corinth, wherein we achieved such signal victories, has cleared away. The dead have been buried. The wounded have been gathered to hospitals. Our late esteemed commanders, Gen'ls Rosecrans and Stanley, have been removed from us to more important commands."[1]

At last, cavalryman David Stanley was given a cavalry command in the Union army. Over the past year, he had demonstrated his ability to command and train volunteer infantry. He had performed well in all his engagements since the war began and had won the trust of William Rosecrans. In fact, the Union high command had focused their eyes on Stanley to command the cavalry since January 1862, when George McClellan was chief of the Union army. McClellan wrote to Henry Halleck on January 29, 1862: "Can you spare Stanley to Buell as chief of cavalry, or shall I look elsewhere to get him one? He has not asked for him, but I know him to be a first-rate officer."[2]

When his division was informed of his leaving for duty with Buell, Stanley was showered with gifts from the various regiments. Maybe one of the most notable gifts was a horse from the 63rd Ohio Infantry, and as important as the horse was to Stanley, the letter which accompanied the gift was even more meaningful: "The officers of the 63d Regt. Ohio Volunteers having served under you for nearly eight months and feeling deeply grateful for your uniform kindness and gentlemanly bearing towards us and all of your command, and having witnessed your gallantry and ability on the field of battle ... [t]he Officers of the 63d Regt. whose signatures do not appear to this communication participated with us in procuring the testimonial—but they are dead or absent from wounds received in the late Battle fighting under your eyes and some of them fell by your side."[3] His remaining regiments gave "horse equipments," field glasses, a sword, a sash, and numerous other items.

Stanley in return wrote a short message to the Second Division: "I can refer with pride to your labors, to your valor, at New Madrid, Island 10, the siege of Corinth, at Farmington and on the 28th of May, unmentioned in history but creditable in the highest degree to those engaged in that gallant affair, and finally, soldiers, to Iuka and Corinth, as your last

6. The Battle of Stones River

great successes in your country's cause. Of your marches and exposure, far more trying to you than the field of battle, I can speak only to praise you. In all these I have felt for you and suffered a soldier's lot with you. If you feel any of the gratitude for me I do for you, let me pray of you, brave men, to serve my successor with the same zeal, the same discipline, you have me. Remember that discipline is the bond of brotherhood among soldiers, and that disregard of it would disgrace the holy cause we serve."[4]

Charles H. Smith, historian of John Fuller's First Brigade, described David Stanley as brave and cool in battle and well respected, not only by the men of his division, but also by his peers and commanding officer. Smith also mentioned Stanley's need to have discipline within the ranks of those he commanded. Under Stanley, his men "were brought to the highest point of military perfection. It was their superb precision in military movements, their fighting and staying qualities during the battles of Iuka and Corinth, Mississippi, during the months of September and October, which led General Stanley to exclaim, 'These troops can never be beaten in battle.'"[5]

When Rosecrans took command of the Army of the Cumberland, he was desperately in need of an effective chief of the cavalry. He was barraged, almost daily, with messages from his commanders about lack of communication with the cavalry and the need for an effective cavalry arm to meet the challenges of Major General Nathan B. Forrest, Brigadier General John Hunt Morgan and Brigadier General Joseph Wheeler's Confederate cavalry. The Confederate cavalry was clearly Rosecrans' most immediate challenge. Only three days into command of the Army of the Cumberland, Rosecrans was firing off messages to Major General Henry Halleck, general-in-chief of the Union army, pleading for assistance with his cavalry: "Will keep you advised. Please send me the nine companies of Anderson Cavalry, raised in Pennsylvania, by the Governor's authority, given to the one company now here. We need them greatly, and shall need them more. As the rebel infantry gets in winter quarters, they will scatter, steal horses, and commence roving the country for living and plunder. We must have cavalry and cavalry arms, and a capable division commander. If possible, give me Stanley."[6] Rosecrans was assembling his cavalry and needed David Stanley. In his message, he requested the Anderson Cavalry. Little did he know how much trouble he and Stanley would have with this cavalry regiment when they finally arrived in December 1862.

Rosecrans wanted numerically more cavalry and he particularly wanted David Stanley as his chief of cavalry. The next day after Halleck received Rosecrans' request, he communicated that Grant had been ordered to send Stanley to the Army of the Cumberland. It would be three weeks before Stanley arrived, but Rosecrans' need for him was recorded in a series of messages. Six days after his last message Rosecrans wrote to Halleck: "I have considerable cavalry in much confusion for want of a head. I am greatly in need of General Stanley, and request that you order him to join me at once. General Grant is pushing him south."[7]

Upon his arrival at the Army of the Cumberland, Rosecrans organized his army into three corps: Major General Alexander McCook, a West Point classmate of David Stanley, commanded the Right Wing; Major General George H. Thomas commanded the Center Wing; and Major General Thomas L. Crittenden commanded the Left Wing. This army had been tested in only two major battles—the Battle of Shiloh and the Battle of Perryville. The latter cost the army its commander, Don Carlos Buell, who had been relieved of his command; and now the newly created Army of the Cumberland was in pursuit of Braxton Bragg's retreating army in Tennessee.

Rosecrans' wing commanders were driving the need for Stanley. The Left Wing commander, Major General Thomas Crittenden, was asked on November 6 to "communicate often, and know that the communication is kept up. Push rapidly to Gallatin. Do you hear anything of Colonel Kennett or his cavalry force? Where is your advance, and when can you reach Gallatin."[8] Colonel John Kennett of the 4th Ohio Cavalry was commanding the cavalry division until Stanley arrived and Kennett was overwhelmed with challenges from all quarters. The cavalry was trying to rid the countryside of guerrillas and was greatly outnumbered by the regular Confederate cavalry.

Kennett was a native Russian, born in St. Petersburg in 1809. He attended Harvard College and returned to Russia after his education. Later, he returned to Cincinnati and became a United States citizen. Kennett had assisted in the organization of the 4th Ohio Cavalry and served as the first colonel of the regiment. Subsequently, Kennett was promoted to command the cavalry division of the Army of the Cumberland. From the messages Rosecrans was already sending to Halleck, it was clear Kennett was not providing the support the army needed.

Kennett had the unenviable task of trying to command the cavalry which was distributed throughout the various corps of the Army of the Cumberland. The small Union cavalry was under the command of the various corps commander and it was virtually impossible for any major cavalry missions to be accomplished under this type of organization.

On November 6, Rosecrans received information that John Hunt Morgan commanded 2,400 troopers and was preparing to raid into Kentucky.[9] Colonel A.A. Stevens, post commander in Mitchellsville, was ordered to communicate this intelligence to Colonel Lewis Zahm, who commanded a brigade of cavalry. Colonel Zahm commanded the Second Cavalry Brigade and was second-in-command to Kennett. Born in Bavaria on August 7, 1820, Zahm came to America with his two sisters and travelled to Ohio, where his brother lived. When the Civil War began, Zahm was urged to raise a regiment of cavalry, which he did after some deliberation, and became the first colonel of the 3rd Ohio Cavalry, which was mustered into service in September 1861.

It soon became apparent to Rosecrans there was also a very weak courier service between the wing commanders, headquarters and the cavalry. Due to the dominance of the Confederate cavalry, couriers who maintained a steady flow of communication often had a difficult time reaching one commander or another. The role of Union courier service was very difficult. The *New York Times* reported the plight of a courier captured by guerrillas and ultimately taken to Nathan B. Forrest. When the courier was captured, his captors "placing his revolver at his forehead told him to go on his knees and say his prayers, if he had any to say, for he had but a moment to live."[10] He was not shot, but the courier service was certainly perilous in late 1862.

Again, on November 6, Rosecrans received a disturbing communication from one of his subordinates, J.B. Anderson, about the dominance of the Confederate cavalry in Tennessee: "The whole country from Richland to Gallatin has been occupied by bands of mounted men, who will cut off working parties and destroy their work unless a sufficient force is placed on the line."[11] The message continued, saying unless a large enough force of Union cavalry was present to intimidate the Confederate raiders, much of the necessary work would not be completed.

The seriousness of the Southern cavalry was communicated to Rosecrans from Major General Alexander McCook, commanding his Right Wing, on November 6. McCook observed that John Hunt Morgan's cavalry had attacked Edgefield, Tennessee, the previous day but was repulsed. While the Union infantry was dealing with this, a simultaneous attack was made at Nashville, which McCook noted was also repulsed. It seemed all the Union army could do was to act defensively. McCook wrote that Morgan was next seen six miles north of Nashville heading for Gallatin and that McCook had dispatched some of his cavalry to observe Morgan's movements and promised to relay the information to Crittenden.[12]

The Confederate cavalry seemed to be everywhere. Rosecrans' frustration was evident when he responded to McCook through his acting chief of staff, Arthur Ducat: "We have nothing from Colonel Kennett as to where he is: did he go toward Scottsville, as ordered? He has not communicated with General Crittenden, and the general does not know whether he has cavalry on his front or not. One regiment was ordered to go on General Crittenden's front. When Colonel Kennett marched it was never reported to him."[13]

On November 7, General Thomas Crittenden was still in the dark regarding Colonel Kennett's location or objective, but he had been in communication with Colonel Lewis Zahm, who reported Morgan was still located at Gallatin, Tennessee. Upon receiving this information, Crittenden gave one of the most frustrating orders of the war when he ordered Brigadier General Thomas J. Wood's Division to "catch" Morgan and his cavalry. "I have this moment received information that Morgan, with his cavalry, is still in Gallatin: Now, if this is true, I want you to catch him, and, although you have marched 20 miles today, you will send a brigade of picked men at 2 o'clock tomorrow morning to Gallatin, so as to reach that point at daylight, with instructions to capture whatever force may be there. March with the remainder of your command at 6 o'clock. General Van Cleve will march at 6, and will be prompt in supporting distance of you. This is hard on the men, but no chances are now to be lost, and I count on you."[14] Chasing cavalry with infantry was one of the most difficult tasks of the Civil War.

Rosecrans wrote a communication to Crittenden on November 7 criticizing Kennett's silence. Rosecrans realized the intent of the Confederate cavalry was to prevent the use of the road to Nashville. He wrote to Crittenden to order Kennett to strongly defend Hartsville from the enemy's cavalry. Rosecrans told Crittenden to use some of the cavalry assigned to his corps to serve as a screen near Lebanon. He continued: "At this distance you must be the best judge of the position of the rebel cavalry, and the general commanding leaves much in this respect to your judgment and discretion. Order Colonel Kennett to keep up communication."[15]

Frustration continued to be the order of the day for Rosecrans. In another communication to Crittenden, Rosecrans reported Colonel Zahm had found John Hunt Morgan's cavalry at Gallatin, Tennessee, and Rosecrans wanted Crittenden to "crush the devil." While Rosecrans was getting communications from Zahm, not everyone was. Speed F. Fry also wrote to Rosecrans on November 7: "I have heard nothing from Colonel Zahm since I left Bowling Green. I will get a correct account of the various roads leading south from the railroad. I have not had time as yet to do so. I learned from citizens at Franklin this morning that Morgan was at Edgefield, and so dispatched from Franklin."[16]

At 10:00 p.m. Rosecrans, through his acting chief of staff, Arthur Ducat, sent a message directly to Kennett. Rosecrans had endured enough silence. If Stanley had been present, he would have let him handle the problem of lack of communication from the Union cavalry. Rosecrans ordered Kennett to put a strong force of cavalry at Hartsville and then to dispatch additional troopers to Crittenden as he crossed the river near Lebanon, Tennessee. Next,

Rosecrans directed Kennett to use his best judgment while carrying out these orders. The distance was too great and Rosecrans had more to do than give Kennett detailed orders for each action. Ducat continued: "The general commanding expects that you will exercise your own judgment in many respects, governed by the several movements ordered. You will, on receipt of this, communicate rapidly with General Crittenden, and co-operate with him.... The general wishes me to state that he does not consider your dispatches satisfactory, and would like them oftener; that communication with his headquarters must at all times be kept up, wherever they are."[17]

Colonel Lewis Zahm, who soon grasped and accepted the need to increase communication, did so on November 7, reporting to Rosecrans the location of McCook's corps and the information of Morgan's 3,000 cavalry at Gallatin. Zahm reported to Ducat he had only 600 troopers and could not engage Morgan. He indicated he was unaware of the exact location of the wings of the army and had to send troopers to try to find Crittenden's corps and open communications with him. Ducat reinforced the information flow from Zahm and encouraged him to keep the messages going: "Inform him [Crittenden] of all you know, and keep up communications with him. If you have to communicate, will Colonel Kennett act on the principle that the cavalry are the eyes of the army. Take orders for co-operation from General Crittenden. Always keep up your communication with headquarters."[18] While Zahm was acting on Rosecrans' wishes that his cavalry work in conjunction with the entire army, it was disturbing that Ducat had to urge Zahm to influence Kennett to serve the army through his role as a commander of cavalry.

Finally Rosecrans had enough of the cavalry operating without communication. He had gotten one of his cavalry brigades on board but he could wait no longer. He issued General Orders No. 7 announcing Captain Elmer Otis, 4th U.S. Cavalry, as chief of the courier lines. One way or another, he was going to get information from his "eyes of the Army" and between his three corps.

Meanwhile, Thomas Crittenden's frustrating order of sending Thomas Wood's infantry to capture Morgan was fruitless. Morgan just scampered away while Crittenden further exhausted his men. Crittenden reported on the efforts of his infantry to capture Morgan and said that the infantry, Harker's brigade, and Zahm's cavalry reached the location where Morgan was last reported at daylight only to find him gone. They did manage to capture eighteen men, some horses, and equipment. "The want of cavalry greatly embarrasses my operations. Colonel Kennett has not yet reported, so I have none to send to General Smith, as you have ordered. Without a cavalry force at Hartsville, I fear a single regiment would not be safe here, and I have no means of opening communication with General McCook."[19] Crittenden lamented the lack of cavalry to support his actions and the continued lack of communication from Kennett.

Stanley was still not present with the Army of the Cumberland and on November 9 Rosecrans wrote again to Halleck: "Our great wants are arms and a chief for the cavalry. Nothing yet from Stanley."[20] He also appealed to Edwin Stanton, secretary of war, the same day: "General Halleck has ordered Stanley for a chief. He has not reported. No promise of arms. What can you do for us?"[21] Bad blood had arisen between Grant and Rosecrans during the Corinth and Iuka campaigns in Mississippi before Rosecrans assumed command of the Army of the Cumberland. Grant was dragging his feet in releasing the experienced and highly prized Stanley, and Rosecrans was suffering because of want of a commander of the cavalry of his newly formed army. Grant finally issued orders for Stanley's transfer on November 11.[22] Stanley would not arrive until November 24. During the intervening weeks the constant struggle of communication with Kennett on one hand and the hit and run tactics of Morgan, Forrest, and Wheeler on the other was enough to distract Rosecrans. By the middle of November, Kennett's communications were somewhat improving.

Rosecrans' commander of his center wing, General Thomas, arrived in Gallatin, Tennessee, on November 12, offering experience and stability to his newly forming army. Thomas' first questions went to the heart of the struggle Rosecrans was facing: "Arrived here today.... Where is Crittenden and the cavalry?"[23] Almost immediately, the weakness of the cavalry was evident. Thomas needed to know how to position his troops and he needed to know where the Union cavalry was placed. On November 12, Kennett, with 2,000 Union cavalry, was in Hartsville, Tennessee, and Thomas was informed Kennett was "requested to keep up communications."

On November 13, Brigadier General James Negley reported Nathan B. Forrest's cavalry of 4,000–5,000 troopers threw aside the pickets of the 4th Ohio Cavalry. Kennett's days were numbered within the Union army. Again, on November 14, Rosecrans wrote to Thomas: "Have you any news from Kennett today? He was anxious on yesterday. Satisfied there was no cause. Find out how much of a train it will take to haul his spoils from Hartsville, and send for them. Direct your infantry at Hartsville to collect the stores discovered by Colonel Kennett."[24] Thomas responded disparagingly of his interactions with Kennett: "A dispatch from Colonel Kennett, just received, states that one of his scouts had just returned from Lebanon, and tells him that Morgan and Forrest are at Lebanon with 4,200 men and eight pieces of artillery. Colonel Kennett thinks it will be an unequal fight, and, therefore,

Confederate cavalry harassed the Union supply line almost daily (from Frank Leslie's *Illustrated Famous Leaders and Battle Scenes of the Civil War* [New York: Mrs. Frank Leslie, 1896], p.3).

would return to Hartsville. He thinks a combined movement should be agreed upon to move from this place and Lebanon on the rebels. Confess I do not understand him, and his dispatch has something of the appearance of a stampede."[25]

Within three days of Thomas' arrival in Gallatin, he had summarized the cavalry situation of the Army of the Cumberland Rosecrans had desperately tried to remedy. Thomas wrote to Rosecrans on November 15: "When will Stanley arrive? It is a great pity he is not now in command of the cavalry."[26] On November 18, Arthur Ducat slapped Colonel Kennett verbally with an unpleasant and thinly veiled message about the way the cavalry was being handled: "Dispatch received. Had information some time before of the affair at Gallatin. It is to be regretted that our cavalry has proved too slow for Morgan. It is hoped that you will execute your orders promptly."[27] On November 17, Halleck came through on his promise to furnish new and effective cavalry arms to the Army of the Cumberland. Although the type of cavalry arms was not specified in his message, the new and technically superior revolving rifles were also being sent to Rosecrans. Edwin Stanton promised 1,600 of the revolving rifles were being sent by passenger train to Louisville for use by Rosecrans.

Stanley Arrives

At long last, on November 24, Rosecrans issued General Orders No. 22 which stated, "Brig. Gen. D.S. Stanley having reported for duty, in acceptance with the orders of the Secretary of War, is announced as chief of cavalry, and assigned to the command of all the cavalry in this department."[28] Stanley arrived at an army desperately in need of a chief of cavalry. Communication, organization, and reliability of the cavalry were poor under the command of Colonel Kennett. Almost immediately upon the arrival of Stanley, all messages about communication and coordination with the cavalry ceased.

When Stanley arrived at the Army of the Cumberland, he brought with him an intimate friend who would serve with him throughout the remainder of the war, Major William Henry Sinclair. Sinclair was born near Akron, Ohio, and enlisted in the Seventh Michigan Infantry. Soon thereafter, he was promoted to the rank of lieutenant in Dees' Third Michigan Artillery. Stanley became acquainted with Sinclair during the Siege of Island No. 10, and when Stanley moved to Nashville in the fall of 1862, Sinclair came along as his adjutant general and remained in that role until the end of the war. During the Battle of Corinth, Sinclair had been sent with a message for Stanley. As he arrived, Stanley's aide was killed and he turned to Sinclair and appointed him to his staff at that moment. Stanley had no more efficient, loyal subordinate or better friend than Sinclair.[29]

Stanley had traveled by riverboat to Louisville and then by rail to Rosecrans' headquarters at Nashville. Despite the urgency for him in Nashville, he spent a few days with his wife in Louisville. The railroad was in such bad condition he had to ride on horseback the last 40 miles to the headquarters, where he found Rosecrans a very busy man. What was thought to be one of the more pleasant bits of news which awaited Stanley was that the Anderson Pennsylvania Cavalry had been requested for the Army of the Cumberland. The Anderson Guards was an independent cavalry regiment formed in Pennsylvania and it served primarily for escort duty for the commanding generals of the army. The Anderson Cavalry was made up of eleven companies of cavalry which officially comprised the 15th Pennsylvania Cavalry.

The 15th Pennsylvania would serve in the cavalry reserve brigade for the Army of the Cumberland and did not reach the army until December 24. Stanley's assessment of the cavalry when he arrived at the Army of Cumberland follows:

> The cavalry had been sadly neglected. It was weak, undisciplined and scattered about a regiment to a division of infantry. To break up this foolish disposal of cavalry and to form brigades and eventually divisions, was my first and most difficult work. Generals commanding divisions, declared they would not give up their cavalry regiments, but I insisted that they do so and General Rosecrans sustained me. I soon had three pretty substantial brigades formed and commanded by good officers. We made several sudden marches upon the enemy's outposts, where they were collecting provisions and running mills and we ran the enemy away. Our cavalry had been poorly instructed and depended upon their carbines instead of the saber. I insisted on the later. I sent grindstones and had the sabers sharpened, each squadron being provided with the means for this work. This soon gave confidence to our men, and the opportunity was only lacking to show their superiority over the enemy.[30]

(Brigadier General John Beatty was impressed with David Stanley upon his arrival at the Army of the Cumberland. Beatty recorded in his diary, "Major-General Stanley, the cavalryman, is of good size, gentlemanly in bearing, light complexion, brown hair.")[31]

Both Stanley and Rosecrans wanted time with their new troops to drill and train them in preparation for the upcoming campaign, but by December 4, Henry Halleck was telling Rosecrans the president was becoming impatient with the Army of the Cumberland's stay in the area around Nashville. In return, Rosecrans had several issues of his own and he felt these needed to be rectified before he could march, including obtaining a supply of shoes, arms, and tents. In regard to the cavalry, he lamented the lack of horses; he felt he had about half the number the cavalrymen needed. On December 7, handpicking good cavalry units, Rosecrans and Stanley requested the 7th Michigan Cavalry, but they were turned down. When Stanley arrived he had 3,038 troopers present for duty and a total number of cavalrymen of 4,534. The 15th Pennsylvania (Anderson) Cavalry which was en route, as well as two regiments of Tennessee cavalry totaling another 2,883 men. The new total of cavalry was 7,400, and even with the new arms received from Washington there were still 1,300 troopers without arms.

Not only was Rosecrans happy to have someone with the skills of Stanley in charge of the cavalry, so were many in the Union cavalry. W.L. Curry, 1st Ohio Cavalry, wrote, "General D.S. Stanley, a cavalry officer of long, active service in the regular army, had just been assigned to duty as Chief of the Cavalry, Army of the Cumberland, and as he was very active and aggressive, a long felt want in that arm of the service seemed to have been supplied. He was always on the alert for duty required of his command, and he did not propose to settle down and wait for the enemy to come to him, but went after the enemy, and usually found him, as Forrest, Wheeler and Morgan were tireless riders and were making raids on the railroads almost daily."[32]

COMPOSITION OF THE UNION CAVALRY, ARMY OF THE CUMBERLAND—DECEMBER 20, 1862

	Officers	Men	Present	Present and Absent
Cavalry—Stanley	203	4,090	4,860	7,464

The need to neutralize the Confederate cavalry was emphasized on December 7 when the Union command became aware Morgan was again on the move. In a message full of foreboding, Rosecrans asked George Thomas, "Where is Dumont's division now lying?" This message referred to Brigadier General Ebenezer Dumont, who commanded the 12th Division. One of Dumont's brigades, commanded by Colonel Absalom B. Moore, held the town of Hartsville, Tennessee. John Hunt Morgan's cavalry attacked Moore's brigade on December 7 and virtually the entire brigade surrendered by 9:00 a.m. to a force half their size. The Union prisoners totaled about 1,800 men. The dominance of the Confederate cavalry was again demonstrated.

Stanley's adversary in central Tennessee—John Hunt Morgan (Library of Congress).

Stanley's adversary in central Tennessee—Joseph Wheeler (courtesy Wilson's Creek National Battlefield; WICR 31412).

The next important step by the Confederate cavalry was, again, taken by John Hunt Morgan. Morgan's movements were detected by the Army of the Cumberland on December 19, 1862. Morgan was observed with 4,000 troopers near Lebanon, Tennessee. David Stanley received an order through Colonel Julius P. Garesche, Rosecrans' chief of staff, to distribute his cavalry along the north side of the Cumberland River and to probe Morgan near Lebanon to discern his strength and intentions. Garesche, a West Point graduate of 1841, was well liked and efficient and had twenty-one years' experience in the regular army. The close of 1862 was going to be busy for Stanley and his cavalry; but the real challenge lay in store for the Union forces in Kentucky as Morgan began what was to be called "Morgan's Christmas Raid." While the Army of the Cumberland was involved in occupying Tennessee, the Confederates saw an opportunity to create havoc in communications, supplies and morale by raiding into Kentucky using their cavalry, which could strike fast and disappear before

Union troops could react. The Confederate intent was to isolate or draw Union forces from Tennessee to defend Kentucky

The Confederate cavalry raiding Kentucky was under overall command of General John Hunt Morgan, an Alabama native who had close ties to Kentucky. Morgan was born in Huntsville, Alabama, and was the grandson of John Wesley Hunt, an early founder of Lexington, Kentucky. Morgan attended Transylvania College for two years but was suspended in 1844 for dueling. He enlisted as a private in the U.S. Army cavalry during the Mexican War. Afterwards, he became a hemp manufacturer and took over his grandfather's mercantile business in Kentucky. In 1857, Morgan raised an independent infantry company known as the "Lexington Rifles," and in September 1861 he took his militiamen to the Confederacy. Initially, he was promoted to colonel of the 2nd Kentucky Cavalry; he had just been promoted to the rank of brigadier general on December 11, 1862.

Stanley's adversary in central Tennessee—John Pegram (Library of Congress).

By Christmas 1862, Morgan and his 3,900 troopers had reached Glasgow, Kentucky, and then began their grim task of disrupting Union transportation and communications. The Union forces in Kentucky and also in Tennessee immediately knew of Morgan's presence. General George Thomas ordered Colonel John Harlan to load his infantry brigade onto the rail cars of the L&N Railroad at Gallatin, Tennessee, and travel north to prevent Morgan's cavalry from continuing their activities, and particularly preventing them from reaching Louisville.[33]

The Union army, still short of cavalry, relied on infantry to try to capture Morgan. Despite the failure of the infantry to "bag" Morgan's raiders, Union units were rapidly converging on him. The Union objective, now, was preventing Morgan's return to Tennessee. To confound Morgan's troubles, the weather was turning cold and unfavorable. On the evening of December 30, Morgan stayed at Bardstown and the next day moved east to Springfield, Kentucky. As the Union army converged on him, he was able to elude capture and move back to the safety of Tennessee after a very successful raid.

While Morgan was in Kentucky, Nathan Bedford Forrest's cavalry, with 1,900 troopers, had also left middle Tennessee to harass Ulysses Grant's supply line from western Tennessee to northern Mississippi.

Four cavalry brigades remained in middle Tennessee: Brigadier General Joseph Wheeler, Brigadier General John Wharton, Brigadier General John Pegram and Brigadier General Abraham Buford. Wheeler had overall command of Bragg's Confederate cavalry. While Morgan moved throughout Kentucky and Forrest in western Tennessee, Wheeler's Confederate cavalry continued their usual tactics of frustrating the Union troops. Despite the reduction in numbers of Confederate

Stanley's adversary in central Tennessee—John Wharton (courtesy Wilson's Creek National Battlefield; WICR 31620).

cavalry, Wheeler's troopers were still formidable. David Stanley was warned by Rosecrans on December 23 of a cavalry force of 3,000–4,000 men moving near Crittenden's wing. Stanley acknowledged the threat but only had 1,300 troopers available to meet the enemy.

The Stones River Campaign

Slightly over a month into his new command, General David Stanley was soon to lead his cavalry in the Battle of Stones River. His organization on December 26 included two active brigades and a reserve brigade. The First Brigade was commanded by the highly regarded Colonel Robert Minty and the Second Brigade was commanded by the capable Colonel Lewis Zahm. The Reserve Brigade would be commanded by Stanley and included the green and untested regiments. John Ken-

Stanley's adversary in central Tennessee—Abraham Buford (Alabama Department of Archives and History, Montgomery, Alabama).

nett still had nominal command of the entire cavalry division, but his role was diminished when Stanley assumed command.

The Stones River Campaign[34]

BRIGADIER GENERAL DAVID S. STANLEY
CAVALRY DIVISION
COLONEL JOHN KENNETT

First Brigade
COLONEL ROBERT H. G. MINTY

2nd Indiana, Company M, Captain J.A.S. Mitchell
3rd Kentucky, Colonel Eli H. Murray
4th Michigan, Lieutenant Colonel William H. Dickinson
7th Pennsylvania, Major John E. Wynkoop

Second Brigade
COLONEL LEWIS ZAHM

1st Ohio:
Colonel Minor Milliken
Major James Laughlin
3rd Ohio, Lieutenant Colonel Douglas A. Murray
4th Ohio, Major John L. Pugh

Artillery
1st Ohio, Battery D (section), Lieutenant Nathaniel M. Newell

RESERVE CAVALRY

3rd Indiana, Battalion (4 companies), Major Robert Klein
15th Pennsylvania, Major Adolph G. Rosengarten/Major Frank B. Ward
1st Middle (5th) Tennessee, Colonel William B. Stokes
2nd Tennessee, Colonel Daniel M. Ray

UNATTACHED
4th U.S. Cavalry, Captain Elmer Otis

It would soon become clear that thirty days were just not enough time to overcome the neglect of the cavalry which continued from the Army of the Ohio; however, Stanley had good material to transform it into an effective cavalry arm. If anyone could lead this cavalry force successfully, it was Stanley. The importance of having the right person in command of even a marginal force was immeasurable. Stanley clearly identified concerns about his cavalry: the mutinous 15th Pennsylvania Cavalry (Anderson Cavalry) and green regiments and cavalry commanders who were yet to be tested, including the inconsistent John Kennett.

Rosecrans had been pushed by Halleck to begin a campaign against Bragg and he finally decided it was time to move. Many of the Confederate cavalry which had been so troublesome to the Union forces in middle Tennessee were gone. Morgan was raiding Kentucky and Forrest was in western Tennessee. The Union command also believed the Confederates would be complacent, having settled into winter quarters. The Union campaigns in the Virginia and Mississippi were bogged down. The Battle of Fredericksburg had just concluded in a decisive Confederate victory, Holly Springs had just fallen to Earl Van Dorn, and Sherman was struggling in Mississippi. The Union army needed good news and Rosecrans decided it was time for the Army of the Cumberland to be the source of the good news.

On December 26, Rosecrans' army of 43,000 seized the opportunity to attack Bragg's army of 37,000. Rosecrans' plan called for Alexander McCook, with three divisions, to move toward Triune along the Nolensville Pike. General Thomas' divisions of Negley and Rousseau were to advance along McCook's right by the Franklin and Wilson pikes to Nolensville. Crittenden's divisions commanded by Wood, Palmer and Van Cleve were to advance along the Murfreesboro Pike to La Vergne. McCook planned to attack Hardee at Triune with the support of Thomas. If there was enemy resistance from the east, Crittenden was to attack.

Stanley organized his cavalry to meet the requirements of the advancing infantry. He received a message from Rosecrans' chief of staff and started moving 1,300 of his men on December 24 and allowed the remainder to complete foraging their horses.[35] Stanley wrote of his actions:

> On December 26 I divided the cavalry into three columns, putting the First Brigade, commanded by Colonel Minty, Fourth Michigan Cavalry, upon the Murfreesborough pike, in advance of General Crittenden's corps. The Second Brigade, commanded by Colonel Zahm, Third Ohio Cavalry, was ordered to move on Franklin, dislodge the enemy's cavalry, and move parallel to General McCook's corps, protecting his right flank. The reserve cavalry, consisting of the new regiments, viz, Anderson Troop, or Fifteenth Pennsylvania Cavalry, First Middle Tennessee, Second East Tennessee Cavalry, and four companies of the Third Indiana, I commanded in person, and preceded General McCook's corps on the Nolensville pike. Col. John Kennett, commanding cavalry division, commanded the cavalry on the Murfreesborough pike.[36]

Stanley faced Brigadier General Joseph Wheeler's cavalry of 4 brigades and 22 regiments with 3 brigades and 11 regiments of Union cavalry. The Confederate cavalry totaled 10,070 troopers compared to 4,849 for Stanley.[37]

The Mutiny of the Anderson Cavalry—15th Pennsylvania Cavalry

Before David Stanley could implement his cavalry support of the army, he and Rosecrans were going to have to deal with the Anderson Cavalry, whose arrival had been so highly anticipated.

On December 24, 1862, the Anderson Cavalry arrived in Nashville for service in the Army of the Cumberland, specifically requested by William Rosecrans; but soon there was a great dissatisfaction within the regiment, and the regiment expressed the dissatisfaction by refusing to perform its duty. Major N.H. Davis, assistant inspector general, recorded, "The grievances complained of by the insubordinate portion of the Anderson Cavalry are, in substance, that they enlisted to form but one battalion, to serve exclusively as body guard to General Buell; that they have not properly been mustered into service; that they have not been properly officered; that they were not well armed; that they have not been assigned to duty as promised, and, in fine, that deception has been practiced in their enlistment, organization, and service."[38]

A more inopportune time cannot be imagined as this cavalry regiment was on the brink of the Battle of Stones River. The Union cavalry was undermanned and had, so far in the campaign, been outmatched by the Southern horsemen. Rosecrans, trying to appease the regiment, appointed 23 officers for the regiment and promised others would be appointed more permanently once the conditions were more suitable to handle this issue. He then ordered Brigadier General Robert Mitchell to move the regiment for duty on December 28 and "he would not submit to their whim." The next day Mitchell ordered the regiment to move with the army, and 200 of the regiment refused to follow the order. In response, Mitchell ordered the Fourth Division under command of General James D. Morgan to provide enough soldiers to compel the Anderson Cavalry to move to the front. On December 30 about 100 troopers complied with the orders and the remainder "refused to obey the order and go to the front, but finally were prevailed upon to march, in obedience to orders, conditionally."[39] The remainder of the regiment refused to camp in the field and returned to their old camp, but they promised to move to the front when they were again called. When they were ordered to the field the next morning, they refused to go even though their task was only to escort supplies. As a result, the ones who refused to go were imprisoned. On the night of 31st of December 1862, and on January 1, 1863, the members of the Anderson Cavalry who had gone to the front were ordered back to Nashville. By January 4, three hundred fifteen members of the Anderson Cavalry were housed in the county jail; on January 4 another 95 were confined in the jail yard due to lack of space and 5 were placed in the local penitentiary. Thus a total of 415 members of the regiment were incarcerated.

The Anderson Cavalry was organized as a single company in Pennsylvania in the fall of 1861 of "select and intelligent" young men for the purpose of serving as a bodyguard of Major General Robert Anderson. The cavalry regiment subsequently provided the same service for Major General Don Carlos Buell while serving in the Army of the Ohio. N.H. Davis, an officer assigned to investigate the situation, the following:

> [A]nd, after being equipped, well drilled, and disciplined, [the company] was assigned to duty at his headquarters, where it rendered valuable and efficient service as guards, escorts, scouts, &c., which service was appreciated and highly commended by the general commanding. The high character as soldiers gained by this company, and the want of more efficient cavalry, induced General Buell to ask authority to have raised three more companies of like class of men, all to be officered from the old troop on his selection and united with it as a battalion. This authority was granted.... Accordingly a recruiting party from the old troop was detailed; their success was unprecedented, and the recruiting continued until two more battalions were enlisted, making a regiment of nearly 1,000 men.[40]

For some reason, when the Anderson Cavalry reached Louisville on their way to Nashville, they remained there and drilled. The regiment remained in Louisville for five to six weeks before they could be fully supplied but the regiment did continue training while in Louisville. There was dissatisfaction that the officers of the regiment did not concentrate on their duties while in Louisville, which caused a deficiency in training and discipline for the members of the regiment.

The officers who recruited the troopers stated there was no deception used when enlisting the new recruits. Authority was given to muster into services companies B-G, and the new troopers were mustered into service by Captain Hastings of the 1st U.S. Cavalry. The regiment was well-armed and given solid mounts. The dissatisfaction began with this regiment when the governor of Pennsylvania wanted to keep the regiment in the state, but the men of the regiment wanted to serve in the war. Once the Anderson Cavalry reached Louisville, they became aware the regiment was destined to serve in the regular Union cavalry. The unhappiness escalated as the regiment got closer to the front and the complaints of the regiment fell upon sympathetic ears, and the troopers were encouraged to refuse to serve in the fighting cavalry. Although the men of the regiment were dissatisfied, they had performed their duty well until they reached Tennessee. Once the troopers reached Nashville, the men realized their new role could result in a real fight with the enemy, and the troopers balked:

> The regiment arrived at Nashville December 24, 1862. On the next day a foraging party was sent out, which had a skirmish with the enemy, in which 1 man was lost. That night there was considerable excitement, and complaints made that their officers were inexperienced and incompetent. Officers who have had experience in the service state that the officers of this regiment will compare favorably with any in the volunteer service. There was at this time evidently much disaffection and demoralization, and a decided objection to do duty, and a determination to be disbanded or discharged, and pretexts sought to justify acts which their dispositions prompted. Insufficiency of officers and incomplete organization were given as reasons for disobeying orders; also that they had been so often and much deceived they did not know who to believe. Their mode of complaint and redress, instead of being through the ordinary military channels, was by caucuses and committees.[41]

As David Stanley proceeded on the Stones River campaign, he had part of a regiment of cavalry only partially committed to doing their duty and wholly unreliable even when convinced to do it. He needed more time.

The Advance on Murfreesboro

For Stanley, the Battle of Stones River was to be a frustrating fight. He was facing twice his numbers in Confederate cavalry, he had green troops and untried commanders and he was dealing with a mutinous regiment. For a strict disciplinarian like Stanley the latter had to be the most frustrating of all. He understood his enemies, but to have a fully outfitted cavalry regiment refuse to fight because its duty was unsuitable to them was almost unforgivable. Stanley wrote of the Anderson Cavalry: "They were men of superior intelligence—mostly clerks or young men of leisure and fortune.... The officers of this regiment had been mustered and had no authority. The regiment refused to march when ordered and as the move commenced, I sent an officer to call for volunteers, when two hundred ninety-four of eight hundred, followed me. They were active brave young fellows, but had no discipline."[42]

The army began the advance on December 26, and McCook and Crittenden met heavy skirmishing throughout the day.

Second Cavalry Brigade Action Advances to Stones River

As the advance on Murfreesboro began on December 26, Colonel Lewis Zahm's 950 troopers rode eastward in search of General George Thomas along the Wilson Creek Pike. Upon determining Thomas's location, Zahm was unable to meet with him and proceeded

6. The Battle of Stones River

to Franklin as ordered. He ran into John Wharton's Confederate pickets about a half mile from Franklin. After heavy skirmishing Zahm was able to send dismounted skirmishers of his own while he flanked the Confederate cavalrymen. The Confederates—4th Tennessee and Davis' Tennessee Battalion—retreated, followed by Zahm's troopers close behind. The chase continued for two miles. Zahm reported he had surprised them and, therefore, they were disorganized and he never gave them a chance to prepare a proper defense. As a result, the Confederate troopers scattered in several directions while trying to stop to slow the Union pursuit, but to no avail.

Among the prisoners captured was a member of General Braxton Bragg's escort and it was determined the defenders totaled about 900 in strength.[43] Zahm also discovered a large number of infantry nine miles from Franklin and another infantry concentration near Triune. Still unable to find Thomas, he made his report of General Rousseau and the two decided the Second Cavalry Brigade would best serve by scouting the front and right, until further orders could be received. Zahm wrote, "I shall therefore send some 500 men toward Petersburg and Triune to reconnoiter; shall likewise send a smaller force over toward Franklin, to ascertain whether the enemy has come back again or not.... My command behaved nobly, both officers and men. The Third [Ohio] Cavalry had the advance, and did the principal part of the fighting; there was no flinch to them."[44]

Due to his proximity to Stanley, the next day Lewis Zahm coordinated his column with the actions of Stanley's reserve cavalry brigade. On December 27, Zahm diligently worked to be the eyes of the Army of the Cumberland. After discovering two large concentrations of Confederates on the previous day, he set out to determine the identity of the units and the concentration of the enemy he was facing. He sent the 1st Ohio Cavalry and most of the 4th Ohio Cavalry to reconnoiter the situation at Triune. These regiments scouted to within two miles of Triune when they encountered enemy pickets and the Confederate artillery began to shell them. After bagging six pickets they returned to camp. Meanwhile, the 3rd Ohio returned to Franklin only to find the rebels had returned in force and were prepared to meet them. They skirmished about two hours but could not drive the Confederates away. The next day Zahm moved his brigade along with the infantry to Triune.

On December 29, Zahm's brigade served as an effective screen for the infantry. His three regiments formed three columns preceding the infantry, 1st Ohio Cavalry on the left, 3rd Ohio Cavalry in the center and 4th Ohio Cavalry on the right. The regiments advanced about a mile apart. The cavalry screen paced the infantry advance toward Murfreesboro moving on a front between the Franklin Road and Bole Jack Road preceding McCook's Corps. After marching for five miles, enemy pickets were encountered and driven before them. Zahm recorded, "[W]e came upon the enemy's cavalry [Wharton's brigade], engaged them for three hours, some time the right wing, then the left, then the center, receiving several charges, which were repulsed, driving the enemy some 2 miles, when the brigade concentrated, repelling a heavy charge from the enemy, driving him back under his guns, which were only a short distance from us. We then retired some 2 miles and went into camp."[45]

By the end of December 29, Zahm and McCook were within 4 miles of Murfreesboro. The next morning, Zahm personally commanded the 3rd Ohio and 2nd Tennessee and moved forward, quickly encountering more enemy pickets. The 4th Ohio Cavalry was sent on reconnaissance southward and met another strong force. Soon, heavy concentrations of cavalry and artillery were being moved forward to meet Zahm's probes.

Zahm recorded a clash with Wheeler's Confederate cavalry just south of the Franklin Road. The Union cavalry approached the enemy camp through heavy timber and then Zahm returned to his column, where there was a better position for cavalry to maneuver: "I soon formed a line of battle. The enemy made his appearance. Skirmishers engaged him pretty briskly. The enemy maneuvered with the design to outflank us, but did not succeed. I forestalled him every time. With the exception of severe skirmishing, nothing transpired."[46] Both cavalry columns returned to their respective lines. After riding another few miles, Zahm found David Stanley in the company of Colonel Philemon P. Baldwin's brigade of infantry. Both cavalry and infantry advanced until they encountered the Confederate defenses. The entire Army of the Cumberland was not in place and Stanley withdrew and camped for the night.

First Cavalry Brigade Advances at Stones River

While Zahm was dealing with the Confederate cavalry on the right, Colonel Robert Minty was providing service on the left flank of the army. A native Irishman, Minty was born in County Mayo, Ireland, on December 4, 1831. Following in his father's footsteps, Minty enlisted as an ensign in the British Army and served five years in the West Indies, Honduras, and the west coast of Africa. Minty's service in the Union army began when he was commissioned major of the 2nd Michigan Cavalry in 1861. He was subsequently commissioned lieutenant colonel of the 3rd Michigan Cavalry shortly thereafter and finally was commissioned as colonel of the 4th Michigan Cavalry in July 1862. Stanley had great respect for Minty and enjoyed his style of horsemanship, both officers realizing the need to wield the saber when fighting in close quarters with enemy cavalry. Minty's brigade would ultimately be nicknamed the "Saber Brigade" because of his insistence on the use of this weapon. David Stanley and Robert Minty would remain lifelong friends.

Robert Minty, Stanley's trusted cavalry commander (Joseph Vale, *Minty and the Cavalry*).

Minty's First Brigade began its advance toward Murfreesboro on December 26 along the Murfreesboro Pike. Colonel John Kennett officially commanded the Cavalry Division and advanced with the First Brigade. Minty's brigade, through December 30, provided reconnaissance and screened Crittenden's Corps on the left and right while the infantry pushed Confederate resistance in front of the column.

Minty ran into Confederate skirmishers as the march began toward Murfreesboro on December 26. The 3rd Kentucky Cavalry covered the left flank, the 7th Pennsylvania on the right and the 4th Michigan moving along the road in the center. Minty recorded, "Ten miles from Nashville I met the enemy's pickets, who, as they fell back before us, were continually re-enforced, until, arriving at La Vergne, they disputed our progress with a force of 2,500 cavalry and mounted infantry, supported by four pieces of artillery, under the command of General Wheeler."[47] As the skirmish intensified, Minty moved his cavalry to protect a knoll where a section of First Ohio Artillery was unlimbering to return the barrage. He ordered two companies of the 4th Michigan to dismount behind a fence and provide cover of the artillerymen. The artillery of General John Palmer's Second Division moved forward and added their guns to the artillery duel for an hour-and-a-half exchange. Lieutenant Nathaniel M. Newell, 1st Ohio Artillery, Battery D, reported that his artillery fired sixty rounds as he wheeled his artillery to the right of the pike and opened fire. The Union infantry began an advance but the darkness put an end to the fighting. The next morning the Confederate cavalry was gone.[48]

On December 27, the 4th Michigan Cavalry of Minty's First Brigade captured the bridge over Stewart's Creek, chasing 200 troopers of the 51st Alabama Cavalry to the rear. Ninety troopers of the 4th Michigan Cavalry under command of Captain James Mix preceded Crittenden's advance toward Stewart's Creek. Three miles north of Stewart's Creek, Mix encountered enemy cavalry and the chase began with Confederates giving way. Mix chased the enemy past the bridge, securing an easy march for Crittenden over the creek.[49]

Minty's advance continued on December 28 with little action, but skirmishing increased on December 29 as he approached Murfreesboro. On December 30, parts of the 7th Pennsylvania and the 3rd Kentucky performed duty in the rear of Crittenden's Corps, pushing the stragglers to their regiments. Minty accompanied the 4th Michigan and a battalion of the 7th Pennsylvania along the Nashville Pike to defend Crittenden from the ravages of Wheeler's cavalry, which had just wreaked havoc on a Union supply train. Minty recorded, "I met the enemy, about 100 strong, and dressed in our uniforms. The Seventh Pennsylvania drove them until after dark."[50] Minty and his cavalry would be at Stewart's Creek when David Stanley joined them very early the next morning.

Reserve Cavalry Brigade Advances Stones River: Stanley—The Center

General David Stanley commanded the reserve cavalry regiments and marched with the center column of the cavalry. His more experienced regiments were given duty on the flanks of the army. Stanley stayed within supporting distance of each cavalry column should they need assistance, and he also gave himself the duty of personal command of his greenest troops. He met with his old classmate and friend Major General Alexander McCook on the evening of December 26 to coordinate his cavalry with McCook's infantry on their march to Nolensville. Due to congestion on the road Stanley's cavalry did not precede McCook's advance. After a two-mile march, he encountered enemy cavalry and infantry supported by artillery. The fog was very dense and it was impossible to see the enemy. McCook was at a decided disadvantage being unfamiliar with the geography. As his troops moved forward, they were pelted with fire from the Confederate defenders. Finally, the march was halted until the conditions improved and prisoners revealed William Hardee had been in battle line in his front.[51]

McCook did not advance until the fog lifted about 1:00 p.m. on December 27. He sent word to Stanley that Zahm's Second Brigade had encountered stiff resistance, and he ordered a brigade of infantry from his reserve division to aid Stanley and Zahm to push the Confederates back. Stanley, an experienced infantry commander, was given loan of the Philemon Baldwin's brigade of infantry in a coordinated advance with the cavalry. Stanley put the Anderson Cavalry to work in conjunction with the 3rd Indiana Cavalry. He had stopped to talk to Major Robert Klein, 3rd Indiana Cavalry, and remarked the 3rd Indiana "knew how to take these rebels."[52] Certainly the remark served as an inspiration for the upcoming fight. The Anderson Cavalry and the 3rd Indiana were sent toward Triune and soon encountered a large force of Confederates in line of battle: "Here we were ordered by General Stanley, with one company of the Fifteenth Pennsylvania Cavalry, to attack the enemy on the right side of the pike. They were posted behind a stone wall, heads only visible, one or more regiments strong. We advanced across the open fields, and were pouring in a steady fire at easy range, when two pieces of artillery on our left, about 500 yards, and two in front, opened on us, obliging us to retire to the cover of the woods from where we advanced. This movement was done promptly, but in good order."[53] Stanley complimented Major Rosengarten and Major Ward of the Anderson Troop for their leadership during the fighting: "Tell the Anderson Cavalry I am extremely pleased with their behavior today."[54]

On December 29 Stanley and Zahm's cavalry moved together and Zahm was ordered to advance his brigade toward Murfreesboro by the Franklin Road while Stanley's column moved along the Bole Jack Road. Another clash of cavalry occurred at Wilkinson's Crossroads. The Union cavalry pushed the defenders beyond Overall's Creek and within a half mile of the Confederate line manned by the 10th and 19th South Carolina Consolidated Infantry. Stanley recorded, "The Anderson Cavalry behaved most gallantly this day, pushing at full charge upon the enemy for 6 miles. Unfortunately their advance proved too reckless. Having dispersed their cavalry, the Troop fell upon two regiments of rebel infantry in ambush, and after a gallant struggle were compelled to retire, with the loss of Major Rosengarten and 6 men killed, and the brave Major Ward and 5 men desperately wounded. With the loss of these two most gallant officers the spirit of the Anderson Troop, which gave such fine promise, seems to have died out, and I have not been able to get any duty out of them since."[55] Stanley later wrote this charge was "the result of rashness and should have been avoided."[56]

The next day, Stanley's cavalry protected the flanks of Rosecrans' army, and light skirmishing occurred throughout the day. As McCook's corps advanced on Murfreesboro, David Stanley brought information which could have changed the battle. At 2:00 p.m. on December 30, he sent a local citizen who had knowledge of the Confederate concentration of forces to McCook, who subsequently sent the citizen to Rosecrans. The civilian stated, "I was up to the enemy's line of battle twice yesterday and once this morning, to get some stock, taken from me. The enemy's troops are posted in the following manner: The right of Cheatham's division rests on the Wilkinson pike; Withers is on Cheatham's left, with his left resting on the Franklin road; Hardee's corps is entirely beyond that road, and his left extending toward the Salem pike." McCook recorded, "This made me anxious for my right. All my division commanders were immediately informed of this fact, and two brigades of the reserve division, commanded, respectively, by Generals Willich and Kirk, two of the best and most experienced brigadiers in the army, were ordered to the right of my line, to protect the right flank and guard against surprise there."[57] At 6:00 p.m. Rosecrans sent an order to McCook to work in conjunction with Stanley to try to deceive the enemy. McCook and Stanley made very large campfires, some outside the camp, to make the enemy think there were more soldiers on the Union right.

Ever diligent, Stanley wanted to determine the veracity of the citizen's description of the Confederate position. He "rode, with only an escort, beyond our extreme right and so I reported to McCook and Rosecrans. One division of two brigades, sent this evening to support Johnson's right would have averted disaster. McCook seemed utterly indifferent and laughed, joked and rolled around his pen, filled with fodder or to make a soft bed, with the good nature and love of fun of a big boy on his first picnic," noted Stanely.[58]

While the Union army had been settling for the night, General Joseph Wheeler had been causing havoc for a Union supply train moving along the Jefferson Pike in the rear of Rosecrans' army. Wheeler had attacked a 64-wagon train and Union regiments were sent to repulse further attacks. Robert Minty had been dispatched earlier in the day with the 4th Michigan and parts of 7th Pennsylvania and 3rd Kentucky to protect the Union rear.[59]

Stanley had returned to his bed after meeting with McCook, only to be roused by a message from Colonel Garesche, Rosecrans' chief of staff, about the attack of Confederate cavalry on the supply train on the Nashville Pike. Stanley was ordered to see to the protection of the trains. At 11:00 p.m. on December 30, Stanley left for La Vergne with the 5th Tennessee and the Anderson Cavalry and was met by Minty with the 4th Michigan and one battalion of the 7th Pennsylvania Cavalry. Stanley rode toward the supply train, arriving there about 5:00 a.m., at Stewart's Creek. He met Colonel Joe Burke of the 10th Ohio Infantry in the company of two other infantry regiments safe and sound. Father O'Higgins, chaplain of the 10th Ohio Infantry, was also present and they were in the company of a pot of tea and some Irish whiskey. Stanley visited with the colonel and the chaplain until his scouts returned reporting the train was safe. No Confederate cavalry was found lurking in the countryside. Soon, Stanley received a note from Colonel Garesche: "The enemy have attacked McCook's corps in great force, and the Corps is falling back in a good deal of disorder. Fasten to the right and do your best to restore order."[60] The Battle of Stones River had begun.

The Union Cavalry at the Battle of Stones River—December 31

Colonel Lewis Zahm had his brigade up and moving early on December 31 and had the misfortune of being on the right flank of the Army of the Cumberland. Zahm had bivouacked his brigade along Overall Creek and behind a small church. By 6:00 a.m. he had sent two squadrons on reconnaissance and soon was alarmed by heavy firing and cannonading to his left and front. He observed what was left of General Richard Johnson's 2nd Division of McCook's wing in full retreat being chased by Major General J.P. McCown's Confederates. Zahm saw the Confederate infantry in close pursuit of McCook's soldiers and observed Wharton's cavalry moving to his right. McCown had crushed the Union right, which was flowing to the rear.

Zahm had several options. He could attempt to rally the retreating troops, engage the enemy, or keep the Confederate cavalry from gaining the Union rear. He could not do all at once. In command of his brigade, he watched and tried to determine where he could be most useful. He wrote, "[T]he enemy pressing hard on me; kept him at bay with my skirmishers. I retired in this wise for a mile, when I formed a line of battle with the First and Third [Ohio Cavalry], when the enemy charged on them with their cavalry, but were repulsed by my men. About this time the enemy began to throw shells into my lines pretty lively."[61] The first barrage of artillery mortally wounded Major David A.B. Moore, 1st Ohio, setting the stage for a difficult day for Zahm's cavalry. Facing superior numbers and being shelled, Zahm fell back and formed a new screen only to be charged by the Confederate cavalry. Zahm recorded the Southern attack was repulsed and again the Confederate artillery found his position. The Union cavalry again retreated and found support from Brigadier General Augustus Willich's First Brigade of Johnson's division. The Confederate cavalry again charged Zahm's troopers only to be repulsed, but Zahm was giving way throughout the morning being attacked by Wharton's cavalry and artillery. In addition, the Confederate infantry's success left Zahm in a position of holding the enemy's cavalry but being nearly cut off by the advance of the Southern infantry. Zahm noted that no matter what successes he made in repulsing the cavalry charges there were more than enough replacements on their heels.

Zahm was facing infantry and cavalry pressing hard on the Union right flank. He set up a screen with the 1st Ohio Cavalry and the 3rd Ohio Cavalry covering the extended right flank of the army while sparring with Brigadier General John Wharton's Cavalry Brigade consisting of a mixture of Tennessee, Alabama, Georgia, Texas and Confederate troopers. White's Battery (Tennessee) was the unit which shelled Zahm's cavalrymen.

While Zahm was withdrawing with too many things to handle, Stanley was unaware of the situation. Having been ordered to the rear of the army to handle the protection of the army's train, he was far from the action. Upon being informed of the Confederate attack, Stanley rode, as ordered, back to the main Union line, but he would not arrive until after missing the morning's combat. He recalled being delayed as he encountered soldiers running from the battlefield. As he got closer to Murfreesboro he had to leave some of his troopers to protect the supply trains which were sent to the rear. He also detached his cavalry to round stragglers and send them forward.[62]

Back at the battlefield Zahm's three cavalry regiments were performing remarkably well and only slowly gave way while being heavily pressed, repulsing three charges from Wharton. By 9:00 a.m. they were pushed back to Overall Creek and by 11:00 a.m. they were pushed further north, losing contact with the creek. As Zahm withdrew his cavalry with the collapsing right flank, an officer rode up to him with a message. Zahm noted, "When we arrived on the open ground, General McCook's aide told me the whole of General McCook's ammunition train was close by, on a dirt road running by that point, and that I must try to save it."[63] The withdrawal was over for Zahm and his cavalry, and he had found the place to stand and fight.

Zahm was successful in a counterattack on Colonel John Cox's 1st Confederate Cavalry and part of the 8th Texas Cavalry, which had captured some guns of the 1st Ohio Light Artillery and men of Colonel William Gibson's First Brigade. Gibson had assumed command of the brigade because August Willich has been captured during the early morning attack. Zahm's charge "threw the greyclads in momentary confusion. Taking advantage of the situation Johnson and most of his men made good their escape."[64]

Robert Klein commanded the 3rd Battalion Indiana Cavalry during the battle on

6. The Battle of Stones River 113

December 31. The 3rd Indiana Cavalry had an atypical organization, with half the regiment serving in the Army of the Ohio and the remainder serving with the Army of the Potomac. Klein recorded his command had been posted to the right and rear of Richard Johnson's Second Division. As the Union right collapsed, Klein lamented that "the efficiency of my battalion was destroyed in being divided by one of our own cavalry regiments running through our ranks and scattering the men. This movement, had it been in the opposite direction, would have been a most gallant charge, and, doubtless, from its determination, an efficient one. We kept falling back, forming and charging at intervals, until forced across to the Murfreesborough pike, where one of my companies was first to form to drive the enemy from our train."[65]

The position held by the Union cavalry on the right was saved by two timely counterattacks. The first was from the 4th U.S. Cavalry. Captain Elmer Otis' 4th U.S. Cavalry, detached from Stanley's cavalry division, was ordered to assist on the right flank of the collapsing Union army, which task Otis hastily attended to. He made two timely and successful charges into the Confederates. The first charge was made just as Colonel Henry Ashby's 2nd Tennessee Cavalry prepared to attack Zahm's cavalry. Otis did not wait for Ashby's cavalry to attack, but rode directly for the Confederate cavalry. The two regiments crashed together and Otis won the exchange, capturing about 100 Southern troopers. Next, Otis prepared to take on White's artillery that had caused so much damage to Zahm throughout the morning, but Otis was ordered to the duty near the ammunition train before he could make the attack. Later, he noticed the supply train being attacked and launched a second charge. Otis wrote,

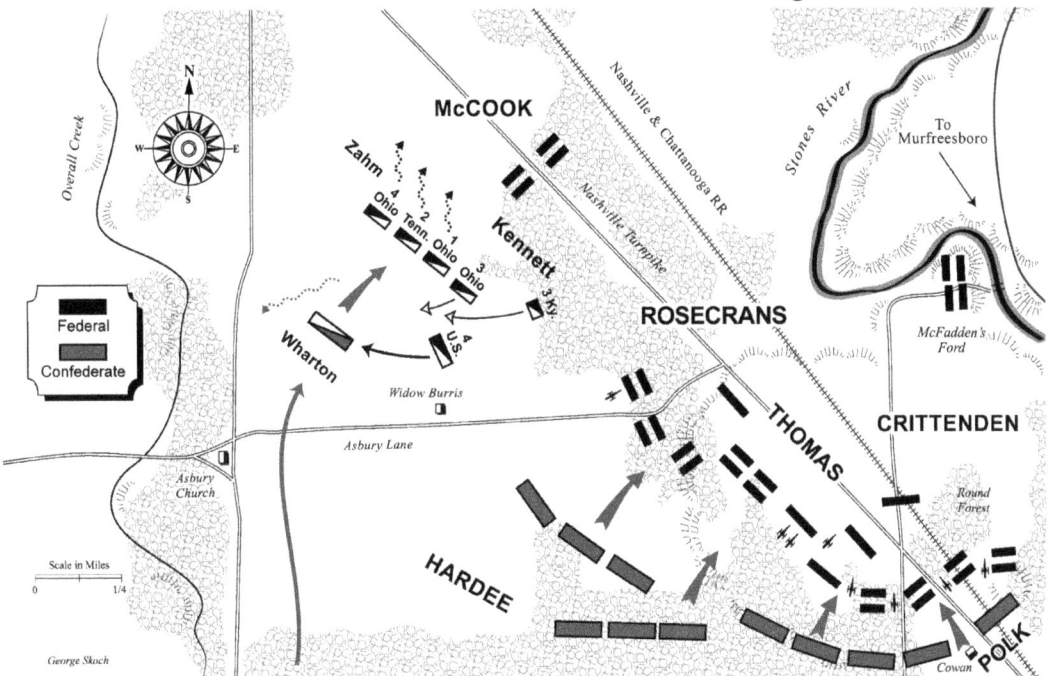

The Union Cavalry at the Battle of Stones River (Morning)

"The train on the pike, I have since learned, was in possession of the enemy, with a large number of stragglers, who were being disarmed at the time. These stragglers did nothing at all to protect the wagons, scarcely firing a shot. From prisoners taken I have learned that the Fourth U.S. Cavalry charged at this time an entire brigade of cavalry, and routed them to such an extent that they disappeared from the field at that point entirely."[66]

By noon Zahm was in position near McCook's supply train and had withdrawn as far as he could go. He formed his line, 3rd Ohio, 1st Ohio, 2nd Tennessee, and 4th Ohio (left to right), and waited for Wharton's move:

> The enemy made his appearance in a position occupying two-thirds of a circle. They prepared to charge upon us; likewise commenced throwing shells, at which the Second East Tennessee broke and ran like sheep. The Fourth, after receiving several shells, which killed some of their men and horses, likewise retired from their line, as it became untenable. The First had been ordered to proceed farther on into another lot, to form and to receive a charge from another line of the enemy's cavalry. The Third moved to the left, in the vicinity of a white house. About the time the First was formed, the enemy charged upon the Fourth, which, being on the retreat, owing to the shells coming pretty freely, moved off at a pretty lively gait. The Third moved farther to the left, and, somewhat sheltered by the house and barns, the First charged upon the enemy; did not succeed in driving them back.[67]

The 1st Ohio's charge was a result of Colonel Minor Milliken's stated desire to lead his regiment in a full-blown sabre charge:

> His officers and soldiers were falling around him rapidly, Major Moore had been mortally wounded early in the day by a shell while the regiment was maneuvering for position, and Adjutant W.H. Scott had been severely wounded in attempting to capture a rebel flag, and Lieutenant Sam Fordyce, of Company B, was also wounded.... He must act at once, or his regiment would be stampeded and driven from the field, as they were being pushed and crushed ... then Colonel Millikin ... gave the command 'Charge!' which was repeated to right and left along the line .... Commending their souls to God, they charged home.[68]

The 1st Ohio's charge cut through the Confederate cavalry, and in the process Milliken was shot in the neck and killed.

Captain Valentine Cupp of the 1st Ohio Cavalry recalled the charge into the Confederate cavalry that resulted in Milliken's death, the serious wounding of his adjutant, Lieutenant William Scott, and the death of Lieutenant Condit. After the charge of the 1st Ohio, the regiment was forced to retire and was attacked again by their pursuers and repulsed the charge. The Confederate cavalry then took possession of a wagon train. Zahm had performed admirably considering his situation during the morning; but he just didn't have the numbers. He had clashed with Wharton throughout the morning and finally his four regiments, facing too many numbers, fled. Louis Zahm wrote of it:

> At this juncture the First and Fourth retired pretty fast, the enemy in close pursuit after them, the Second East Tennessee having the lead of them all. Matters looked pretty blue now; the ammunition train was supposed to be gone up, when the Third charged upon the enemy, driving him back, capturing several prisoners, and recapturing a good many of our men, and saved the train. I was with the three regiments that skedaddled, and among the last to leave the field. Tried hard to rally them, but the panic was so great that I could not do it. I could not get the command together again until I arrived at the north side of the creek; then I found that only about one-third of the First and Fourth Regiments were there, and nearly all of the Second

East Tennessee. These I marched back across the creek, when, joined by the Third, we had several skirmishes with the enemy's cavalry all day long; received several charges, and repulsed them.[69]

Of Zahm's cavalry, the 3rd Ohio Cavalry held its ground. Major J.W. Paramore, 3rd Ohio Cavalry, recorded the action of the regiment after they retreated as far as McCook's ammunition rain after the collapse of the Union right:

> We had been forced back as far as General McCook's ammunition train, and were drawn up in front of it for its protection, the furious charge of the enemy's cavalry, preceded by a shower of shells, caused a pretty general stampede of our cavalry, led off by the Second Tennessee on our right, and followed by the Fourth and First Ohio, and the First Battalion of the Third Ohio Cavalry. At that juncture an aide of General McCook came up to me, and informed me that "that was their entire ammunition train, and must be held at all hazards." I gave orders accordingly to the left wing of the Third Ohio Cavalry, under my command, and I am happy to report that they held their position and did not break their lines nor join in that stampede, but received the galling fire of the enemy with the firmness of heroes, and maintained their ground till all the wagons, except a few that were disabled or deserted by the teamsters, had safely reached the lines of our infantry.[70]

As the enemy moved away from the 3rd Ohio, the Union cavalry was able to charge the retreating cavalry. Paramore recorded the charge was effective, as his troopers killed some of the retreating Southern cavalry and claimed 10–12 prisoners.

The 3rd Ohio encountered another group of Confederate cavalry, near the Union hospital, intending to capture a supply train. Paramore ordered his troopers to attack and Klein estimated he faced twice his numbers. The battle was severe and several were lost on both sides. Another squadron of Paramore's cavalry engaged another group of Southern cavalry further along the pike in what was an effective counterattack led by Colonel John Kennett. Paramore proudly wrote in his after action report: "Then be it spoken to their praise, that the Second and Third Battalions of the Third Ohio Cavalry did not run nor break their lines during that day's severe fighting."[71]

Kennett's Counterattack

Kennett's service to the Army of the Cumberland had been inconsistent at best and by all indication he had been shelved as divisional commander of the Union cavalry. However, Colonel John Kennett showed his value by doing the right thing at the right time. Without question he helped save the Union supply train.

During the battle on December 31, Rosecrans ordered Kennett, in Stanley's absence, to attempt to rally the collapsed right wing and organize the cavalry in an effective screen. Rosecrans had to have realized the error of sending his chief of cavalry to deal with raids on his supply train. Kennett was up to the task and performed exemplary service on this day. He wrote, "I found Colonel Murray, of the Third Kentucky, in command of about a squadron of men. With that we made our way to the right. We found a complete stampede—infantry, cavalry, and artillery rushing to the rear, and the rebel cavalry charging upon our retiring forces on the Murfreesborough pike."[72]

Kennett recorded, "Colonel Murray, with great intrepidity, engaged the enemy toward the skirts of the woods, and drove them in three charges. His men behaved like old veterans.

Between his command and the field the space was filled with rushing rebel cavalry, charging upon our retreating cavalry and infantry, holding many of our soldiers as prisoners. I rallied the Third Ohio, some two companies, which was falling back, and formed it in the rear of a fence, where volley after volley had the effect of driving back the rebels upon the run, they (the Third Ohio) charging upon them effectually, thereby relieving the pike of their presence, saving the train, one piece of artillery, and rescuing from their grasp many of our men taken as prisoners."[73] Kennett was in the middle of the battle, was nearly killed by Confederate troopers, and had his orderly to thank for saving his life. Corporal James Farrish, the orderly, shot two Southern troopers converging on Kennett and captured a third that had a pistol leveled in Kennett's face.[74]

The nineteen-year-old, Colonel E.H. Murray of the 3rd Kentucky Cavalry, recorded the following:

> I found our whole train of baggage and ammunition in possession of the enemy. Captain Wolfley, with part of his battalion, and Captain Breathitt, commanding the First Battalion, with a squad of his command, in all about 80 men, in a moment were engaged charging down the train. We came upon the enemy in all directions. Here were engagements hand-to-hand, but dashing onward my men were doing in earnest the work before them. The open field gave us the place for charging. The enemy were marching about 250 of our men to their rear as prisoners. These we recaptured. We also recaptured a portion of the Fifth Wisconsin Battery; also a section supposed to be the First Ohio.[75]

The hospital of General John Palmer was still in the hands of the Confederates, but Murray's charge reclaimed it. Murray pulled his regiment together and again repulsed a cavalry charge on his position and held the enemy at bay. After some time the Confederate cavalry facing Murray, their intent the Union ammunition train, moved to the right. Murray followed their movement and an exchange of gunfire convinced the Confederate cavalry not to attack. The Confederate cavalry finally withdrew, leaving Murray with 50 prisoners. Murray over zealously claimed, "In the engagement the 80 men of my command drove from the field Wharton's brigade of rebel cavalry; saved the baggage and ammunition of a great part of our army; recaptured a portion of the Fifth Wisconsin Battery and a section of, I think, the First Ohio Battery, and, at least calculation, 800 of our men."[76]

Major John Wynkoop commanded part of 7th Pennsylvania that remained near Murfreesboro, while Minty was with Stanley at Stewart's Creek. During the morning, Wynkoop's command screened the left flank of the army and served as couriers. The 7th Pennsylvania performed a yeoman's task of rallying the retreating troops. Once the Union right collapsed, Wynkoop pulled his troopers together and began the duty of stopping the panic-stricken solders running to the rear. He noted it was almost impossible to stop the stampede of men running away. In exasperation, he asked for orders from Rosecrans, who directed him to proceed to the rear and try his best to pull the troops together into fighting units. The 7th Pennsylvania rallied the troops until about 2:00 p.m. when the regiment was ordered back to the front by Kennett. Wynkoop recorded, "We were thrown upon the front, and were for some time under a heavy fire from the enemy under cover."[77]

Stanley's Reserve and First Cavalry Brigades

David Stanley's reserve cavalry and portions of Minty's First Brigade were the last to arrive to assist Zahm's and Kennett's troops after a ten-mile ride. David Stanley and Minty rode hard to the collapsing wing of the army with the 1st Middle (5th) Tennessee and a portion of the Anderson Cavalry. With Minty's First Brigade in tow (4th Michigan and Jennings Battalion, 7th Pennsylvania), the combined cavalry moved to the right to support McCook's damaged flank. Minty left 130 men of the 4th Michigan to provide cover for the Battery D, 1st Ohio Battery, and as they hastened to Overall Creek Stanley's cavalry came under friendly fire.

As Stanley reached the right wing of the army he met many stragglers, "first a few dozen, then a hundred and finally not less than five thousand." He left a troop of cavalry to rally the troops and return them to their lines. "I learned afterwards that my cavalrymen brought back two thousand," he said.[78] Stanley consulted with Rosecrans and then he joined Minty's fresh cavalry before deciding to attack. Stanley was faced with a difficult situation but he was itching for a fight. His blood was up when he realized Zahm's cavalry had been scattered.

Once at Overall Creek, the 4th Michigan dismounted and formed a line of skirmishers and drove some Confederate cavalry from a wooded area to their front. The 4th Michigan was supported by a portion of the 1st Middle Tennessee, which was dismounted. To the right and rear of the 4th Michigan, Captain Jennings' battalion of the 7th Pennsylvania and two companies of the 3rd Kentucky Infantry joined in the preparation for battle. The Anderson Cavalry was immediately behind the 4th Michigan. The entire Union cavalry defense comprised 950 men, and they soon were approached by troopers of General Wheeler's cavalry. Stanley rode among the cavalry, encouraging them to maintain the line.[79]

Minty described the action: "The enemy advanced rapidly with 2,500 cavalry, mounted

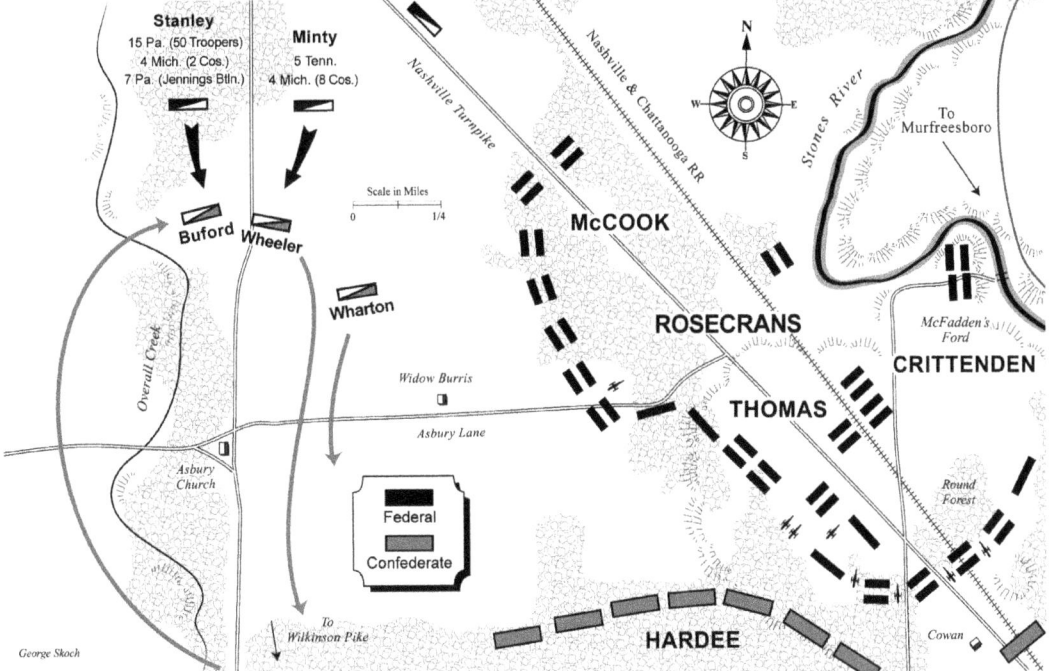

and dismounted, with three pieces of artillery, all under the command of General Wheeler. They drove back the Fourth Michigan to the line of the First Tennessee skirmishers, and then attacked the Seventh Pennsylvania with great fury, but met with determined resistance. I went forward to the dismounted skirmishers and endeavored to move them to the right, to strengthen the Seventh Pennsylvania, but the moment the right of the line showed itself from behind the fence where they were posted, the whole of the enemy's fire was directed on it, turning it completely around."[80] The unreliable 15th Pennsylvania Cavalry continued to be so, rapidly riding to the rear. This left the 7th Pennsylvania Cavalry dismounted, without any support and in a very vulnerable position. The Union cavalry fell back and re-formed unseen and outside the range of the Southern artillery.

The Union cavalry was not to be pushed aside so easily. Together, Minty and Stanley led a coordinated charge that would end the day. At four o'clock, Minty noted that Wheeler's cavalry, in force, moved to the right, collecting more Union infantry as prisoners. Shadowing the Rebel cavalry, Minty moved to the right also and at a distance of about six hundred yards.[81] Minty noted, "My first impression was that these covered infantry, but I learned soon that they were only dismounted cavalry. We successfully held them at bay for one-half an hour with the Fourth Michigan and Seventh Pennsylvania, dismounted, when, being outflanked, I ordered our line to mount and fall back to the open field. The enemy followed here, and being re-enforced by detachments of the Anderson and Third Kentucky Cavalry, and the First Tennessee, we charged the enemy and put him to rout."[82] Minty recorded the remainder of the action: "The rebel cavalry had followed us up sharply into the open ground, and now menaced us with three strong lines, two directly in front of my position and one opposite our left flank, with its right thrown well forward, and a strong body of skirmishers in the woods to our right, and threatening that flank."[83]

Simultaneously, David Stanley was leading his own charge. The adjutant of the 15th Pennsylvania observed of Stanley, "General Stanley was everywhere, and in a moment he saw the best that could be done was to order a charge: "Let's charge them boys! Let's charge them!"[84] Robert Minty recorded David Stanley commanded the Union cavalry defense and gave the order to charge. Stanley and Minty split the leadership of the cavalry in the attack. Stanley rode at the head of the two companies of the 4th Michigan Cavalry and what group he could rally of the 15th Pennsylvania Cavalry. The attack was successful and the Confederate troopers hustled away. While Stanley was leading his troopers, Minty charged with his regiments of cavalry, which made two charges. Minty recorded the capture of one stand of colors and noted "the enemy was again broken and driven from the field."[85]

At this point in the day, Stanley was fearless and he decided to put the fighting spirit in his horsemen despite the odds. He knew he had to inspire whatever part of the Anderson Cavalry that would fight. As he divided the assignment of the cavalry, he said to Minty, "You look after those fellows in the front and I will take care of this force," pointing at Wharton's cavalry.[86] Stanley was preparing to lead two companies of the 4th Michigan. He stopped, considered and, Minty recalled, Stanley told the men of the 4th Michigan, "'Wait here and I will bring you assistance." He rode over to the men of the troublesome 15th Pennsylvania. He told the men of the 15th Pennsylvania to prepare to charge the Confederates: "There was hesitation in Gen. Stanley's, and I then witnessed one of the most heroic scenes of the war. Stanley, standing in his stirrups, his soldierly figure erect, his saber raised straight above his head, in a voice distinctly heard above the noise of battle exclaimed, 'The man who does not follow me is a——coward!' and wheeling his horse dashed back to the two companies of the 4th Michigan. The 15th followed and the 4th, and with a raging cheer this little band of heroes, led by the gallant Stanley, charged into the center of Wharton's Brigade and drove it from the field."[87] When the charge was over, Sergeant Eugene Bronson, 4th Michigan, recorded, "The number of horses that was killed almost covered the ground."[88]

At the end of a difficult day, the small Union cavalry had stabilized the extended right flank of the army. The 4th Michigan Cavalry, 5th Tennessee, and 7th Pennsylvania held the Union line and while Wheeler had gotten some booty from the Union supply train, it was minimal. General John Wharton recorded, "Owing to this and to my being detained to defend the battery, we were able only to bring off a portion of the wagons, 5 or 6 pieces of artillery, about 400 prisoners, 327 beef cattle, and a goodly number of mules cut from the wagons."[89]

After the day's battle Rosecrans met with his commanders on the evening of December 31. He asked the question, "Shall we fight it out here, or withdraw to an advantageous position covering our depots at Nashville?" Crittenden declined to offer an opinion but agreed to obey any orders of Rosecrans, and Thomas gave a similar answer. It was McCook who said, "I therefore advise that we retire on Nashville and await reinforcements." The officers looked toward Stanley, who said, "I agree with what Gen'l. McCook has recommended." Rosecrans thanked the officers for their opinions and inspected the ground he held with Stanley for two hours.[90] At 1:00 a.m., Stanley asked him, "'General, what are you going to do.' He immediately answered, 'By God's help, I am going to beat the enemy right here.' No more was said and we immediately went to bed."[91] Rosecrans returned to headquarters and told the commanding generals, "Well, gentlemen, we shall not retreat, but fight it out here and to the front. Go at once to your posts and hold your commands ready to receive any attack from the enemy."[92] Rosecrans had concluded to establish a defensive position and not resume his advance until the arrival of ammunition and supplies from Nashville.

Cavalry Actions: January 1–January 5

While the Union and Confederate cavalries clashed, it was the infantry regiments that suffered the carnage of the hard-fought battle on December 31. On January 1, the two opposing armies stared across the fields and streams at each other; and on January 2, Bragg ordered John C. Breckinridge to attack Rosecrans. Breckinridge's attack was initially successful; however, as the Confederates advanced, fifty-seven Union cannons decimated the advance, resulting in the loss of more than 1,800 Confederate soldiers, killed or wounded. After suffering this loss and the fear Rosecrans would continue to receive reinforcements, Bragg withdrew southward from Murfreesboro. Rosecrans marched into Murfreesboro, claiming the victory, on January 5.

For Lewis Zahm's Second Cavalry Brigade, January 1 began early after the difficult time his troopers had experienced on the previous day. Zahm's brigade was saddled and moving at 3:00 a.m., having been ordered to ride to Nashville to escort badly needed supplies to replenish those destroyed or captured on the previous day. Wheeler took three brigades of cavalry north and to the rear of Rosecrans' army and was rewarded with a wagon train along the Nashville Pike defended by the 2nd Tennessee Cavalry and the 22nd Indiana Infantry. Wheeler and Buford rode together to attack the train and Wharton's brigade was sent north to cut off the retreat. Seeing the large number of enemy cavalry, the 2nd Tennessee rode for their lives, the teamsters panicked, and ninety-five of the infantrymen surrendered to Buford. With the 2nd Tennessee Cavalry riding for their lives after burning 30 wagons, Wheeler sought more booty.

Zahm accompanied a large supply train with the 3rd Ohio Cavalry, 4th Ohio Cavalry, and the 15th Pennsylvania Cavalry. As the supply train passed La Vergne, the ever-present Confederate cavalry attacked the train. Zahm repulsed the Confederate attack twice at the cost of only 2 or 3 wagons and he was able to save some cannons which were almost captured. He noted, "The Anderson Troop, I am sorry to say, were of very little benefit to me, as the majority of them ran as soon as we were attacked."[93]

At the second attack, Zahm continued to pull his command together and advanced another two miles when he observed the Confederate cavalry charging on the Union rear. Zahm's troopers rode to meet the charge and repulsed the attack, killing 9, wounding 11 and capturing 2: "I had a few men slightly wounded. After this they troubled my train no more. Not a wagon fell into their hands ahead of the escort. Some four or five wagons broke down, which we left and destroyed. The enemy's forces were Wheeler's brigade, with two pieces of artillery, which they played upon us pretty lively."[94] Prior to the last attack, Zahm discovered he was being attacked when he found the 2nd Tennessee Cavalry riding hard toward him and toward the rear. Zahm threw a company of cavalry across the road to stem the retreat. Zahm proceeded to stop the Confederate attack, only to see the 2nd Tennessee again race to the rear "like sheep." While the 2nd Tennessee showed no willingness to fight, the Anderson Cavalry showed even less. When the Confederates attacked, the Anderson Cavalry ran off in every direction to avoid the fight. It was the retreat of the two regiments which stampeded some of the supply wagons resulting in the breakdowns. Despite the poor performance of the 2nd Tennessee and Anderson Cavalry, Zahm coordinated with the infantry and drove the raiders off. This clearly was not a proud day for these two regiments, despite Zahm's efforts. Zahm was later threatened by Confederate cavalry. The enemy again appeared and engaged the Union skirmishers. The enemy formed a line in preparation to attack, but before they moved, Zahm ordered a charge of his own. However, the enemy wasn't ready for a fight and withdrew.[95]

While Zahm was escorting supply trains, Minty's First Cavalry Brigade stayed at the front with the Army of the Cumberland and was involved in skirmishing with enemy cavalry pickets. Minty maintained this duty on January 1, 2, and 3. Stanley's Reserve Brigade also remained with the army on January 1 and had little to report, except "about 9 o'clock New Year's morning the enemy showed a line of skirmishers in the woods to our front, and soon after brought a six-gun battery to bear upon my cavalry. As we could not reach the enemy's skirmishers, nor reply to his artillery, I ordered my cavalry to fall back."[96]

On January 2, Zahm found time to gather his troopers and forage the horses after two days of activity. Stanley's reserve brigade maintained its position and scouted the flanks of the army. On the next day, somewhat rested and replenished, Zahm was again guarding hospital and ammunition trains supplying Rosecrans' army and again found himself fighting the Confederate cavalry. Lewis Zahm's brigade was back on duty on January 3 after such a dismal performance on January 1. Much to his relief, he had the 1st Ohio, 4th Ohio and 3rd Tennessee Cavalry to perform this duty, with much better results. The cavalry formed the escort around a hospital supply and ammunition train, and, with two-and-a-half regiments of infantry, the train began to move southward at 11:00 a.m. After marching for eight miles, Wheeler's cavalry attacked and was repulsed and then attempted a second attack later. Fourteen hours later the train arrived safely and Zahm recorded he had killed 15 Confederate troopers, wounded an unknown number and captured twelve prisoners. This was a much better day for Zahm.[97]

On the 4th, Zahm scouted toward Murfreesboro and found Bragg had withdrawn. On January 5, Stanley was pursing Bragg's army. Minty advanced through Murfreesboro and down the Manchester Pike southward and within a mile encountered Confederate pickets. David Stanley took command of the advance and drove ahead, riding with the 4th U.S. Cavalry. As the advance continued, the Union cavalry crossed a creek another mile forward and came under attack from Confederate artillery. The advance, which included the 1st Tennessee, 3rd Kentucky, 7th Pennsylvania, 4th Michigan, 4th U.S. and 2nd Tennessee cavalries, pushed onward. Six miles south of Murfreesboro, a stiff skirmish resulted, with most of the fighting being successfully done by the 4th U.S., 5th Tennessee and 7th Pennsylvania. Afterward Stanley and the cavalry camped just south of Murfreesboro.[98] Alexander McCook wrote of the actions of Stanley and the cavalry after the battle was over:

> To Brig. Gen. D.S. Stanley, chief of cavalry, my thanks are particularly due. He commanded my advance from Nolensville and directed the cavalry on my right flank. A report of the valuable services of our cavalry will be furnished by General Stanley. I commend him to my superiors and my country.[99] [Rosecrans also lauded the role of the cavalry.] Brig. Gen. D.S. Stanley, already distinguished in four successful battles—Island No. 10; May 27, before Corinth; Iuka, and the battle of Corinth—at this time in command of our ten regiments of cavalry, fought the enemy's forty regiments of cavalry, and held them at bay, or beat them wherever he could meet them. He ought to be made a major-general for his service, and also for the good of the service.[100]

In Rosecrans' report of the Battle of Stones River, he mentioned specific individuals for special services performed during the battle and recognition for their efforts. Among those mentioned in the cavalry were David Stanley (chief of cavalry), Robert Minty (First Brigade), Eli Murray (3rd Kentucky Cavalry), Lewis Zahm (Second Brigade), Major Robert Klein (3rd Indiana Cavalry), and Elmer Otis (4th U.S. Cavalry).

Stanley mentioned in his report those individuals who in his opinion deserved recognition for their actions during the battle:

Major Robert Klein	3rd Indiana Cavalry	For Action on December 27
Major Frank Ward	Anderson Cavalry	Great Bravery
Major Adolph Rosengarten	Anderson Cavalry	Great Bravery
Colonel Robert Minty	4th Michigan Cavalry	Command in Several Actions
Captain Elmer Otis	4th U.S. Cavalry	Important and Distinguished Service
Colonel Eli Murray	3rd Kentucky Cavalry	Important and Distinguished Service
Major John Wynkoop	7th Pennsylvania Cavalry	A Model to Faithful Soldiers
Colonel Lewis Zahm	Second Brigade	Personal Example
Colonel John Kennett	Divisional Command	Rendered Good Service

Of the Battle of Stones River, Stanley wrote, "The battle of Stones River was no great victory but retreating to some extent demoralized, the rebel army, and coming about the time of Burnside's miserable failures in the east, our victory helped to sustain the courage of the country."[101]

Stanley and Rosecrans, both Roman Catholics, spent their first Sunday at Murfreesboro giving thanks for the victory recently won. T.F Dornblaser, 7th Pennsylvania Cavalry, recorded, "The first Sabbath in Murfreesboro, we looked into the Catholic church, during the hour of service. In front of the altar, on his knees, was Rosecrans, the general of the army. Long and devoutly he knelt in prayer. He had abundant reason to thank God for the salvation of his army, and for the wonderful preservation of his own life. Near him knelt General D.S. Stanley, Chief of Cavalry. We honor these men, though Catholics, for acknowledging their dependence on Him who rules the armies of heaven."[102]

Summary

David Stanley's cavalry was outmanned and outperformed at the Battle of Stones River; however, this was a beginning. A change in the Union cavalry had started under Stanley's command, with the help of William Rosecrans. These Union generals worked well together and had an excellent relationship. Wheeler, Hunt and Forrest generally ran the Union army in circles at this point in the war. But this would end, and it would end with David Stanley in command of the cavalry of the Army of the Cumberland. That day had not yet arrived.

The aftermath of the battle deeply touched Stanley, who rode across an area of heavy fighting, and he wrote, "The dead lay strewn upon the ground by the hundreds, the blue and the gray about equally mingled.... Frost had fallen the night before and the bearded men lay with their upturned whiskers whitened with the hoar frost, whilst the boys with clear faces looked like the boys of the farmer household not yet waked from their morning's sleep. And there were so many of these boys! It seemed as if they formed one half of Death's harvest, strewn mush like sheaves of wheat upon the ground."[103]

During the Battle of Stones River and the following days, some of Colonel Louis Zahm's cavalry ran, and the Anderson cavalry was still an embarrassment. But the 3rd Ohio cavalry held their ground, Elmer Otis's 4th U.S. Cavalry demonstrated its professionalism, and even Colonel John Kennett added to the successes of the day. Colonel Robert Minty was clearly Stanley's best commander, and his cavalry—2nd Indiana, 3rd Kentucky, 4th Michigan and 7th Pennsylvania—performed in an excellent manner. Outmanned two to one, the Union cavalry, while pushed back, gave respectable service at Stones River. The image of Stanley standing in his stirrups, sword above his head, rallying his troopers into a charge was a highlight of his career, although he made little of the affair.

The entire campaign revealed how Stanley viewed the use of the cavalry. He felt the cavalry should be the eyes and ears of the army, with specific assignments in relation to the movements of the infantry. Then, at the opportune moment, the cavalry should become an offensive arm of the army. Stanley was opposed to countless, pointless raids for the sole purpose of keeping the cavalry moving.

Finally, to this point in the war, Stanley had been a complete success. This success was based on his years of experience and his need to perform as a professional soldier. He was operating in an environment which allowed him to make good decisions in conjunction with his commander and subordinates. Stanley was not a good politician and he felt he had no need to be such. He was a soldier, and in such an environment he would flourish. A correspondent of the *Cincinnati Commercial Newspaper,* William D. Bickham, recorded the following of David Stanley after the Battle of Stone's River: "He is an active, enterprising soldier, familiar alike with the abstract science, and the practical art of war.... It was his good fortune to be loved by all whom he commanded. The soldiers had faith in his zeal and skill, and his fiery courage inspired them with confident enthusiam [*sic*]. They compared him not inaptly with Murat, and airily applied to him the soubriquet of 'gay old Stanley'—singing merrily at festive board or cheerful bivouac fire 'Here's to gay old Stanley[,] Pass him round, Pass him round.'"[104]

While David Stanley was fearless in battle, he held strong convictions about the Divine and the progress of mankind. Stanley supported the principle that "all nations have their progress, and the progress of a nation is like the growth of a tree, bearing its fruit in due season. If the trunk of a tree is wounded, the vigor of the tree is stayed.... The good and pure see God's power in the storm, in the cataract, in the earthquake. They see His wisdom in the laws which govern the boundless universe; His beauty in the flower, in the sun-beam, and in the many-tinted window." Clearly Stanley, was a complex individual.[105]

7

Middle Tennessee and Tullahoma

Under Stanley, always forward, efficient and brave.

As David Stanley sat on his horse on the cold morning of January 1, 1863, he contemplated the previous day. He had rallied his cavalry and was able to maintain his position on the right on the Union line. He had stood in his stirrups inspiring his troopers and personally led a cavalry charge into the Confederate cavalry. Within a few days Murfreesboro was in Union hands and he was praised for the efforts of his command during the Battle of Stones River. He was beginning one of his most important years of his life and one which would define him. He was a West Point-trained, professional soldier who believed in discipline, traditional methods of waging war, the hard life of the soldier, and he felt that the best leaders were chosen to command. In all these areas he was about to be challenged to the core of his being and he would never be the same person. Stanley, if he was nothing else, was a realist. On January 5 he knew he faced superior numbers of enemy cavalry, but he welcomed the challenges.

Immediately upon the Union's taking possession of Murfreesboro, the work of Stanley's cavalry began again as they faced the strong Confederate cavalry just south of the town protecting the retreating infantry along the Shelbyville and Manchester pikes. Faced with the same old problem of a strong Confederate cavalry that had faced the Union army before the Battle of Stones River, Stanley and Rosecrans sought a numerical and technological solution to the problem. On January 14, Rosecrans outlined to secretary of war Edwin Stanton that the Confederates outnumbered his cavalry by four to one and were plaguing his communications and supply lines. One solution planned by Rosecrans was to mount an infantry brigade. He wanted to be able to move quickly like cavalry, but bring to bear the new technology of repeating rifles, which would increase the firepower of the mounted infantry as a way to tame the Confederate cavalry. Rosecrans wrote, "I must have horses and saddles to mount some infantry, and have asked authority to buy the horses and saddles for 5,000."[1] Upon receiving the request in Washington, the wheels began to turn to fill Rosecrans' need.

Colonel John T. Wilder's brigade was selected to become the mounted infantry Rosecrans would use against the Confederate army. Wilder's Brigade—17th Indiana Infantry, 72nd Indiana Infantry, 98th Illinois Infantry, 123rd Illinois Infantry—was the 2,000-man Second Brigade of General J.J. Reynolds's division. Wilder had failed in his attempt to trap Brigadier General John Hunt Morgan during his Christmas raid of 1862 and had been very frustrated and unable to contain his disappointment since that time. He wanted a way to fight the Confederate cavalry and he had argued his case with Rosecrans. Once mounted, Wilder's brigade proved a valuable resource used to complement the traditional cavalry.[2]

In the meantime, on January 20, Stanley had 5,500 traditional cavalrymen present for duty and another 3,500 absent for various reasons.[3] Much of the spring involved skirmishes and encounters between his cavalry and the Confederates, but Stanley worked hard to increase the number of trained cavalry which would be effective against his Confederate adversaries. He centered his activities in middle Tennessee because Rosecrans had, so far, refused to move his army. Rosecrans was determined not to advance further until his supply line was secure, but the Confederate cavalry continued to harass it.

Throughout the winter, Rosecrans increased the number of infantry, artillery and cavalry for the Army of the Cumberland. In February 1863, he recommended seven of his subordinates be promoted to the rank of major general. Among them was David S. Stanley. Rosecrans' report of the Battle of Stones River stated he felt Stanley had proved himself worthy of the rank. In addition to Rosecrans' recommendation, a group of citizens from Ohio and the officers of his command petitioned Abraham Lincoln to promote Stanley to the rank of major general. In the petition, Stanley's prior actions were cited: "On behalf of the soldiers of his command, we ask it! In the name of justice and for the country's good we ask his promotion." The officers ended their request this way: "Under Stanley, always forward, efficient and brave."[4] Along with this rank, which was formally accepted on April 10, 1863, Stanley was also introduced to new personnel whom he found difficult, including Rosecrans' new chief of staff, James A. Garfield, who would later be elected president of the United States. Stanley was soon to meet others who had gained their positions through influence and not merit.

A final issue which lingered from before the battle was the fate of the 15th Pennsylvania Cavalry and it was decided the best solution was to reorganize the regiment. This process began in February 1863 for the highly demoralized group. Some of the regiment was mustered out of service, but when the reorganization was completed in March the 15th Pennsylvania Cavalry was a detached regiment in Rosecrans' army. The regiment would not be part of Stanley's cavalry in the upcoming year but was assigned to Rosecrans' headquarters for his specific purposes, most notably as couriers.

Stanley used his leadership abilities

James A. Garfield, Rosecrans's chief of staff and future president of the United States (Library of Congress).

to mold the Union cavalry of the Army of the Cumberland into a well-trained, spirited force, which was so desperately needed. In February and March 1863, the cavalry remained in camp most of the time and Stanley became greatly liked because he did not believe in drilling veteran cavalry just for purpose of drilling. Nor did he feel military reviews were routinely necessary for his cavalry, which was a marked contrast from the previous cavalry commander. Captain Joseph Vale, 7th Pennsylvania Cavalry noted "the change from the constant irksome drills and reviews of the preceding year to the rest and recuperation of camp life now permitted was highly appreciated by the soldiers, and endeared their commander to them, as one who cared for their comfort rather than for display."[5]

But officers were officers, and soldiers were soldiers. On February 24, the commanders of the Army of the Cumberland had a large dinner and speeches were made during the event. Sergeant Daniel Prickitt, 3rd Ohio Cavalry, humorously recorded in his diary, "Speeches by Gen. Stanley, Chief of Cavalry, Gen. J.A. Garfield, Chief of Staff to General Rosecranz, Col. Paramore of 3rd O.V.C., Col. or Gen. Wagner of Brigade in Wood's Div. After the toasts dinner served—guests getting the best course. If the Generals & Officers crush the rebellion, what will the privates do?"[6]

Brigadier General James Garfield, an Ohioan, had been a member of the Ohio senate and professor at Western Reserve Eclectic Institute. Stanley generally liked soldiers from Ohio; however, he did not like Garfield, whom he called a meddler. Rosecrans, on the other hand, liked him, noted historian Larry Daniel, because "Garfield possessing the political savvy that Rosecrans lacked, the partnership was to be complementary."[7] Perhaps the reason Stanley disliked Garfield so much was the very reason Rosecrans liked him. Stanley was very similar to Rosecrans in many ways and also lacked the refined political skills Garfield possessed. Stanley was also a favorite of Rosecrans and the relationship with Rosecrans would soon become strained due to Garfield's influence. On the other hand, some of the other officers of the Army of the Cumberland looked a little jadedly at what they thought was Stanley's unfair advantage. "Rosecrans swears and swallows more whiskey in a day than I do in a month, but his headquarters are the resort of the priests. General Stanley is a Catholic and must go up," lamented General John Palmer.[8] While Stanley disliked the advantages of officers appointed for political reason, some officers believed Rosecrans gave unfair advantages to his Roman Catholic friends, which included Stanley, his godson. Despite the perceived advantages to the Rosecrans' Roman Catholic friends, "letters and journals abound with references to both quality and quantity of the [religious] services at headquarters on the Sabbath. There is no doubt that in the days preceding the Tullahoma Campaign through those following the battle of Chickamauga, the Army of the Cumberland was provided as moral a living environment as could be expected," noted historian, Robert Delassandro.[9]

In the meantime, Stanley's cavalry was involved in some skirmishing almost weekly. Most notably, Colonel Robert Minty's actions in the direction of Versailles, Middleton, and Unionville; Colonel Paramore and Colonel Eli Long's action of protecting 400 wagons near Bradyville; Colonel Thomas Jordan's cavalry action at Spring Hill; and Stanley with the Second and Third brigades near Columbia. The Union cavalry also had a significant victory on April 3 at Snow Hill, Tennessee. What was missing from the Union reports after the Battle of Stones River were the repeated records of the successes of the Confederate cavalry that had been so prominent in the past. This was not to say the activities of the Confederate cavalry were not felt, but there were more and more Union cavalry successes.

On February 16, 1863, John T. Wilder was given permission to mount his brigade, and he began to train it in this new type of warfare. Not only were the upcoming days ones of change for Confederate cavalry and infantry, but the traditional Union cavalry also needed to change to work in a coordinated manner with the mounted infantry. At 35 years of age, David Stanley was by no means old and inflexible, but he was a traditionalist who trusted in the established practices of the professional army and cavalry.

Major General Stanley, ever the disciplinarian, continued to train his cavalry, and his more inexperienced troopers needed as much drill as possible. Fortunately, a good portion of his cavalry was composed of veterans and an excellent experienced regiment was the 4th Michigan Cavalry. In March, the 4th Michigan was reviewed by commanders of the Army of the Cumberland. On March 17, 1863, Captain Henry Albert Potter of this veteran regiment described the review, including a description of David Stanley and his yellow sash: "We had a grand review and inspection of all the Cavalry Force in the Department or nearly all by Maj Gen Rosecrans yesterday at 12 M. It was a grand sight. The Review was on a large common 2 miles from town. There was one large flag with the Gen'l and then the 'star' flags of each Brigadier or Commander of Brigade numbered to show which each commanded and then most of the different Companies had their Guidons. All together made a handsome show with the officers with their full uniforms and white gauntlets and red sashes. Gen Stanley wore a Yellow Sash."[10]

Stanley was a sincere, professional soldier and was never happier than when serving in that capacity, but his new rank gave him much more exposure to the politics of war. Unknown to Stanley, he had been used as a pawn in a disagreement which arose between General John M. Palmer and Rosecrans. Palmer had been harboring a grudge against Rosecrans since the Stones River battle when Rosecrans had ordered him to occupy Murfreesboro. Rosecrans reported Stanley had found Murfreesboro to be free of the enemy and Rosecrans ordered Palmer to move into the town. Palmer refused to do so because he observed the enemy still firmly entrenched. When Palmer sought to find the source of the report that Murfreesboro was free of Confederates, it was found "the report, first ascribed to Stanley, had later been attributed to him, and [Palmer] was furious when this later version of the story was included in Rosecrans' official report." Palmer wrote, "'The truth is, I sent him no message whatever and, in his order, he states that he received his information from General Stanley. I have the dead wood on him [Rosecrans]. He selected me because he thought that as I was the only civilian, he might destroy me with impunity.'"[11]

Engagement at Franklin, Tennessee

On April 10, Stanley had just returned from Louisville, where he was trying to find horses, and when he returned he brought new cavalry regiments. Since he had assumed command of the cavalry for the Army of the Cumberland he had been outmanned by the Confederate horsemen, but he was slowly, with the weight of Rosecrans' support, equaling the odds. He was now able to expand his cavalry to include two divisions, which was excellent news, but he was soon to be disappointed with the selection of the commanders for the two divisions.

On April 10 Stanley took a large cavalry force of 1,600 troopers in conjunction with

Major General Gordon Granger's Corps with the intent of repulsing Major General Earl Van Dorn's army, reportedly at a strength of 10,000–18,000 men, located near Franklin. In fact Van Dorn had about 6,000 men. This affair at Franklin was a rare case of over aggressiveness on Stanley's part, which almost cost the cavalry dearly. Stanley's force included the First Brigade—4th Michigan, 7th Pennsylvania, 2 companies of the 1st Middle Tennessee, 2nd East Tennessee, 4th U.S. Cavalry—and Newell's artillery and his Second Brigade with 3 companies of the 3rd Indiana, and two Ohio regiments (3rd and 4th) commanded by Lieutenant Colonel Oliver Robie.

Stanley camped about 4 miles east of Franklin on the evening of the 9th and reached Franklin at 10:00 a.m. on April 10. General Granger estimated Van Dorn's force "consisted of about 9,000 cavalry and mounted infantry and two regiments of infantry proper."[12] Though greatly outnumbered, David Stanley was confident in the ability of his cavalry to meet Van Dorn. He sent a message to Rosecrans on the morning of April 10: "At 7 o'clock this morning Van Dorn was still at Spring Hill. Steedman thinks he has 18,000 men. Granger put it at 12,000. I think this latter probably about right. With one of our old divisions we could whip them out of their boots. I do not know whether it would be judicious to attack with this green force, but if you think 'the game is worth the candle,' we will slap away at them."[13]

Van Dorn marched on Franklin and met the 40th Ohio Infantry, which held its ground in the town. Stanley watched the advance and recorded, "As soon as I saw that the attack was in force, I immediately ordered a counterattack by the way of the ford at Hughes' Mill and the Lewisburg pike. The road, after crossing the ford, divides, one fork, the right one, reaching the pike about 1 mile from the ford; the other, the left, 1 1/2 miles from the same point. The Second Brigade was commanded by Lieutenant-Colonel Robie, and supported by the Second East Tennessee, Colonel Ray, and a detachment of the Third Indiana, Lieutenant-Colonel Klein, supporting. On the left-hand road the Fourth Regular Cavalry moved. This last column soon became engaged, and, charging promptly, dispersed a great part of Forrest's division, taking his battery of six pieces and some 300 prisoners."[14]

As Stanley's cavalry was advancing on the Confederate cavalry, an ex-slave was taken to Stanley and reported he had just escaped from the enemy. Stanley had ordered his cavalry to swing around Van Dorn's flank, and much to his consternation he was told Van Dorn was moving between Stanley's troopers and Franklin with 4,000 men. To prevent this Stanley rushed the 4th Kentucky Cavalry with two cannon to Ewing's Ford on the Big Harpeth River, but by the time they reached the ford, Van Dorn was already crossing. Stanley's cavalry needed the ford to prevent being encircled by Van Dorn's troopers. Fortunately, the 4th Kentucky (U.S.) was able to capture the crossing. The Union cavalry, being outnumbered, hastily moved to the ford to escape capture. The 4th U.S. Cavalry had captured a battery of enemy artillery but the Confederate advance prevented the Union cavalry from escaping with the guns. The cavalry cut the spokes on the wheels and tried to spike the guns and then headed back to the ford. The Union cavalry fought off three attacks before they reached the ford. Fortunately, darkness prevented any further action. Although this was a close affair for Stanley, he was able to extract his troopers.

Rumors abounded about David Stanley on April 11 after the battle. Lieutenant Lewis Hanback, a member of the 27th Illinois Infantry, wrote a letter to his family about the action at Franklin: "They [Confederates] also attacked Franklin, Tenn. with a large force. But were repulsed with severe loss though I learn this evening that Gen. Stanley who commanded our cavalry, a brave and skillful officer was captured."¹⁵ The rumors were false, but the letter reflects the feeling of soldiers for Stanley.

Captain Potter of the 4th Michigan Cavalry wrote of the engagement at Franklin on April 14: "We were over near Franklin. Van Dorn is hovering around to see what he may devour. He made a dash into Franklin on Friday. But got rather severely handled. We killed about one hundred, officers and all, while our loss was but a trifle compared to theirs. The Fourth Regulars captured a Battery of six pieces but they were not supported and consequently were obliged to give it up again."¹⁶ Granger's report of the affair also recognized Stanley's efforts. He noted Van Dorn was advancing on his infantry at Franklin, and Stanley's flanking action, while dangerous for the cavalry, had caused Van Dorn to divert his attack from Franklin. Although Stanley was pushed back across the river, the Confederates moved back toward Spring Hill. Granger wrote, "Since Van Dorn's repulse, he facetiously calls his attack an armed reconnaissance in force."¹⁷

Gordon Granger commanded Union infantry at the engagement at Franklin (Library of Congress).

Although Stanley's cavalry was roughly handled by Van Dorn, the confidence and aggressiveness of the Union cavalry was evident. Stanley stymied the Confederate advance and relieved the pressure on Granger's infantry as a result. On April 17, Stanley was ordered to Louisville along with 1,200 of his cavalrymen who were without horses. The purpose of the trip was to, at last, secure mounts for his cavalry. Yet on April 24, Rosecrans wired secretary of war Edwin Stanton that Stanley was still in Louisville and horses were not to be found.

As the situation in the Army of the Cumberland developed in the spring of 1863, the issue of mounted infantry took an unfortunate turn when Colonel Abel D. Streight led a mounted infantry brigade too far to the rear of Bragg's army. Streight and infantry under the command of Colonel Grenville Dodge marched together, then separated with the hope General Nathan B. Forrest would follow Streight's mounted infantry. This was exactly what happened, and in May Streight, isolated and exhausted, surrendered his entire force of 1,446 men and officers. Stanley felt this was another example of poor judgment by Garfield and, through him, Rosecrans. It has been implied Stanley resisted the concept of mounted infantry, but this does not appear to be the case. He never criticized the mounted infantry and the U.S. Cavalry frequently utilized dragoons prior to the war. He was, however, always a proponent of well-trained and disciplined soldiers in all actions. In Stanley's criticism of the Streight affair, he clearly places the blame not on the mounted infantry but on the unwise decision by Garfield and Rosecrans that resulted in the loss of such good soldiers. Stanley also severely criticized Streight for advocating such an attempt to ride through Confederate territory.

By May 1863, Stanley was informed of the men selected to command his two divisions, and he was ever so angry at the outcome. Perhaps at the rank of major general the politics of the army was more intense and perhaps this was the source of Stanley's intense dislike of James Garfield. But as a result of the reorganization of the cavalry, Stanley was shackled with two divisional commanders who were totally unsuitable to him, Brigadier General John B. Turchin and Brigadier General Robert Mitchell. Turchin, a native Russian, was born Ivan Turchaninoff in 1822. Turchin had been involved in the "rape of Athens," Alabama, the previous year and had been court-martialed for actions taken in Athens. Immediately after the conclusion of the court martial Lincoln promoted him to the rank of brigadier general, although the court recommended he be dismissed from the service. The presiding officer of the court-martial was none other than Brigadier General James A. Garfield.[18]

His commanding officer, Major General Don Carlos Buell, was so disgusted by the actions being taken on Turchin's behalf he wrote, "If as I hear, the promotion of Colonel Turchin is contemplated I feel it is my duty to inform you that he is entirely unfit for it. I placed him in the command of a brigade, and now find it necessary to relieve him from it in consequence of his utter failure to enforce discipline and render it efficient."[19] Regardless of this, on April 17 Turchin was given command in Stanley's cavalry. Stanley's other divisional commander was Brigadier General Robert B. Mitchell, a man Stanley had known since the beginning of the war and had served with during the Wilson's Creek campaign. Mitchell, a native Ohioan, was living in Linn County, Kansas, at the beginning of the war. He was wounded while leading the 2nd Kansas Infantry at the Battle of Wilson's Creek and had most recently commanded the garrison at Nashville. Stanley rightly appraised Mitchell as a political appointee without the skills to lead a division of cavalry.

These appointments, and obvious battles fought by Stanley to resist them, jaded Stanley's outlook. He resented Garfield's meddling in the selection of divisional officers, which alienated Stanley, who believed, correctly, it weakened the cavalry. It is important to note Stanley lays the blame of the selection of the division cavalry officers at the feet of Garfield, but this blame was made many years after the war. It was Rosecrans who made the final decision on the appointment of Turchin and Mitchell. There is little evidence to demonstrate the full extent of Garfield's involvement in making these decisions. Stanley and Rosecrans had struggled from November through April to develop a skilled cavalry which could meet the superior Confederate cavalry. Both Lewis Zahm and John Kennett had resigned from the cavalry after the Battle of Stones River and had been replaced with improved commanders. Stanley had excellent commanders capable of commanding divisions, Eli Long, Robert Minty, and Elmer Otis, but he felt he was shackled with Turchin and Mitchell after making so much progress. Certainly for the remainder of 1863, David Stanley was less pleased with his time in the Army of the Cumberland than at any other time in the war. He clearly disliked the political aspect of the war.

Stanley's unhappiness could not be expressed more clearly than his report demonstrated after the expedition to Middleton, Tennessee, which occurred from May 1 through May 22. He discovered "a force of the cavalry of the enemy was lying about carelessly at Middleton,

I started on the evening of the 21st, with a portion of General Turchin's division and Colonel Thomas Harrison's 39th Indiana Infantry (Mounted) regiment, to attack them. I was furnished by General Sheridan with the best guide I have ever yet followed."[20] Stanley approached the Confederate camp during the evening and remained about three miles away as he intended to attack at dawn. On the morning of May 22, Stanley rode along with Lieutenant O'Connell of the 4th U.S. Cavalry, which was the advance element of his cavalry. He ordered the remainder of the cavalry to follow his advance.

General Turchin was commanding the cavalry and Colonel Harrison's regiment of mounted infantry, which was to follow. After riding for about a mile and a half, Stanley looked to his rear:

> [T]o my surprise and indignation, [I] saw no one following. At the same instant I heard shots in front. I sent one orderly after another, and finally rode as fast as my jaded horse could carry me back, and found the entire column at a walk and turned upon a by-road at direct right angle to the road we were going on. By tours, by companies, and by squadrons I turned them back, and soon arrived in the enemy's camp, to find that Lieutenant O'Connell, to whom the word gallant applies, not as a compliment, but in its true old English signification, had, with his intrepid squadron, whipped the enemy out of his three camps. The rebels, with the exception of a few men in the Eighth Confederate Regiment and some Georgians, escaped to the cedar thicket—literally sans culottes. An attempt at a stand was made by the fugitives 1 mile from Fosterville, but they fled upon the approach of our support.[21]

Although this was a successful attack by the 4th U.S. Cavalry, the Confederate cavalry escaped and Stanley had to settle for "800 stand of arms, all the camp equipage and saddles, blankets, and clothing in all the camps, some wagons, and, perhaps, captured about 300 horses."[22] However, the reports of some of Stanley's regiments—4th Ohio Cavalry, 3rd Ohio Cavalry, 3rd Indiana Cavalry, and 7th Pennsylvania Cavalry—all contain notations suggesting the embarrassment of not being in position to support the 4th U.S. Cavalry. The wrath of Stanley certainly fell on Turchin in Stanley's sharp report to James A. Garfield as chief of staff.

Turchin was described by Stanley as "a fat short-legged Russian, who could not ride a horse."[23] The apologetic reports which were submitted by Stanley's regimental commanders carried the same message. Stanley noted,

> My staff officers came and told me that General Turchin, was not supporting me and indeed had not followed me. I was in the presence of two thousand rebels with only one hundred men. Turchin, after receiving the order to gallop, had deliberately commanded trot, and although the road we were on was broad and plain, he deliberately led his column into a wood road at right angles to the main road and leading away from the sound of the battle. The fight for our small force, was becoming perilous, when relief came in the shape of a charge over the fields by Colonel Eli Long's and Colonel H. G. Minty's Brigades. The valiant and brilliant soldiers heard our firing and without waiting for orders, threw down fences and charged across the fields to our rescue.[24]

After this incident, Stanley reported directly to General Rosecrans and marched into his tent and declared Rosecrans could choose between Stanley or Turchin. Rosecrans chose to keep Stanley. Turchin would be formally relieved of duty in the cavalry in July 1863. William H. Sinclair, assistant adjutant general, informed Stanley by messenger of Turchin's exit from the cavalry: "Turchin relieved of duty this morning. Good!"[25] Once Stanley had an opportunity to reflect on Turchin's lack of support at Middleton, Tennessee, he concluded Turchin simply could not ride. Stanley described his riding style as one who is sitting in a rocking chair; he concluded that the fact Turchin did not gallop or charge was because he was afraid he would fall off his horse. More disturbing was Stanley's description of Turchin's leadership style, which called to mind the actions in Athens, Alabama: "A perfectly cold bloodied foreigner—he did not care a fig what became of me or of the few men who followed me. He did not care to be jostled in a rush of cavalry for anybody's sake.... Garfield who was everlastingly looking out for votes, had imposed Turchin on the cavalry without any inquiry as to his fitness."[26] (Turchin's wife recorded her feelings about her husband's time in the cavalry: "My husband—despite his learning (which they cannot deny, ignorant as they are), despite his distinguished manners and his noble bearing does not count for much with them.")[27]

The unhappiness of Stanley with the way the cavalry was handled was evident in his writings after the Battle of Stones River. In his reflections later in his life on the organization of the cavalry Stanley included disappointment in Garfield and also Rosecrans. He would write, "Garfield disgraced himself eventually on Rosecrans' staff and the latter did himself great discredit by listening to such humbugs.... Neither Rosecrans, Sherman or Grant ever understood the true uses of cavalry. All these commanders were given to sending cavalry upon aimless raids, invariably resulting in using up their cavalry without accomplishing anything. Generals Thomas and Sheridan had more correct views of cavalry and used it to protect their flanks, to keep themselves in order of battle, and then ... threw the whole cavalry upon the enemy's flank at the critical time of the battle and crushed the opposing force. This is true application of cavalry."[28] Despite Stanley's unhappiness with Garfield—Mitchell and Turchin aside—the troopers of Stanley's command had great affection for him. Henry Albert Potter, 4th Michigan Cavalry, wrote on May 26: "Maj. Gen. Stanley visited us and is visiting with the Col. now. The band are getting out now to serenade him."[29]

Stanley's time after the Battle of Stones River was not totally devoted to the affairs of the army. Anna Maria Stanley, Stanley's wife, spent time with him during the lull between campaigns. Sergeant Daniel Prickitt, 3rd Ohio Cavalry, recorded in his diary, "Mrs. Gen. Stanley in camp when we had dress parade."[30] Anna Stanley joined her husband in Tennessee after the Battle of Stones River when newspaper reported he had been wounded.

By June 1, Stanley had assembled quite an impressive cavalry arm for the Army of the Cumberland and despite his disappointment in his division commanders he had a combination of excellent brigade and regimental commanders mixed with new and untried commanders. The days of dominance of the Southern cavalry were coming to an end and the Union cavalry would have the ability to meet its opponents on equal terms.

Rosecrans had lingered long enough in his position, and the urging from Washington convinced him it was time to advance against Bragg. On June 8, Rosecrans sent a set of questions to three corps commanders and thirteen division commanders regarding the feasibility of advancing against Bragg[31]: "Thirteen of the seventeen generals did not believe that Bragg had been substantially weakened, while two, Stanley and Brannan, disagreed," noted historian William Lamers. General John Turchin agreed that Bragg had lost some strength, but not enough to make him vulnerable. Garfield also responded and the "line officers resented Garfield's trespass."[32] David Stanley wrote to Rosecrans: "I believe the enemy is so reduced by detachments sent to reinforce Johnston, that we may hope to defeat him, provided we can meet his force fairly upon the field.... I believe an advance upon the enemy at this time would prevent their sending any more detachments from their force.... I have reasoned that an advance would bring on a decisive battle. Battles must be fought for political or military reasons. Had Hooker succeeded upon the Rappahannock, there would have been no political reason for now fighting a battle. Should Grant succeed at Vicksburg there will be no reason of such nature for a battle. Should Grant fail, the necessity would in my humble view be imperative.... The time has passed when the fate of armies must be staked because the newspapers do not sell well. I think our people have now comprehended that a battle is a very grave thing."[33] After receiving the answers to his questions, Rosecrans decided to march against Bragg and determined the march would begin on June 23, 1863. At that time, Stanley had assembled an impressive cavalry corps, complemented by mounted infantry.

CAVALRY CORPS[34]
MAJOR GENERAL DAVID S. STANLEY

FIRST CAVALRY DIVISION
BRIGADIER GENERAL ROBERT B. MITCHELL

First Brigade

COLONEL ARCHIBALD P. CAMPBELL

4th Kentucky, Col. Wickliffe Cooper
6th Kentucky, Col. Louis D. Watkins
7th Kentucky, Col. John K. Faulkner
2nd Michigan, Maj. John C. Godley
9th Pennsylvania, Col. Thomas J. Jordan
1st Tennessee, Lieut. Col. James P. Brownlow

Second Brigade

COLONEL EDWARD M. MCCOOK

2nd Indiana, Lieut. Col. Robert R. Stewart
4th Indiana, Lieut. Col. John A. Platter
5th Kentucky, Lt. Col. William T. Hoblitzell
2nd Tennessee, Col. Daniel M. Ray
1st Wisconsin, Col. Oscar H. La Grange
1st Ohio Artillery, Battery D (one section), Capt. Andrew J. Konkle

SECOND CAVALRY DIVISION
BRIGADIER GENERAL JOHN B. TURCHIN

First Brigade

COLONEL ROBERT H.G. MINTY

3rd Indiana, Lieut. Col. Robert Klein
5th Iowa, Lieut. Col. Matthewson T. Patrick
4th Michigan, Maj. Frank W. Mix
7th Pennsylvania, Lieut. Col. William B. Sipes
5th Tennessee, Col. William B. Stokes
4th United States, Capt. James B. McIntyre
1st Ohio Artillery, Battery D (one section), Lieut.

Second Brigade

COLONEL ELI LONG

2nd Kentucky, Col. Thomas P. Nicholas
1st Ohio, Col. Beroth B. Eggleston
3rd Ohio, Lieut. Col. Charles B. Seidel
4th Ohio, Lieut. Col. Oliver P. Robie
10th Ohio, Col. Charles C. Smith
Stokes' (Illinois) battery, Capt. James H. Stokes
Nathaniel M. Newell

UNATTACHED
39th Indiana Infantry (mounted), Col. Thomas J. Harrison

Tullahoma

While Stanley commanded the cavalry of the Army of the Cumberland, he projected a formidable appearance: "General Stanley was well on six feet in height. He had a rugged boldly modeled brow, which was deeply furrowed. His hair, mustache and beard were full and grizzled. From underneath bushy eyebrows beamed a pair of knowing gray eyes. The carriage of his head and a high arched nose showed his spirit and his dash."[35] Although Stanley and Rosecrans were eagerly planning the advance toward Bragg, a cloud hung over the Army of the Cumberland. David Stanley wrote of Major General William S. Rosecrans: "Rosy was powerful then, but his head was marked and it only awaited the slightest excuse to bring his dooms day."[36] Stanley was never so prophetic in describing not only Rosecrans' but also his own position as a chief of cavalry in the Army of the Cumberland. The final six months of 1863 were months which would redefine Stanley's military career. He was a close and trusted subordinate of Rosecrans and if Rosecrans' failed, he would be tied to Rosecrans, as would the other major generals under Rosecrans' command. The lofty position of major general was one of increased scrutiny. Whatever the decision, the impact on so many soldiers and the resulting successes and failures, by definition, brought the inevitable judgments of those decisions.

THE ADVANCE ON TULLAHOMA

Having made the decision to begin his advance on Bragg, Rosecrans moved the Army of the Cumberland in a southeasterly direction toward Tullahoma, Tennessee, beginning on June 23. While the Union army remained in Murfreesboro, Bragg had entrenched his army and constructed abatis as defenses. Rosecrans knew the cost which would be associated with attacking well-constructed defenses and he had to find a way around the defenses. Leonidas Polk's corps was located near Shelbyville, William Hardee was near Wartrace and the Confederates also had the advantage of holding the highland passes along the three primary roads—Shelbyville Pike, Wartrace Road and Manchester Road—leading to Tullahoma. Rosecrans estimated Polk commanded about 18,000 men, Hardee had 12,000 and the Confederate cavalry was thought to have about 8,000 troopers. Rosecrans planned to push Bragg southward and then quickly capture the bridge at Estill Springs or at Pelham, trapping Bragg before he could cross the Elk River. But before that could happen, Rosecrans was going to have to move the bulk of his army through Hoover's Gap and Matt's Hollow, which could be easily defended by his Confederate foe.

Rosecrans' plan called for Thomas' XIV Corps to move along the Manchester Pike and seize and hold Hoover's Gap. Thomas and McCook were ordered to advance so that each corps was within supporting distance of the other. Meanwhile, Crittenden's XXI Corps was to advance and concentrate at Bradyville, forming the left flank of the Army of the Cumberland. A brigade of cavalry under the command of General Turchin was ordered to operate in conjunction with Crittenden. David Stanley and the remainder of the cavalry were ordered toward Versailles, west of the Shelbyville Road, and then to move southward to unite with Mitchell's division. The cavalry was to seek and attack the Confederate cavalry at Middleton, Tennessee.

Initially, Rosecrans sent Major General Gordon Granger's reserve corps and David Stanley's cavalry to Triune in a feint to confuse Bragg as to his true plan. He hoped Bragg would send troops to an area Rosecrans did not plan to attack. Interestingly, Granger commanded the reserve corps and had overall supervisory command of the cavalry. On June 23 Granger ordered General Robert Mitchell's first cavalry division along the Eagleville and Salem roads, pushing the enemy's cavalry and pickets in front of them. Granger marched

Brannan's division to Salem and Palmer's division and a brigade of cavalry to Readyville. Mitchell had a sharp fight but accomplished his task. Then Rosecrans called a meeting of his corps commanders to explain their orders. McCook's XX Corps was to begin its march on the Shelbyville Road and then advance on Wartrace along the Wartrace Road. One of McCook's divisions was to cover Granger's left flank. Next Granger was to march along the Middleton Road, covering the movement of the Thomas' XIV Corps.[37]

On June 23 and June 24, General Robert Mitchell's cavalry engaged the 2nd and 4th Georgia Cavalry, 7th Alabama Cavalry and 51st Alabama Cavalry regiments as he advanced. Stanley, becoming aware of the resistance Mitchell was facing, rode with Minty's Brigade and Stoke's Battery to join Mitchell. After riding to Mitchell, Stanley recorded, "That day the rain set in, which has continued to this present date, and which, converting the whole surface of the country into a quagmire, has rendered this one of the most arduous, laborious, and distressing campaigns upon man and beast I have ever witnessed."[38] On June 25, Stanley's 5th Iowa and 4th Michigan cavalries skirmished with Confederate cavalry near Guy's Gap. The following day, Stanley rested his horses and rationed his men.

Stanley recalled "one of the ridiculous things that sometimes happen to lighten up the death roll [during the skirmish on June 23].... The Confederates made a charge on our line of skirmishers, but recoiled when they met a brisk fire. One trooper continued to charge straight down our lines. As he passed across the line of skirmishers of the 1st Tennessee cavalry (Union) every man took a shot at the bold horse soldier. He dashed into our lines with his gray clothes full of bullet holes but with a whole skin, when it was discovered that a bullet had cut both his reins, and it was the horse that did the charging, the trooper being an unwilling participant."[39]

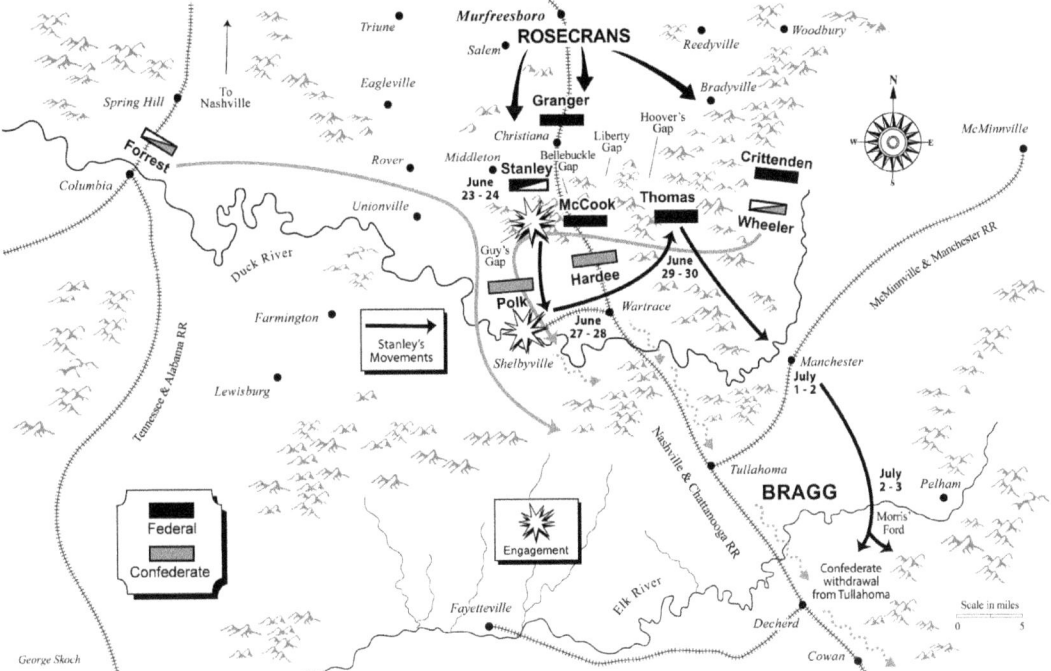

Union Cavalry Advance, Tullahoma Campaign

June 27 was a long day for the cavalry. Stanley, commanding 5,000 cavalrymen, set out in search of their enemy. Captain Joseph Vale, 7th Pennsylvania Cavalry, recalled, "Here was presented a scene of grand military pageantry, as rare as it was inspiring. The sun, for a few hours after rising, shone out clear and bright, reflecting in full splendor the bright sabers and arms, and kissing the flags, banners, and steamers, as a harbinger of victory."[40] At 9:00 a.m. Stanley advanced on Guy's Gap under Rosecrans' orders to "dislodge the enemy" at that location. Stanley, commanding Mitchell's Division and Minty's Brigade, approached Guy's Gap. He sought Granger's permission to make a direct attack on the defenders and later stated Granger "acquiesced in this, and, pushing forward, our forces deployed. The enemy abandoned their position and fled toward Shelbyville, closely pursued by the First Middle Tennessee Cavalry, Colonel Galbraith commanding, supported by the Fourth Regular Cavalry, Captain McIntyre commanding."[41] Playing it safe, Stanley placed his favorite brigade commander, Colonel Minty, with the 4th U.S. Cavalry in front of the gap while the 7th Pennsylvania, 4th Michigan, and 3rd Indiana were positioned to flank Confederate defenders. Historian Michael Bradley noted, "Observing that not much defensive fire was coming out of the place Lieutenant Colonel Galbraith sent forward some men from his 1st Middle Tennessee Cavalry (U.S.), cleared the barricade off the road, and then charged the earthworks mounted. The few Confederates holding the place immediately scattered and for about two miles there was a horse race."[42] Stanley also gave credit to the two columns of infantry from Granger's reserve corps which were deployed and attacked the defenders. As the Union cavalry pursued the Confederates toward the critical engagement at Shelbyville, no one knew the results there would change the balance of power in the Civil War. Stanley recorded the action:

> Immediately afterward I directed Colonel Minty to support this movement with his whole brigade. The enemy in considerable force, consisting of Martin's division and a part of Wharton's, all under command of Wheeler, made a stand at the fortifications 4 miles north of Shelbyville, where they commenced shelling our advance. Colonel Minty immediately sent the Fourth Michigan to the right, dismounted, but, finding the distance they must necessarily travel was very great, they remounted and advanced through the abates on horseback, and, after a severe skirmish, they succeeded in getting in on the enemy's left flank, when they fled in haste. As the enemy began to mount, the Seventh Pennsylvania charged up the pike, supported by the Fourth Regulars, and, deploying to the right and left as they passed through the earthworks, succeeded in capturing many of the rebels. From this point up to the time that our advance reached the precincts of Shelbyville the whole brigade pursued them closely, but when they again opened with their artillery, our men being much scattered in the long charge, fell back out of range and reformed. General Granger and myself were still at Guy's Gap when the state of affairs came to us by couriers. I immediately wrote an order to Colonel Minty to charge their battery and take it, at the same time General Mitchell being ordered to support the movement with his entire division. A section of the Eighteenth Ohio Battery, Captain Aleshire commanding, preceded Mitchell's division. Shortly afterward General Granger and myself started to Shelbyville, but before arriving at the place, the energy of General Mitchell and Colonel Minty, nobly seconded by the gallant troops under their command, had won for us a decided victory over the rebels. The latter had been dislodged from the stand they made at the line of intrenchments.... This regiment attacked them with revolving rifles.[43]

After breaking the Confederate defenses in Shelbyville, the defenders retreated from the town after unsuccessfully attempting to stop the Union attack by preparing a defensive line at the public square. Minty was charging directly into the mouths of the cannon and

Colonel Archibald Campbell's brigade was swinging around to cut off the retreat at the bridge over the Duck River. The defenders had been totally defeated and lost the artillery; 591 men who were prisoners and an estimated 200 troopers had chosen to take their chances in the swollen Duck River rather than being captured. Stanley observed, "The charge upon the enemy's battery was led by the Seventh Pennsylvania Cavalry, headed by Captain Davis, and, as the charge was made down a stone pike, by fours, upon a three-gun battery, supported by mounted infantry (dismounted), the annals of this war will not probably show a more gallant charge. The enemy threw away their arms in their flight, and two of their generals— Wheeler and Martin—escaped by swimming the river. Some five or six hundred stand of arms and a considerable amount of commissary and ordnance stores fell into our hands."[44] The Union cavalry's ability to defeat Wheeler at Shelbyville revealed the results of increased numbers of troopers, mounts and efficient weapons. The engagement at Shelbyville also demonstrated the benefits of being properly trained, as the Union cavalry had just implemented two successful saber charges.[45] They had finally come into their own.

While Stanley and Minty's insistence on training the cavalry in the use of the saber has been discounted by many, the battle at Shelbyville showed the value of this weapon. It has also been noted that the saber charges had occurred by troopers of the same battalion which had just "demonstrated comparable skill as dismounted skirmishers."[46] As one of the defenders later wrote, "On either side of the highway, in columns of fours, they advanced at a steady gallop.... The Union troopers, with sabers high in the air, made no sound whatever, beyond the rumbling tattoo which their horses' hoofs played upon the ground.... No more gallant work was ever done by any troops than was done this day by the Seventh Pennsylvania."[47]

Wheeler was able to escape the Union cavalry and move across Skull Camp Bridge, which provided escape over the Duck River. However, he was informed Forrest was rushing to his aid with two full brigades of cavalry and he was on the north side of the Duck River. Wheeler had planned to burn the bridge and prevent Stanley's cavalry from crossing the river, but he knew this would trap Forrest and his Southern cavalry. So he took two guns and 500 troopers back on the north side of the river and prepared to hold the bridge until Forrest arrived. He was in a very uncomfortable position, as Archibald Campbell's brigade, with the 9th Pennsylvania Cavalry leading the way, swung to the left and came charging directly into his right flank. Wheeler had already had enough to deal with as Minty charged his front. Campbell's flanking movement proved too much. Two cannons had been ordered across the bridge, but during the excitement they had overturned and the bridge was blocked. Any Confederates not across the bridge were trapped. "After a four-day downpour, Duck River was a roaring Torrent, with it crest fifteen feet below the level of the streets of Shelbyville and with a nearly vertical drop from the riverbank to the water below. Wheeler 'saber in hand, shouted to his men that they must cut their way through and swim the river, ordered the charge, and, with General Martin, led in the desperate venture,'" observed Stephen Starr, author of *The Union Cavalry in the Civil War*.[48]

David Stanley was having a good day, because at midnight he learned the formidable Nathan Bedford Forrest's cavalry had struggled through the mud and had crossed the Duck River downstream as he retreated toward Tullahoma. The day belonged to Stanley and his cavalry. The aggressive Stanley was satisfied with what he had gained but with this blood up, he decided to go after Forrest. Unfortunately, Rosecrans had shackled Stanley to Granger. Stanley pleaded with Granger for permission to pursue Forrest, but Stanley recorded Granger "was of the opinion that the command was too much wearied to move in the night. As the matter turned out, I think it was very unfortunate that this attack was not made, as I think we could have completely routed this part of Forrest's force."[49] Stanley had to have been particularly frustrated when he received a message from Lt. Colonel C. Goddard, assistant adjutant general, which encouraged to him to take the battle to Wheeler and Forrest—"Pitch in and use them up"[50]—Only to find out he had been ordered not to pursue Forrest by his new commanding officer, Granger.

The three infantry corps of the Army of the Cumberland united after crossing the highland gaps and pushed southward through the rain and mud. While this army marched toward Tullahoma, Stanley and Granger were still to the west of the main army. Rosecrans was very complimentary regarding Stan-

Nathan Bedford Forrest, Confederate cavalry (Library of Congress).

ley's actions at Guy's Gap and Shelbyville: "From their intrenchments the rebels fled to town, where they made another stand, but in vain. Our cavalry came down with resistless sweep and drove them in confusion into the river. Many were killed and drowned, and Shelbyville, with large numbers of prisoners, a quantity of arms and commissary stores, were the crowning results of the cavalry operations that day."[51]

The engagement at Shelbyville, while not really significant in terms of the tactical situation during the Tullahoma Campaign, carries great significance in terms of the strategic situation in future campaigns in the central theater of the Civil War. It is generally recognized as a point where the dominance of Confederate cavalry over the Union cavalry ended. David Stanley wrote, "The Confederate cavalry never recovered from the demoralizing effect which it experienced that day of being ridden down by the Union cavalry."[52] Rosecrans and Stanley had worked diligently to bolster the Union cavalry in terms of men, horses, training and firepower. They could now stand on their own, on equal terms, against the Confederate cavalry. This was a critically important event in the career of David Stanley. He gave credit for the success of the engagement at Shelbyville to the confidence and training of his cavalry. He would write that the "superior nerve" of the Union cavalry "unnerved" his opponents on the field.

The infantry advance had also moved smoothly. McCook seized Liberty Gap, and General Reynolds' division, including Wilder's mounted infantry, claimed the critical Hoover's Gap. The infantry struggled through the same mud as the cavalry, and the rain continued for the remainder of the Tullahoma campaign. On June 26, Bragg had retreated to Fairfield and Wilder's brigade captured Matt's Hollow, another very important position. By July 27, Rosecrans' army had crossed the Duck River and Rosecrans ordered Wilder's brigade to destroy the bridge over the Elk River, therefore preventing Bragg's escape.

On June 28, Stanley resupplied and rested the horses, but on June 29 he sought Forrest's cavalry and was unsuccessful in locating the Confederate horsemen. He sent Mitchell with the First Brigade to Beech Grove while he moved the remainder of the cavalry to Fairfield and Turchin remained on duty on the army's left flank. Rosecrans advanced his infantry and ordered Stanley to join the army at Manchester.

First Rosecrans needed to maneuver Bragg into his fixed defenses at Tullahoma, and second he wanted Thomas and Crittenden to swing south and cut railroad and turn the Confederates, trapping and forcing them into a weaker line of defense. Rosecrans hoped Stanley's cavalry could work in concert by capturing bridges over the Elk River, preventing Bragg from retreating. Wilder was unable to destroy the Elk River Bridge, but his expedition along with the line of Federal march revealed Rosecrans' intent. On June 30, Bragg realized he could not hold Tullahoma, and by July 1, he had successfully retreated from Tullahoma.

Also on July 1, Robert Minty's brigade rode back to Walker's Mill and Stanley was informed Bragg had evacuated Tullahoma. Then the cavalry was in pursuit of the retreating army, with Pelham, Tennessee, as the intended destination in hopes of cutting off the retreat at Elk River, trapping Bragg's army. Rosecrans did not want to lose contact with Bragg's retreating army and on July 2 he ordered his infantry corps to aggressively follow the Confederates. "Additional instructions to Thomas indicated Rosecrans expected Stanley to work for Thomas. Thomas and Stanley were then to cooperate to destroy the Confederate cavalry and trains," noted military historian, Richard Brewer.[53] More practically, Rosecrans needed Stanley to capture the bridges to insure he could pursue Bragg even if he could not trap him.

Turchin started for Hillsboro, and Mitchell's division rode for Manchester. The next day, it was confirmed the route of retreat was not through Pelham. Upon this discovery, Turchin was ordered to ride to Decherd, but his advance was blocked at Morris' Ford by a Confederate rearguard. Turchin had crossed the ford and attempted to protect the crossing, but enemy artillery forced him to retreat to the north side of the river. Mitchell's cavalry was dispatched to assist in the crossing. Stanley recorded, "General Turchin, having arrived in advance of my column, immediate measures were taken to force the passage. General Mitchell was directed to cross the upper and General Turchin the lower ford. This was effected with little opposition—a fortunate circumstance, as the current was swift, and almost swam a horse. Colonel Long's small brigade crossed first, and was soon engaged in a very heavy skirmish with the enemy's cavalry, driving them in the direction of Decherd."[54] Once across the ford, Turchin and Mitchell pressed the pursuit until nightfall, and Stanley's cavalry claimed a Confederate colonel killed and mortally wounded a second, in addition to another twenty soldiers killed.

The reports by Turchin and Stanley fairly drip with the animosity felt between the two men. Stanley stated a simple crossing of the Elk River was unable to be accomplished by Turchin. He also makes almost no reference to Turchin himself in his overall report, except this incident. Turchin lamented the fact that his cavalry brigade "was scattered by battalions, under command of majors and lieutenant-colonels, on the front of the two army corps, the regimental commanders and the brigade commanders remaining in camp with twelve companies of different regiments, and at the head of all was the division commander himself."[55]

In regard to his failure to cross the Elk River, he felt he faced an entrenched enemy with superior numbers of men supported by cavalry. He also wrote he decided to guard a second ford to prevent the enemy from threatening the army's flank. Clearly Stanley had not forgiven Turchin for abandoning him to die in the face of the enemy earlier in the summer.

By the end of the day on July 2, the Army of the Cumberland had successfully claimed several points to cross the Elk River despite Bragg's attempts to destroy bridges and guard the fords. However, the high water and Confederate resistance at the fords had accomplished what Bragg desperately needed—time to withdraw his army.

Rosecrans wrote in his after action report, "It affords me pleasure to return my thanks to Major-General Granger and Major General Stanley, commanding the cavalry, for their operations on our right, resulting in the capture of Shelbyville."[56] Opinions vary on the success of the Tullahoma Campaign. Some hold this campaign as a model of maneuver to achieve success with the least amount of loss, while others point out that Bragg's army slipped southward to fight again. Stanley agreed with the latter opinion but quickly pointed to weather as the primary reason Bragg was able to escape.

Summary

The Union cavalry performed well during the Tullahoma Campaign and David Stanley aggressively drove his horsemen to victory. One additional accomplishment would have claimed a major victory—if Stanley could have captured the bridges over the Elk River. Historian Michael Bradley wrote of the possibility of the Union cavalry's trapping Bragg's infantry along the Elk River: " ... the idea that blue cavalry would have trapped the Army of the Tennessee asks too much of the Union cavalry. Rosecrans' mounted arm had improved vastly during the first six months of 1863 but his troopers did not have the firepower or the élan to hold a river line against Reb infantry and artillery. Wilder's Brigade of mounted infantry could have held a bridge, but Stanley's cavalry could not have held the line of the Elk."[57]

Another interesting event occurred during the campaign when Rosecrans assigned Stanley as a subordinate to Gordon Granger. Historian Stephen Starr wrote, "For reasons Rosecrans has not explained, he gave Gordon Granger, also at Triune with his Reserve Corps, what appears to have been supervisory authority over Stanley and the cavalry. Rosecrans may have become disenchanted with Stanley's performance as an adequately aggressive cavalry commander ... or he may have decided that it would be convenient to have the commander of the infantry corps with which the cavalry was to work, control the operations of all three arms."[58] However, messages from Garfield on June 26 were directed to Stanley and the wording appeared to show Stanley and Granger as relative equals: "The above order to feel the enemy at Guy's Gap will not be carried out if there are reasons why Generals Stanley and Granger regard the expedition as fruitless or too hazardous; in that case, General Stanley will come forward at once."[59] Once Bragg began his retreat, Stanley was again placed in a position to "work for Thomas" in the pursuit. This strongly suggests a decision by Rosecrans to put the cavalry at the disposal of his infantry corps commanders as situations changed in the campaign to achieve the desired result and as a way to improve communications.

The other interesting point made in Stanley's reports was that he was definitely on his good behavior, but he made a few veiled remarks directed at Granger's cautious command style. And clearly he was under Granger's command early in the campaign. One remark was directed at the action taken by Stanley at Guy's Gap which resulted in the Union army gaining this critical position. Stanley stated he urged Granger to allow his cavalry to make a direct attack on the position and Granger "acquiesced." A second comment was made after the success at Shelbyville. Stanley wanted to battle Forrest and felt Granger's reluctance kept him from further successes. These reports clearly showed Stanley shackled when he aggressively wanted to move forward. If Rosecrans had been disenchanted with Stanley, the general's performance during the Tullahoma campaign allayed any concerns. Stanley's philosophy was to face his opponents with "hindward feather and with forward toe."[60]

Historically, the success of Stanley's cavalry in the Tullahoma Campaign is overshadowed by the success of John T. Wilder's Lightning Brigade. There can be no doubt Wilder's brigade was a hugely successful experiment which contributed directly to Rosecrans' victory at Tullahoma. David Stanley is often referred to as a sarcastic fellow and he was certainly an officer who believed in the traditional cavalry methods. But as a regular cavalry officer, he was comfortable with the role of dragoons. There are no historical records from Stanley about his thoughts on Wilder's Brigade, but Wilder stated Stanley referred to his brigade as "tadpole" cavalry. In a conversation with Rosecrans, Stanley is quoted as saying he did not expect Wilder's brigade to return from the attempt to cut the Confederate retreat. Rosecrans had earlier allowed Abel Streight to have a sweeping maneuver in Confederate-held territory only to be captured and Stanley felt the same was likely to occur. Stanley was wrong. Wilder returned to enjoy the successes of the campaign. Based on Stanley's experience with dragoons and his stated opposition of large sweeping maneuvers, his comments are most likely an opposition to the tactics rather than the establishment of mounted infantry.[61]

Clearly the Tullahoma Campaign was a great success for Stanley. He was described by historian Robert Delassandro as "not the stereotypical cavalryman. Stanley was an apt leader described as 'bold and dashing, his action tempered and guided by skill and prudence, which make him a successful commander.' Stanley was universally liked by his subordinates."[62] Despite Stanley's later assessment of Garfield, there is evidence Garfield liked Stanley and had sent a photograph of Stanley in a letter to his family on June 21, 1863, saying, "a photograph of my friend General Stanley, our chief of cavalry. He is an able and gallant officer."[63] This strongly suggests that, at the time, Garfield held no ill feeling for Stanley, and questions whether Stanley's judgment of Garfield was one held at the time or more likely ill will produced by events which occurred after the war.

8

The Advance on Chattanooga and the Battle of Chickamauga

It was most unsatisfying and annoying.

On July 5, 1863, the president and the secretary of war must have been ecstatic, or so Major General William Rosecrans thought. The Battle of Gettysburg had been fought and won, Vicksburg had fallen, and the Union army in Tennessee had pushed Bragg to Chattanooga. Rosecrans was to be surprised and enraged by the message he received from Washington stating he now had the opportunity to finish the job he had started. Rosecrans felt he had just performed a remarkable piece of generalship by pushing Bragg out of middle Tennessee at a cost of less than 700 casualties, but Washington wanted more results.

Once the advance on Tullahoma was over, Stanley had been released from Granger's command and was soon on the road in pursuit of Bragg. Rosecrans wrote on July 5, "Stanley is pressing enemy with cavalry."[1] Also on July 5, Louis Watkins, Third Cavalry Brigade commander, communicated that the citizens reported Bragg's retreating army was heading toward Chattanooga. Stanley concentrated his cavalry and pursued Bragg. On July 7, Rosecrans again wrote: "Stanley occupies Salem with a cavalry force that will crush the rebel cavalry."[2] Rosecrans had sent Stanley on a hopeful expedition of gaining Bragg's rear and preventing the Army of Tennessee from crossing the Tennessee River; but a message from Alexander McCook reminded Rosecrans that if the railroad bridge had been burned as Bragg retreated the cavalry raid and infantry pursuit were pointless.

McCook's chief of staff, G.P. Thurston, called on Stanley for assistance in reconnoitering the bridge. The cavalry assigned to McCook, the 5th Kentucky, and also the 39th Indiana Mounted Infantry, had horses in such poor condition they could not possibly make the reconnaissance. The recent muddy campaign had taken its toll.

On July 10 Garfield sent Stanley orders about limiting his expeditions and working toward getting the Union cavalry horses in good condition for future action. He also wrote, "The lawlessness of which you speak on the part of our soldiers on foraging parties will make bushwhackers faster than any other thing. I have already mentioned, in a former dispatch, that the general commanding desires you to gather and send in to the provost-marshal-general all the able-bodied male negroes (slaves of rebel masters) you can find. Your proposed expedition will probably be fruitful in this respect, as well as in the collection of horses and mules."[3] Garfield was responding to a question from Stanley about the discipline of the Union troops. He also tried to maintain the peace as much as possible, and in some cases he used fear tactics. Stanley wrote, "I scared Jackson County, I think, by my savage threats."[4] Stanley observed the local citizens generally opposed the actions of the bushwhackers and guerrillas. He noted there were many who held a strong allegiance to the Union in eastern Tennessee and northern Alabama.

Stanley took the cavalry to Huntsville, Alabama, and collected as much forage, horses and mules as he could find. He had also been ordered by Rosecrans to "impress every able bodied colored man I could find to use as teamsters and for work upon the fortifications of Nashville and Murfreesboro. My provost marshal arranged to capture the congregations of the negro churches as they were emptied after service on Sundays."[5] Stanley was also able to impress another 600 ex-slaves during various cavalry expeditions. Brigadier General John Beatty recorded in his diary, "General Stanley has returned from Huntsville, bringing him about one thousand North Alabama negroes. This is a blow at the enemy in the right place. Deprived of slave labor, the whites will be compelled to send home, or leave at home, white men enough to cultivate the land and keep their families from starving."[6] Stanley's actions from the Southern point of view seemed to be achieving the desired effect. Local Huntsville resident Mary Jane Chadwick wrote, "They are stealing all the Negroes and confining them in the Seminary building. Seventy have just passed by under a strong guard. All the good horses have been taken."[7] Stanley promised the local civilians that he would keep the ex-slaves overnight and if any wanted to return to their old masters he would allow them to do so. None agreed to return.

While Stanley was confiscating mules as well as ex-slaves, he came in contact with many of the local citizens. A correspondent of the *Chicago Times* recorded one incident:

> A Mrs. Pruitt, whose husband is a volunteer in Col. Russell's regiment of fleet-footed rebels, who are far more discreet than daring, made application at headquarters for the return of her mules and cornmeal, captured by a foraging party. There was a submissive weakness in her manners when she first entered, which, together with a fluency of well-selected words, and a beauty of feature that would stir the feelings of an anchorite, would have pled her cause with partial success at least. But a casual reference to the proverbial cowardice of the command to which her husband is attached roused the dormant hostility that she had artfully concealed and partially denied, and she showered upon the authorities a perfect volume of vituperation, couched in terms as opprobrious as though it had been her business to vilify and denounce. The success that her feigned gentleness of disposition and excellency of character was about to secure, was swept away by this violent disclosure of her true character, and the General informed her that he would retain the mules and meal. Though she was left destitute of provisions almost, she continued furious, and, displaying an abundance of gold, proposed to purchase the property refused her.[8]

Stanley also captured a Confederate captain who had just been married the day of his capture. The captain pleaded with Stanley to parole him, which Stanley did. The captain, true to his word, returned within two weeks and was sent to Johnson's Island until he was exchanged.

Stanley, while he strove to make life as good as possible for his men, was a strict disciplinarian and was ever aware that lack of discipline could quickly turn into chaos and pillaging. To demonstrate he would not allow this type of behavior on the part of his troops, he endorsed the verdict of a court-martial of Corporal George W. Mercer, 1st Ohio Cavalry, who had been found guilty of "willfully and maliciously setting fire to a certain cotton factory."⁹

Stanley's mandate for discipline was communicated to his subordinates. He reminded his two division commanders, Mitchell and Turchin, of the importance to maintaining a tight rein on their soldiers. He wrote in a very thinly veiled jab at Turchin, who was involved in the "Rape of Athens in 1862, that "irregularities and insufferable outrages in the war of foraging having been practiced by soldiers on former expeditions." He issued orders that if a soldier was found inside a civilian's house or acquiring a horse or mule in a method that was not according to regulations, the soldier "will be whipped, the uniforms stripped from him, and be drummed out of camp." In addition, "the attention of subordinate officers was especially called to the order, and violations on the part of the soldiers detected in two instances, resulted in the dangerous wounding of one, and the sentencing of another, by a Drumhead Commission, of two years' confinement in the Penitentiary at Jeffersonville, after having one half of his head shaved as a mark of disgrace."¹⁰ While Stanley was not a severe disciplinarian, like Gordon Granger, he required his soldiers to act like soldiers and not like bandits.

In the July 22 communication to Rosecrans, Stanley asked, "Have you received my communication concerning General Turchin?"¹¹ It is unclear to what Stanley referred, but Turchin was relieved of duty with the cavalry on July 29.¹² The historian of the 7th Pennsylvania Cavalry wrote of Turchin: "General Turchin, as a cavalry officer, was not a success. He was personally brave, and had a good deal of dash in his mental make-up, but was physically out of place on horseback, the circumference of his body being equal to his height. His failure as a commander of cavalry was due, more than anything else, to the fact that he marched with too long a tail, orderlies and escort numbering nearly four hundred men."¹³ George Crook, a West Point classmate of Stanley, assumed command of the Second Cavalry Division upon Turchin's removal. Crook served early in the war in western Virginia, at the Second Battle of Bull Run and the Battle of Antietam. He and his division had been transferred west, and he had commanded an infantry brigade in the XIV Corps during the Tullahoma Campaign.

In early August, the Union cavalry was disrupting Confederate communications, a task the Confederate

George Crook replaced John Turchin as division commander of cavalry (Library of Congress).

cavalry had enjoyed for the past year. Captain James E. Love, 8th Kansas Infantry, wrote to his fiancé on August 6: "Our men and Stanley's Corps of Cavalry, regular daredevils, are swarming down here. Stanley's men are bent on destroying railroads—we are merely supporting them."[14]

Stanley returned to Nashville on July 25 and then went to Winchester, Tennessee, and established the cavalry headquarters there. On August 10, he had 6,645 men in Brigadier General Robert Mitchell's cavalry division at Fayetteville, Tennessee, and 5,391 troopers in Brigadier General George Crook's Second Cavalry Division headquartered with Stanley in Winchester, Tennessee. The 472 troopers of the detached 15th Pennsylvania Cavalry, while not a part of the cavalry corps, were present for duty in Winchester. While operating from Winchester and Fayetteville, the Union cavalry sparred with the Confederate cavalry, and on August 11, Stanley's cavalry struck Brigadier General George Dibrell's Confederates in Sparta, Tennessee.

Stanley made his headquarters in the home of a Mr. McGee in Winchester. Even though McGee was an ardent Southern supporter, he and his new Union general became good friends. Huntsville, Alabama, resident Mary Jane Chadwick recorded in her diary, "Mr. McGee from Winchester was here tonight. The most amusing gentleman I have ever met. Gen. Stanley was quartered in his house ... and it appears he took quite a fancy to him, although he is a great Rebel."[15]

The Advance on Chattanooga

On August 15, William Rosecrans presented his plan to march against Bragg at Chattanooga. General Thomas' XIV Corps was to march two divisions to Stevenson, Alabama, and two divisions into the Sequatchie and Battle Creek valleys near Jasper, Tennessee. Thomas Crittenden's XXI Corps would march to various locations: Wood's Division to Therman, Palmer's Division to Dunlap, and Van Cleve's division with Minty's cavalry brigade to Sparta. The main body of Minty's cavalry brigade would then march to Pikeville, while the remainder of his cavalry would operate in conjunction with Van Cleve's division in the Sequatchie Valley. Minty, Wilder and Wood were to push forward and reconnoiter towards Chattanooga. Alexander McCook's XX Army Corps was ordered to move Richard Johnson's division toward Stevenson, Alabama. Jefferson C. Davis' division was ordered to select a good camp for forage and water between the Mud and Raccoon creeks and open communications with McCook at Stevenson.[16]

Stokes' 5th Tennessee Cavalry was ordered to operate in cooperation with the Carthage Brigade still located in central Tennessee. Stanley was ordered to post Minty's cavalry brigade under orders of General Van Cleve. Stanley, with the reserve brigade and the remainder of the cavalry, was to follow Rosecrans to headquarters and act under Rosecrans' command as the situation developed. This order assigning Stanley near headquarters but without specific objectives set the stage for a confrontation between Rosecrans and Stanley later in the campaign. During the advance on Chattanooga, Stanley operated without the ability to use his own initiative but rather fulfilled direct orders from headquarters. Only Minty was free to operate somewhat independently.

Granger's Reserve Corps was ordered to "advance to Fayetteville to protect the depot;

a column of two brigades of infantry and all the spare cavalry to Athens; an advance to Decatur, to be called 'the advance of the Reserve Corps,' numbering 25,000 strong, and to remain there in observation with all means of transportation and movement on hand for advancing to cover our rear on the Tennessee, or protecting any point threatened within this State."[17]

On August 15, David Stanley's cavalry had complied with Rosecrans' orders. In the absence of Brigadier General Robert Mitchell, the First Cavalry Division, now under Colonel Edward McCook, had ridden from Fayetteville beginning on August 11, and Crook's Second Cavalry Division was supplied and ready to ride from Winchester. Archibald Campbell's First Brigade of the First Cavalry Division was soon riding toward Stevenson, Alabama, with orders to guard the fords on the Tennessee River to his front. By August 18, Campbell reported his various regiments were positioned on the fords.[18]

Minty was riding with Van Cleve on August 16, and Van Cleve watched Minty begin an expedition (to Pikeville) according to Rosecrans' orders. Van Cleve wrote of Minty, "He is certainly an able and efficient officer."[19] Rosecrans was also pleased with Minty's efforts: "Minty's cavalry had a fight with Dibrell's brigade, of Forrest's, at Sparta, on Monday night; whipped and drove them to Yankeetown and Kingston. We lost 15 wounded."[20] While some of the cavalry were performing well, Stanley received a message from Gordon Granger regarding the 5th Tennessee Cavalry: "Colonel Galbraith's command has left Shelbyville. I will send them back in a few days. They are terribly lax in their discipline."[21] Of course, Granger was notoriously for the level of discipline he required and had already alienated many in the Union army.

On August 24, Minty scouted the left flank of Crittenden's XXI Corps near Washington, Tennessee, about 40 miles north of Chattanooga. Minty found two Mississippi infantry regiments consisting of 700–800 soldiers entrenched along the Tennessee River near Blythe's Ferry. Although he was able to drive the pickets before them, he did not engage the infantry. Two days later Minty, exposed on the extreme left flank, was concerned about the Southern infantry moving towards him while Confederate cavalry surrounded him. He withdrew somewhat closer to the rest of the army and was soon urged to move back to the left to protect the flank. Minty and Van Cleve continued to work well together.

Edward McCook commanded Mitchell's division during much of the advance on Chattanooga (Library of Congress).

8. The Advance on Chattanooga and the Battle of Chickamauga

The Advance on Chattanooga
(August–September 1863)

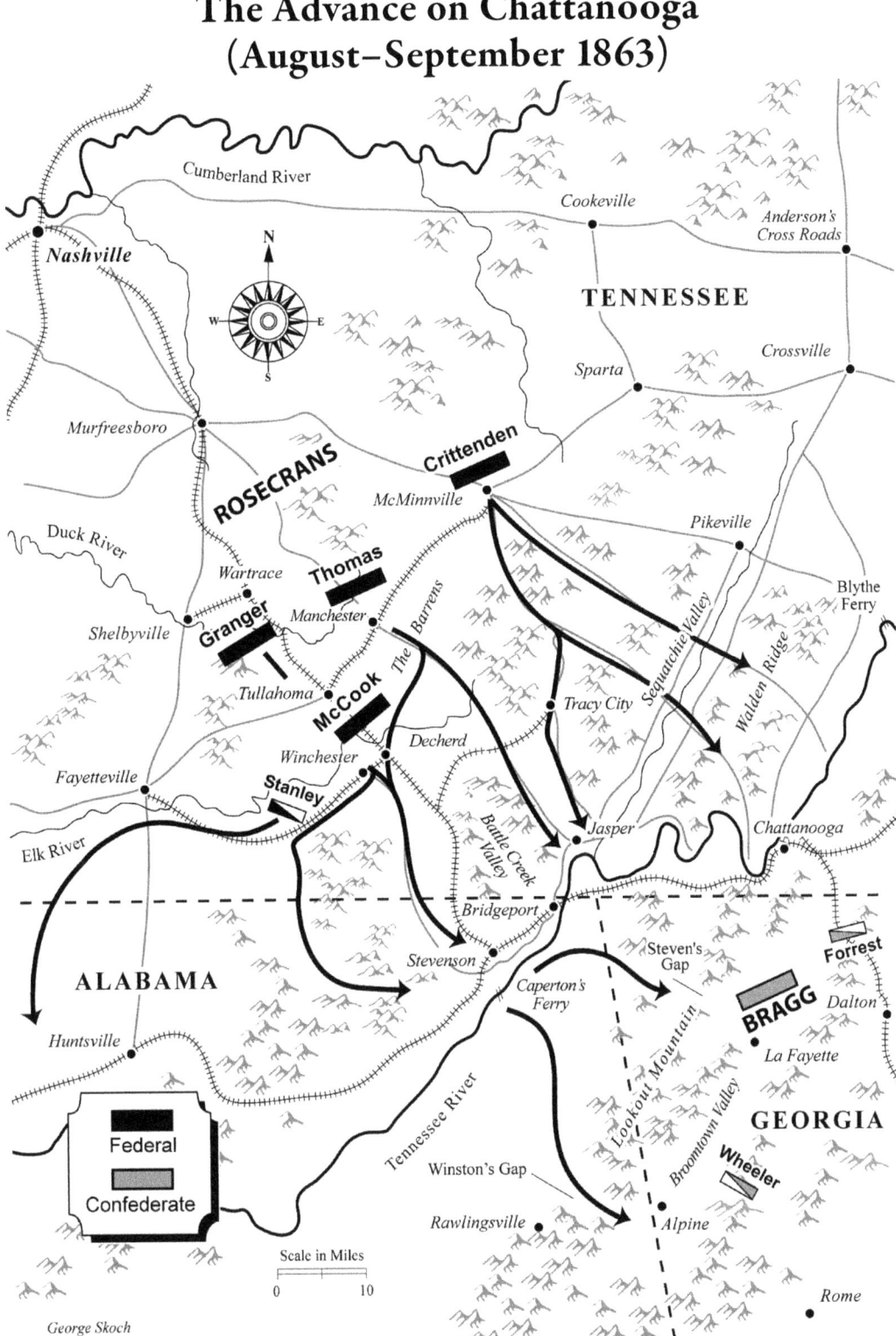

When Minty was urged back to the extreme left flank, Van Cleve came to his defense in a message to Crittenden: "I have every confidence in Colonel Minty's vigilance and judgment, and believe you will be perfectly satisfied with his movements."[22]

On the other flank, Stanley, while dealing with the Confederates to his front, was suddenly faced with Confederate cavalry in the rear, near Winchester and Decherd. At the same time, Colonel Louis Watkins reported he had information at his position in Huntsville, Alabama, that Chattanooga was to be evacuated. On August 26 Colonel Edward McCook confirmed Watkins' report that Bragg was evacuating Chattanooga and the Confederate army was reported to be demoralized.

On August 24, the 4th Indiana Cavalry skirmished with Confederates at a ferry opposite Fort Deposit, and five troopers of the 6th Kentucky Cavalry were taken prisoners by bushwhackers. Two days later, Minty reported the Confederate cavalry was moving on his left, and he lamented the fact he had so much territory to cover he was able to place only 12 pickets on each road. It was especially important now to keep the horses in top condition as, throughout this campaign, the Union cavalry was constantly on the move. It was difficult for the men to handle the routine duties while called upon to be ever in motion. In certain cases the men and horses were pushed to the point of exhaustion.[23]

By August 30, Rosecrans' army crossed the Tennessee River as he advanced on Chattanooga. He ordered Crittenden to start crossing his XXI Corps on August 30 and reported Alexander McCook's XX Corps was already crossing. Wilder and Minty were ordered to cooperate and protect the crossing. The cavalry had been riding constantly for two weeks, and it was beginning to take a toll. Minty had been ordered to aid in the crossing of the XXI Corps, which he agreed to do but lamented. "I trust General Van Cleve will send me the Third Indiana Cavalry the moment it arrives in Pikeville. My scouts traverse about 150 square miles daily, which, together with picketing, makes the duty too heavy on both men and horses."[24] As the infantry corps began their crossing, Stanley ordered the remainder of the cavalry forward to aid in the crossing, even assisting in locating fords.

CAVALRY CORPS—AUGUST 31, 1863[25]

MAJOR GENERAL DAVID S. STANLEY

Escort

4th Ohio Cavalry, Company D, Captain Philip H. Warner

FIRST DIVISION

COLONEL EDWARD M MCCOOK

First Brigade

COLONEL ARCHIBALD P. CAMPBELL

2nd Michigan, Maj. John C. Godley
9th Pennsylvania, Lieut. Col. Roswell M. Russell
1st Tennessee, Lieut. Col. James P. Brownlow

Second Brigade

COLONEL OSCAR H. LA GRANGE

2nd Indiana, Maj. Joseph B. Presdee
4th Indiana, Col. John A. Platter
2nd Tennessee, Col. Daniel M. Ray
1st Wisconsin, Lieut. Col. Henry Pomeroy

Third Brigade

COLONEL LOUIS D. WATKINS

4th Kentucky, Col. Wickliffe Cooper
5th Kentucky, Lieut. Col. William T. Hoblitzell

6th Kentucky, Maj. Louis A. Gratz
7th Kentucky, Lieut. Col. Thomas T. Vimont

Artillery

1st Ohio, Light, section Battery D (2d Brigade), Lieutenant Nathaniel M. Newell

SECOND DIVISION
BRIGADIER GENERAL GEORGE CROOK

First Brigade
COLONEL ROBERT H. G. MINTY

3rd Indiana (battalion), Lieut. Col. Robert Klein
4th Michigan, Maj. Horace Gray
7th Pennsylvania, Maj. James J. Seibert
4th United States, Capt. James B. McIntyre

Second Brigade
COLONEL ELI LONG

2nd Kentucky, Col. Thomas P. Nicholas
1st Ohio, Lieut. Col. Valentine Cupp
3rd Ohio, Lieut. Col. Charles B. Seidel
4th Ohio, Lieut. Col. Oliver P. Robie

Third Brigade
COLONEL WILLIAM W. LOWE

5th Iowa, Maj. Alfred B. Brackett
10th Ohio, Lieut. Col. William E. Haynes
5th Tennessee (1st Middle), Col. William B. Stokes

Artillery

Chicago (Illinois) Board of Trade Battery, Capt. James H. Stokes

September 1863—Missed Communications

Also on August 30, secretary of war Edwin Stanton announced he was sending one of his assistants, Charles A. Dana, to Rosecrans. Earlier in 1863 Dana had been sent to observe Grant during the Vicksburg Campaign. Little did Rosecrans or David Stanley know that the impact of having this person in their midst would affect both their careers in the Army of the Cumberland. Stanton wrote, "Mr. Dana is a gentleman of distinguished character, patriotism, and ability, and possesses the entire confidence of the Department. You will please afford to him the courtesy and consideration which he merits, and explain to him fully any matters which you may desire, through him, to bring to the notice of this Department."[26] The purpose of Charles Dana with the Army of the Cumberland is not fully known, but the army received him as a "bird of ill-omen"[27]

As September began, the Union cavalry corps had a respectable 12,700 troopers present for duty. As the Army of the Cumberland moved closer to Chattanooga, the order of advance was unchanged. Minty operated on the left flank and Stanley and the remainder of the Union cavalry operated on the right. Stanley's second-in-command, Brigadier General Robert Mitchell, was absent and more important, David Stanley had contracted dysentery.

On September 2, Minty recorded activities in conjunction with Burnside's army about 100 miles northeast of Chattanooga. Minty and Van Cleve were watching the fords to insure Bragg did not surprise the left flank north of Chattanooga. Minty patrolled and found the Tennessee River strongly picketed by Confederate cavalry and infantry. Meanwhile, Edward McCook reported his cavalry was ready to cross the river after daybreak on September 3.

On the same day, Stanley was ordered to take Crook's cavalry to Rawlingsville, Alabama, about 50 miles southwest of Chattanooga. The purpose of this movement was to reconnoiter towards Rome, Georgia, to determine the position and strength of Bragg's forces. Parts of Edward McCook's division and Minty's brigades were also assigned to screening duty with the infantry brigades. Major General Alexander McCook and Stanley worked well together, and perhaps this friendship explains a note in McCook's message to Garfield on September 3: "Tell general about distance mentioned in Stanley's letter."[28] McCook, an old classmate of Stanley, supported him in communications to Rosecrans throughout the remainder of the advance on Chattanooga. Stanley's cavalry corps was operating over a wide area, a 150-mile front, and the long reconnaissance stressed the men and animals.

The next day, September 4, Stanley sent a message to Garfield outlining the position of the cavalry and hinted that the distances his cavalry had been requested to ride were unrealistic: "We found the march too long to go through today. As soon as I get the cavalry well together I will move Wheeler. There has been no important information collected today. It is well for the general to know that Winston's is 20 miles from Trenton instead of 10, as the general supposed. My train will not get up to this place until the morning of the 5th."[29] The First Division reported on September 3 Wheeler's cavalry was at Alpine, Georgia, and identified Martin's Confederate cavalry regiments of about 2,000 men between Alpine and Gadsen. He went on to report, "Wheeler has not been at Lebanon or Rawlingsville at all. No infantry in the vicinity of Gadsden."[30]

Robert Mitchell commanded the Union cavalry due to Stanley's illness (courtesy Wilson's Creek National Battlefield; WICR 31630).

Stanley was without an effective second-in-command. Robert Mitchell was on sick leave and missed much of the campaign. General John Beatty recorded in his diary his thoughts about Mitchell's absence: "The papers state that General R.B. Mitchell has gone home on sick leave. Poor fellow! He must have been taken suddenly, for when I saw him, a day or two ago, he was the picture of health. It is wonderful to me how a fellow as fat as Bob can come the sick dodge so successfully. He can get sick at a moment's notice."[31]

On September 3, an important message was sent by Alexander McCook, commander of the XX Corps and Edward McCook's cousin. The purpose of the letter was to define the exact route Garfield had identified for Stanley's advance, but McCook closed his letter with this question: "I hope you are better. Have you any news?"[32] This message is important as a point which identifies the beginning of the illness of David Stanley.

The next two weeks would be detrimental to Stanley's reputation because the illness caused his performance to suffer. If McCook was asking about Stanley's health on September 3, it is likely Stanley had been ill for some days prior to this message. In light of Beatty's message about Mitchell's absence and his inability to command, Stanley felt he could not afford to be sick. Otherwise, the cavalry he had worked so hard to perfect would fall under the command of Mitchell upon Mitchell's return.

On September 4, Alexander McCook's XX Corps was at the base of Lookout Mountain. He reported, "Ed McCook is on my right. Crook with about 600 men is here. My headquarters will be at the mouth of a little gap, about one-half mile from this place. General Stanley will be with me. All goes on well. The rebel cavalry has all moved toward Chattanooga."[33] Stanley and his cavalry caught Thomas' infantry on the morning of September 4, and Alexander McCook's Infantry also opened communications with Thomas the same day. Stanley was in constant communication with McCook, who did an excellent job of keeping Rosecrans informed of the movements of the infantry and the cavalry. Alexander McCook wrote of his positive view of the work Stanley was doing: "I do not know what Stanley's instructions are, but he wrote me that he could carry them out as well on that side of Lookout Mountain. He has 5,800 sabers and can whip all before him."[34]

On the same day, David Stanley reported the efforts of the cavalry and location of the various brigades. Crook's camp was at Winston's Gap about 30 miles southwest of Chattanooga, and Edward McCook had ridden to Rawlingsville. Stanley wrote, "Four miles this side of Rawlingsville a road crosses the mountain, but it is a bad road. The crossing here is also bad; no depression in the mountain. Between this and Easley's are traces every 4 or 5 miles which cavalry may cross, single file. In Broomtown Valley Wheeler's forces have been scattered, but from all I can learn, Martin's force has moved toward Chattanooga."[35] Later that night, Stanley wrote to Garfield that little had occurred but McCook had been unsuccessful in locating the enemy beyond Rawlingsville, discovering only some local home guards but no significant cavalry or infantry presence.

Stanley planned to send a force into Broomtown Valley the next morning. He stated, "This cross-tug of the mountain is said to be the best; it is quite bad; about the same as the mountains at Caperton's Ferry. Distance to Rome, 48 miles; to Dalton, 45 to 50; to La Fayette, 25. Our trains are not up yet; must be guarded."[36] In his message

Alexander McCook, West Point classmate of Stanley, assisted Stanley during the advance on Chattanooga (Library of Congress).

Stanley stressed the distances his cavalry was operating from the main army. When Edward McCook reported later, he said he had reached Rawlingsville and found nothing there. At that time Stanley ordered McCook to move to Winston's Gap unless he found something on his scout. Stanley wanted the cavalry closer to the army after days of fruitless searching at such distances from the main body. McCook reached Winston's Gap by the evening of September 5. Also on September 5, Brigadier General William B. Hazen pulled Minty's cavalry closer to the infantry of the XXI Corps on the left, stating, "There is considerable activity opposite. I am bringing down Minty."[37] Wilder's mounted infantry, which was working in concert with Minty, discovered the Confederate forces north of Chattanooga were withdrawing southward.

While Hazen needed Minty, so did Stanley; but Stanley was not able to convince Rosecrans to allow him to combine the cavalry. Stanley wrote to Garfield: "I do not want to start to interrupt the enemy's communications until Minty joins, unless the general desires me to go sooner. Ask the general to let me know tomorrow by cipher how far I am to regulate my movements by those of the infantry."[38] Garfield responded that the infantry was moving slowly, but he still encouraged Stanley to move 75 miles south of Chattanooga to Rome, Georgia. Garfield wrote to Stanley: "The general commanding hopes that your instructions in regard to the movement on Rome can be successfully carried out."[39] It may never be known the problems which were occurring between Garfield, Rosecrans, and Stanley at this point in the campaign. Stanley appears to be seeking agreement to begin a more aggressive cavalry action, but he felt he needed to have his entire corps together before he did. Rosecrans insisted on continuing with Minty's command of Union cavalry on the left of the army between Knoxville and Chattanooga and the right wing of the cavalry serving to probe and strike at the Confederate communications and supply lines. Thus began four days of conflict between Stanley and Rosecrans that resulted in a severe censure of Stanley.

Edward McCook reported that his reconnaissance on the extreme right of the army found nothing of importance: "The scout has returned from Lebanon; nothing there. We struck their pickets with another scout at Davis Gap, on top of the mountain 10 miles from here, and pursued them to within 6 miles of Alpine, capturing the outposts, a sergeant, and 10 men. Will send them to you in the morning. The brigade stationed at Alpine is Crews, Second, Third, and Fourth Georgia and Fifth Tennessee Cavalry. They have no force south of this."[40] McCook, following Rosecrans' orders, moved toward Rome, and he gladly reported the results of his expedition. The 2nd Indiana Cavalry and the 4th Indiana Cavalry located three regiments of Confederates about twenty-eight miles from Rome and then sent them scattering. McCook recorded that the action "will lead the enemy to think that we have moved in the direction of Rome, and I suppose cause them to send at least part of their infantry from Summerville to re-enforce that place."[41]

The Rome expedition was one of missed communication. Stanley obviously wanted his entire cavalry force together before he raided the Confederate communications in earnest. He said this in his message, and Garfield responded in an uncharacteristically amiable manner. Stanley calmly stated he was going to wait for Minty to arrive, and Garfield, in return, replied Rosecrans hoped Stanley would fulfill his orders. Rosecrans thought Stanley should be destroying the railroad and bridges and wreaking havoc on Bragg's rear. Stanley appeared to be under the impression his objective was to continue to be the eyes for the army and feint toward Rome to screen the real purpose of Rosecrans' advance—Chattanooga. The two were at cross purposes. Stanley was on record of opposing cavalry raids deep behind enemy lines without specific objectives and his reluctance to carry out this raid was evident.[42]

William Sinclair of Stanley's staff wrote McCook on September 5: "The general-commanding desires to know if you have any claw-hooks, crowbars, or any other means of tearing up a railroad track; also have you any torpedoes in your ordnance train—for blowing up railroad bridges, culverts, etc.? If you have not some of these instruments, and cannot make them here, they must be sent for to Stevenson immediately and hurried forward. Make inquiries and reply at once, and if you have not got any of these things and cannot make them, send back tonight."[43] To this message, McCook responded he had no such tools with his command nor any way to obtain them in the field, but he would send for the necessary tools to accomplish the task at hand. He wrote he had a trustworthy man who could get the job done: "He is a man who will not sleep until his mission is accomplished, and will enforce to the letter any order you may give."[44] However, the raid did not take place until September 10, much to Rosecrans' unhappiness, after McCook was able to acquire the tools. Stanley decided to continue with his original plan of waiting for Minty to arrive and delayed the raid.

Meanwhile, for Minty, the Confederate presence on the left flank of the army seemed to have lessened, and the Confederate pickets were moved back south and east. Minty was being stretched along the left flank of the Army of the Cumberland while being asked to cooperate with Burnside's army in Knoxville. Nevertheless Minty was able to maintain good communications and a good understanding of the objectives he needed to accomplish. In response to Stanley's request for orders about striking the Confederate supplies and communications lines, Rosecrans responded on September 6: "The general commanding desires you to. Rush the enemy sharply, and if possible strike the railroad. It will probably be a week before Minty can join you, possibly more, and we cannot wait. The enemy appears to be preparing for making a stand at Chattanooga, and it is of the utmost importance that his line of communication be broken. Forrest and a part of Wheeler's force being in the neighborhood of Chattanooga, you can attack with impunity any mounted force the enemy may have in the direction of Rome and the railroad. The general commanding hopes soon to hear that you have struck a heavy blow."[45] Stanley had to have known he had missed Rosecrans' intent for the cavalry raid, and this message directed Stanley, at last, to shift to an offensive role.

Stanley had realistic expectations for the cavalry which faced Wheeler's and Forrest's cavalries. However, confusion was the order of the day on September 6, and confusion seemed to be taking hold of the entire Union advance on Chattanooga, as explained by historian Major Paul Shelton: "In two hours Rosecrans and Garfield had painted three distinctly different pictures of the enemy. They prompted Sheridan, the demonstrated master of intelligence collection, to find out what was going on. They then tasked Stanley to break the enemy's communications as the Confederates prepared to make a stand. Halleck was told the enemy had concentrated considerable force in the area and left to draw his own conclusion regarding the enemy course of action, and Crittenden was told the enemy was preparing to fall back to Dalton!" Shelton suggests two explanations for these various messages: Garfield and Rosecrans were so exhausted they could no longer keep up with intelligence reports coming into headquarters or they were using projected (anticipated) movements as a basis to deliver orders to the commanders in the field.[46]

Conditions Worsen for Stanley

Alexander McCook was ordered to support Stanley's movement to cut railroad communications between Chattanooga and Atlanta on the evening of September 7: "The general commanding directs you to send one brigade, or such force as may be necessary to hold the mountain pass, to cover the movements of General Stanley, who has been ordered to cut the enemy's railroad communication between Chattanooga and Atlanta. He also directs you to send two brigades, with three days' rations, to Alpine to support General Stanley and cover his return."[47]

Rosecrans again planned for Stanley to strike the rear of the Confederate communications and supply line on September 8 in the large wheeling movement of the Army of the Cumberland designed to capture the Confederate army at Chattanooga. The Union cavalry was important to this movement, but Stanley seemed to be unaware of the plan to close the door on Bragg, preventing his retreat from Chattanooga. Again, Stanley appeared to be puzzled by the order received from Rosecrans to launch a full cavalry raid on Bragg's railroad. His cavalry had been working diligently for three weeks without relief covering a one hundred-mile front. He still had much of his cavalry on duty screening the flanks, and he did not have access to his much-valued Robert Minty and Minty's brigade. Stanley seemed to be pleading that if only Rosecrans knew the correct status of the cavalry, he would not give this order. His response to Garfield on September 7 follows:

David Stanley suffered from dysentery during the month of September before relinquishing command on September 15 (Library of Congress).

I will start in the morning and endeavor to strike the railroad. I regret exceedingly that I cannot have the aid of Minty's brigade, as I deem my present force entirely inadequate to the work to be performed. I fear the general is not aware that I have but thirteen small regiments here, reduced by battalions guarding the Nashville and Huntsville Railroad. To seriously affect the railroad we should be able to hold it for at least half a day. My force is so small that I cannot make proper detachments for striking the road and at the same time fight the force of the enemy. The entire force of Wharton's and Martin's divisions lie between me and the railroad. I will do the best I can. If the general wishes any modification, send a courier through to-night. To make success certain I should have my whole force, Wilder at the same time making a diversion to attract the attention of the enemy.[48]

Garfield replied later that night and denied Stanley's request to wait:

8. The Advance on Chattanooga and the Battle of Chickamauga

> Your dispatch of 10.30 a.m., 7th, is received. The general commanding thinks it practicable for you to make a successful expedition against the enemy's line of communication. Considering the relative strength of the enemy's cavalry and our own, and the additional fact that Forrest's whole force and nearly all of Wheeler's are in the neighborhood of Chattanooga and cannot be brought to bear against you, he has the more confidence in your ability to succeed in the expedition. Even should you fail in thoroughly breaking the railroad, you would at least make a strong diversion in that direction.... The general commanding directs you to push forward rapidly and with audacity. The severing of the enemy's railroad communication with Atlanta will be the most disastrous to him.[49]

Seeking to comply, Stanley ordered Edward McCook's division to prepare to march at daybreak on September 8; but for the first time in his career, Stanley did not move. On the afternoon of September 8 Rosecrans informed general in chief Henry Halleck that the Confederates had not fought at Chattanooga but had evacuated the town, avoiding the trap Rosecrans hoped to spring. Rosecrans' great wheeling movement of his army had missed its prey. He wrote that Stanley and Alexander McCook would be in pursuit the next morning. While Rosecrans calmly wrote to Halleck, he was livid about Stanley's lack of action on September 8, writing him a scathing message:

> The messenger brings nothing from you, but I learn from him that your command lies at the foot of the mountain on this side, intending to move in the morning. I am sorry to say you will be too late. It is also a matter of regret to me that your command has done so little in this great movement. If you could do nothing toward Rome, nor toward the railroad, you might at least have cleared the top of Lookout Mountain to Chattanooga and established a patrol and vedette line along it, which I should have ordered had I not trusted to your discretion, expecting something more important to be done. But what is worse than this, you had peremptory orders to move, which were reiterated yesterday, expecting you would move this morning. It appears that the enemy have sent a large infantry and cavalry force to Alpine. Your cavalry ought to have full control from your position to that place. This you do not appear to have done. Had you gone according to orders you would have struck the head of their column, and probably inflicted on them irreparable injury. So far your command has been a mere picket guard for our advance. Orders accompany this, which I hope to see effectually executed. Let me always hear from you fully.[50]

On September 8 Stanley failed to carry out Rosecrans' direct order that had been sent and then repeated. Stanley replied to Rosecrans in a weak and conciliatory message: "I could not get off this morning on account of deficiency of horseshoes. I am in pretty good trim now, and gain 600 men by delaying today. Crook is on the mountain this evening, and McCook will move at 3 a.m. We should strike Alpine at 11 a.m. to-morrow. Wheeler and Wharton were at Alpine yesterday evening. Martin's headquarters are said to be at La Fayette. I expect to fight them at Alpine. Wharton has with him a full battery. If he can get them on good ground you need not fear the result."[51] After this rebuke from Rosecrans, there was still the question of what was to be the assignment for the cavalry and especially in light of the new information that the Confederates were retreating southward. Rosecrans decided to return the cavalry to the picket duty for which he had just criticized Stanley. The cavalry was again sent to reconnoiter the retreat of Bragg's army.

Several questions arise about Stanley's failure to act. Clearly, Rosecrans was disappointed with him in regard to the expedition to Rome. Edward McCook made the desired raid on September 10 and 11, but was only able to reach to within twelve miles of Rome when he ran into enemy defenders. Rosecrans was irritated with Crittenden as well and had already verbally abused his chief engineer, James S. Morton, who resigned and was replaced with Baldy Smith.[52] It is unclear why Stanley did not advance on the morning of September 8 when orders had been given the night before to prepare for the raid; and Rosecrans was justified in his anger at him. Rosecrans was probably overly harsh when he wrote, "So far your command has been a mere picket guard for our advance." In fact, the cavalry had been assigned just that duty. Rosecrans' criticism may reveal a more deep-seated unhappiness with Stanley, or it may just reveal the pressure Rosecrans faced seeking a deadly enemy in the mountains around Chattanooga. Stanley was clearly ill and it was commendable he was trying to keep the cavalry going. However, if he was too ill to handle the job, it was incumbent on him to step aside. Unfortunately, he had no confidence in Robert Mitchell, who would assume command of the cavalry, and Stanley's ego or will to serve blinded him to the reality that he himself no longer functioned at the level required of a corps commander. In addition, as Stanley asserted in his initial reply and in his apologetic follow-up message, he did not have enough troopers to successfully fulfill the mission.

But Rosecrans had counted on Stanley to aid in the army's "great wheeling movement to bring Rosecrans upon the roads and railroad to Bragg's rear. Crittenden's two brigades before Chattanooga formed the axle, the cavalry under Stanley many miles to the right, the rim. On September 8 and 9, Union cavalry near Alpine, supported by a division of McCook's infantry, swung eastward to Summerville in Broomtown Valley. Alpine lay about twenty miles southerly of La Fayette; Summerville about fifteen miles due south. Both places gave access to the rear of La Fayette, and on roads leading from Broomtown Valley to the railroad in Bragg's rear."[53] Before the Federals could swing into place trapping Bragg in Chattanooga, he had abandoned the town and moved twenty miles south. Although neither Stanley nor Rosecrans was aware of this, Stanley's raid on Bragg's rear might have been for naught; as it was, Rosecrans felt if Stanley had followed orders he would have done great injury to the retreating Confederates.

Stanley was not the only subordinate to incur Rosecrans' ire. General John Beatty had received a tongue lashing in April 1863: "His [Rosecrans] face was inflamed with anger, his rage uncontrollable, his language most ungentlemanly, abusive and insulting. Garfield and many officers, commissioned and non-commissioned, and possibly not a few citizens, were present to witness my humiliation. For an instant I was tempted to strike him; but my better sense checked me."[54] Rosecrans, famous for some of his rages, had never before directed them at Stanley in this manner. Brigadier General George Crook offered his firsthand account of the receipt of the letter rebuking Stanley on September 8:

> Some time in the early part of September, Gen. Stanley, who was in command of all the cavalry, was ordered to make an advance on the enemy, and in case of his retreat to harass him, fall on his flanks and rear, and cut him to pieces, etc. On our march across Lookout Mountain to Broom Corn [sic] Valley we overtook Gen. A.D. McCook's corps, who were destined for the same place. He was halting, resting his men, and we also halted to rest. The officers were together when Gen. Stanley received a letter from Gen. Rosecrans, accusing him unmercifully of procrastination, unnecessary delays, and of wants of appreciation of situation, etc. stating that the enemy was in full retreat, and that instead of his cavalry being on their flanks, destroying them, he had by his delays lost the fruits of all the campaign, etc. Gen Stanley was taken sick. In fact, he was sick then. He was shortly afterwards compelled to go off duty.[55]

The Cavalry Returns to Duty

On September 9, Stanley was back on track. Edward McCook told his commanders to aggressively follow the orders by starting reveille at 2:30 a.m. and to be in the saddle at 4:00 a.m. Stanley sent orders to Crook: "The general commanding directs that you send your two pieces of artillery and ambulances on top of the mountain via Winston's this evening, in order that there may be, no delay in getting speedily over the mountain tomorrow morning, sending with them a battalion of cavalry to act as escort and assist the infantry regiment now on top of the mountain in doing picket duty tonight."[56] After the rebuke by Rosecrans, Stanley was back in control of the cavalry and ready to fulfill his orders.

The cavalry made a reconnaissance to Summerville on September 9 and fought its way through a barricade thrown up by the Confederates at Henderson's Gap. Stanley fought Confederate resistance beyond Alpine through to the Rome Road, claiming a dozen prisoners while losing two men killed and seven wounded. He was also able to capture three dispatches carried by Wheeler's couriers. The cavalry was again in the saddle on September 10, heading towards Rome and capturing Confederate mail verifying Walker's Division was south of Chattanooga. Crook's division determined Bragg's army was concentrating near La Fayette. Colonel Louis Watkins' Kentucky Cavalry brigade also determined Bragg was drawing his cavalry toward La Fayette. Stanley ended his report on September 10: "I have been very sick and confined to my bed all day, but hope to be up to-morrow or next day."[57]

On the left flank of the army, Minty had been probing the Confederates to his front, and he discovered two brigades of Brigadier General John Pegram's cavalry division. Minty was ordered to carefully observe and lightly probe the positions. Minty also determined John C. Breckinridge's infantry was in the vicinity and had joined with Forrest's cavalry. On September 9, Crittenden had entered Chattanooga without any fighting; but Minty was worried the Confederates would cross the river and attempt to gain the rear of the Union army.

On September 10, Garfield ordered Crook's division of cavalry to Bridgeport to protect the Union supply line and to keep the crossings open. Stanley was clearly suffering from his illness by this date. Alexander McCook took over the role of reporting the actions of the cavalry on September 10 and reported Edward McCook was on a reconnaissance toward Rome: "His main body is at Melville, and he has ordered six companies to go to Dirt Town to intersect the road from Summerville to Rome.... I am having the Neal's Gap road opened, which is on the road leading from Valley Head to Broomtown. General Crook was ordered to march on this road but did not do it. I can open the road in a few hours. I heard casually today that your headquarters had been moved to Chattanooga, and have heard nothing from you since leaving Will's Valley. Colonel Watkins' brigade has been ordered to support Harrison and to push through to La Fayette at all hazards. Summerville is 23 miles from Rome and 16 miles from La Fayette. Roads reported good. Rome has lately become a fortified place, occupied now by infantry and artillery."[58]

Rosecrans included his XIV Corps commander, George Thomas, in a verbal censure when on September 10 he wrote though Captain J.P. Drouillard, his aide-de-camp: "The general commanding directs me to say that General Negley's dispatch forwarded by you at 10 a.m. is received. He is disappointed to learn from it that his forces move tomorrow morning instead of having moved this morning, as they should have done, this delay imperiling both extremes of the army. Your movement on La Fayette should be made with the utmost promptness. You ought not to encumber yourself with your main supply train. A brigade or two will be sufficient to protect it. Your advance ought to have threatened La Fayette yesterday evening."[59] No one appeared to be meeting Rosecrans expectations.

With Chattanooga in Union hands, Minty continued to screen and scout on Crittenden's left flank; but things were not going well for Stanley. Alexander McCook continued to cover for Stanley by forwarding a message from Thomas, who was complaining about the want of cavalry and almost writing the orders to achieve the necessary action: "I have just received a dispatch from General Thomas, dated at 8 a.m. this morning (McKaig's Gap, Lookout Mountain), stating that he was working along as best he could, and that he would try to get into La Fayette tomorrow. I would send a courier at once after Colonel Watkins, and order him back to camp, leaving patrols well out on that road. Inclosed you will find an order to Colonel Harrison also to return to camp. I will be much obliged if you will forward it to him with Colonel Watkins' order. I would recommend that you keep your patrols well out, for if the enemy are concentrating at Rome, our troops here are exposed to the entire force of the rebel army."[60] Despite whatever failings Alexander McCook had, he was truly Stanley's friend. Stanley was trying to redeem himself in Rosecrans' eyes. Colonel Edward McCook's division had returned to the area just west and north of Rome. George Crook ordered McCook to "occupy their attention" if he encountered the enemy.

David Stanley's time with the cavalry was over. He was again censured by Rosecrans, in perhaps the harshest tones yet, in Rosecrans' aide-de-camp Major Frank S. Bond's September 12 message in which both Alexander McCook and David Stanley were taken to task: "The general commanding directs me to say that after the most explicit order to connect with and keep open courier lines, he finds that neither your own nor General McCook's headquarters are connected with the headquarters of the department or of General Thomas. He directs me to say there is no military offense, except running from the enemy, so inexcusable as a neglect to keep up communications with headquarters. Our lines are now much extended, and we must husband our resources."[61]

Stanley was so ill he was either unaware of the message or could not respond; however, Alexander McCook struck back on both their behalves. McCook retorted to Garfield that the lack of communication was a result of Rosecrans' headquarters being moved to Chattanooga without informing McCook or Stanley. He went on to put the blame on the Rosecrans' 15th Pennsylvania Cavalry, which served as Rosecrans' courier service, for the delay in informing the army of the movement of headquarters.[62]

The next day, September 13, Stanley sent a message to Garfield: "I am still confined to my bed, and have had to ride in an ambulance today coming over the mountain. Unless I get better I shall have to turn over the command to General Mitchell and go where I can have rest and quiet. General Mitchell is here and will take command of his division in the morning."[63] Rosecrans was increasingly irritated with all his corps commanders. "Thomas used the day to form a defensive position at Steven's and Cooper's Gaps. Rosecrans continued to express irritation with his senior corps commander due to Thomas's lack of information regarding his position and that of the enemy.... McCook ... remained huddled around Alpine," noted Larry Daniel.[64]

On the evening of September 13, Stanley was trying to continue with his duties, reporting Crook's reconnaissance to be within 3 miles of La Fayette attempting to determine Bragg's position and strength. Stanley also reported Colonel Edward McCook's force returned from an unsatisfactory reconnaissance near Summerville and along the La Fayette Road.

Stanley's Illness and Transfer of Command

On September 15, Stanley again wrote to Garfield: "I am so prostrated that I am not able to sit up, and I will this morning turn the command over to General Mitchell, and go to some place where I can have rest and an opportunity to recover my health. I desire to go to Nashville for treatment."[65] Robert Mitchell assumed command of the cavalry and wrote to Garfield on September 15: "General Stanley will go to the rear tomorrow. He is very sick, and I am fearful that he will have a serious time. Give me specific directions with regard to cavalry movements, and I will endeavor to carry them out. The cavalry are badly used up, both men and horses. We have sent today, and will send tomorrow to Stevenson 300 sick soldiers."[66]

David Stanley was not physically transported from the Chattanooga area until September 17. The Battle of Chickamauga began on September 18 and continued through September 20. The result was a decisive Confederate victory, and an important contributing cause of the Federal defeat was an errant order given by Rosecrans on September 20. Major General George Thomas commanded a desperate defense at Horseshoe Ridge and Snodgrass Farm and saved the Army of the Cumberland. After the battle, the Union army withdrew to Chattanooga and began to build defenses. Bragg besieged Rosecrans' forces to the point of starvation. While the battle was being fought and during subsequent actions, Stanley had been moved to a Union hospital and returned home to his family in Ohio while he recuperated from dysentery.

David Stanley was in the army hospital at Stevenson, Alabama, on September 18 when the Battle of Chickamauga began and then he was transported to Wooster, Ohio, where his wife had been staying with Stanley's old teacher, Dr. Leander Firestone. Stanley was fed a milk diet and was able to overcome the effects of dysentery. He was away from the army for about a month. So close was the relationship between Stanley and William Rosecrans that his wife moved to Yellow Springs, which was the home of Rosecrans and where his brother, the Reverend Sylvester Rosecrans, lived.

On October 9, 1863, Rosecrans relieved both Alexander McCook and Thomas Crittenden of their commands. Although the infantry and artillery components of the army were reorganized, the cavalry was untouched. On the next day, Brigadier General James A. Garfield left the army to serve in Congress, and Rosecrans wrote of him: "Brig. Gen. J.A. Garfield has been chosen by his fellow-citizens to represent them in the councils of the nation. His high intelligence, spotless integrity, business capacity, and thorough acquaintance with the wants of the army, will render his services, if possible, more valuable to the country in Congress than with us."[67] While David Stanley detested Garfield, Rosecrans had nothing but high praise for him. Perhaps this is why Stanley had fallen from favor with Rosecrans. Stanley's impression of Garfield might better have been heeded by Rosecrans, who sought to gain political mileage from his chief of staff. Garfield had been the only one of these three men whose career had benefited from their interaction. Military historian, Robert Dalessandro, wrote, "Although generally loyal to Rosecrans, Garfield made the unforgivable military *faux pas* of voicing his displeasure to his friends in Washington, particularly Secretary of the Treasury Chase. Garfield's criticisms of Rosecrans would ultimately be a contributing factor to Rosecrans' relief as army commander."[68]

Stanley still held the position of chief of cavalry for the Army of the Cumberland in October, even though General Robert Mitchell had served in that capacity since Stanley's exit. Mitchell's days were also numbered as chief of cavalry. Mitchell wrote on October 14, 1863, "I am out of rations and my horses are breaking down, but will do the best I can. I am as near a dead man on horseback as you ever saw."[69] A replacement needed to be found, and Henry Cist, acting assistant adjutant general for the Department of the Cumberland, on October 17 wrote, "General Stanley has not yet returned. Do not know where he is."[70] The next day, Mitchell again appealed to Rosecrans to be relieved of duty: "The severe service devolving on me since having been on duty in this arm of the service has rendered the state of my health much worse than formerly, and the chances of my ultimate recovery more remote, and I feel that in justice to myself I should not expose myself any longer as I have been obliged to do for the last four months. When I last saw General R.S. Granger he expressed a desire and seemed very anxious to be assigned to the cavalry command. I should like to see him assigned to that duty."[71] After only a month in command of the cavalry, Mitchell had had enough and sought to give up command.

Major General Joseph Hooker inquired about the cavalry under Mitchell's command on October 18: "I have good reason to believe that Roddey is still on the north side of the Tennessee, and have so informed General Crook in the hope that he will be able to strike his trail, follow, and destroy him. Colonel Stokes was here on the 16th, and informed me that General Mitchell knew but little of the cavalry and its late operations, as he had not been with the command. I don't know how this is."[72] Despite Stanley's failings during this campaign, he had been right in trying to keep the cavalry from Mitchell's control. Subsequently, Mitchell was also taken to task during the court of inquiry of Alexander McCook's actions during the Battle of Chickamauga for failing to move his cavalry to assist in the battle.

Finally, on October 19, 1863, Major General William S. Rosecrans was relieved of command of the Army of the Cumberland and replaced by Major General George H. Thomas. Two days later Brigadier General Washington L. Elliott was ordered to report for duty in Chattanooga, and three days later Elliott was given command of Mitchell's cavalry division. On November 12, 1863, Special Field Orders No. 303 officially relieved David Stanley of command of the cavalry and assigned him to command the First Division of the IV Army Corps, serving under Major General Gordon Granger.[73] Stanley would later write of his demotion: "I did not regret being relieved of the command of the cavalry. It was most unsatisfying and annoying."[74] Stanley's reassignment to the infantry was decided by Major General George Thomas, who had been Stanley's instructor at West Point.[75]

On November 20, Stanley received his first orders as part of the IV Corps. He was given command of the portion of the IV Corps near Bridgeport and would remain there through the Battles of Lookout Mountain and Missionary Ridge, essentially taking no part in these actions. On November 20, Stanley sent a message to the troopers of the Cavalry Corps:

> In parting with you, your late commander takes occasion to express his regrets that the changes of services should separate his fortunes from your own. For a year we have served together most pleasantly, and I am happy to congratulate the Cavalry upon their achievements

8. The Advance on Chattanooga and the Battle of Chickamauga 161

in that time. My poor efforts to render you efficient have been zealously seconded by both officers and men. As to our success, the testimony of our enemies is the more flattering to you, it being forced from them, they now admit you are dangerous and have left material proof of it upon many a field. Though separated from you, I shall serve in the same army with you and shall always water your course with confident pride. Your success and glory is assured.[76]

Stanley had left a strong legacy with the cavalry. He had taken an outnumbered, demoralized group and transformed it into an excellent fighting corps.

Allegations of Stanley's Drinking

An underlying question that shadows Stanley from the Tullahoma Campaign through the advance on Chickamauga is whether he was drinking to such an extent that it impacted his ability to command. On November 20, Charles Dana wrote to the secretary of war:

Brigadier-General Mitchell, just relieved from command of cavalry, Department of the Cumberland, is incapacitated by ill health, resulting from severe wounds, for field service. He will not ask for leave of absence, and desires duty as commander of some post. Thomas

Charles Dana, assistant secretary of war and a "bird of ill omen" (Library of Congress).

has no such command to give him, and would be glad if you could employ him on some board or court. He is a shrewd, energetic man, might be used advantageously on Crittenden and McCook court. Thomas has been much embarrassed by Stanley, who gets drunk and is lazy and careless. Still, he is a major-general assigned to this department by the Administration, and Thomas has not felt himself at liberty to order him away. Accordingly, he has very reluctantly appointed him to command a division. Can I tell Thomas that he must follow his own judgment in such cases?[77]

This message followed Dana's of October 16 that accused Stanley of alcoholism and implicated Rosecrans as refusing to take appropriate action to remove him, therefore jeopardizing the operation of the army. Dana also reported as follows:

> The general organization of this army is inefficient and its discipline defective. The former proceeds from the fact that General R[osecrans] insists on personally directing every department, and keeps every one waiting and uncertain till he himself can directly supervise every operation. The latter proceeds from his utter lack of firmness, his passion for universal applause, and his incapacity to hurt any man's feelings by just severity. It is certain that if it had been left to him, McCook and Crittenden might have lost other battles and fled from other fields without a word of censure. As I have already reported, McCook got from him a whitewashing letter, and Crittenden might have got one had he not been too proud to ask for it. In the same way he gave Negley a similar letter, although he had repeatedly declared that he ought to be shot, and although the official reports of General Brannan, General Wood, and Colonel Harker leave no doubt of his guilt. I learn, on the best evidence, that a few months ago General Stanley defeated an important operation by being drunk at the critical moment, and that he has repeatedly been guilty of that offense while in the discharge of most important duties in the field, yet General Rosecrans has never taken any notice of the fact. He cannot bear to hurt Stanley's feelings, and prefers, instead, to jeopardize the cause of the country.[78]

There is no question David Stanley liked his drink. The shadow of alcoholism would follow him throughout his career, and indeed, from June through September, the cohesiveness of Rosecrans and his chief of cavalry seems to have diminished. Was Rosecrans disenchanted with Stanley's performance in general, was he concerned about Stanley's ability to command being limited through the consumption of alcohol, or did Garfield's meddling cause a breach in the close relationship between the two generals? Stanley did not address his demotion in November 1863 in his memoirs, other than to say he never regretted losing command of the cavalry. He did make a reference to Rosecrans' alcohol consumption however: "He [Garfield] doubtless gave C.A. Dana the information which caused Dana to write defamatory letters about his [Rosecrans] drinking. Dana told me afterwards that the three great scandal mongers were Garfield, T.J. Wood, and Gordon Granger."[79] Stanley's remarks could easily have applied to himself.

What is particularly disturbing is Dana's assertion that George Thomas had lost all confidence in Stanley due to his drinking, and Thomas only reluctantly agreed Stanley would have command of a division in the IV Corps. We have this opinion from Dana, but not from Thomas himself, whose papers were destroyed upon his death. It is also important to note Dana's high regard for Robert Mitchell, who Stanley, Crook, Beatty and Hooker all agreed to be unsuitable for command of the cavalry. Dana, himself was considered a "spy" for the War Department and was admired for his excellent insight as well as hated for his highly judgmental decisions about generals and other matters in the Army of the Cumberland. Stanley's only defense made against this charge was this: "It is frightful to think what havoc a set of scandal mongers who have access to the ears of the officers, may produce. Had not General Thomas known these men were falsifiers, I should have been left out of the reorganization."[80]

The facts show Stanley, a major-general, was placed under the apparent command of Gordon Granger during the Tullahoma Campaign. It was reasonable for the cavalry to work in conjunction with the infantry corps during campaigns. The records also show excellent duty performed by Stanley and the cavalry during the Tullahoma Campaign. In fact, Stanley was much more aggressive than Granger, and Stanley's actions at Guys Gap and in pursuit of Forrest were driven by Stanley's desire to push the cavalry. In addition, Rosecrans put the cavalry at the service of George Thomas. The reason for this appears to have been to shorten communication lines rather than a loss of confidence.

The facts also show Stanley's performance declined after September 5. There has been no reasonable explanation for his not conducting a raid on Bragg's communications on September 8. This seems to have been the only incident Dana could have been referencing when he wrote that Stanley "defeated an important operation by being drunk at the critical moment." If Stanley was so drunk on the evening of September 7 as to be ineffective, then his excellent staff would have directed the cavalry's actions through the equally excellent brigade commanders. No one knows what happened, but it is clear Stanley was not on a binge during this time. Alexander McCook was inquiring about his health on September 3, and even Robert Mitchell reported Stanley was dangerously ill. It is also in Stanley's favor that the account made by George Crook fails to suggest any drunkenness by Stanley. Crook made only one comment regarding Stanley in his entire memoirs, and it referred to his being ill enough to be hospitalized. Stanley was finally admitted to a Union military hospital for dysentery two weeks after he was clearly too ill to command.

David Stanley was a plainspoken man. He minced no words in expressing his dissatisfaction with James A. Garfield. Historian Peter Cozzens described Garfield as chief of staff: "Garfield's colleagues saw him for what he was—an ambitious man who would measure his loyalty to commander by its utility in furthering his political or military career. Few [would be] as taken with Garfield's military abilities as he himself would.... Rosecrans was doubtless impressed by the Ohioans letters of introduction from Chase, and as Garfield's biographer has speculated, Rosecrans probably reckoned the political advantages that might accrue to him from having patronized an officer bound for Congress."[81] Stanley was less critical of Dana; but presumably Dana was more detrimental to Stanley's career than Garfield. Of Dana, Cozzens wrote, "Dana may not have known a cap from a cartridge, but he knew what Stanton wanted. He was to apprise the secretary confidentially on a regular basis of all he saw and heard, to pass judgments freely on the commanding general and his subordinates and their management of the campaign. Clearly, Stanton hoped to use Dana as the instrument of Rosecrans' destruction."[82] "Gordon Granger dismissed Dana as a 'loathsome pimp.' Smith Atkins labeled him as an 'interloper, a marplot, a spy upon rival generals.' "He was received by the army as if he was a bird of evil omen," wrote journalist William Shanks. It was whispered at headquarters that he had come as the spy of the War Department and to find justification for Rosecrans' intended removal. The rumor spread through the army; officers looked upon him with scowls, and the men ridiculed him by pretending to mistake him for a sutler."[83] Dana was not beyond Machiavellian maneuvers of his own in regard to Thomas, "Thomas spelled things out in such excruciating detail for Hooker in large part because Dana had poisoned the waters between the men," wrote Cozzens.[84]

Certainly David Stanley, at some point in his life, grew to dislike Garfield, and Dana did considerable damage to Stanley's reputation. In the 1870s, Dana publicized that Garfield's criticism of Rosecrans contributed to Rosecrans' removal from command of the Army of the Cumberland. In 1880, Garfield wrote in regard to Dana's article that appeared in the *New York Sun*: "I have been told its substance by two or three persons who have seen it. I can only say, in absence of the article itself, that any charge, whether it comes from Dana or any other liar, to the effect that I was in any sense untrue to you or unfaithful to your friendship has no particle of truth in it." It is interesting to note the low regard Dana and Garfield had for each other. Stanley, and Rosecrans, would have been better off without these two men.[85]

Finally, it should be remembered Stanley was a recently converted Roman Catholic, with his spiritual advisor as close as the 4th U.S. Cavalry. Father Trecy was ever close to Stanley and it was noted: "General Stanley was ever remarkable for his truly Christian piety and zeal. Though Father Trecy engaged a kind of moving commission in the army, passing from command to command attending the spiritual duties of the soldiers he had his headquarters with General Stanley." It is very difficult to reconcile these two very different descriptions of Stanley.[86]

The conclusion is that Stanley liked his drink, as did many other generals. Stanley's relationship with Rosecrans in September deteriorated, which could have been a result of excessive drinking. But it could have just as well been a result of Stanley's loss of influence due to the "meddling" of Garfield or even the confusion which was evident at army headquarters. Most likely Stanley's illness reduced his efficiency. His character was stained through two messages sent by Charles Dana, whose role was to provide information to displace Rosecrans. There are no other records to support the allegation of drunkenness, nor are there any specific examples which demonstrated Stanley was not fit for duty due to alcohol. During the Chickamauga Campaign, he made one genuine mistake—failure to attack on September 8. It would be too great a jump to dismiss Stanley as an incompetent drunk based on the unsubstantiated remarks of Charles Dana.

David Stanley wrote a letter to Rosecrans from Cincinnati immediately after the Battle of Chickamauga:

Dear General
   I intended writing to you from Nashville, but did not for the several reasons that I was too ill to sit up to do so, and the affairs of the Army of the Cumberland were yet so critical on the 22nd that I did not know what to think of matters. As the smoke has now cleared off the scene, I can, I believe, consistently congratulate you.... The first news which came to Nashville was most frightful as the true state of the case came in during the night many anxious hearts were relieved—Of course we cannot but regret that we could not have been granted a victory complete; But we had the position and I hope with a little assistance from other sources we may soon take the offensive again.
   The energies the enemy experienced upon us must be lost to him at some other vital point, and after all the accomplishments of the one great end is what we all labor for—
   For the last five days my health has been improving and I think I shall be able to join by the 10th of October perhaps sooner. I go tomorrow to Wooster to my old home where I think I can soon regain my strength in the pure country air.
   I have seen very few people being confined to my room. Upon my return I think I can give you very satisfactory reasons for my delay in moving the cavalry of the right wing further south at an earlier day than I did.

> I shall defer explanation until I rejoin you.
> With much esteem,
> D.S. Stanley Maj. General[87]

Whatever explanations Stanley made to Rosecrans are unknown, but he wrote that he had a reason for his actions during the advance on Chattanooga. Although his explanation was not recorded by either Stanley or Rosecrans, they were such that Rosecrans modified his after action report to give Stanley a favorable report and recognition for the improvement in the cavalry during the past year. From the evidence of the correspondence and actions taken, Rosecrans was unaware of the extent of Stanley's illness. Peter Cozzens wrote an excellent summary of the interactions between Rosecrans and Stanley during the campaign and explained the apparent reconciliation of the two after the battle: "Rosecrans might as well have been lecturing his horse. Stanley's health had taken a turn for the worse, and he was so sick with fever and dysentery that he could barely stand up. Mitchell had not yet reported in, however, and Stanley was apparently unwilling to relinquish command to either of his division commanders. Rosecrans must not have known of Stanley's incapacity, if he had, he presumably would have peremptorily ordered the Ohioan to the rear rather than issue him a reprimand that he was probably too sick to read."[88]

Stanley understood the pressure Rosecrans experienced and he knew how Rosecrans pushed himself. Perhaps this understanding helped Stanley remain so amiable in his relations with Rosecrans. Stanley explained that a commander could push himself only so far, and in describing Rosecrans, he wrote, "Rosecrans habitually used himself badly in time of excitement. He never slept, he overworked himself, he smoked incessantly. At Iuka, at Corinth and Stone [sic] River, the stress of excitement did not exceed a week. His strong constitution could stand that, but at Chickamauga, this strain lasted a month and Rosecrans' health was badly broken."[89] This is supported by others who analyzed the Chickamauga Campaign. Robert Richardson noted Rosecrans was assuming too much direct control over the myriad duties required in commanding the Army of the Cumberland during this campaign. He concluded, "Rosecrans also selected, trained, and poorly utilized his staff officers. The adverse environment within the staff was the responsibility of Rosecrans. However, the inability of his chief of staff to remove the administrative burden from the commander, coupled with the numerous distractions created by the inefficient staff significantly and directly contributed to Rosecrans' loss at Chickamauga." In many ways, Rosecrans and Stanley were functioning in the same manner by taking all the responsibilities on their own shoulders rather than giving up control to their subordinates.[90] Seven days of illness and his failure to hand over command to his subordinates cost Stanley the command of the Union cavalry of the Army of the Cumberland.

Summary

Stanley was haste itself as the Chattanooga campaign began although he was tied to the main body of Rosecrans army under no specific orders. The advance on Chattanooga for David Stanley and his cavalry was truly frustrating. Stanley made serious mistakes during the campaign and the fact he was not alone in making mistakes does not absolve him of responsibility. He performed admirably during the advance on Chattanooga except for a four day period, September 5–8. In his messages, Rosecrans criticized Stanley for two mistakes: failure to strike what was thought to be Bragg's rear on September 8; and failure to communicate with Rosecrans on September 12.

On both September 5 and 8, Stanley stated he needed his entire cavalry, including Robert Minty's brigade, then operating on the left wing of the army. Stanley felt he was outnumbered and when the expedition was finally made Stanley was only able to send two brigades, which would have faced Wheeler's two divisions. He also recalled Rosecrans' previous order regarding Abel Streight's disastrous April-May raid through enemy lines and the results; and Stanley was on record as disapproving of Wilder's raid behind enemy lines during the Tullahoma campaign. If Stanley was going to be part of a Rosecrans-ordered raid, he wanted the best chance he could get; but Rosecrans refused to release Minty to join Stanley. Further, Stanley and Edward McCook did not receive clear instructions on September 5. Stanley's orders were, "General Stanley will send such force from Rawlingsville as he may deem sufficient for the purpose to Rome, Ga., or as far in that direction as practicable, to ascertain the position and intentions of the enemy. This force should push forward with audacity, feel the enemy strongly, and make a strong diversion in that direction."[91] Also, Rosecrans opined that Stanley should have been able to do considerable damage to Bragg's retreating army, but in fact, Bragg's army was not retreating to Rome. Based on his actions, Stanley followed these orders exactly as they were given. He believed he was serving as a feint toward the Confederate rear, just as he had done during the Tullahoma Campaign. Edward McCook's communication also supported this objective when he stated that his presence would surely divert some troops away from Chattanooga. It is clear Stanley was not intentionally acting contrary to Rosecrans' intent, because once he was aware that Rosecrans wanted his troopers to destroy the railroads he ordered Edward McCook to accomplish the task. The attempt to carry out Rosecrans' orders demonstrated a lack of communication and not insubordination.

It is puzzling Stanley failed to follow a direct order to make the raid on Rome on September 8 and there is no doubt this was a direct order. Stanley does not address this in his memoirs, nor does his apologetic message sent on September 8 with the promise to attack the next day offer a satisfactory explanation. The only explanation ever offered was that the horses needed to be reshod. There are no references to a planned cavalry movement on September 8 from any of the Union cavalry reports.

In regard to the lack of communications with Rosecrans on September 12, certainly this was a mistake, but not one that required the intense rebuke he received from Rosecrans. Rosecrans' message to Stanley and Alexander McCook completed a series of harsh messages that included all of Rosecrans' top commanders during the days before the Battle of Chickamauga. As noted previously, one factor in the loss of communication with Rosecrans was that headquarters had been moved without informing McCook or Stanley of the change.

The best explanation for Stanley's mistakes is attributable to his debilitating illness. It is unclear when the illness of dysentery began with Stanley, but Alexander McCook was inquiring about Stanley's health on September 3. The September 21 surgeon's certificate issued when Stanley entered the hospital recorded he had been suffering from his illness for three weeks, thus it commenced on or about September 1.[92] Stanley was so ill he was confined to his bed and had to be moved in an ambulance. Even Robert Mitchell, who was not well liked by Stanley, wrote, "He is very sick, and I am fearful that he will have a serious time."[93]

Stanley had no confidence Mitchell could lead the cavalry in the complex campaign in the mountains around Chattanooga, and he was correct. However, if Stanley ceased to be effective as a commander on September 7, he should have passed command to someone else. His reputation suffered because he would not cede command, and he ultimately was relieved of command as chief of cavalry for the Army of the Cumberland as result. Whether this was ego, animosity, or devotion to duty, his failure to relinquish command was probably his greatest failing in September 1863.

Stanley wrote of the meddling of Garfield in his cavalry corps, and in particular in the selection of the cavalry division commanders. Stanley was successful in having Turchin removed but remained shackled with Mitchell. General John Beatty and others were aware of Mitchell's shortcomings. George Crook was also dissatisfied with Mitchell. Crook recounted his interaction with Mitchell on September 21: "General Mitchell came to me and said, 'General, you are a military man, I wish you would take charge and straighten things out and make the necessary dispositions.... [Later] I was present when Gen. Mitchell made his verbal report to Gen. Rosecrans and to hear him recount the valorous deeds of his command. How he could have the cheek, after what had passed, surpassed my understanding. It was humiliating to see persons wearing the uniforms of general officers to be so contemptible."[94]

William Rosecrans and David Stanley had been working long and hard to make the cavalry arm of the Army of the Cumberland a force equal or superior to that of the Confederate cavalry. The parity of the two cavalries has been recognized by many during the Tullahoma Campaign. Despite Stanley's medical problems for three weeks in September, the Union cavalry was a formidable force and worked diligently in August and September 1863. Rosecrans criticized Stanley for the limited action of the cavalry, alleging it has served as a "mere picket guard" for the Army of the Cumberland. In fact, Rosecrans was criticizing Stanley for doing the duty Rosecrans had ordered his cavalry to do. Stephen Starr agrees in his *The Union Cavalry in the Civil War,* "The duties given General Stanley and the bulk of the cavalry—five of the six brigades of the Cavalry Corps—go a long way to justify Stanley's previously quoted opinion that Rosecrans 'had no idea of the use of cavalry.'"[95] Rosecrans' campaign report stated, "The cavalry for some reason was not pushed with the vigor nor to the extent which orders and the necessities of the campaign required. Its continual movement since that period and the absence of Major-General Stanley, the chief of cavalry, have prevented a report which may throw some light on the subject."[96]

In John Londa's analysis of the Union cavalry during the Chickamauga Campaign, he asserts the Union right wing of the cavalry was less successful than the left, which was commanded by Minty. He concludes the efforts of the right wing should have been more aggressive and Rosecrans was right to chastise Stanley on September 8 for his lack of action. He also states the "problems that the cavalry suffered through were in a large measure caused by the initial plan for the cavalry's employment.... Rosecrans preferred to give directions rather than missions. He robbed the commanders of the latitude to make decisions on the employment of their forces.... The blame of the dispersal of the Cavalry Corps must rest with Rosecrans."[97]

Stanley never produced an official report for the cavalry during this campaign. Rosecrans reconsidered his initial report in January 1864 and rewrote his report of the actions of the cavalry. Whatever demons had possessed Rosecrans and Stanley during the campaign had departed. Of the cavalry and of Stanley, Rosecrans' reconsidered reported noted as follows:

> I cannot forbear calling the special attention of the General-in-Chief and the War Department to the conspicuous gallantry and laborious services of this arm. Exposed in all weather, almost always moving, even in winter, without tents or wagons, operating in a country poorly supplied with forage, combating for the most part very superior numbers, from the feeble beginnings of one year ago, when its operations were mostly within the infantry lines, it has become master of the field, and hesitates not to attack the enemy wherever it finds him. This great change, due chiefly to the joint efforts of both officers and men, has been greatly promoted by giving them arms in which they had confidence, and by the adoption of the determined use of the saber.
>
> To Maj. Gen. D.S. Stanley is justly due great credit for his agency in bringing about these results, and giving firmness and vigor to the discipline of the cavalry. It requires both nature and experience to make cavalry officers, and by judicious selections and promotions this arm may become still more useful and distinguished.[98]

9

The Atlanta Campaign

Gen'l Stanley has taken the corps, and I don't believe there is a general in the army thought any more of by his troops than General Stanley.

When David Stanley assumed command of the First Division of the IV Corps, he was satisfied with his assignment. A professional soldier, he landed on his feet and found himself commanding veteran soldiers of twenty infantry regiments. He recounted a story while posted at Stevenson:

> Now we had amongst the Kentucky and Ohio officers, a pretty gay set, and one night they sat up drinking whiskey toddies long after they should have been in bed. Finally getting out in the air, they investigated the horizon and discovered a fire on Sand Mountain. In their condition this fire seemed to them to wag, and so they finally came to my cabin, woke me up, and informed me that the enemy were signaling and no doubt intended to attack. They thought I had better send for our signal officer and see if he could take their message. "Don't you see," said one of them, "There they go—7, 14, 14, 22, don't you see it?" Here one of my sides [aides] who had been awakened, called out, "General that light [is] the log fire of one our videttes, it is the heads of those follows [fellows] that are wagging; they cannot see straight, and their boozy condition converts a log fire into a swinging torch." And such was the truth.[1]

Stanley was getting his sense of humor back and was ready to meet the new year commanding an infantry division of veterans.

Stanley's division included veteran regiments from several states and his commanding officer was Major General Gordon Granger, a man Stanley knew well. Stanley's three brigade commanders were Brigadier General Charles Cruft, Colonel Jesse Moore, and Colonel William Grose. Stanley commanded about 8,500 soldiers, present for duty, in his new assignment. The Second Division commander was Brigadier General Phil Sheridan, Stanley's old West Point classmate, and the Third Division commander was Brigadier General August Willich, a Prussian by birth and late colonel of the 32nd Indiana Infantry. Stanley was ordered to move his division from Bridgeport to Blue Springs, Tennessee, during the winter months of 1864, and he remained headquartered there until May 1864 when the Atlanta Campaign began. During the winter Stanley marched his division to Cleveland, Tennessee, and "converted a flat topped mountain into a strong fort."[2]

FOURTH ARMY CORPS[3]
MAJOR GENERAL GORDON GRANGER
First Division
MAJOR GENERAL DAVID S. STANLEY

First Brigade

BRIGADIER GENERAL CHARLES CRUFT

21st Illinois, Maj. James E. Calloway
38th Illinois, Capt. William C. Harris
29th Indiana, Lieut. Col. David M. Dunn
31st Indiana, Col. John T. Smith
81st Indiana, Lieut. Col. William C. Wheeler
1st Kentucky, Col. David A. Enyart
2nd Kentucky, Lieut. Col. John R. Hurd
90th Ohio, Capt. Nicholas F. Hitchcock
101st Ohio, Col. Isaac M. Kirby

Third Brigade

COLONEL WILLIAM GROSE

59th Illinois, Lieut. Col. Clayton Hale
75th Illinois, Col. John E. Bennett
80th Illinois, Lieut. Col. William M. Kilgour
84th Illinois, Col. Louis H. Waters
9th Indiana, Col. Isaac C.B. Suman
30th Indiana, Capt. Joseph W. Whitaker
36th Indiana, Lieut. Col. Oliver H.P. Carey
24th Ohio, Lieut. Col. Armstead T.M. Cockerill
77th Pennsylvania, Capt. Joseph J. Lawson

Second Brigade

COLONEL JESSE H. MOORE

96th Illinois, Col. John C. Smith
115th Illinois, Col. George A. Poteet
35th Indiana, Col. Bernard F. Mullen
84th Indiana, Maj. Andrew J. Neff
8th Kentucky, Capt. Coleman D. Benton
21st Kentucky, Col. Samuel W. Price
40th Ohio, Col. Jacob E. Taylor
51st Ohio, Maj. David W. Marshall
99th Ohio, Lieut. Col. John E. Cummins

Artillery

CAPTAIN PETER SIMONSON

Indiana Light, 5th Battery, Lieut. Alfred Morrison
4th United States, Battery H, Lt. William H. Heilman
4th United States, Battery M, Lt. George W. Dresser

Stanley took interest in the welfare of the citizens around Cleveland, Tennessee. He wrote to Granger about the situation of Confederate raiders attacking civilians and asked that the Confederate authorities be contacted to reduce the destruction:

> I have the honor to address you for the purpose of calling the attention of the general commanding the department to the sad condition of the inhabitants of the belt of country lying between our lines and the lines of the Confederate forces south of us. These people are divided in sentiment, some adhering to the Confederate cause, many more professing Union sentiments. The latter are the subjects daily of gross outrages at the hands of Confederate soldiers, being driven from their homes and having their houses and buildings destroyed. Two cases of burning Union men's houses have occurred within a few days; one, a Mr. Lusk, near Red Clay, the other, a Mr. Southerland, near Spring Place. From all I can learn this was done in a spirit of wantonness, and although I cannot say by the orders of any Confederate officer, a very considerable body of Confederate troops were present. I would respectfully suggest that this matter be made the subject of a communication to the commander of the Confederate forces at Dalton, as I have every confidence that he would promptly exert his authority to suppress this needless and wanton vandalism.[4]

Eastern Tennessee had strongly supported the Union since the beginning of the war, but the Confederate raiders made life difficult for those supporters.

While the area around Blue Springs, Tennessee, was being fortified, a court of inquiry had been convened regarding Major General Alexander McCook's actions at the Battle of Chickamauga. Both Brigadier General Jefferson C. Davis and Stanley were summoned to appear at the inquiry. Thomas and Grant both wanted these generals in the field. Thomas wrote on February 15, "I have been considerably embarrassed by having Generals Stanley and Davis summoned before the McCook court of inquiry, just at this time; but if it continues to rain through the day, as it did all night, I think nothing will be gained by starting just yet. In the meantime, Stanley and Davis can get back by Wednesday."[5] The record of the inquiry did not include testimony from Stanley, who had not been present during the battle.

On March 9, Grant met with President Lincoln at the White House, received his promotion, the rank of lieutenant general, and was made general in chief of all the Union armies. When Grant received his new command, he selected Major General William T. Sherman to succeed to command of the Military Division of the Mississippi, which gave Sherman command of the Union armies in the west. Sherman made several command changes, and Gordon Granger was relieved of command on April 28 of the Fourth Army Corps. Sherman wrote of his reasons for relieving Granger: "General [Granger] has notified me that he has a sixty days' leave from the War Department, of which he proposes to avail himself now, and that he is willing to give up his corps. I would therefore ask that a new corps commander be appointed for the Fourth Corps."[6] Granger's removal from command was not what it appeared to be in Sherman's communication and the real reason was explained by historian Larry Daniel: "Sherman next went after the profane and hard-drinking Granger, who so irritated him with his grousing and lethargy in chasing Longstreet past Knoxville that he determined to be rid of him."[7] To command the IV Corps, Sherman, in consultation with the Army of the Cumberland's commander, Major General George Thomas, selected Major General Oliver O. Howard, who had lost command of the XI Corps when Sherman consolidated the XI and XII corps into the new XX Corps. Stanley's new commander was devoutly religious, a teetotaler nicknamed the "Christian General." If alcohol was a problem for Stanley, Howard might be the best commander Stanley could have to help moderate his habits.

In late April 1864, David Stanley was informed his third daughter, Anna Huntington Stanley, had been born at

O.O. Howard, the "Christian General," commanded the IV Corps during the first part of the Atlanta Campaign (Library of Congress).

Wilkes-Barre, Pennsylvania. To everyone's relief, both Anna Stanley and daughter were well after the birth.

For the Confederates, Braxton Bragg resigned after his defeat at Missionary Ridge. In December 1863, General Joseph Johnston was given command of the Army of Tennessee, then in camps around Dalton, Georgia. Johnston was shocked at the condition of the Southern army and immediately began to rebuild it by improving discipline, rations and supplies, and granting furloughs. In March, newly promoted Lieutenant General John Bell Hood, having recuperated over the winter in Richmond from his Chickamauga wound and made himself more familiar to important people, including President Davis, joined the Army of Tennessee. This brought an aggressive, combat-proven officer to that army, but it would cause resentment among the officers who had long served in the west and hoped for a corps to command themselves.

On March 19, as Grant and Sherman traveled by train north from Nashville, they discussed the overall plan for the coming spring campaigns. Grant would direct the several armies in the east towards destruction of Lee's Army of Northern Virginia, and Sherman would focus the Federal forces in the west on destruction of Johnston's Army of Tennessee. To this end, Sherman began assembling around Chattanooga the force that he would lead against Johnston. By far the largest was the Army of the Cumberland under George Thomas: 62,000 infantry, including Stanley's division, and 10,000 cavalry. From Kentucky and eastern Tennessee, Sherman brought the newly reconstituted Army of the Ohio, under Major General John Schofield, consisting only of the XXIII Corps with 11,000 infantry, many of whom had far less combat experience than Thomas' men, and 2,000 cavalry. From Mississippi, Sherman was able to bring only part of the Army of the Tennessee, under Major General James McPherson, with 24,000 infantry but no cavalry. Sherman had chosen McPherson as his successor, but a substantial portion of Sherman's favored army had to remain in the Mississippi Valley to garrison Memphis and Vicksburg, protect against Confederate cavalry raids, and participate in the Red River Campaign.

Sherman's specific plan was for part of his force to fix Johnston's Confederates in place near Dalton while another part of his force swung to the west and south through Snake Creek Gap to cut Johnston's railroad supply line at Resaca. To occupy Johnston, Sherman had Thomas' Army of the Cumberland, including Stanley, approach Dalton from the northwest and Schofield's Army of the Ohio approach from the north, while McPherson's Army of the Tennessee was chosen for the envelopment through Snake Creek Gap. As the campaign began, Stanley had a new commander for his second brigade, Brigadier General Walter Whitaker. Whitaker, a Kentuckian and past colonel of the 6th Kentucky Infantry, had been in several fights and had been wounded during the Battle of Stones River, at Chickamauga and at Chattanooga in November 1863.

The IV Corps left Catoosa Springs on May 7 and, as the corps approached Tunnel Hill, Stanley's First Division advanced on the right and Newton's Second Division on the left with Thomas Wood's Third Division in reserve. Howard wrote, "Steadily our men pressed forward, driving back first the Southern cavalry pickets and outer lines till, awakening opposition more and more, about nine o'clock our foe crowned Tunnel Hill with considerable force and fired briskly upon our advance. The same angry reception was given to the Fourteenth Corps, coming up simultaneously southward beyond our right. Then I saw that the Confederate artillery had only cavalry supports, so that immediately I ordered a charge along our lines. Our troops promptly sprang forward and carried the 'crowned hill.'"[8] After taking Tunnel Hill, Rocky Face Ridge could be seen in the distance, a formidable ridge over 500 feet high.

The next day, Sherman pushed his armies forward. McPherson's Army of the Tennessee was pushing south and east toward Resaca, the Army of the Cumberland was pushing slowly forward in a diversionary role and Major General John Schofield's Army of the Ohio was pushing the Union left toward Dalton. As Howard advanced the IV Corps on May 8, General Newton's Second Division was able to get a brigade to the top of Rocky Face Ridge about two miles north of Buzzard's Roost Gap. Newton's men surprised the Confederates posted on the ridge and claimed about a third of the Confederate position. Howard recorded, "Stanley and Wood, on Newton's right, stretched out their own lines to some extent, and gave Newton all the support they could in that difficult ground near the west palisades of the ridge. During the night his men dragged up the steeps two pieces of artillery, and by their help gained another 100 yards of the hotly disputed crest."[9]

While Newton was approaching the Confederates along the ridge, Stanley marched his First Division to within 400 or 500 yards of the west face of Rocky Face Ridge. Stanley's division was pelted with fire from the Confederates at Buzzard's Roost Gap and along the ridge. Brigadier General Jefferson C. Davis' XIV Corps division attacked the defenders at Buzzard's Roost Gap in the afternoon and Stanley added the support of his artillery under Captain Peter Simonson, a highly regarded commander. On the next morning Stanley's skirmishers pushed ahead and skirmishing continued throughout the day. In the evening, Stanley was ordered to advance against the strong enemy positions in the gorge at Buzzard's Roost. He selected Colonel Thomas Champion, 96th Illinois, and Major Andrew Neff, 84th Indiana, to lead the movement toward the enemy positions. Stanley noted, "Our men drove the rebels quickly to their main lines, and pushed up to the foot of the perpendicular rocks of the mountain and maintained themselves until night, when all but the pickets were withdrawn. The fire of the enemy was severe, much of it coming almost from overhead."[10]

Howard recorded the difficulty of making the advance on the ridge. He also recorded a near miss as he, Stanley, and Captain G.C. Kniflin were planning the assault: "On May 9th another experiment was tried. Under instructions I sent Stanley's division for a reconnaissance into that horrid gap of Buzzard's Roost, until it had drawn from the enemy a strong artillery fire, which redoubled the echoes and roarings of the valleys and caused to be opened the well-known incessant rattle of long lines of musketry."[11] Howard recalled the officers thought they were beyond the range of the enemy sharpshooters, but they were soon surprised. A shot rang out and a bullet passed through the group of officers, narrowly missing them. Howard had holes in the back of his coat, then the bullet went through Captain Kniffin's hat and finally struck a tree nearby. The group quickly found a safer location to discuss strategy

In addition to the near miss with Howard, Stanley again had a close call, much to the amusement of some of his soldiers. First Lieutenant Chesley Mosman, 59th Illinois Infantry, recorded Stanley and his staff rode forward to observe the Confederate defenses when they became the targets of musket fire from the enemy. The staff quickly dispersed and Mosman recorded, "Gen. Stanley was run into a thicket, and he kept kind of shady (out of sight) till out of range. But oh my, didn't the boys enjoy the scattering of that staff. They just fairly shook with laughter at the ludicrous performance."[12]

On May 11, Stanley relieved Davis' division, which was in position around the entrance of Buzzard Roost Gap, but little Confederate activity had been noticed throughout the day. Stanley probed forward that evening with his First Brigade, commanded by Brigadier General Charles Cruft. Stanley's infantry sent skirmishers forward and pushed the enemy's entrenched pickets back, only to be greeted with heavy fire from infantry and artillery. Stanley moved his infantry to within 600 yards of the enemy and began constructing defenses. Stanley recorded, "During the 12th we watched the enemy closely, the Fourth being the only corps before Dalton. Early on the morning of the 13th we learned the rebels had left their works."[13] Johnston, fearing he would be cut off by maintaining his position, withdrew southward on the evening of May 12. In possession of Buzzard's Roost and Rocky Face Ridge, Stanley placed some artillery on the ridge the next day and began bombarding what he thought were the Confederates positions in the valley on the other side of the ridge.

Stanley's First Division entered Dalton on the morning of May 13 to find the town deserted but the railroads intact. The Union army would soon use the town as a supply depot. Stanley was grateful for the movement threatening Johnston's rear because of the strength of the defensive position at Dalton. He wrote, "I do not see how we could have forced his line at Dalton. It was the strongest military position I saw during the war."[14] After leaving Dalton, the Confederate troops rushed to Resaca to prevent Sherman from gaining their rear. Stanley later complained Sherman would have been more successful if he had sent the Army of the Cumberland toward Resaca because of the larger number of troops. Nevertheless, Stanley pressed hard after the retreating Confederates toward Resaca.

The Battle of Resaca

Stanley encountered only a few Confederate pickets to slow his march. By the evening of May 13, he camped nine miles south of Dalton, but being cautious his troops slept in battle line with their back to Rocky Face Ridge. The pursuit continued the next day and the First Division proceeded toward Resaca, a small town on the north side of the Oostanaula River, bordered by the Conasauga River to the east. As Stanley marched southward he formed the eastern most flank of the advancing Union army and because there were no other troops near, the march was easy and unencumbered. By 2:00 p.m. Stanley's three brigades had formed a battle line about two miles north of Resaca. Being the left flank of the army, Stanley began to build defenses and had orders to hold the line along the Dalton Road. Thomas Wood's division soon fell into line, connecting with John Newton's division on his right flank, while Stanley's First Division continued to maintain its position on the extreme left flank. Stanley placed Cruft's brigade on the left of his line connecting with the Dalton Road and instructed the troops to begin entrenching. Before the defenses were completed, Stanley observed Confederate infantry massing for an attack. He wasted no time in reporting his observations to the IV Corps commander, Howard, who rode in person to George Thomas to report the situation. Wisely, Stanley withdrew his artillery commanded by Captain Peter Simonson to a position that would cover the open ground in front of his lines.

Stanley's transition back to divisional command of infantry had been smooth and he was again loved by his troops. On May 14, he would need all his leadership abilities and his troops' regard during the Battle of Resaca. He was in a dangerous position, being on the

Hood's Attack on Stanley's Division (Battle of Resaca)

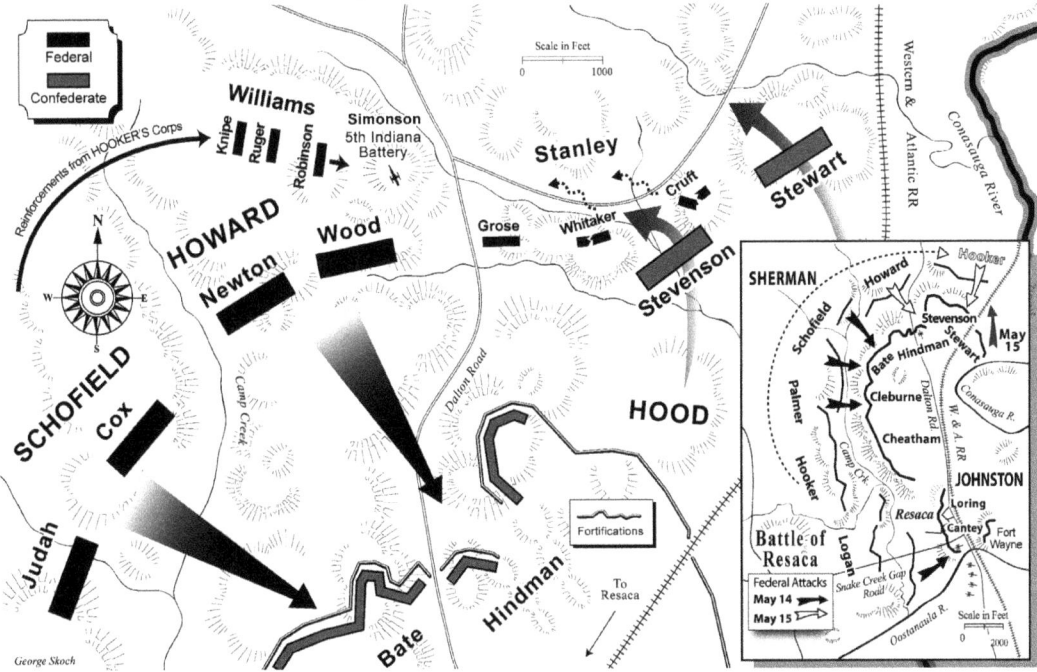

exposed flank that the Confederate cavalry had reported as vulnerable, offering Johnston an opportunity to attack. Historian Albert Castel, author of *Decision in the West*, wrote "there is another Union division commander who is facing a far greater immediate danger than Sweeny. He is Major General David S. Stanley of the IV Corps, whose 'splendid presence' causes his troops to refer to him proudly as 'Our Stanley.' Stewart's and Stevenson's divisions move out of their works and formed a double line of battle. As they did so, two of Walker's brigades came up from the south side of the Oostanaula.... Johnston is putting everything he can into this attack, which by good fortune, will be conducted by the best general in the Confederacy for such an enterprise: Hood of Gaines' Mill, Hood of Second Manassas, Hood of Antietam, Hood of Chickamauga."[15]

Castel also wrote that Stanley was "capable, steady, and certainly experienced enough to know what to do when scouts bring word that the Confederates are massing in large numbers on his front and flank; he sends a courier to Howard to notify him of the impending assault, and he orders his chief of artillery, Captain Peter Simonson, to post the six Napoleons and Rodman cannons of the 5th Indiana so as to cover the rear of Cruft's brigade on the extreme left."[16]

As Stanley was being flanked, he attempted to make his line as long as possible by stringing his men in a single file. He even had large spaces between his regiments. He was greatly outnumbered and was being approached on three sides by long lines of Confederates that swept over and past Cruft's and Whitaker's defensive positions when the attack began. Some regiments broke immediately and others held on, but the sea of gray was too much. The attack on Stanley's division began about an hour before sundown and perpendicular to his line. Stanley recalled the following:

The Thirty-first Indiana, stationed upon the round-topped hill, found itself fired into from three directions. They did the best they could under the circumstances; they got out of the way with such order as troops came hurrying through a thick brush. Directing their attack more to our rear than flank, the One hundred and first Ohio and Eighty-first Indiana were soon driven back, and the enemy was bursting exultingly upon the open field when Simonson opened on them with canister, which soon broke and dispersed that attack. The enemy formed in the woods and attempted to cross the open field again, but met the same savage shower of canister.... The broken regiments of the First Brigade had reformed near the battery.... The troops of the brigade did as well as could be expected, situated as they were. Attacked in flank, and greatly outnumbered, they could only get out of the way the best they could.[17]

Three brigades of Confederate Major General Carter Stevenson's division broke through Stanley's line and claimed the trenches Cruft's and Whitaker's brigades had been preparing. Once they regrouped they pressed into the vulnerable Union flank. As they streamed through a wooded area onto the open field, Simonson's artillery opened up on the mass of Confederate attackers. Simonson's six cannons were located at the other end of a field about a half mile away and they were pouring shells into their Confederate targets. So effective were Simonson's barrages that the artillery became the next targets for Stevenson's brigades. As they ran for the guns, Simonson's men continued to pour the shells into the advancing line and as they got closer Simonson switched to canister causing a devastating effect. Stanley was with Simonson urging him to keep the firing going. The effect of the canister was terrible: "Simonson, realizing that they will be sure to make another charge, rapidly turns his pieces in that direction.... Soon Stevenson's troops emerge from the forest, advancing at a quick pace. Simonson's gunners double-shot their cannons with canisters, then fire, reload and fire again with a speed that an Illinois infantryman finds 'marvelous to witness.' Each salvo tears holes in the ranks of the attackers, who waver, then turn and run back into the forest, ignoring the pleas of their officers to keep going. Six cannons have repulsed 5,000 infantry."[18] The surgeon of the 40th Illinois Infantry, John Beach, wrote, "The writer was in position to witness the exciting scene, and until then, had no conception how rapidly guns could be fired. As the stream of fugitives from the front came drifting back to the left of the battery, closely followed by the enemy in overwhelming numbers, the six guns were brought

Union artillery played a key part in Stanley's success in maintaining the Union left flank at Resaca (Library of Congress).

into action, and for a half an hour there was almost a continuous stream of fire from their muzzles, hurling grape and canister, a fire so hot and steady that the enemy halted."[19]

After the barrage of Stanley's artillery, the Confederate infantry began to re-form and again headed for the Union line, knowing they still had the same cannons to face. The last attack began at twilight. Stanley was aware he had, through sheer brashness and the skill of some brave artillerymen, temporarily averted disaster. He rode among Simonson's artillerymen encouraging them to hold on for a few more minutes, exclaiming reinforcements were on the way and they were the last hope of the Union left flank. As Stanley finished his encouragement to the troops, long lines of blue infantrymen were seen rushing to their defense. Hooker had dispatched his best fighting division under Brigadier General Alpheus Williams to Stanley's aid. What the Confederates had so desperately tried to avoid was becoming reality. Seven thousand fresh, battle-hardened Union soldiers were reinforcing the Union flank. Albert Castel wrote, "The Confederates rush forward. One of them, shooting into their flanks, yells at a small group of Stanley's troops, 'We don't care anything about you; we are after that battery!' Simonson's cannons belch forth canister even faster than before, but the gray mass keeps coming. Then, just as it seems the battery will be overrun. William's lead brigade arrives and, in the proud words of its commander, Colonel James S. Robinson, puts on a display of the 'Army of the Potomac fighting.' Its five regiments are formed in as many ranks. At Robinson's order the first rank fires a volley and drops to the ground, the second does the same, and so do the third, fourth, and fifth. Shocked, staggered, and shredded, the Confederates turn and flee."[20] Stanley understated the intensity and danger of the battle in a message to Edward McCook: "Had a brash little fight this p.m., and by the timely arrival of General Williams' division saved our left from being turned. Keep a sharp lookout on our left."[21] There is little doubt the timely arrival of Williams' infantry secured the Union line, which had been in peril of collapsing.

As the battle was being fought, Stanley was talking with Brigadier General William Grose, commander of the Third Brigade, about the disposition of his troops and observed the death of one of his officers. As the two generals were talking, another officer nearby was struck with grape shot between his shoulders. Stanley recalled, "It knocked him down and he gave an exclamation of pain and yet the skin was not broken. He was carried to the rear and died of this contusion."[22]

Howard wrote his approval of how Stanley handled the battle against Hood. It was hoped the Union left flank would be able to form a solid line with the Conasauga River on the east, but the river was too far away. As a result, Stanley's division formed a vulnerable left flank. Howard wrote, "It was quite impossible for my left regiments to reach that river, so that, after examining the ground, I was again forced to have the left of my line 'in the air.' But Stanley's excellent division stationed there, by refusing (drawing back) its left brigade and nicely posting its artillery, formed as good an artificial obstacle against Hood as was possible."[23]

Stanley had followed Howard's orders before the battle but Howard did not know the terrain. Stanley had been expected to provide a connection to the Conasauga River but also needed to connect with the Union line to his right. There was nothing Stanley could use as an anchor for the end of his line. Howard, seeing what was impossible for Stanley to accomplish, wrote, "The bend of the river was so great that an entire corps, thrust in, could hardly have filled the opening."[24]

Howard noted the loss was severe from Hood's attack with about 400 killed or wounded. The IV Corps commander was grateful to Joseph Hooker and Alpheus Williams, who came to his support. Howard rode to Hooker's headquarters the next morning and paid his respects. Hooker and Howard coordinated the alignment of their corps and Howard vowed to support Hooker in any way he could.[25]

The Battle of Resaca was the first major conflict in the Atlanta Campaign, and though Stanley had little to say about the battle, his experience saved the day. Visions of Chancellorsville, where Howard's XI Corps had been overwhelmed, and Chickamauga, where Union flanks collapsed, came to mind. Stanley was placed at the end of the Union line with his "flank in the air," and Johnston took advantage of it. He had faced a similar situation during the advance on Corinth in May 1862 when his division was assaulted by Confederate infantry. Having faced the same situation as before, he reacted in the same manner at Resaca by directing his artillery to slow the enemy's attack until he could piece together a suitable defensive line and await reinforcements. This was a gutsy call and required considerable composure to watch rows of advancing enemy soldiers with nothing to stop them but six cannon. While Stanley was not happy that two of his brigades broke, he was greatly outnumbered by Hood's soldiers that had flanked his line. Stanley remained on the field encouraging his troops, and providing the leadership needed to insure the flank did not collapse.[26]

After the battle on May 14, Stanley reestablished his line and fully fortified his division. The artillery fired throughout the night. The two sides continued to fire throughout the next day. At 11:00 a.m. the next day, Johnston again demonstrated against Stanley's line, only to be greeted with a "general discharge of cannon and muskets along the whole line. Soon after, early on the morning of the 16th, it was found the enemy had evacuated under cover of the night," observed Stanley.[27] Hooker's corps had reinforced the Union left flank and the Union attacked on May 15 but made little progress. However, over the night of May 15–16, Johnston had retreated across the Oostanaula River, leaving Resaca to the soldiers in blue.

Although the Union army fought to a draw at Resaca, the morale of the army was high as the soldiers marched into the abandoned town. Stanley thought the battle had little strategic impact and he understated the contribution he had made during the battle. Johnston was compelled to retreat toward Atlanta, and the armies would battle another day. General Joseph Johnston decided to withdraw his army southward and find a place to stop Sherman on his chosen ground. He decided to make his next stand at Adairsville, about fifteen miles south of Resaca. On May 17, Stanley's division was approaching Adairsville, reaching to within two miles of the town, where part of William Hardee's corps was found in battle line. Stanley's division marched in the rear of Newton's division and was not engaged in the skirmishing. Stanley recorded, "Our advance to Adamsville [Adairsville] was stubbornly resisted, but skirmishing amounting to a battle. Several times we had to deploy and bring up the batteries to drive their rear guard."[28] While Johnston had intended to fight Sherman at Adairsville, he found the valley where he planned to fight too wide to properly fight a battle to his advantage against the number of Union troops he was facing.

Cassville

Next, the Confederate command decided to attack Sherman at Cassville. Johnston, after consulting with his commanders, decided to march to Cassville by two roads, one via

Kingston and the other directly over the Gravelly Plateau to Cassville. His plan depended on the Union army to also divide and march down the same roads. His intent was to strike the Union column marching down the Cassville Road and destroy it before the other column marching via Kingston came to its aid.

Stanley began his march to Cassville on May 18, passing through Adairsville, but his division became entangled in the march of the Army of the Tennessee on the way to Kingston. Early the next morning, with McPherson's army having moved farther to the west, Stanley marched along the Kingston Road with the XIV Corps and encountered the ever-present Confederate cavalry pickets slowing the march. Hardee made the intended demonstration at Kingston, then withdrew towards Cassville with the bulk of the Army of the Cumberland following. The Confederate main line was soon found in the hills east of Cassville and the IV Corps marched toward it. Stanley placed Cruft's and Whitaker's brigades in line facing the enemy, while William Grose's brigade moved down the Western & Atlantic Railroad track in an attempt to push the Hardee's Confederate infantry back into the main Confederate line. After some stiff skirmishing the Confederates were pushed back toward Cassville. Then Stanley saw what was before him:

> [T]he enemy was discovered, formed in three lines of battle perpendicular to the road, and very soon after the appearance of the head of the column the entire rebel line advanced toward us. The division was deployed as hastily as possible; batteries were put in position, and other troops were coming up to form upon the flanks of the division, when the enemy was seen to be withdrawing. Some volleys from the rifled batteries caused them to move off in a good deal of confusion, and the whole division advanced in line to the rebel position. Finding the enemy had left, the division moved on in accordance with orders, with a view of reaching Cassville. When within about a mile of that place and while changing the direction of the skirmishers, the head of the column received a sudden volley from the enemy across an open field. The division was again deployed, and as night had arrived, the men were instructed to fortify their position. Very sharp skirmishing was kept up the early part of the night, and early in the morning we found the enemy had again abandoned his works and retired across the Etowah.[29]

Lieutenant Colonel Chesley Bailey, 9th Kentucky Infantry, Wood's Third Division, also recorded the march without an understanding of the imminent threat. As Wood's Division followed Stanley's Division, Bailey recorded in his diary, "Moved out at 9 a.m. Stanley's Div. in advance. Moved steadily forward until reaching Kingston where we lay some time. Skirmishing going on in front. Moved on at 1, 2 miles, when we went in order of battle. Formed in open field near Cassville, moved forward into wood. Sharp firing attended with some loss."[30]

Stanley arrived at Cassville after the Confederate attack plan had faltered when Federal cavalry approached Cassville from the northeast. Reacting to reports that cavalry was in his rear, Hood moved his corps to address this threat and thereby ruined the chance to launch a flank attack on Schofield's XXIII Corps, approaching the town over the direct road from Adairsville. Still, Stanley was approaching the veterans of Hardee's Corps, who felt capable of making their own attack against the Federals approaching from the west; however, Hood's failure to spring the trap caused Johnston to pull the Confederate line—including Hardee's Corps—onto the hills east and south of Cassville. Stanley's division was leading the Union column approaching from the west and around noon encountered three enemy battle lines that advanced, then suddenly stopped and withdrew. Historian Albert Castle described events at the engagement at Cassville: "This seemingly inexplicable retrograde action puzzles but also relieves Stanley's troops, who were bracing for a ferocious, Chickamauga style charge by the Rebs; it also puzzles but (so some say later) disappoints the Confederates who have made it. Having listened to the stirring words of Johnston's general order, they were all set to hurl themselves against the yanks."[31]

Johnston extended his army to a three-mile front with Hood on the right, Polk in the center, and Hardee on the left. In the meantime, the Union XX Corps moved into position left (north) of the IV Corps at 5:30 p.m. Parts of the XIV Corps were positioned to the right of the IV Corps and next Cox's division of the XXIII Corps arrived. Then 40 Union cannon were ordered to open fire and continued until after dark. During the evening, Polk and Hood convinced Johnston of the vulnerability of the Confederate position and Johnston decided to withdraw again. By the end of May 20, the Confederates were across the Etowah and deploying along the Allatoona Range, destroying bridges as they retreated.

Pickett's Mill and Pine Mountain

Sherman paused for three days to repair the railroad and build up supplies, because he was about to "plunge into the wilderness," in his words, leaving the line of the railroad and relying on wagons to supply his forces as they advanced around Johnston's left flank, hoping to seize an important crossroads to Johnston's left and rear. Stanley's division remained in place from May 19 until May 23 when his division crossed the Etowah River. It was rushed forward on May 25 when he was informed that part of Hooker's XX Corps had found the enemy at New Hope Church, where five roads came together, near Dallas. Stanley's division crossed Pumpkinvine Creek at sunset on May 25 and moved to Hooker's left flank. Grose's Third Brigade of Stanley's division connected with the left flank of Hooker's Corps on May 26. The next day Stanley's division replaced Wood's division in the line so that Wood could be part of a flanking movement to the northeast at Pickett's Mill. Larry Daniels wrote, "Remarkably, Howard chose Wood's division, to be withdrawn and replaced by Stanley's, then in reserve. Wood, perhaps with the specter of Chickamauga still in his mind, protested, but to no avail. This time the Federals were lucky, the exchange of units occurred uneventfully."[32]

General O.O. Howard led the flanking force consisting of Wood's IV Corps division and Richard Johnson's division of XIV Corps. After a difficult march through the dense woods, Howard reported that he thought he had reached the Confederate right flank and ordered an assault at Pickett's Mill. Hazen's brigade of Wood's division began the attack, but Howard never achieved a coordinated assault from six available brigades. Hazen's brigade of 1,500 veterans lost 467 men within forty-five minutes, and the other units that did attack fared similarly. Stanley and his men were not to be part of this action. He wrote of the affair: "[It] led to many scandals and accusations. One brigade commander could not be found at the critical moment to say whether to go ahead or to retreat. Another divisional commander stayed so far in the rear he could give no command; another shocked General Howard by drinking whiskey out of a black bottle before the men. All in all, the affair was a miserable failure."[33] The Union loss in the attack was estimated as a total of 1,600 men in Hazen's, Gibson's and Knefler's brigades.

The advance to Atlanta was becoming one of endless days and nights of marching and skirmishing, with occasional larger battles. The skirmishing, rain, and diminishing supplies resulting from more difficult transport caused the Federals to designate the area from Dallas to Pickett's Mill as "The Hell Hole." On June 3, Stanley relieved Brigadier General Jefferson C. Davis' division and was then subject to constant musket and artillery fire. Stanley's division remained in line near Dallas until the evening of June 4 when the enemy evacuated their position. The division rested near New Hope Church on June 6 and then pressed forward, finding the enemy on June 10 entrenched at Pine Mountain. Stanley entrenched his men and remained in line until June 15.[34] During Stanley's time before Pine Mountain, he was visited by General Sherman, who angrily noticed Confederate soldiers were moving around in full sight of the Union line. Stanley told Sherman the pickets had a truce, which made Sherman even more angry. He ordered Stanley to scatter the Rebels, which Stanley ordered his men to promptly do, but not before the pickets warned their enemy the truce was over by order of General Sherman.[35]

On June 14, Sherman noticed a group of Confederate officers on the crest of Pine Mountain observing the Federal positions below. "How saucy they are," remarked Sherman and ordered Major General Howard to find the nearest artillery battery and have it throw a few rounds at the Confederates. The nearest battery was Peter Simonson's 5th Indiana of Stanley's division. Simonson's first cannonade was noticed by the Confederates atop the mountain, and they separated. But three shells were already on their way, and the third struck Lieutenant General Leonidas Polk in the left side and ripped through his chest, killing him. Unknown to Sherman and the Federals, the group atop the mountain included Joseph E. Johnston and two of his subordinate corps commanders, Hardee and Polk, who were discussing whether or not to evacuate Pine Mountain. Simonson, who had proved so valuable at Resaca under Stanley's command, had killed the Confederacy's second most senior lieutenant general.[36]

On June 15, Stanley found Pine Mountain had been evacuated as the Confederate division that had been on the mountain moved back to the main Confederate line near Gilgal Church. As men of Stanley's division marched past Pine Mountain, they found a paper that read, "Right here is where you Yankee *** killed Bishop General Polk."[37] Sadly for Stanley and the Federal army, Captain Peter Simonson was killed by a Confederate musket shot just two days later.

Stanley approached the main Confederate line shortly after noon as he followed Newton's division. The terrain was such that forming a battle line was difficult. Howard ordered his divisions to form a line and entrench opposite the enemy. On June 16, the Union artillery attempted to soften the resistance of the enemy and then the IV Corps moved forward until severe fire from the entrenched enemy stopped them. "On the morning of the 17th it was found the enemy had again evacuated his line, and we advanced to find that he had abandoned his hold on Lost Mountain with his left. Again we had the experience of feeling for the position of the rebels and found him, as usual, strongly intrenched on one of the small branches of Noyes' Creek. On the 18th the rain poured in torrents. Kirby's brigade was sent to support General Newton's division, which engaged the enemy's lines closely all day. This night the enemy again abandoned his line, and on the 19th we moved forward and found him in his intrenched line of Kennesaw Mountain."[38] The stops and advances were a daily challenge for the advancing army. Lt. Colonel Chesley Bailey, 9th Kentucky Infantry, recorded in his diary, "Enemy fell back during the night. Moved out at 8 a.m. Stanleys Div. in front. Found enemy in less than 2 miles when heavy skirmishing began. lasting all day."[39]

Even in the endless days and nights of the Atlanta Campaign, the men of the Union occasionally heard the music of their own band play at night. Along the march, as Stanley's division settled down for the night, the band of the 36th Indiana began to play. The band was within earshot of the Confederate line, and the Southerners could tolerate Union music only for so long. Soon, there was the echo of "Dixie" being played by a Confederate band. But the reality of war exacted its toll. The Confederate artillery decided to add its music to the night and the shells exploded in the trees above the Union band. One man was killed as a result, and Stanley concluded that no more music would be played in the evening until the campaign was over.

The Battle of Kennesaw Mountain

David Stanley's part in the fighting along the Kennesaw Mountain line was mostly done before Sherman's decision to assault the line directly on June 27. Stanley was not a general to direct an attack from behind the lines. Lewis Day, 101st Ohio Infantry, recorded that "wherever help was needed, or the fight was thickest, there Stanley, brave, true, generous, big-hearted Stanley was sure to be found."[40] At 4:00 p.m. on June 20, Stanley pushed his entire line forward, encountering stiff skirmishing. The skirmishers took the hill to their front only to be attacked as they began to build their defenses, but they were able to repulse the attack. A second attack was made but again Stanley's infantry repulsed the attack. The third attack on the position occurred at 8:00 p.m. and part of the 35th Indiana Infantry was pushed backward. The 99th Ohio saved the brigade when the 99th scrambled forward and, according to Stanley's report, "coolly formed a flank and poured a fire into the rebel force which had broken our line, saved the brigade. The Fortieth Ohio was brought up and charged the rebel force which had broken through, restoring our lines. This affair, which was a very severe fight, reflects great credit upon Whitaker's brigade. The men fought with great coolness and resolution.... Colonel Kirby's brigade carried the bald hill in his front, but the enemy rallied and drove him back. This occurred three times, when, night having arrived, I directed the contest to stop."[41] Major General George Thomas recorded that Stanley had been attacked seven times but held the line throughout the afternoon. The severity of the battle on June 20 was described by Corporal George Washington Herr, 59th Illinois Infantry: "On came the moving mass, steady and silent, sweeping through the darkness like the huge and measureless spirit of evil. Not a shot was fired, for the charging column was ordered to depend wholly upon the bayonet.... Suddenly the stillness was broken by such an unearthly chorus of whoops and yells as only the rebel soldiery could utter, and, with a rush, abrupt and swift as the sweep of an avalanche, the charging column hurled itself against Whittaker's barricades. The shock was terrific, and the melee savage, bloody, indescribable.... The men on both sides—lost in the darkness, without officers to control or direct—knew not what to do save—kill—kill! The slaughter was appalling."[42]

On June 21, Kirby's First Brigade moved forward at the same time as Wood's division and claimed the hill they had battled for possession. The next day Stanley again battled the Confederates while a much larger Confederate attack occurred near the Kolb Farm to the south. At 5:00 p.m. Stanley, after strengthening his defenses during the day, charged ahead and captured forty Confederate skirmishers. The enemy counterattacked and pushed Stanley's force back with a loss of 60 men. Lieutenant Louis Hanback of Newton's division watched the action. He wrote to his family: "Our lines were to be advanced and the probabilities were that it would be heavily contested. However, in our front we were mistaken, but Stanley's division on our right had a hard fight. He charged and took a strong position from the enemy and was in turn charged but repulsed the enemy with severe loss after a very obstinate fight."[43] Stanley's sarcastic humor was evident as he told Captain Hubert Dilger, 1st Ohio Artillery—whose battery was effective in cannonading the enemy and was a target of enemy fire in return—"he was going to order bayonets for Dilger's guns."[44]

The Battle of Kennesaw Mountain took place on June 27. Stanley was part of a meeting with George Thomas and the other commanders of the Army of the Cumberland prior to the attack. After the meeting, Stanley and Thomas discussed the prospects and Stanley said, "General, I am sorry this assault has been decided on, and I know it will fail." Thomas replied, "I fear it will be so, but General Sherman has decided it and we must do our best. If we do possibly succeed it will lead to a great victory."[45] Stanley's First Division was ordered to support the attack of Newton's Second Division but due to the failure of the first assault, Stanley's division did not participate in the battle: "From the failure of the assault the troops of this division were not engaged, Kirby's brigade only passing out of the works, and yet so severe was the fire of the enemy that the division lost over 100 men killed and wounded while waiting the movement of the Second Division."[46]

Being chief of artillery under David Stanley was dangerous. The highly regarded Peter Simonson was killed earlier in the month. Stanley's second chief of artillery, Captain Samuel McDowell, Independent Pennsylvania Battery, was killed at his post on June 27 with his batteries just before the attack at Kennesaw Mountain.[47]

Stanley also recounted a blunt remark made by General John Newton during a lull in the fighting. Sherman, Stanley, and Newton were observing the enemy from Stanley's position and were soon observed by the enemy. Stanley suggested they move to the protection of some large oaks and all moved to safety except for John Newton. Stanley wrote, "He was mad and did not care for bullets." It was John Newton who remarked to Sherman, "Well this is a d__d appropriate culmination of one month's blundering."[48] Brigadier General Charles Harker, commanding a brigade in Newton's division, was killed and Colonel Dan McCook, commanding a brigade in Davis' division, was mortally wounded during the June 27 assault.

From June 27 through July 2, Stanley's First Division maintained its position. On June 28, again an informal truce was struck between some of the Union regiments and the opposing Confederates units. Part of the truce specified a cessation of building defenses, movement of troops and artillery. Colonel John T. Smith, 31st Indiana Infantry, observed the Confederates sneaking some cannons into position behind a barrier of timbers. Smith reported this to Stanley, who decided to match the movements of the enemy and called for a pile of brush to be stacked and a section of artillery rolled into position. A large number of Confederate soldiers lined the timbers concealing the newly positioned Confederate artillery. Stanley ordered his artillery to fire. Colonel Smith recorded, "At the first shot from our guns, these timbers, and the men that were on them, were knocked several feet into the air. After a few shots the firing ceased, and the guns moved back. In a little while the rebel officer of the day called again to the Colonel, and told him he need have no further fears in regard to artillery, for their guns would hardly make good kindling-wood. He said they intended to play a trick on us, and they had got beat at their own game."⁴⁹

On the evening of July 2, Stanley's division relieved Newton's division on the line. Stanley found the enemy gone the next morning. His division led the corps through Marietta and that evening found the enemy entrenched at Smyrna. At 5:00 p.m. on July 2, Stanley's division attacked Major General W.H.T. Walker's Confederate division and breached the Confederate line. Stanley knew a counterattack was to come or the Confederates would have to retreat again. He hastened to fortify the new position and was not disappointed by Walker, who attacked at 10:00 p.m. in a spectacular battle. Two Georgia regiments passed his right flank and struck the 40th Ohio Infantry in Stanley's rear. One of the Confederate regiments was the 54th Georgia Infantry and the fight was primarily with Whitaker's brigade. The 99th Ohio Infantry was cited as performing exceptional duty during the fight. The Union loss was about 250 men in the bloody affair.

At 11:00 a.m. on July 4 near Ruff's Mill, Grose's Third Brigade skirmishers pushed forward. Howard and Sherman were convinced Johnston would not make a stand with the Chattahoochee River to his rear, but as Grose's skirmishers advanced, they received a concentrated fire from the Confederates.⁵⁰ The day was very hot and the men were suffering severely from the heat. Grose's infantry broke through the Confederate skirmish line, and then Stanley ordered his entire division forward. His infantry then came under the most devastating artillery and infantry fire they had encountered up to that time. Stanley recounted the Rebel skirmish line amounted to almost a full battle line and the removal of the skirmishers was an arduous task which resulted in over 100 casualties. Later in the day the enemy withdrew.

The fighting on July 4 at Smyrna and Ruff's Mill two miles to the west resulted from Sherman's assumptions about what Johnston would do. He insisted the Confederate line in front of Stanley and the IV Corps was just a skirmish line. Over the objections of his commanders, he ordered the attack only to find the Confederate skirmish line was heavily supported by artillery and infantry. David Stanley received a commendation for the efforts of his division in this futile attack, which resulted in over one hundred casualties in his division. He would write in his memoirs that he was always puzzled by the commendation, except perhaps it was awarded for his efforts during the advance and for the fact that he, in true, humble, Stanley style, had exposed himself to the direct fire from the enemy. From July 5–10, Stanley remained on the north bank of the Chattahoochee River along the railroad about halfway between Smyrna and the Chattahoochee River. On July 12, Stanley's division crossed the river on pontoon bridges at Power's Ferry.

The Seige of Atlanta

On July 17, Sherman had all his forces moving towards Atlanta. The XIV Crops was farthest to the west, then the XX Corps, both having crossed at Pace's Ferry. The IV Corps, having crossed a few miles farther upriver, was next in line and marched south through Buckhead separated from the left of XX Corps. Stanley's division was following Newton's. That evening, a telegram relieving Johnston of command arrived at his headquarters behind the Confederate lines. In Johnston's place, President Davis had appointed John Hood and promoted him to full general. Hood was selected in part because Davis believed he was more likely to take action than many of the other possible commanders. Davis was correct in his assumption. On the morning of July 20, Stanley's and Wood's divisions marched along the Decatur Road and crossed over Peachtree Creek. Stanley's advance pushed enemy skirmishers before him: "The enemy made an effort in the afternoon to retake his picket line but was badly repulsed and late in the evening Colonel Suman, Ninth Indiana, of Grose's brigade, charged their picket-line, farther to our right, and took 43 prisoners without losing a man."[51]

While Stanley and Wood were marching with Howard towards Decatur, Newton and his division were detached and operating directly under Major General Thomas. Newton's men were heavily engaged during the Battle of Peachtree Creek, fought in the late afternoon of July 20.

Stanley faced enemy skirmishers all day on July 21 but the enemy withdrew that evening. The next day the division was within sight of the Atlanta defenses observing the enemy in force behind the abatis, palisades, and other obstructions. As Stanley's division advanced, it came under "very annoying artillery fire to the nearest point we could occupy without driving the enemy from his lines, and breastworks were thrown up to shelter the men from the enemy's shells. This same day, July 22, the rebels attacked the Army of the Tennessee heavily upon the left [Battle of Atlanta], but made no demonstration upon our position."[52] Stanley and his men had thus not participated in either of the two major battles near Atlanta.

With the death of Major General James McPherson on July 22, Sherman consulted with Thomas about who should take command of the Army of the Tennessee. Upon Thomas' recommendation, Sherman chose Major General Oliver O. Howard, so a new commander was now needed for IV Corps. Prior to selecting a new commander of the IV Corps, Lieutenant Chesley Mosman, 59th Illinois, wrote, "I think General Stanley will soon command our Corps. He is able and energetic."[53] Stanley was now the senior officer in the corps and had a record that warranted his selection. On July 26, Stanley was assigned to command IV Corps.

Of the torturous marching and battles that had taken place from May 1 until July 26, Stanley wrote his final divisional report, "I have thus imperfectly traced out the marches, fights, and labors of the division. It would be difficult to give a description which would adequately show the services rendered for nearly three months. But few days had passed that every man of the division was not under fire, both of artillery and musketry. No one could say any hour that he would be living the next. Men were killed in their camps, at their meals, and several cases happened of men struck by musket-balls in their sleep, and passing at once from sleep into eternity. So many men were daily struck in the camp and trenches that men became utterly reckless, passing about where balls were striking as though it was their normal life, and making a joke of a narrow escape, or a noisy whistling ball."[54] The Atlanta Campaign was one of the most difficult and important military campaigns of the Civil War. The units were in almost constant action from May to early September in situations where slight mistakes could lead to disasters. Through the end of July, Stanley's division recorded a total of 1,537 casualties.

On July 27, David Stanley was again corps commander. Captain Jay Butler wrote, "Gen'l Stanley has taken the corps, and I don't believe there is a general in the army thought any more of by his troops than General Stanley was by his division. In passing some of our boys the other day, one says to the other, 'I wonder what time it is.' The Gen'l stops, takes out his watch, gives the desired information, and passes on. He is not too high up to notice any soldier, and in time of need, he is cool and cautious, and in the advance—a splendid soldier

John Schofield commanded the Army of the Ohio during the Atlanta Campaign (courtesy Wilson's Creek National Battlefield; WICR 30699).

and perfect gentleman."[55] Colonel Emerson Opdycke agreed with Butler's assessment, writing, "Stanley now commands our Corps, I think he will do well with it; he has been commanding our 1st Division. Cap. Steele is on his staff. Gen. Newton drinks hard, I have seen him tipsy when trying to direct his troops in the face of the enemy; his division succeeds in spite of him, not from any merit of his."[56] William T. Sherman stated in his memoirs Stanley was given command of the IV Corps due to the recommendation of George Thomas.[57]

Stanley's IV Corps was positioned northeast of Atlanta with Newton's Second Division forming his right flank, Wood's Third Division his center and Grose's First Division on the left. On July 28, Stanley ordered his divisions to move forward and penetrate a portion of the Confederate line if possible. Wood's and Grose's divisions were able to capture the Confederate rifle pits, but the artillery was very heavy and the large concentration of Confederate soldiers before them convinced Stanley any attempt to carry the main line would be futile. Stanley remained in line throughout the remainder of July. On August 3, Brigadier General Nathan Kimball of Newton's division was appointed commander of the Stanley's First Division.

With command of IV Corps came new obligations of command. One of the first things Stanley had to address was a squabble between General John Newton and Lieutenant Adolphus Erdmann, 15th Missouri Infantry. During the July 20

Battle of Peach Tree Creek, Lieutenant Erdmann withdrew the regiment's supply train—which was under enemy artillery fire—contrary to the orders of his captain. Newton described Erdmann's refusal to obey the order as tantamount to mutiny; but Colonel Joseph Conrad, commander of the 15th Missouri, came to Erdmann's defense, saying the charges were untrue. With Conrad on his side, the scrappy lieutenant wrote to then corps commander Howard that Newton was unjustly persecuting him. When Howard left command of the IV Corps, the matter fell to Stanley. But Stanley refused to be drawn into the argument and flatly stated if Newton and Erdmann wanted to continue their squabble they needed to do so as part of a formal court-martial, which, fortunately, was not pursued by either party.[58] Privately, Stanley and George Thomas discussed the actions relating to Erdmann's case in which Newton had ordered the lieutenant's hands tied behind his back and that he be marched through the regiment. This action thoroughly disgusted Stanley.

When the Army of the Ohio was withdrawn from Stanley's left on August 1, the IV Corps became the left flank of Sherman's entire force. Stanley conducted demonstrations on the Confederate lines on August 3, 4, 5, and 6. These demonstrations revealed Cheatham and Cleburne were to Stanley's front. The actions also were designed to keep the Confederates guessing about Sherman's intentions. At the same time, Stanley, as the extreme flank of the army and recalling Resaca, was ever vigilant and aware of the potential of being attacked.

Lieutenant Chesley Mosman, 59th Illinois, was somewhat frustrated by the demonstrations and he wrote in his journal, "I wonder if Gen. Stanley will want the Rebel rifle pits this afternoon again, and why he don't keep them when he gets them. Should think any Johnny of ordinary intelligence would understand the meaning of these demonstrations."[59] Corporal George W. Herr, also of the 59th Illinois Infantry, recorded his view of the siege of Atlanta: "Day after day, and day and night the measureless roar continued. With Hood's artillery added to Sherman's more than 300 cannons, many of them rifled ordnance, fed the volume of concussion that terrified Atlanta, shook the earth and reverberated along the neighboring hills."[60]

David Stanley was widely respected by the common soldier. Charles Partridge, 96th Illinois Infantry, recorded that after one of the demonstrations before Atlanta, Ned Malone of the regiment had been shot in the leg. Malone limped backed toward the line and encountered General Stanley. Stanley asked, "'Well, corporal, I hope you are not badly wounded'; to which Ned replied; 'If I thought I had been pecking away at them all these years and hadn't hurt them worse than they've hurt me I'd go hang mesel!' and then, looking his commander square in the face, he added, 'I say Gineral, have yez ary drap of whisky wid yez?' Ned was promptly handed a flask, and Gen. Stanley never tired of repeating the story of the Irish corporal of the Ninety-sixth who asked him for whisky."[61]

It wasn't until August 18 that Stanley's IV Corps was moved and massed behind the line of the XIV Corps, but the planned movement was cancelled because Sherman had been persuaded to let cavalry, this time led by Brigadier General Hugh Judson Kilpatrick, try once more to cut the two remaining railroad lines that the Confederates were using to supply the Army of Tennessee in Atlanta's defenses. Stanley conducted demonstrations against the city defenses to hold the Confederates in place while Kilpatrick made his raid. Kilpatrick's raid was only partially successful and within a few days the trains were again bringing supplies to Atlanta.[62]

The Battle of Jonesboro

After cavalry raids failed to cut the two remaining railroads supplying Atlanta, Sherman determined to accomplish the task using six of his seven infantry corps. Sherman issued the orders for the movement on August 25. Sherman left Major General Henry Slocum's XX Corps to guard the most important Chattahoochee River crossings northwest of Atlanta. For the other six corps, Schofield's XXIII Corps would have the shortest march, moving on an arc to the south, then east to strike first the Atlanta & West Point Railroad and then the Macon & Western Railroad. Thomas's two remaining corps would be on Schofield's right (west): Stanley's IV Corps, closest to Schofield, and Palmer's XIV Corps on Stanley's right. Howard's Army of the Tennessee (XV, XVI, and XVII corps) would traverse the longest arc and march for Jonesboro, about twelve miles south of Atlanta. The disappearance of the Federal infantry from the trenches north and west of Atlanta caused brief excitement among the Confederates and the few citizens remaining in the city; but Hood's remaining cavalry quickly discovered the mass movement of Federals. Hood could not defend the entire length of the railroads and decided that Jonesboro was a likely Federal objective. He dispatched both Lieutenant General William Hardee's and Lieutenant General Stephen Dill Lee's corps by rail and foot to Jonesboro, with Hardee in overall command.

On August 30, Howard's three corps (XV, XVI, XVII) stopped for the night near Renfroe's Place, just north and west of Jonesboro. Confederate cavalry had been skirmishing with Howard's advance. Howard did not know that the town was only lightly defended at that point. Hardee and Lee's weary troops arrived in the town overnight and into the morning of August 31. By late morning, Major General Logan's XV Corps was a "mere eight hundred yards" from the Jonesboro depot and the Union soldiers watched as the Confederate reinforcements poured into the town.[63]

William T. Sherman and David Stanley developed a long-term dislike of each other due to the events at Jonesboro (National Archives).

Knowing the Confederates would attempt to drive his forces away because his artillery was already within range of the railroad, Howard had his men prepare defensive positions. By 2:00 p.m. the Confederates began forming for the attack. The Confederate line stretched for about a mile and a half, roughly the length of Jonesboro, and about 20,000 men stretched along the line of battle. On the afternoon of the 31st the Confederate artillery began to pound the Union forces. Around 3:00 p.m. Lee's corps on the right and Hardee's corps on the left attacked, but they were handily repulsed. Several Confederate officers remarked that the spirit of attack seemed to be gone from their troops. The Southerners were forced to withdraw with heavy losses of 2,200 men, almost ten times as many as Howard's.[64]

Stanley's IV Corps began its movement against the railroads on August 25. If there was any question about the intensity of Stanley's desire to follow orders and advance quickly, it was dispelled by the tactics he used to keep his troops on schedule after a particularly heavy rainstorm. Stanley had arrived at William Grose's headquarters at 3:00 a.m. when he was informed by staff officers that all the IV Corps was not keeping up. After the lead two brigades marched forward, the remainder of the corps came to a particularly large mudhole. Stanley recalled the following:

> [T]hey halted, and now they have lain down to sleep.... I mounted and called my staff and Colonel Grose's staff about me and rode back. In less than a mile I found the head of the column in the woods where they had gone to sleep. I tried to get hold of the officers but it was very dark and they easily evaded me. However armed with such clubs as I and my staff officers could find, we gave the sleepers the rudest awakening of their lives. A big lieutenant belonging to Colonel Grose's staff, a provost marshal.... had a long club. "Get up and form ranks," the lieutenant would say after awakening a man. "I won't do it," replied the sleeper. Whack came down on the head, arms, shoulders, legs, anywhere, and the fellow was wide awake. I wonder some of those fellows did not shoot us. They threatened to do so, but we waked the obstructionist and soon had twelve thousand waiting behind, marching on.[65]

The advance of the IV Corps stretched four miles long and the early part of the march was exceedingly tense. Stanley lamented that his flank was exposed during the march from Atlanta, but, luckily, no attack was made. Early on August 31, the IV Corps approached the Macon & Western Railroad about five miles north of Jonesboro, by way of Thorn's Mill. On his left, Schofield's XXIII Corps had already hit the railroad at the village of Rough and Ready; and on his right, Davis's XIV Corps was still some miles from the railroad because it was curving away to the east. Stanley's corps encountered the enemy's breastworks as he advanced. He formed a battle line and advanced on the works only to find dismounted cavalry that quickly "abandoned the works and took to their heels."[66]

As Stanley turned southward along the railroad at 4:00 p.m. on August 31, he connected with the XXIII Corps and formed a *V* with the XXIII Corps facing Jonesboro: "The troops were strongly barricaded in this position, and a strong force, including all the pioneers of the corps, was ordered to commence breaking up the road at 3 o'clock in the morning. General Schofield sent me a copy of his instructions from district headquarters, and proposed that Cox's division should go back on the road in the direction of Rough and Ready, assisting Garrard to break up the road, and that I should move on in the direction of Jonesborough, breaking the road, and that he would follow with his corps and make the work complete. In answer to this, I objected to his plan of separating forces, not knowing the position of the enemy."[67]

Stanley finally received orders at 10:00 p.m. to march toward Jonesboro early the next morning and to destroy the railroad along the way. Early on September 1, Kimball's and Newton's divisions advanced southward along the railroad. "In starting out in the morning I passed General Schofield's headquarters. In conversation he asked me if I ranked him; I told him I did. He then said if a battle occurred he would be under my command. I said to him that there was little likelihood of any battle until reaching Jonesborough, and that our common superiors would probably be near at hand. No intimation from any quarter was

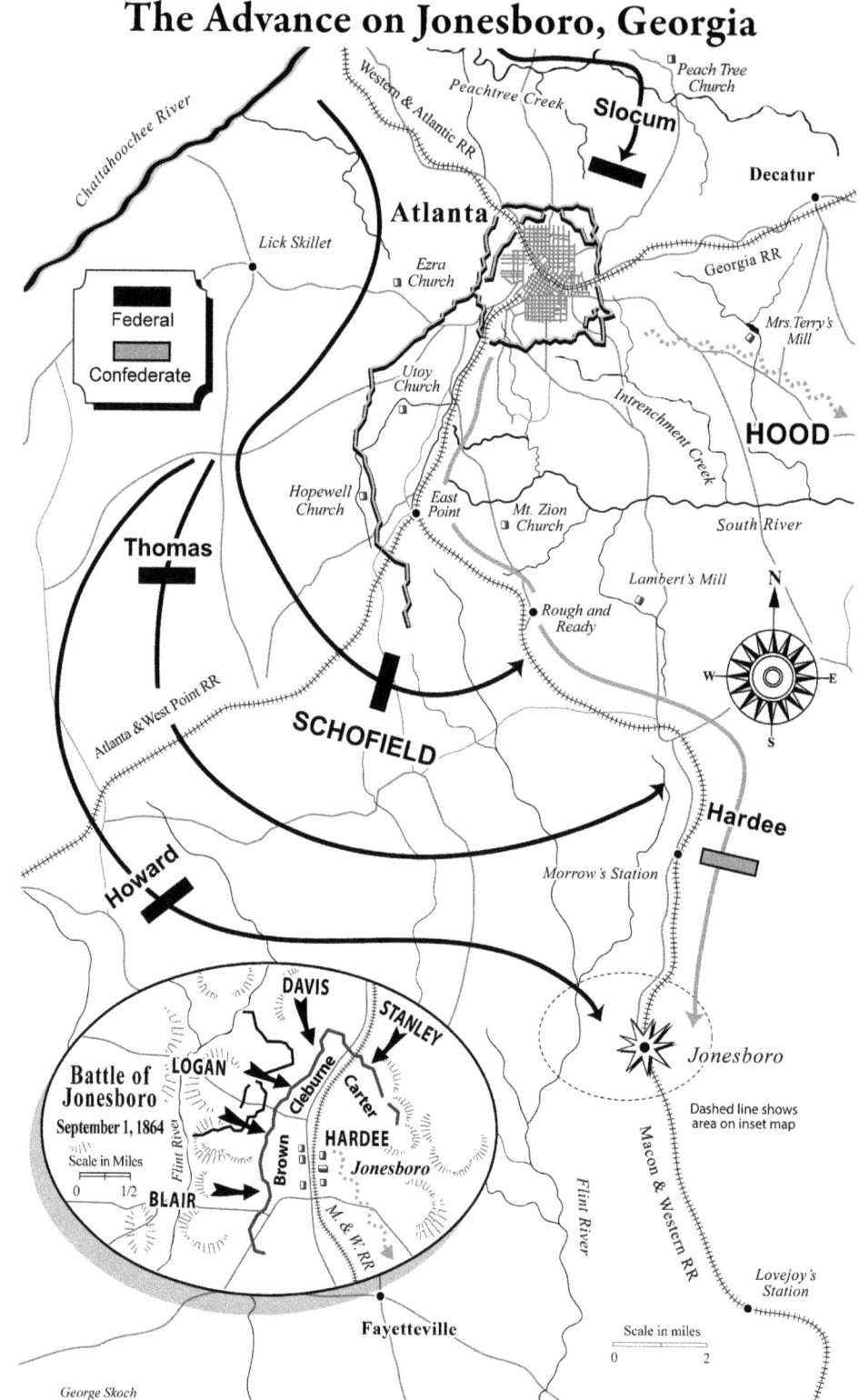

given me that General Schofield was under my command, nor did I so consider him. I had no right to command him unless so instructed from competent authority."[68]

At 10:00 a.m. on September 1, the right of the IV Corps connected with the left of Brigadier General Absalom Baird's division of the XIV Corps. Stanley continued to destroy the railroad. He was ordered by General Thomas to wait for the arrival of Wood's division and then to inform Thomas. At 4:00 p.m. Thomas ordered Stanley to advance his corps down the railroad to Jonesboro. Kirby's and Grose's brigades marched in battle line and Newton's division was ordered to quickly move to the left of Kimball. It was after 5:00 p.m. when Stanley approached the enemy's entrenchments. He later wrote of his actions:

> General Grose and Colonel Kirby both reported they could not carry the position in their fronts owing to the perfect entanglement made by cutting down the thick undergrowth in front of the rail barricade the rebels had hastily thrown up. Newton's division had a much longer circuit to make, and, when moved forward, the right brigade (Wagner's) found no enemy in front but received a fire from the rear of their right flank. The flank of the enemy had been found and turned, but it was now pitch dark and nothing more could be done. Very early in the night the enemy retreated. The formation and advance of the troops of Kimball's and Newton's divisions was done under a severe cannonade, and, although the men were perfectly cool and behaved well, I have no doubt but this delayed the deployment. Just before dark General Davis sent me word that he had positive information that we were on their flank, which was the [first] intimation I had of the position of the enemy. No one regrets more than myself the escape of Hardee's corps, and it is easy after the facts are revealed to see how he might have been caught; but the position of the enemy was entirely unknown to me and had to be developed, and the time necessary to overcome the difficulties brought us to night, and with night the opportunity for the enemy to escape. I carried out all orders and instructions received without delay, and when the enemy was found used all the personal exertions in my power to push the troops rapidly forward. I believe the subordinate commanders put their troops in position and advanced them to the best of their ability and understanding. That we did not succeed was simply because the daylight was not an hour longer.[69]

By the next morning, September 2, Hardee had withdrawn and Stanley was in pursuit. His troops found the Confederates around noon throwing up defenses about a mile north of Lovejoy's Station. In a coordinated movement with Howard's Army of the Tennessee, Stanley advanced his IV Corps at 3:30 p.m. on September 3, against the enemy position near the railroad. As Stanley advanced, he and General John Newton discussed the planned attack and found the Confederate artillery was in position to control the ground the Union divisions would have to cross. They concluded a successful attack could not be made. Stanley had planned to use Wood's and Kimball's divisions to attack Hardee's right flank:

> Generals Wood and Kimball met very bad ground in their advance. The country about the head of Indian Creek over which they passed is very broken and intersected by difficult little streams and marshes. Owing to these difficulties, it was nearly 6 o'clock before Kimball's and Wood's divisions arrived at the enemy's position. Their skirmishers were soon driven in, and General Wood was engaged selecting a point of attack, when, he was severely wounded and disabled from attending to the management of his advance. Colonel Knefler's brigade, placed on the left of Wood's division, charged and carried the enemy's work, but was unable to maintain its position, owing to a sweeping enfilading fire coming from both flanks. General Kimball pushed his brigade well forward, but was struck in flank by a sweeping artillery fire, and finding that he would have to cross the open field to gain the enemy's work, which they were laboring might and main to complete, the assault was countermanded; indeed, the enemy had concen-

trated force enough to hold nearly as long a line as ourselves, and from our observations Kimball's left brigade was about opposite the rebel flank. As night had fallen at this time, the troops were ordered to intrench and remain in the position gained. The Twenty-Third Corps came in sight behind our right flank during the engagement, but gave no support to our movement. The loss in Knefler's brigade was quite severe.[70]

Just as Stanley began his attack, Howard received orders from Sherman not to attack; but neither Thomas nor Stanley was aware of these orders. While Sherman was present on the battlefield he chose not to send orders to the Army of the Cumberland. Accordingly, Albert Castel offered only two plausible reasons for Sherman's actions: "One, highly unlikely, is that Sherman has left it up to Howard to notify Stanley.... [T]he other, much more probable, is that Sherman, bitter over what he deems to be the inexcusable failure of the IV Corps to attack yesterday."[71] A third explanation might be that Sherman thought the IV Corps could carry the position alone, but this also was not likely.

On September 4, Stanley was informed Atlanta had been evacuated and the Union army had possession of the city. Stanley's corps remained in place until they were withdrawn to Jonesboro and then he marched to Atlanta on September 8. The entire Atlanta Campaign resulted in 7,226 casualties for the IV Corps.

Controversies at Jonesboro

David Stanley was involved in two controversies relating to the advance on Jonesboro. The first concerned whether a general of equal rank but earlier promotion date commanding a smaller unit, e.g. corps vs. army, has command when the general commanding the larger unit is present in the field. Sherman had confronted this question in a particularly aggravating way about a month earlier. The situation facing Sherman at Jonesboro related to Stanley, commander of the IV Corps with an earlier promotion date, and Major General John Schofield, commander of the Army of the Ohio.

In the operations around Utoy Creek, Sherman had directed Major General John M. Palmer's XIV Corps of the Army of the Cumberland to take orders from Major General John M. Schofield, commanding the Army of the Ohio. Palmer refused, indicating that his promotion to major general was earlier than Schofield's.[72] In fact, Palmer was incorrect, but Palmer had another motivation. Palmer was a citizen soldier who had acquitted himself well and justifiably rose to corps command, but he resented the influence and favoritism of West Point Military Academy graduates. He had recently seen West Point graduate Howard chosen to succeed West Point graduate McPherson as commander of the Army of the Tennessee, those choosing passing over fellow citizen soldier John A. Logan, who had temporarily commanded upon McPherson's death. Much to his disgust, Sherman had to spend time adjudicating the dispute and finally allowed Palmer to resign his command despite the political ramifications back in Illinois during an election year. Consequently, Sherman was sensitive to the issue when he realized Stanley and Schofield would need to operate in concert on September 1. He issued the following order:

> In the Field, Couch's House, August 31, 1864 — 9.15 p.m.
>
> General Schofield: As the question of rank will come up, I will decide it now, and beg you to acquiesce whatever your present opinion may be. Whenever two or more officers happen

together on a common duty calling for a common head, even for a minute, the officer highest in rank present must give the necessary orders. Your own, Stanley's, and Davis' commands will tomorrow form a common movement requiring a common head in case of battle or extreme danger, and whoever happens to rank must command and be held responsible. The real point is your being a separate army commander, but the overruling necessity of the well established principle before recited takes precedence, or in a combined army like this, embracing three, the latter lose their separate character and become parts or components of the single army. I have and shall continue to keep each army separate, employed as far as may be on tasks proportioned to the strength of each, but when these unexpected combinations arise from the nature of things a fixed rule had better be established now. My decision, I repeat, is that when current events carry your corps and another together in a common object your rank is then determined by the well established rule, and as a separate army commander you have no legal right to exercise that authority over an officer of superior rank in another separate army, but the one having the highest commission must command the whole. Please act on this decision.[73]

Schofield wrote to Stanley the same night "proposing" to act in concert and forwarded a copy of Sherman's orders, thus alleviating a more volatile situation. This communication resulted in Stanley's visit to Schofield on the morning of September 1. In Stanley's after action report, he calmly revealed the position he took in his meeting. His many years of experience also helped to decrease the tension which could have resulted from the order. He calmly did not insist he was in command and further stated that, because it was unlikely any combat would occur until more senior officers were present, the issue was not important. Schofield's recollection of the matter showed Stanley in a favorable light. Schofield wrote of Stanley's position, "He [Stanley] said General Sherman was wrong; that he was not entitled to the command and did not want it; and urged me to accept the chief command, and let him act under my orders. I replied that General Sherman's order was imperative, and I could not relieve him (General Stanley) from the responsibility of executing it."[74] Although Sherman wanted to avoid another command controversy, he probably need not have worried since both Stanley and Schofield were Military Academy graduates and professional soldiers, and they handled the situation in a gentlemanly manner.

The second, and much more serious, controversy was the accusation Sherman made about Stanley's failure to attack Hardee's right flank on the afternoon of September 1. Stanley recorded Sherman angrily accused him of failing to crush Hardee's troops and therefore allowing him to escape at the Battle of Jonesboro. To this Stanley replied, "'If I did so sir, it was owing to you own orders.' And with that the subject dropped." Stanley was not pleased with the performance of the IV Corps during the afternoon of September 1: "I was not satisfied myself with the affair. I believed that General Newton was unnecessarily slow and I tried to hurry his troops forward. In doing so I received a bullet in my left groin. It proved a slight wound but at the time it was exceedingly painful, and made me very sick. I have always resented Sherman's imputation of my being slow, but my conscience is clear on the subject."[75]

Stanley is supported in his actions on September 1. Instead of directing Stanley toward Hardee on September 1, Sherman ordered Stanley to put his corps to work destroying the railroad toward Atlanta. At 1:00 pm., Major William Warner of Sherman's staff rode to Stanley and told him Sherman desired him to put all his troops' efforts into destroying the railroad. Warner said, "The General says our army has engaged in destroying the railroads before and has only half done it; now let this be thorough."[76] The IV Corps marched three miles to reach the railroad and set to work on it. Stanley was not in place opposite the Confederate line along with Davis' XIV Corps on the afternoon of September 1 because the IV Corps had farther to travel as Stanley followed Sherman's direct order. Stanley commented in his memoirs that if he had been in place four hours earlier he could have taken Hardee's defenses. Historian Albert Castel agreed: "The basis of this belief is Sherman's utter ignorance of the actual military situation, an ignorance that is compounded by his having returned to Howard's headquarters, which is on the Flint River, two miles northwest of Jonesboro. Sherman asserted he had Captain Audenried, aide-de-camp, then engineer, Colonel Poe, and finally General Thomas himself to order Stanley to envelope Hardee and attack his flank and rear." Castel pointed out that "although Audenried and Poe did go over to the IV Corps' sector, Sherman's own nighttime letter to Thomas indicates they did not do so until after the fighting had ended."[77] In the after action reports, neither Thomas nor Stanley recorded Thomas having ridden to Stanley to give him the order to attack Hardee.

As previously mentioned, Sherman's appraisal of the Army of the Cumberland was not favorable, even though he had been roommates with Thomas at the military academy and had a good personal relationship with him. He wrote to Grant in June in an unofficial manner about his problems with Thomas and the Army of the Cumberland:

IV Corps Officers. Front row, left to right: Samuel Beatty, Thomas Wood, D.S. Stanley, Nathan Kimball; back row, left to right: Ferdinand Van Derveer, Washington L. Elliott, Luther Bradley, Emerson Opdycke (U.S. Army Heritage and Education Center).

> My chief source of trouble is with the Army of the Cumberland, which is dreadfully slow. A fresh furrow in a plowed field will stop the whole column, and all begin to intrench. I have again and again tried to impress on Thomas that we must assail and not defend; we are the offensive, and yet it seems the whole Army of the Cumberland is so habituated to be on the defensive that, from its commander down to the lowest private, I cannot get it out of their heads.... I ordered Thomas to move at daylight, and when I got to the point at 9:30, I found Stanley and Wood quarreling which should not lead. I'm afraid I swore, and said what I should not, but I got them started, but instead of reaching the Atlanta road back of Marietta which is Johnston's center, we only got to a creek to the south of it by night, and now a heavy rain stops us and gives time to fortify a new line.[78]

Someone needed to be blamed for the failure to destroy Hardee, and Stanley was to receive the blame in Sherman's eyes. Many years after the Battle of Jonesboro, Sherman still tried to justify his admonition of Stanley by stating the IV Corps should have enveloped Hardee because the corps faced a mere "skirmishline."[79] In fact, the IV Corps was facing four well entrenched brigades. For all of Sherman's visionary concepts and strategies, he chronically assessed military situations as he thought they should be rather than as they were.

Finally is the question of whether Stanley would have been successful if his infantry had been able to make a timely attack. Historian Albert Castel considered this possibility also: "Possibly, but not likely. The breastworks are there, and Rebel troops behind them. Hardee, having received word that a strong enemy column was approaching Jonesboro east of the railroad, has sent three brigades ... from Cheatham's Division to extend the Confederate right further to the east and south. These three brigades, along with McCullough's, face Kimball's and Newton's divisions and are fully capable of holding them in check. Far from having turned Hardee's flank, the IV Corps has not even found it."[80] Historians James Lee McDonough and James Pickett Jones wrote, "Rather than waiting for Stanley, Sherman might have used the Fifteenth and Sixteenth corps to aid Davis. He did not do so, and the Battle of Jonesboro was over."[81]

In summary, Stanley was not satisfied by the actions of the IV Corps on the afternoon of September 1, particularly the slowness of John Newton's Second Division. However, the failure to crush Hardee's flank rests with Sherman, not Stanley. Even if Stanley had made a timely attack, Hardee had reinforced his line with brigades that could have repulsed it. Certainly Sherman had other forces available to use against the Confederate left rather than blaming Stanley for failing to collapse the Confederate right. The questionable accusations of tardiness and the failure to act would follow Stanley as Sherman unjustly painted a poor picture of him.

10

Spring Hill and Franklin

Come on, men, we can go wherever the general can.

The fall of Atlanta did not signal the surrender of the Confederate army. Sherman had failed during the Atlanta Campaign to force Johnston or Hood into a decisive battle, nor was he able to trap the Confederates; but he had succeeded in capturing Atlanta. After the battle at Lovejoy's Station, the Atlanta Campaign was concluded and Sherman reorganized the army. As the Union army moved back to Atlanta in September, General John Bell Hood decided to advance northward, trying to draw the Union army from further intruding into the South. Sherman decided to deal with Hood by dispatching George Thomas to Nashville and assigning him command of Stanley's IV Corps and the XXIII Corps commanded by John Schofield. Stanley recorded the reason the IV Corps was assigned to Thomas at Nashville: "It was the largest corps and my spat with Sherman over the Jonesboro affair still rankled in his breast. He liked the way his failures sat on other shoulders and when the scapegoat attempted to explain or argue the case he was never forgiven."[1] When Thomas went to Nashville, Stanley became the commander of the Army of the Cumberland in the Field, as it was designated.

The calm which lasted after the battle at Lovejoy's Station was not to continue. On September 20, Confederate cavalry were observed crossing the Tennessee River at Waterloo, Alabama, and on September 23 the railroad was destroyed between Athens and Decatur, Alabama. Major General Nathan Bedford Forrest captured five regiments of Union infantry on September 24 during his raid northward. Next, Forrest continued his foray by severing the Nashville-Chattanooga Railroad near Tullahoma. General Lovell H. Rousseau had the unenviable task of trying to stop Forrest's mischief in Tennessee; and Major General James B. Steedman along with 5,000 troops of the District of Etowah was dispatched to protect the railroad in Tennessee. Two divisions were sent from the IV and XVI Corps, Newton's and Morgan's, to Chattanooga replacing Steedman. Sherman concluded not to be baited into following the Confederates as they backtracked into Tennessee, but he effectively dismantled the Army of the Cumberland when he sent General George Thomas to Nashville to deal with Hood and Forrest while he began his famous "march to the sea" in mid–November. The XIV Corps and the XX Corps of the old Army of the Cumberland joined Sherman.[2]

David Stanley's IV Corps was on the move following Hood and Forrest on October 3. The IV Corps led the Union pursuit along a path of familiar places: Marietta, Pine Mountain, Altoona, Kingston, Rome, Resaca, and Rocky Face Ridge. The IV Corps was joined by the XIV Corps near Rocky Face Ridge and pushed the Confederates from Snake Creek Gap and then proceeded to Gaylesville, Alabama. Stanley recorded the pursuit: "The marching was severe, but in the entire campaign, though the enemy could be seen on two occasions from the mountains, I do not know that a gun was fired in the corps at the enemy."[3]

Stanley marched faithfully along with his soldiers up, down and around the hills and mountains in pursuit of Hood. Lieutenant Chesley Mosman, 59th Illinois, recalled Stanley's march: "Gen. David S. Stanley, was nearby and I had the pleasure of giving him a drink of water from my canteen. In return Stanley offered me a drink of whiskey which I respectfully declined. Lieut. Col. Hale was considerably disgusted. He swears that Bonaparte did not cross the Alps without resting. The valley is called 'Snicker's Gap.' We have boiled beef for supper. Gen. Stanley's mess chest not up and his staff parched corn for supper. Pretty tough on a Corps Commander."[4]

The allegations of slowness on Stanley's part at the Battle of Jonesboro lingered during the pursuit of Hood, although without basis. On October 17, Charles Wills, 103rd Illinois Infantry, wrote, "In Snake Creek Gap, but for General Stanley's laziness, we would have got enough prisoners to make Hood howl. He rested his corps three hours, just as he did when entrusted with a critical piece of work at Jonesboro."[5]

On October 26 Stanley received orders to move to Chattanooga, and from Chattanooga the IV Corps was transported by rail to Athens, Alabama. Then the corps marched to Pulaski, Tennessee, about halfway between Columbia, Tennessee, and Huntsville, Alabama, arriving on November 1. Stanley learned from General R.S. Granger a large concentration of Confederate infantry and cavalry were near Brown's Ferry, Tennessee, and Stanley stopped and began entrenching his position at Pulaski.[6] While Stanley was marching to Pulaski he was required to ford the Elk River because all the bridges were destroyed. The soldiers of the IV Corps crossed the Elk River in only their shoes in water as deep as their armpits, and the soldiers' clothes, blankets and weapons were carried over their heads. The "temperature was at the freezing point." They quickly scrambled into their dry clothes as soon as they reached the other side of the river. Motivated by the cold weather, it took only three hours for the corps to cross the river.[7]

Throughout the war, David Stanley held on to the belief that without discipline an army becomes a rabble and he issued orders in the fall of 1864 emphasizing the importance of protecting citizens and their property as much as possible. He discovered a soldier of the 59th Illinois Infantry inside a house and "struck him with his sword which was in its scabbard."[8] He was not going to tolerate this type of behavior by his men.

Also, Stanley's experience in 1863 taught the value of cavalry well used; and he was very complimentary of the actions of Union cavalry division which provided the observations of Hood's troops and provided timely notice of the movement of the Confederate army.

While Stanley was building defenses at Pulaski, Major General John Schofield's XXIII Corps which had been posted at Resaca, was placed under Thomas' command and was ordered to join Stanley in Pulaski. Hood's objective was to somehow disrupt the Union army in Georgia. His efforts included the destruction of the supply and communication lines, but he also had as his objective to cut off and destroy either Major General George

Thomas' force (19,000 men) in Nashville or defeat the Union forces scattered throughout Tennessee or Alabama. Hood's army totaled greater than 30,000 men. Stanley initially commanded about 5,000 men in Pulaski and could be an ideal target for Hood. Schofield, moving toward Pulaski, Tennessee, also proved an excellent target for Hood. For the Union forces, their hope was to rapidly unite into a force large enough to be able to repel an attack from Hood. Thomas recorded, "Hood's plans had now become evident, and from information gained through prisoners, deserters, and other sources, his intention was to cross into Middle Tennessee."[9]

Schofield Assumes Command

On November 4, Forrest struck Johnsonville, Tennessee, which served as a key supply depot on the Tennessee River and an important railroad center connecting Nashville to the East. More than $6,000,000 worth of supplies, four gunboats, fourteen transports, and twenty barges were destroyed by Forrest. Schofield's XXIII Corps arrived in Nashville on November 7. Thomas sent it directly toward Pulaski and then directed the corps to Johnsonville. As all of Stanley's corps concentrated at Pulaski, he commanded 12,000 men in the IV Corps, and Schofield commanded 10,000 in the XXIII Corps. Thomas sent a request for Major General A.J. Smith's XVI Corps, which has just completed a pursuit of Major General Sterling Price after his raid across Missouri, to hurry to Nashville. As Schofield marched toward the IV Corps, Thomas gave command to Union forces in the field to Schofield even though Stanley's date of service as major general superseded Schofield's. The question which arose at the Battle of Jonesboro of who was in command, Stanley or Schofield, was decided on October 4 by Henry Halleck. The order giving Schofield command cited his departmental command as the reason for granting overall command to him. "By virtue of his position as a department commander, Maj. Gen. J. M. Schofield will assume command of the troops now assembling at Pulaski, Tenn., and operating in front of that place," wrote Halleck.[10] The whole issue of who was in command was never brought up by Stanley. Schofield recorded Stanley told him he never desired to claim command, but Stanley was painted as being petulant by having to serve under Schofield.

However, the entire event seemed to escalate when Grant weighed into affair and wrote on November 7 that perhaps Stanley should be removed from command "if Schofield is likely to be embarrassed by Stanley's feeling soured at serving under a junior, and therefore not giving a hearty support, authority had better be given Schofield to remove the latter, when, in his judgment, the good of the service requires it."[11] As this process continued, Stanley became aware of how he was being portrayed in this affair. He wrote to Henry Halleck on October 20: "General: I have received a copy of your letter to Maj. Gen. W.T. Sherman, dated War Department, October 4, 1864, giving the opinion and decision of the honorable Secretary of War upon the question of rank between army commanders and their seniors serving with them. I very respectfully desire to state that the case upon which this decision is founded is an imaginary one, so far as I am concerned. No dispute upon the subject of rank has ever occurred between General Schofield and myself. He was not under my orders at the battle of Jonesborough, nor was I in any way responsible for the movements of his corps upon that occasion. I deem it necessary to make these statements as there seems to be a misunderstanding in the matter."[12] The entire affair was brought on through the machinations of others and yet Stanley suffered the effects.

Defense of Pulaski, Tennessee

Meanwhile, Stanley was facing Hood's army, which greatly outnumbered his own corps. Perhaps symbolizing the seriousness of Stanley's position in Pulaski, in early November Thomas sent an additional 400,000 rounds of ammunition to the IV Corps. Brigadier General Edward Hatch's cavalry also expressed concern about Hood's army on November 6. Hatch's cavalry had discovered pickets of Armstrong's Confederate cavalry and had driven them back toward the main enemy force. Hatch also noted, "We found some infantry south of the creek; also, three miles down on the creek at White's Ford a division of infantry. Two deserters who came in today say Hood is going to Murfreesborough."[13]

While posted in Pulaski, there were always local citizens coming and going from the town. Stanley humorously recalled "a funny little fellow with a little mule and a little bull broke to harness, drove up in a rickety wagon with a bale of cotton. The fellow had no shoes, and although the weather was cold, had only a cotton shirt and trousers, a single towstring of a suspender, completing his costume. He was a hard looking customer, but the avarice of the northern people, sometime the worldly greed of our own post commanders, always admitted cotton. He was allowed to come in and after selling his cotton he went around to see the soldiers. No one paid any attention to him until he was met by a union soldier from East Tennessee, whose sharp eyes recognized him and he brought him to me. He had concealed in that old shirt a very perfect map of all our lines and fortifications at Pulaski, and was a very bright and intelligent spy. We intended to hang that fellow but in the confusion of our retreat he escaped, and I am not sorry."[14]

While at Pulaski, Stanley kept his eyes open for the movement of Hood, and Schofield dispatched Jacob Cox's division closer to Stanley to offer support should it be needed. Stanley hoped the high water along the rivers would keep Hood from mounting an offensive until he could get his provisions, artillery and ammunition.

Major General John Schofield arrived in Pulaski, Tennessee, on November 14 and assumed command of the Union forces in central Tennessee. Although the temperature was cold enough to freeze, the roads were not frozen enough to adequately support loaded wagons. Stanley spent the time getting his supply trains moving and improving the defenses around the town. It was clear Hood's intention was to advance northward, but the destination was unknown. General Edward's Hatch's cavalry observed Hood's march northward toward Columbia, Tennessee, on November 21; but the traveling was difficult for both armies due to the excessive rain.

November 30, 1864[15]

FOURTH ARMY CORPS
MAJOR GENERAL DAVID S. STANLEY
First Division
BRIGADIER GENERAL NATHAN KIMBALL

First Brigade
COLONEL ISAAC M. KIRBY

21st Illinois, Capt. William H. Jamison
38th Illinois, Capt. Andrew M. Pollard
31st Indiana, Col. John T. Smith
81st Indiana, Maj. Edward G. Mathey
90th Ohio, Lt. Col. Samuel N. Yeoman
101st Ohio, Lt. Col. Bedan B. McDonald
45th Ohio, Lt. Col. John H. Humphrey
51st Ohio, Lt. Col. Charles H. Wood

Second Brigade
BRIGADIER GENERAL WALTHER WHITAKER

96th Illinois. Maj. George Hicks
115th Illinois, Col. Jesse Moore
35th Indiana, Lt. Col. Augustus Tassin
21st Kentucky, Lt. Col. James C. Evans
23rd Kentucky, Lt. Col. George Northup
40th Ohio (6 com), Lt. Col. James Watson

Third Brigade
BRIGADIER GENERAL WILLIAM GROSE

75th Illinois, Col. John E. Bennett
80th Illinois, Capt. James Cunningham
84th Illinois, Lieut. Col. Charles H. Morton
9th Indiana, Col. Isaac C.B. Suman
30th Indiana (three companies), Capt. Henry W. Lawton
36th Indiana (one company), Lieut. John P. Swisher
84th Indiana, Maj. John C. Taylor
77th Pennsylvania, Col. Thomas E. Rose

Second Division
BRIGADIER GENERAL GEORGE D. WAGNER

First Brigade
COLONEL EMERSON OPDYCKE

36th Illinois, Maj. Levi P. Holden
44th Illinois, Lt. Col. John Russell
73rd Illinois, Maj. Thomas W. Motherspaw
74th/88th Illinois, Lt. Col. George Smith
125th Ohio, Capt. Edward P. Bates
24th Wisconsin, Capt. Edwin B. Parsons

Second Brigade
COLONEL JOHN Q. LANE

100th Illinois, Lt. Col. Charles M. Hammond
40th Indiana, Lt. Col. Henry Learning
57th Indiana, Maj. John S. McGraw
28th Kentucky, Lt. Col. J. Rowan Boone
26th Ohio, Capt. William Clark
97th Ohio, Lt. Col. Milton Barnes

Third Brigade
BRIG. GEN. LUTHER BRADLEY (WOUNDED NOVEMBER 29), COL. JOSEPH CONRAD

42rd Illinois, Maj. Frederick A. Atwater
51st Illinois, Capt. Merritt B. Atwater
79th Illinois, Col. Allen Buckner
15th Missouri, Capt. George Ernst
64th Ohio, Lt. Col. Robert C. Brown
65th Ohio, Maj. Orlow Smith

Third Division
BRIGADIER GENERAL THOMAS J. WOOD

First Brigade
COLONEL ABEL D. STREIGHT

89th Illinois, Lieut. Col. William D. Williams
51st Indiana, Capt. William W. Scearce

Second Brigade
COLONEL P. SIDNEY POST

59th Illinois, Maj. James M. Stookey
41st Ohio, Lt. Col. Robert L. Kimberly

8th Kansas, Lieut. Col. John Conover
15th Ohio, Col. Frank Askew
49th Ohio, Maj. Luther M. Strong.

71st Ohio, Col. Henry K. McConnell
93d Ohio, Lt. Col. Daniel Bowman
124th Ohio, Lt. Col. James Pickands.

Third Brigade

Brigadier General Samuel Beatty

79th Indiana, Lieut. Col. George W. Parker
86th Indiana, Col. George F. Dick
17th Kentucky, Lieut. Col. Alexander M. Stout
13th Ohio, Maj. Joseph T. Snider
19th Ohio, Lieut. Col Henry G. Stratton

Artillery Brigade

Captain Lyman Bridges

Illinois Light, Bridges' Battery, Lt. Lyman A. White
Kentucky Light, 1st Battery, Capt. Theodore S. Thomasson
1st Ohio Light, Battery A, Lt. Charles W. Scovill
1st Ohio Light, Battery G, Capt. Alexander Marshall
Ohio Light, 6th Battery, Lt. Aaron P. Baldwin
Ohio Light, 20th Battery, Lt. John S. Burdick
Pennsylvania Light, Battery B, Capt. Jacob Ziegler
4th United States, Battery M, Lt. Samuel Canby

The Battle of Spring Hill

The IV Corps marched from Pulaski to Lynnville, Tennessee, about twenty miles due south of Columbia, on November 23. To their west Colonel Horace Capron's cavalry brigade was pushed out of Mount Pleasant by the advancing Confederate army. This was startling news to Stanley, because Hood was northwest of his position. In response Stanley pushed his corps, beginning the march at 1:00 a.m. toward Columbia to prevent being cut off from Nashville. Hood's intention was do just that—to cut off the IV Corps and XXIII Corps from Nashville and defeat each corps in turn. The information about Hood's advance was sent to the various Union forces in the area. General Jacob Cox's division of the XXIII Corps marched quickly three miles south of Columbia. They attacked the forward units of Hood's army and stopped the advance. Stanley's IV Corps reached Cox's line near Columbia and began entrenching, and although the Confederate cavalry made demonstrations on the line, no major engagements occurred. Stanley's march was strong and urgent; Schofield reported to General George Thomas: "Hood had ten miles the start of Stanley at noon yesterday, but Stanley outmarched him and reached here at ten o'clock to-day. His troops are all here and in position."[16] Two days later Hood's army deployed to Stanley's front and Stanley recorded the enemy "made several attacks upon our pickets; but it became evident very soon that Hood was moving to the east, and most likely with a view of crossing Duck River above us. The intentions of the enemy became so apparent that it was determined to cross the entire of our force to the north bank of Duck River."[17]

As the Union movements occurred in late November 1864, the commanders of the various brigades were back at their posts. Stanley's First Division was commanded by Nathan

George Wagner's division made a heroic stand at Spring Hill (Library of Congress).

Kimball, a favorite of Stanley, and his brigade commanders were Colonel Isaac Kirby (First Brigade), Brigadier General Walter Whitaker (Second Brigade), Brigadier General William Grose (Third Brigade). His Second Division was commanded by General George Wagner and his brigade commanders were Colonel Emerson Opdycke (First Brigade), Colonel John Q. Lane (Second Brigade) and Brigadier General Luther P. Brady (Third Brigade). It would be the Second Division that would be involved in the most action during the upcoming battles at Spring Hill and Franklin. The Third Division was commanded by Brigadier General Thomas J. Wood and his brigade commanders were Colonel Abel Streight (First Brigade), Colonel Sidney Post (Second Brigade) and Brigadier General Samuel Beatty (Third Brigade).

Fearing Hood was making a flanking movement, Stanley again ordered his troops to begin to withdraw, but the rain so severe it wasn't until the night November 27 that this was accomplished. Stanley attempted to burn a fort and magazine, which task was only partially completed due to the dampness. The morning of November 28 found Stanley a mile north of Columbia on high ground. The defenses on the north side of the Duck River were being strengthened when it was learned Forrest had been observed five miles north of Columbia. The likelihood of being cut off from Nashville was becoming more real.

November 29 was a day of high stakes for the Union army, which Stanley would record "was the biggest day's work I ever accomplished for the United States."[18] The outcome of the battles of Franklin and Nashville were set by the actions taken by Stanley and Schofield on November 29. The race for Spring Hill began when Brigadier General James Wilson, commanding the Union cavalry, erroneously reported Forrest had laid a pontoon bridge at Huey's Mill when Forrest had actually crossed at Davis Ford. Nevertheless, the Confederate cavalry was close to cutting off both Stanley's IV Corps and John Schofield's XXIII Corps. At 8:00 a.m. Stanley sent his First and Second divisions marching quickly toward Spring Hill.

General George Wagner's Second Division reached Spring Hill at 11:30 a.m. after a report by a cavalry scout that the Confederates were also approaching Spring Hill. Wagner quickened his march and reached Spring Hill in time and, fortunately, gained control of the town before the main Confederate force could arrive. Wagner's division was able to push the Confederate cavalry out of Spring Hill and quickly set up defenses. Stanley and Wagner

Union artillery again played a key part in Stanley's success in defending Spring Hill (Library of Congress).

positioned the men to cover the road to Franklin and Columbia. Stanley ordered Opdycke's and Lane's brigades to protect as much space about the village as would serve for room to park the trains. Next Bradley's brigade was positioned on a wooded knoll about three-quarters of a mile east of the pike, where he commanded the ground to the southeast.[19] The afternoon battle would pit David Stanley against two-thirds of Hood's army. The stakes were Schofield's army, an 800-wagon supply train and fifty artillery pieces. This was to be one of Stanley's best days in the war.

When Wagner's division was battling the Confederates for possession of Spring Hill, Stanley received a message from Schofield: "Wood's reconnaissance shows a considerable force, at least, on this side of the river. I have halted Kimball's division this side of the creek and put it in position. I will try to hold the enemy until dark, and then draw back. Select a good position at Spring Hill, covering the approaches, and send out parties to reconnoiter on all roads leading east and southeast."[20] Stanley read the last sentence realizing he had a long afternoon ahead if he was to prevent the approaching Confederates from gaining the Union rear with a single division. Stanley had George Wagner's division in Spring Hill facing an increasing number of Confederate lines and he also had 800 wagons to worry about.

Stanley, who initially thought his Second Division was just facing Forrest's cavalry, soon found he faced Confederate infantry. He received a message from Schofield informing him the Confederates were crossing the river, "leaving no doubt but that we now confronted a superior force of rebel infantry.... Thus we were threatened and attacked from every direction, and it was impossible to send any re-enforcements to Bradley's brigade, which had

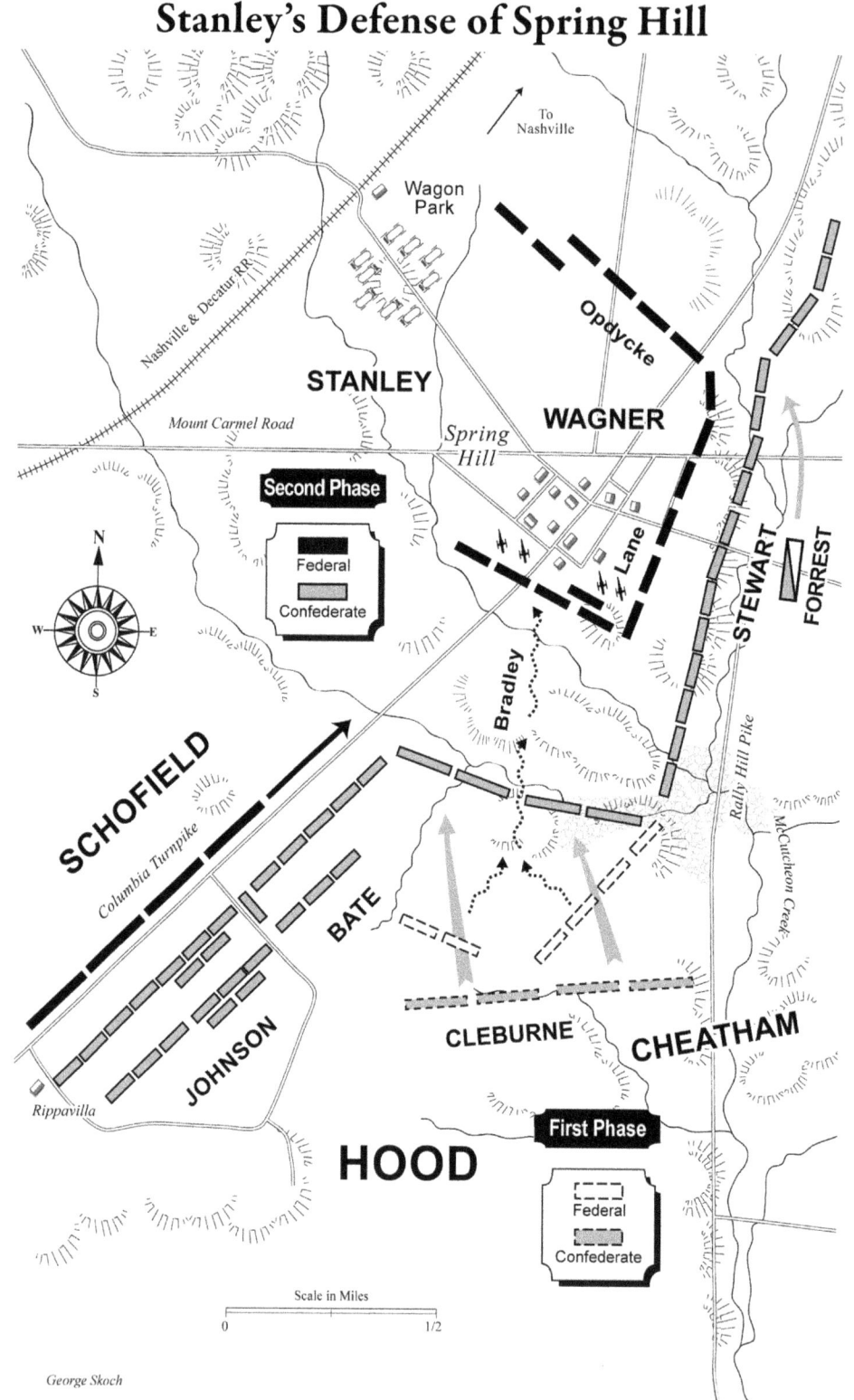

Stanley's Defense of Spring Hill

become quite severely engaged, lest in so doing we should expose the train and artillery park to destruction."[21] With Schofield directing Kimball's First Division and Wood's Third Division, Stanley was in the precarious and extremely important position of guarding the only exit with Wagner's single division.

Stanley was lucky on the battlefield, and his experience paid dividends. On November 29, he was again favored by events on the battlefield. At 4:00 p.m. Hood ordered Major General Pat Cleburne's division to march to the Columbia-Franklin Turnpike then wheel left and strike Schofield's troops marching toward Spring Hill. As Cleburne's division marched toward the Columbia-Franklin Pike, Bradley's Third Brigade loosed a volley in the flank of the advancing Confederate line. The 43-year-old Bradley was a native of Connecticut and had lived in Chicago before the war. He had plenty of experience as he faced the lines of butternut forming to his front. First commissioned as lieutenant colonel of the 51st Illinois Infantry Regiment, he had fought at Island No.10, Corinth, Battle of Stone River, Tullahoma and Chickamauga, where he was wounded twice. On November 29 at Spring Hill he was ready when the attack came.

Brigadier General Mark Lowrey's brigade of Alabamans and Mississippians turned and faced Bradley's brigade. Lowrey's brigade was repulsed, but it was quickly joined by Brigadier General Daniel Govan's Arkansas brigade. The two Confederate brigades charged Bradley's line personally led by Major General Pat Cleburne. The Confederate brigades soon outflanked Bradley's line, which fell back in chaos. Bradley, sensing the collapse, hastened to his old regiment, the 51st Illinois Infantry, to stop the flight and was severely wounded while rallying his soldiers.

The retreat was a rout and with the retreat loomed the loss of the wagon train, the collapse of Stanley's Second Division and the probable loss of the remaining Union divisions under Schofield's command. Stanley scrambled to find a way to re-form his line, and just as he had done so many times in the past, he directed his artillery to blast the advancing Confederate lines with everything they had. This had worked in Corinth in May 1862 and at Resaca in 1863, and the stakes were never higher than at Spring Hill in November 1864. Stanley recorded, "The rebel troops tried to follow but the fire of six batteries appalled them. The ground was planted in corn and was very muddy, and if the Johnnies in gray were not hit with artillery missiles, they were covered with mud.... Our cannonade was simply magnificent."[22] Stanley had positioned his guns at the southern edge of Spring Hill, and as Cleburne charged northward the cannons exploded.

While the battle was raging on the south edge of the town, George Wagner rode to Colonel John Lane's brigade posted on the east side of Spring Hill and ordered two regiments to line up with Stanley's artillery. Lane had a total of 1,600 men, and in addition to giving up his two regiments, he ordered his Second Brigade to change front from the east to the direction of the Confederate attack. Then a portion of the Second Brigade advanced to a line on the south side of Spring Hill to meet the impending attack. This new line hurried to extend the Union line, crossing Rally Hill Pike. But seeing the fresh Union infantry falling into line, the Confederates ceased attacking.

Stanley summarized the battle: "The enemy made two assaults on Bradley's position, and were severely handled and repulsed; but finding his flank the third time they overlapped him on his right, and the general at the time receiving a severe wound whilst encouraging his men, his brigade was driven back to the outskirts of the village, where we rallied them and again formed them in line. The enemy attempted to follow up his advantage, but coming across the corn-field toward the village they fell under the fire of at least eight pieces of artillery, at good range for spherical case-shot, and received a fire in flank from a section of a battery which had been placed on the pike south of the village."[23] Bradley's Second Brigade reported about 150 men killed, wounded and missing during the battle. The estimate of Confederate casualties was attributed to a Southern surgeon who reported the loss at 500.

As the day ended, Stanley stoutly defended the Franklin-Columbia Turnpike, but the full might of Hood's army extended in his front two and half miles. Stanley had been lucky in his defense at Spring Hill, but he had stood his ground. He was able to draw upon his experiences and piece together a defense which was remarkable. If Hood had been able to mount a more coordinated attack on Stanley's position, it is unlikely Stanley would have been able to withstand it. Schofield was racing with the Ruger's, Cox's, Kimball's and Wood's divisions to reach Stanley, who guarded the only route which prevented Schofield from being trapped or Nashville lost if the Union forces could be not united before Hood struck. Stanley reported, "General Schofield arrived from Columbia at 7 o'clock in the evening with Ruger's division. He found the enemy on the pike, and had quite a skirmish in driving them off. My pickets had reported seeing rebel columns passing east of our position as if to get possession of the hills at Thompson's Station, and the anxious question arose whether we could force our way through to Franklin."[24] The tension was palpable.

Schofield's aide-de-camp wrote to General George Thomas about the closeness of the situation at Spring Hill and Franklin: "Their cavalry reached that point at 4 p.m. and their infantry came in before dark and attacked General Stanley, who held the place with one division, very heavily. General Schofield's troops are pushing for Franklin as rapidly as possible. The general ... regards his situation as extremely perilous, and fears that he may be forced into a general battle tomorrow or lose his wagon train."[25] Schofield praised Stanley's defense at Spring Hill, "The gallant action of Stanley and his one division at that place in the afternoon of November 29 cannot be overstated or too highly praised."[26]

In one of the most unlikely and gutsiest calls of the war, Schofield and Stanley decided to try to silently slip past the Confederate camp, in full view of their campfires, and escape toward Franklin. At 11:00 p.m. Jacob Cox's division arrived at Spring Hill while Stanley was questioning a captured Confederate captain. Then the Union divisions began marching northward to Franklin. Jacob Cox's division marched out of Spring Hill by 1:00 a.m. and then came the slow exit of the supply train, 800 wagons long. The supply train included not only ammunition and other supplies but also ambulances and the ever-so-important artillery. Stanley knew only a miracle would save the train. It had to begin its movement north with each wagon passing single file over a small bridge, and all 800 wagons had to be out of Spring Hill by daylight. Stanley recorded the events of the movement toward Franklin:

> So close were the enemy on our flank that, when a column was not passing, it was difficult for a staff officer or an orderly to get through on the road.... Unless this could be done, and the corps put in motion, we were sure of being attacked at daylight and of being compelled to fight under every disadvantage. I was strongly advised to burn the train, and move on with the troops and such wagons as could be saved, but I determined to make an effort to save the train. My staff officers were busily employed hurrying up teamsters, and everything promised well, when we were again thrown into despair by the report that the train was attacked north of Thompson's Station, and that the whole train had stopped.[27]

The disaster Stanley had feared had occurred: the Confederates had attacked the Union retreat north of Spring Hill. Stanley feared the entire Union train would be lost.

Surprisingly, it was Major Steele of Stanley's staff who averted the disaster. Steele and the headquarters guard consisting of thirty-five men organized a group of stragglers to drive off the attackers after ten wagons were set afire. The Union wagon train had been attacked by Brigadier General Lawrence Ross' Texas Cavalry, and as Stanley's guard came running from the dark the Confederate cavalry withdrew, unable to determine the number of men who were attacking. Ross' cavalry remained some distance from the train, and "Stanley had wisely ordered two infantry divisions, Kimball's and Wood's, to escort the main segments of the wagon train, and they were soon observed marching protectively alongside the slow-moving wagons."[28] From 1:00 a.m. until daybreak, the Union artillery and wagon train quietly moved out of Spring Hill and along the Franklin Turnpike toward Franklin. Stanley noted it was a starlit night as the wagon train inched toward the town. Stanley recorded the tension as the wagons left Spring Hill: "It was now 3 o'clock in the morning. General Kimball was directed to push on with the First Division and clear the road. General Wood's division, which had deployed in the night north of Spring Hill and, facing the east, had covered the road, was directed to move on, keeping off the road and on the right flank of the train, and General Wagner's division, although wearied by the fighting of the day before, was detailed to bring up the rear.... At about 5 o'clock I had the satisfaction of seeing the last wagon pass the small bridge."[29]

At last all of the IV Corps and the wagons quietly marched out of Spring Hill by daylight, but still the arduous march to Franklin lay ahead. There were plenty of Confederate cavalry, and the enemy's infantry still had the opportunity to overtake the wagon train. After daylight the Confederate cavalry circled around the Union force and made several demonstrations but Stanley had positioned his infantry around the train and the cavalry was repulsed. At one point Stanley had to unlimber a battery of artillery to fight off the rebel attack. Colonel Emerson Opdycke's First Brigade of Wagner's division formed the rear guard for the entire march to Franklin and skirmished throughout the journey. There was no time to linger for stragglers and the wounded who struggled to keep up the march. Wilbur Hinman of Bradley's Third Brigade recorded, "A few days later he [General Luther Bradley] wrote: 'It was the most critical time I have ever seen. If only the enemy had shown his usual boldness, I think he would have beaten us disastrously.' Indeed, that the Union army had escaped intact soon came to be considered the decree of Providence."[30]

As Stanley watched the retreat of the Union forces toward Franklin, he noticed a battery of artillery still unlimbered and in place at Spring Hill. He rode to the battery and discovered it was the 6th Ohio Battery and he inquired why they had not limbered and moved out. The artillerymen replied they were posted there in the afternoon and had never received orders to move. Stanley said, "You are now relieved. Take your guns and proceed to Franklin; and I desire to say to you that you have not one chance in a hundred of reaching that place. There are more than thirty thousand rebels between you and Franklin, and you will undoubtedly be attacked or cut off before you get through." The battery moved toward Franklin with the battery commander riding along carrying gun spikes and a hammer. Remarkably, the battery made it through the enemy lines.[31]

By the next morning, Hood awoke to find that Ruger's, Cox's, Wood's, Kimball's and Wagner's divisions had simply and quietly walked past the sleeping soldiers of his army and, even more unbelievable, Stanley had been able to withdraw the entire 800 wagons to the rear. The plan to isolate Union forces and destroy them in turn was lost. Now the IV Corps and XXIII Corps were united and marching toward Franklin. When Hood became aware of what had happened he unleashed his anger, much of which fell on Pat Cleburne and Benjamin Cheatham.

Stanley's postwar assessment of the Battle of Spring Hill answered what he considered the result would have been if Hood had effectively cut off Schofield's retreat. He mentioned three points: Schofield could not have effectively battled Hood, being separated from his artillery and ammunition; the Union troops attempting to reach Nashville would have been scattered and without sufficient mass to battle Hood; and the Union forces separated and attacked from all sides would not have made an effective stand. Stanley wrote, "You sometimes read of fellows 'Cutting their way out.' To use an Irish bull, these fellows usually surrender their way out."[32] The fact that Stanley was able to hold the road at Spring Hill, allowing five Union divisions to pass under the noses of their enemy, and then to effectively withdraw 800 wagons along the same route during the night was surely one of the luckiest and brashest maneuvers in the war. Had this failed, the Battle of Franklin, which occurred the next day, almost assuredly would have ended differently, as well as the events at Nashville. Luck favored the bold on the afternoon and night of November 29–30, 1864, in Spring Hill, Tennessee.

The Battle of Franklin

Once Schofield reached Franklin, he quickly distributed his troops with the order to begin construction of defenses around the town should Hood continue his pursuit. The last of the IV Corps reached Franklin by noon and Hood was close behind. If the Battle of Spring Hill was Stanley's best day in the Civil War, the Battle of Franklin was a near second, and one that would nearly cost him his life.

When Schofield arrived at Franklin after the narrow escape at Spring Hill he was faced with another serious situation. The swollen Harpeth River ran through Franklin but he had no expedient way of moving his troops and wagons across the river. The river had some fords which still allowed troops to cross. Pontoon bridges were supposed to have been sent by Thomas but these had not yet arrived. Schofield decided he would hold Franklin until a wagon bridge could be constructed and he ordered Thomas Wood's division of the IV Corps to the north side of the river to protect the crossing. The wagon bridge was finished by noon, but the slow process of getting 800 wagons across the bridge meant it would be nightfall before Schofield could again proceed northward. Schofield was aware he had another difficult day ahead for his command, but he doubted Hood would attack such a well-defended position.

Schofield went through a series of communications with Thomas during the morning of November 30 in which Thomas desired to hold Hood at Franklin while he sent additional troops, namely Major General A.J. Smith's XVI Corps, to support Schofield. Schofield answered, "I have just received your dispatch asking whether I can hold Hood here three days. I do not believe I can. I can doubtless hold him one day, but will hazard something in doing that. He now has a large force, probably two corps, in my front, and seems prepared to cross the river above and below. I think he can effect a crossing tomorrow, in spite of all my efforts, and probably tonight, if he attempts it. A worse position than this for an inferior force could hardly be found."[33]

As the Union position at Franklin was being sorted, confidence began to build with the Union ranks. The wagon train had safely entered the Union lines, the wagon bridge had been completed over the Harpeth River, and the infantry was entrenching around the town. Stanley had been ill during the morning in the residence of Dr. Daniel Cliffe on November 30 after being without sleep for 48 hours. At 1:00 p.m. Stanley and Schofield "rode to the residence of Alpheus Truett, about a half mile north of the Harpeth River on the pike to Nashville. Here Schofield's new headquarters was established."[34] The two generals worked through the final details of the defense and planned their steady retreat the last nineteen miles to Nashville. Meanwhile, Brigadier Jacob Cox had "control of virtually all of the army's infantry except for Wood's division of the Fourth Corps."[35] As the Union defenses were being finalized, George Wagner's brigade, which had fought so stoutly the day before, was halted and ordered to defend Winstead Hill, about two miles south of Franklin, until dark, if possible.[36]

At noon, Wagner noticed lines of Confederate infantry marching toward his position and, being so exposed, he ordered his division to march toward Franklin. As he was marching toward the safety of the Union lines, he received an order from Stanley instructing him to hold Winstead Hill: "The general commanding directs that you hold the heights you now occupy until dark, unless too severely pressed; that you relieve Colonel Opdycke with one of your brigades, and leave his and the remaining brigade as a support; and that you cross the river to the north bank after dark, at which time the position you are to occupy will be pointed out to you."[37] Wagner then began a countermarch back to Winstead Hill. In the meantime, Stanley had received a message from Wagner stating he was abandoning the heights. Since Cox had control of the infantry and the defenses of Franklin, Stanley made no further orders. The luck Stanley had on the previous day proved to be fickle due to the confusion and miscommunication which occurred over command and orders.

As for Wagner, he marched back to Winstead Hill and soon was aware his position was untenable. He was being flanked by Hood's approaching army, and he ordered his division to march quickly to Franklin. About halfway to Franklin, Wagner stopped

Jacob Cox was responsible for the preparation of the Union defenses at Franklin (Library of Congress).

and turned to prepare a defense against the relentless Confederates. He placed Lane's brigade at Privet Knob, a hundred-foot rise, supported by artillery. Another half mile toward Franklin, Wagner deployed Colonel Joseph Conrad's brigade—Conrad had replaced Bradley, who had been wounded the previous day—on a small elevation to the east of the Columbia Pike. Next, Wagner ordered Opdycke's brigade to deploy west of the turnpike, but Colonel Emerson Opdycke had endured enough. He refused to obey Wagner's orders and continued to march for Franklin. Wagner rode alongside Opdycke demanding he follow his orders, but Opdycke continued his march to Franklin. Wagner, remembering Stanley's orders to relieve Opdycke, allowed him to continue on this march.

Wagner rode to Cox's headquarters, where he was for the first time informed he was under Jacob Cox's command and realized why he had received no further orders from Stanley. Wagner reported to Cox the solid lines of Confederate infantry which had caused him to retreat from Winstead Hill. Cox had just received orders from Schofield to prepare to move the XXIII Corps to the north side of the Harpeth River. So he gave Wagner no further orders, but told Wagner to follow his earlier orders.

None of the Union commanders except Wagner seriously considered an attack from Hood to be likely. Historian Wiley Sword observed, "From the evidence, it appears that Cox told Wagner that the appearance of the Confederate infantry was in all probability a sham, a deception to convince the Union army they were about to attack, while actually preparing to bypass Franklin by another flanking march, Cox only added that Wagner should slowly retire his two brigades within the main line if actually compelled to do so. The tenor of Cox's instructions was unmistakable: to hold Hood so as to allow the Federal army to get away."[38] With these orders, Wagner returned to his command on the Columbia Turnpike to

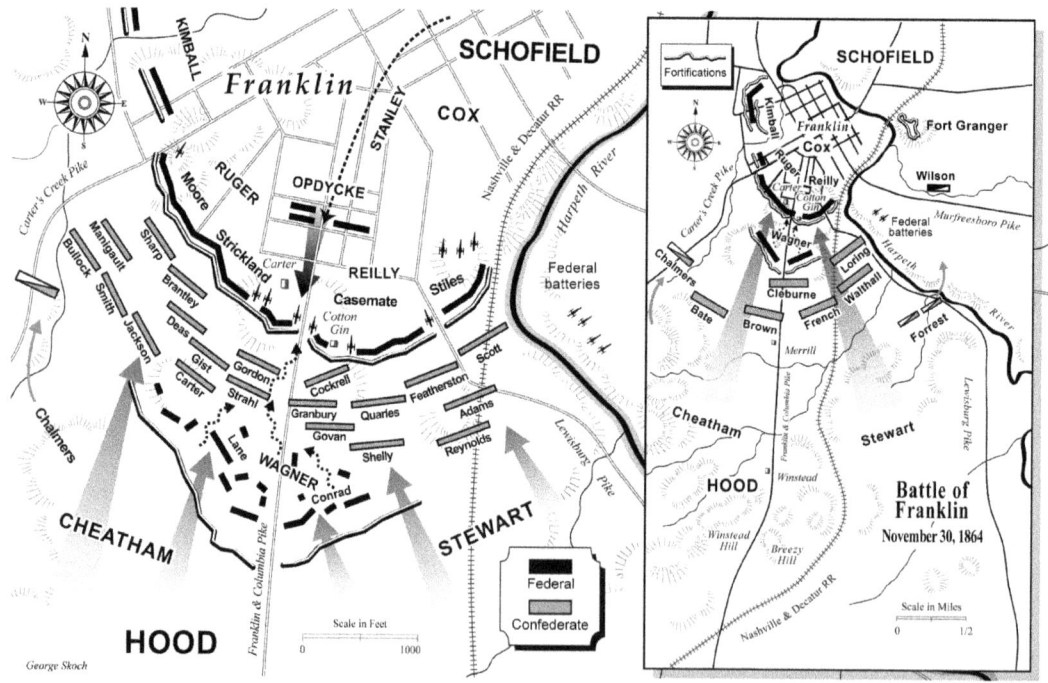

The Battle of Franklin

find Lane and his artillery moving back toward Franklin, and Colonel Conrad explained the need to retreat: "Wagner exploded with wrathful invectives and not only told Conrad to stay put, but to have his sergeants fix their bayonets and forcibly keep the men at their post."[39]

As the Confederates marched toward Franklin, they faced three lines of defenses. Despite the urgings of the divisional commanders, Hood was determined to attack the Union line. On the Union side of the line, despite the warning given by Wagner, when the mass of gray-clad soldiers appeared outside Franklin the Union officers were surprised. Stanley asked the question both the Union and Confederate officers were all asking: "Why try this desperate assault? The fact is that the fight was a result of Hood's charging and pique over the failure of his strategy and tactic the day before. He had indulged in high words with Cheatham and Cleburne as they rode to Franklin that morning and Hood was wrought to that pitch of desperation which only copious bloodshed can assuage."[40]

At 4:00 p.m. the attack began and the Confederate army flung itself at the Union line. Lane and Conrad appealed to Wagner to retire to the Union defenses, but Wagner refused, sending messages to both commanders to "fight like hell."[41] It was impossible for Lane and Conrad to withstand the Confederate attack and the brigades inevitably ran for the defenses at Franklin, with the Confederates on their heels. In some cases the Confederates were intermixed with the running Union soldiers and entered the Union works together, hindering the defenses at the main Union line. All along the remaining Union line, it was a different story. The Union infantry looking across the field and firmly placed behind excellent defenses released a terrible volley into the approaching Confederate lines. It was the Union center, encumbered by Wagner's routed brigades, which threatened the collapse of the Union line.

As Wagner's troops ran to the Union lines, their disorganization unnerved the Union soldiers manning the defenses and some of these soldiers turned and joined the rout. Conrad wrote in his after action report, "Immediately as our men left the works the enemy fired several volleys at us, and then charged after us. Owing to the great number of recruits in the brigade my men became very much confused. As fast as the men reached the inner line of works they halted, and would have been easily rallied, but the works were manned by the Twenty-third Corps, and the men of that corps became panic-stricken when my men rushed over them, and they (the Twenty-third Corps) commenced leaving the works."[42]

Stanley and Schofield were at Dr. Cliffe's house earlier in the day. John Shellenberger, author of *The Battle of Franklin*, wrote, "Stanley and Cliffe had been schoolboys together in Wayne County, Ohio, and as Cliffe was a well known Union man, it was supposed to be unsafe for him to remain in Franklin and he was invited to accompany Schofield and Stanley on their ride to Nashville. General Schofield has claimed that he scored a great success in his campaign against Hood and that this success was largely due to his intimate knowledge of Hood's character, gained while they were classmates at West Point, which enabled him to foresee what Hood would do and then make the proper dispositions to defeat him."[43]

Once the generals became aware of the battle, they mounted their horses and rode in different directions. "When Stanley started for the front Schofield started for the rear, and the most charitable construction that can be placed upon his action is that he interpreted the sound of the firing to mean that the expected flank movement had begun and that his duty called him across the river to provide against that flank movement. His disturbed mental condition at that time is disclosed by the fact that he abandoned in the room of Cliffe's house, where he had slept, his overcoat, gloves, and a package containing the official dispatches he had received from General Thomas."[44] The different actions of Stanley and Schofield were noted by several different soldiers. William Dodge, author of the history of the 74th Illinois Infantry, noted, "Another wrote that he [Schofield] was 'well beyond the range of every rebel bullet that was fired,' and still another veteran bitterly remarked that the general 'possessed the "rascally virtue called caution" in an eminent degree' and was never known to be 'reckless enough to expose his carcass to the fire of the rebels.'"[45] David Stanley heard the roar of the cannon and muskets, and with his years of experience he knew he needed to ride to the sound of the guns as he always did.[46] Stanley and a single orderly rode hard to the battle only to be confronted with the center of the Union line disintegrating before their eyes. Stanley later wrote his report:

> When Wagner's division fell back from the heights south of Franklin, Opdycke's brigade was placed in reserve in rear of our main line, on the Columbia pike. Lane's and Conrad's brigades were deployed—the former on the right, the other the left of the pike—about 300 yards in front of the main line. Here the men, as our men always do, threw up a barricade of rails. By whose mistake I cannot tell, it certainly was never a part of my instructions, but these brigades had orders from General Wagner not to retire to the main line until forced to do so by the fighting of the enemy.... The part of the Twenty-third Corps stationed in the works for a distance of about three [hundred] or four [hundred] yards to the right of the Columbia pike, and which space took in the First Kentucky and Sixth Ohio Batteries, broke and ran to the rear with the fugitives from Conrad's brigade. To add to the disorder the caissons of the two batteries galloped rapidly to the rear, and the enemy appeared on the breast-works and in possession of the two batteries, which they commenced to turn upon us. It was at this moment I arrived at the scene of disorder, coming from the town on the Columbia pike; the moment was critical beyond all I have known in any battle—could the enemy hold that part of the line, he was nearer to our two bridges than the extremities of our line. Colonel Opdycke's brigade was lying down about 100 yards in rear of the works. I rode quickly to the left regiment and called to them to charge; at the same time I saw Colonel Opdycke near the center of his line urging his men forward. I gave the colonel no order, as I saw him engaged in doing the very thing to save us, viz, to get possession of our line again. The retreating men of Colonel Conrad's brigade, and, I believe, the men of the Twenty-third Corps, seeing the line of Opdycke's brigade start for the works, commenced to rally. I heard the old soldiers call out, 'Come on, men, we can go wherever the general can, and making a rush, our men immediately retook all the line, excepting a small portion just in front of the brick house on the pike. A force of the rebels held out at this point, and for fifteen or twenty minutes, supported by a rebel line fifty yards to the rear, poured in a severe fire upon our men.[47]

The initial Confederate breakthrough was stopped. Stanley recalled he saw a large group of soldiers jumping over the Union defenses and he was concerned the enemy was breaking through again and rode to the commotion. As he approached the group he was shot and his horse was killed at the same instant. Stanley fell to the right and the horse to left. Stanley moved to General Cox's position and was given another horse. Stanley noted he stayed and assisted with the defense until 8:00 p.m. when he retired from the field. Later, he found the minié ball which had wounded him lodged in his clothing.[48]

Another Union soldier recorded Stanley's presence on the field at Franklin: "Stanley hurried to the front which he reached just as Opdycke's brigade was starting forward. Spurring his horse to the front of this brigade, he personally led it in its famous charge. A little later his horse was shot under him and he got a bullet through the back of his neck as he was rising to his feet. It was a flesh wound that bled freely, but Stanley declined to leave the front until after the fighting was all over. He then went to the rear to have his wound dressed and after his departure Cox was the senior general on the battlefield."[49] David Stanley was the only Union general to be wounded during the battle.

Lyman Bennett and William Haugh, 36th Illinois Infantry, recalled the order for Opdycke's brigade: "Opdycke sprang to the front, and waving his sword, shouted, 'Up and at them, men!' Just at that moment Gen. Stanley dashed up to the left of the line, and with soul-stirring enthusiasm urging the men forward to the rescue. The efforts of these officers were bravely seconded by the regimental commanders."[50]

The Union counterattack, which included more regiments than just Opdcyke's brigade, stopped Hood's breakthrough on the Union center. Afterward, several additional Confederates attempts were made to penetrate the Union line, but without success. The Confederates still held the outside defenses and in some places the two lines were 200 yards apart. The last Confederate attack took place at 9:00 in the evening, but again

Emerson Opdycke's brigade played an important part in stopping the Confederate breakthrough at Franklin (Library of Congress).

the attack failed. Schofield's plan was to march northward to unite his forces with Thomas, but he had to extricate the troops and march nineteen miles to Nashville. He feared another flanking movement by Hood. So at midnight the Union troops began their march to Nashville, with the Union flanks withdrawing first followed by the pickets, which retreated after the army was across the Harpeth River. One final complication occurred before the Union troops were across the river. Stanley recalled: "Some villain came very near frustrating this plan by firing a house in Franklin; the flames soon spread, and the prospect was that a large fire would occur, which, lighting up objects, would make it impossible to move the troops without being seen. My staff officers and General Wood's found an old fire engine, and getting it at work, the flames were soon subdued and the darkness was found to be increased by the smoke."[51]

Stanley's IV Corps recorded a loss of 1,368 men during the Battle of Franklin, with 1,192 of the casualties from Wagner's Second Division. As it turned out, the Battle of Franklin was a decisive Union victory, but the battle was saved by quick thinking by key Union officers. For General John Bell Hood, the Battle of Franklin was a bloody affair, with an estimated 2,300 casualties for the Union army as opposed to 6,261 casualties for the Confederate army. In addition to the massive losses of Hood's army at Franklin were the great command losses, which included fifteen Confederate generals (six killed or mortally wounded, eight wounded, and one captured) and 53 regimental commanders. The loss of these officers to Hood, particularly Major General Patrick Cleburne, was incalculable because they had shown such an outstanding ability to lead men in battle this late in the war. The losses had been so severe, "in Cleburne's division the highest ranking officer left in Granbury's brigade was a captain."[52]

Schofield's army marched out of Franklin on the evening of November 30 and reached Nashville the next day. Hood was not to be denied, as he marched on Nashville and would fight the Battle of Nashville on December 15–16. Despite Hood's smaller army, he marched toward Nashville and stopped a few miles south of the city where he began to construct a series of defenses on which he hoped the soldiers of the Union army would throw themselves. The battle resulted in a decisive Union victory even though Hood had devised a plan to defensively defeat Thomas. The plan nearly worked, but the Confederate line broke on the afternoon of December 16 when a somewhat impetuous attack made by Brigadier General John McArthur's division of the XVI Corps broke the Confederate line, resulting in a rout of Hood's army.

On December 2, General George Wagner knew he was in trouble for his actions at the Battle of Franklin that nearly caused the Union center to collapse. Although Wagner was not alone in making mistakes, he was to receive most of the blame for the crisis in the Union center. When the army reached Nashville, Stanley, who was suffering from his neck wound, turned over command of the IV Corps to General Thomas Wood. Wagner was ordered to relinquish divisional command, and rather than face formal charges he quietly resigned.

As Thomas faced Hood on the hills south of Nashville, the old animosity between Grant and Thomas began again. This time Schofield, the politically savvy general, was there waiting in the wings. Despite what some consider Schofield's subversive attempts to undermine Thomas and Grant's nearly relieving Thomas of his command, the Union army prevailed at Nashville and the Confederate army was pushed out of Tennessee, resulting in Hood's resignation.

Schofield wrote of Stanley's actions in the campaign: "General Stanley is deserving of special commendation, and has my hearty thanks for his cordial support and wise counsel throughout the short but eventful campaign."[53] General George Thomas wrote, "I would also recommend Generals Schofield and Stanley be brevetted one grade in the regular service, for gallantry and good conduct at the battle of Franklin, November 30, 1864."[54]

Various descriptions would be made of Stanley's wound at the Battle of Franklin, but medical records reported the "ball passed transversely through the skin and the integuments of the posterior and inferior part of his neck and emerged about three inches from the point of entrance.... [B]y late December there was localized inflammation and suppuration of the wound."[55] The wound was painful and would take time to heal, but it was not life threatening.

Emerson Opdycke wrote to Lucy Opdycke on December 2 recounting some important items which would later become points of dispute when credit was claimed for the victory at Franklin. Opdycke wrote, "Stanley was wounded in the neck, but did not retire from the field. He came on to the field and helped me with his presence, and with his owns hands in the desperate work."[56]

Summary

The Battle of Franklin would be the last active engagement for David Stanley in the Civil War. He had been moved aside by Sherman because of the "affair" at Jonesboro. Next, he was placed under the command of John Schofield, who did not have the field experience of Stanley. The politics of the Union army in the west centered on Grant and Sherman, and these generals clearly had no confidence in the Army of the Cumberland and General George Thomas. Stanley was placed in command of the IV Corps by Thomas, and Stanley had the audacity to challenge Sherman over the orders given during the Battle of Jonesboro. However, Stanley clearly showed his abilities during this campaign and did much to save Schofield's reputation and future in the army.

Stanley had little respect for Schofield, seeing him a political general rather than a fighting general. The full measure of Schofield's politics was not to be seen until the Battle of Nashville fought in mid–December 1864. "Two Union generals, D.S. Stanley and Thomas Wood, then at Nashville, warned Thomas Schofield was a Judas on his staff," wrote historian Benson Bobrick.[57] Thomas had come dangerously close to losing his command at Nashville, as Schofield was sending messages to Grant criticizing Thomas' command decisions. Fully aware of the type of general he served, Stanley performed extraordinary duty during this campaign.

One of the unfortunate occurrences of the battles of the Civil War was the effort to claim credit for actions taken or not taken. How a soldier performed his duty was under the scrutiny of the country and the world as the drama of the Civil War played out. The key events at the Battle of Franklin centered on Wagner's brigade stationed outside the Union lines and their unorganized retreat through those Union lines, which nearly caused the Union center to collapse. Of equally, or more, importance was the charge of Opdycke's brigade to plug the center as it was breaking. The three key figures in claiming the credit were David Stanley, Emerson Opdycke and Jacob Cox. Wagner, who had performed so well at Spring Hill, was relieved of divisional command on December 2 and had no part in the controversy which occurred later.

Clearly Cox, Opdycke and Stanley were all key characters in the Battle of Franklin and all played important parts that resulted in the Union victory. However, the verbal battle over the extent to which each individual performed specific duties would last for years after the war. For David Stanley's efforts in rallying the troops and leading the charge, he would be awarded the Medal of Honor, but not until 1893. There were twenty-seven Medals of Honor awarded for action during the campaign in middle Tennessee in November and December 1864. Only three of those commendations would be awarded for bravery; the remainder would be for the capture of enemy flags. Congress approved Stanley's award for "Distinguished bravery in the battle of Franklin, Tenn."[58]

Ill feelings persisted for years after the battle. Stanley sent letters to various commanders after the war seeking their acknowledgement of his part in the battle as other commanders presented varying accounts. For example, Stanley wrote to General Nathan Kimball in 1867 asking him to write his recollections of Stanley's part during the Battle of Franklin, stating, "This I deem necessary from the malignant and persistent efforts of the villain, T.J. Wood, to deprive me of every particle of credit in that affair."[59] This would be just one of many letters Stanley would write after the war defending his record. He also felt slighted by Emerson Opdycke's accounts of the battle, in which he made no reference to Stanley. He felt betrayed by Opdycke, particularly since Stanley had personally written to President Andrew Johnson on May 13, 1865, recommending Opdycke for promotion to brigadier general and requesting he be maintained in the regular army service at the end of the war. Stanley had also personally written a commendation on December 2, 1864, for Opdycke's charge, which had saved the Union line.[60]

The journal of the IV Corps recorded the action at the Union center: "As soon as Wagner's two brigades were drawn back to the main line a large number of Cox's men broke and ran. The enemy, driving hard after these two brigades, entered the lines at this point. Opdycke's brigade, of Wagner's division, being in reserve, was ordered up at this moment by General Stanley. The rebels were driven back and our line of works reoccupied. Here General Stanley was severely wounded. Why were these two brigades left out in such an exposed position, and why did not General Schofield order them in?"[61] Major General Jacob Cox wrote in his after action report, "Major-General Stanley, commanding Fourth Corps, who had been ill during the prior part of the day, came on the field on hearing the sound of battle, and arrived in time to take an active part in the effort to rally Wagner's men, but was soon wounded and his horse shot under him. The most strenuous efforts were made by all officers along that part of the line to rally the men, and were so far successful that the line was quickly restored on the left of the turnpike, and after a sharp struggle."[62] Nevertheless, the battle of words raged between Stanley, Opdycke, Cox and Thomas Wood for years as each tried to craft their version of the Battle of Franklin. The point of contention centered around three items: (1) Who commanded the IV Corps at what point in the battle? (2) Was Stanley, Opdycke or both important in rallying the Union troops and plugging the gap? and (3) How long did Stanley remain on the field after being wounded?

David Stanley's spiritual advisor, Father Jeremiah Trecy, was also present when the battle was fought. "At Franklin, he was beside General Stanley, when a bullet tore across the latter's neck, just touching the carotid artery. The general put up his hand and felt the string of his scapular was cut by the bullet. In his faith and religious belief, he turned to the priest and said, 'Father, this blessed scapular, through Lord's mercy, has saved my life.'"[63] Later in life Stanley was being interviewed by artist James Edward Kelly, and during the interview Stanley was looking for some material for him. Stanley opened a box and to his surprise, "it contained a white scapular, one with the cords cut, also a large minie bullet in Mrs. Stanley's writing." The note said, "This scapular was worn by Gen. Stanley at the Battle of Franklin." Stanley told Allen, "Father Cooney always insisted on it, that it was a miracle, and I was always willing to accept it as so."[64]

11

Post–Civil War

I have fought a good fight;
I have finished my course;
I have kept the faith.

David Stanley was absent from the IV Corps for two months recuperating from his gunshot wound. On January 31, 1865, he returned to the corps and assumed command at Huntsville, Alabama. While in Huntsville, the good and loyal Catholic Stanley attended services in the local Presbyterian church with his wife, Anna. The minister of the Huntsville Presbyterian Church was the Reverend Frederick Ross. When Stanley converted to Catholicism in 1862, his wife remained a Protestant. Through Anna's urging all the local churches were reopened in the town. This was a dramatic step on the part of David Stanley, because many Southern ministers used their pulpits to promote the Southern cause. One example of this was Frederick Ross, who had declared that slavery was ordained by God. The 67-year-old Ross had incensed General James Steedman, when he commanded the District Etowah, when Ross openly retorted from his pulpit, "If every man had done his part, the Yankees might have been whipped out of here in six months." In December, Steedman had intended to banish Ross but relented. When David and Anna Stanley arrived, the orders banning church services were lifted, offending General Gordon Granger in addition to James Steedman by his decision.[1]

Prior to the movement to east Tennessee, David and Anna Stanley had the opportunity to play matchmaker with a local young lady, Jennie Watkins, and members of the IV Corps staff. The young lady accepted only Confederate courtiers and refused all attempts at matchmaking on the part of the Stanleys. Just before Stanley left Huntsville, he jovially commented, "Well Miss Jennie, I commend your course and admire you for it! You have excited the curiosity of my staff and they declare that when the war is over; they are coming to Huntsville expressly for an introduction to you."[2] Soon afterward, the IV Corps was ordered to march to eastern Tennessee to prevent Lee's Army of Northern Virginia from retreating into the mountains. Stanley established his headquarters in Greenville, Tennessee, using the same house that Brigadier General John Hunt Morgan had occupied prior to his death. The IV Corps saw very little action in eastern Tennessee and even the advance and occupation of Asheville, North Carolina, was relatively uneventful.

Stanley's headquarters in Huntsville in 1865 (U.S. Army Heritage and Education Center).

Robert E. Lee surrendered his army on April 12 and Stanley received the glorious news on April 13. His troops reveled in the news throughout the night realizing they had finally achieved the goal for which they have striven for four years. The next day David Stanley issued General Order Number 4 for his command:

> The glorious success of the national arms under Lieut. Gen. U.S. Grant being no longer a matter of any doubt, the army under his command having killed, wounded, captured, and forced the capitulation of the entire principal army of the rebels, including their commander-in-chief, tomorrow, which is the day appointed by the War Department for the raising of the old flag over Fort Sumter, where it was first insulted and pulled down by insolent traitors, will be kept as a holiday and a day of thanksgiving in this corps. A salute of 100 guns will be fired at 12 m. under the direction of Major Goodspeed, chief of artillery. All military duty, excepting necessary police and guard duty, will be suspended. It is recommended that chaplains of regiments hold service in their respective places of worship to render thanks to Almighty God for His goodness and mercy in preserving us a nation and giving us this great victory over our enemies. Let us in our thankfulness remember in tears the many brave men who have fallen at our sides in this great and terrible war. Who among us has not lost a brother, a relative, or a dear comrade? Let us reflect, and we may profit by so doing, that great national, as great personal, sin must be atoned for by great punishments.[3]

At the end of the war, the IV Corps was ordered to Nashville; but for the soldiers who had recently enlisted, their service was not over. Most soldiers thought when the war was over they would be mustered out of service and could return home; however, the IV Corps was ordered to duty in Texas.

Anna Maria Wright Stanley, David Stanley's "messmate, my heart's joy," in 1864 (United States Military Academy Library, Special Collections and Archive).

Prior to announcing the movement of the IV Corps to Texas, Major General George Thomas held a grand review of troops which lasted two hours. The soldiers were so happy about their victory and so excited in their anticipation of returning home that much of their normal restraint was lost. Colonel Lewis H. Waters of the 84th Illinois Infantry gave a speech which negatively reflected on war correspondents and he singled out William S. Furay of the *Cincinnati Gazette* as one who printed lies in his column. Furay verbally defended himself and the only thing which prevented a riot was the intersession for peace by Stanley.[4]

While in Nashville, the soldiers of the IV Corps wanted to express their affection to David Stanley. Isaac Royse, 115th Illinois Infantry, wrote the following: "Without the assistance, knowledge or consent of the officers, about dark one evening the enlisted men formed in line by regiments, brigades and divisions, in charge of marshals of their own choosing, and with flaming torches marched up the pike, presenting a most brilliant spectacle, to the entrance of the general's headquarters, and thence through the grounds, winding around his headquarter tents like the coils of a rope, until the entire corps became a solid mass about him."[5] Stanley was touched and pleased with the affection demonstrated by his troops. He acknowledged the gesture and declined the opportunity to make a speech. H.O. Hardin, 90th Ohio Infantry, also recounted that the adjutant of the 21st Illinois Infantry painted a life-sized portrait of General Stanley on a piece of canvas and below the portrait was inscribed, "The Hero of Franklin."[6]

On June 7, 1865, Stanley issued General Orders Number 71, in which he congratulated those soldiers who had completed their time in the army and thanked them for their contributions to the success of the war. He cited the battles as part of the Army of the Cumberland and concluded their impact would have to be decided by history. The final lines of the order correctly opined that civilian life would be nothing compared to the hardships of the past four years.[7]

The elation of the soldiers of the IV Corps was short-lived. When the orders came about moving to Texas, there were grumblings among the troops but soon the IV Corps was transferred westward. Not all the regiments agreed to march west, Stanley recorded the 31st Indiana Infantry mutinied and commandeered a riverboat only to be subdued by the 77th Pennsylvania Infantry from another riverboat. Ultimately, the IV Corps was transported to Louisiana, where it remained for a month before being transported to the sweltering heat of Indianola, Texas. Thomas J. Wood's division left Louisiana on July 7, 1865, and Nathan Kimball's was the next division to be shipped to Indianola, located midway between Corpus Christi and Houston on the Gulf Coast.[8] Once the divisions disembarked from the transports, they were ordered to march inland until they could find good water and campsites because neither were to be found at Indianola. Brigadier General Joseph Conrad's Second Division left Louisiana on July 16. On July 20, 1865, the various military districts of Texas were created and command was assigned. The Central Military District of Texas was assigned to David Stanley and he reported to Major General Edward Canby.[9] The morale of the soldiers in Texas was low and Captain Alexis Cope, 15th Ohio Infantry, observed David Stanley in an incident with a rowdy soldier: "One afternoon General Stanley was driving along one of the streets when a drunken soldier cursed and applied vile epithets to him. There was no guard in sight, and the general, who did not lack physical courage, alighted from his ambulance and arrested the man, put him in the ambulance and took him to the guard house."[10]

On July 28, 1865, David Stanley was ordered to report to Major General H.G. Wright.

On August 6, Stanley wrote to Wesley Merritt: "The newspapers say General H.G. Wright is assigned to the Department of Texas. If so, I hope he will come soon and regulate this question of supplies."[11] Again, the old question of command arose. General Phil Sheridan wrote, "General H.G. Wright will be entirely acceptable to me for Texas. I would be very glad to have him. General D.S. Stanley, who commands the Fourth Corps, has some claims on account of rank. Either one will answer."[12] If Wright ever had command of Stanley, Stanley failed to mention this in any of his records, but he gave praise to General Edward Canby: "General Canby was in command of the department and a wonderfully dignified and impressive gentleman he was."[13]

The army's presence in Texas served a twofold purpose. First, Texas, like many Southern states, needed a period of transition to establish civil authority once the state returned to the Union. Second, there were concerns that, due to the weakened condition of the United States after the Civil War, Maximilian of Mexico had designs on Texas. Stanley initially established his headquarters at Victoria, Texas, but after two months, in October 1865, he moved to San Antonio. Despite the improvement in living conditions, the morale within the IV Corps was low.

In December 1865, the IV Corps was formally dissolved and the troops were informed they could return home. Prior to the dissolution of the corps, Stanley had the dubious honor of ending the U.S. Army Camel Corps. This experiment had begun in 1856 and, despite some very favorable reports about the service of the animals, was to be disbanded. Some camels had remained in service in Camp Verde, Texas, and they were transported to San Antonio for auction. Many of the animals were sold to Ringling Brothers Circus.[14]

Stanley was called to testify before Congress at the end of his duty in Texas. He and other officers were asked about the conditions in the states where they were garrisoned in regard to establishing a Reconstruction policy for the postwar South. He testified: "'Texas was the worse than any other state because she had never been whipped,' that the women were universally rebels...." Stanley further remarked that in the case of a foreign war almost the entire population of Texas would side against the United States government.[15]

The time spent in Texas was not all work. David Stanley, Wilbur Hinman, 65th Ohio Infantry, and Joseph Conrad went on a fishing trip along with several others of the IV Corps. As the boats moved down the Guadalupe River, the boat carrying Stanley and Conrad capsized and the generals went into the water, much to the amusement of the other fisherman. "After a deal of splashing and floundering, they were hauled into other boats and the capsized craft was righted and bailed out," recalled Hinman.[16] The excursion was a relief from the heat and the mosquitoes which tormented the soldiers, and it offered some much needed amusement.

Dakota Territory

In February 1866, Stanley was mustered out of service of the Volunteer Union army and, like many of the professional soldiers, he scrambled to find a position in the United States Army. There were too many generals, and the officers who were mustered into the army almost universally held a lower rank than their Civil War rank. David Stanley was mustered into service as colonel of the 22nd U.S. Infantry and posted to Fort Rice in the Dakota Territory. The old animosity between Stanley and Sherman still existed. "Sherman gave Stanley a poor posting, sending him to Fort Sully, Dakota, in May 1867. Stanley remained there seven years, a painful assignment for a man intellectually dissatisfied with routine army life," remarked historian, M. John Lubetkin.[17]

Stanley's poor luck at drawing the Dakota Territory as his next command was accompanied by the very good news of the birth of his next child, Alice May Stanley. Alice Stanley was born on March 13, 1866, at Wilkes-Barre, Pennsylvania. She tragically died the following year in the Dakota Territory. Anna Maria and David Stanley made a trip in 1870 to accompany the body of Alice so she could be interred in Pennsylvania. Anna wrote to her children: "I heard the wolves last night. Our tent is pitched and I was sitting on the ground. We travel tomorrow and next days—and then we will go over to Randal on the third day—then to Yankton. This journey seems very long and dreary to me for I think of dear little sister all the time, and miss her so much—but I am happy to think that I shall see my dear little Josie [Josephine] and Lilly [Sarah] before very long."[18]

The old Fort Rice, named for Brigadier General James Clay Rice, who was killed in Virginia in May 1864, was constructed in 1864 during the period of conflict involving the Sioux Indians. Stanley made the fort his home and in 1868 it was rebuilt with 10-foot-high walls. The new fort had four barracks to house four companies of soldiers, seven additional buildings for officer quarters, a hospital, a bakery, five warehouses, a library, a magazine, and a guardhouse.

Stanley's second in command was Lieutenant Colonel Elwell Otis, a native of Maryland and brigade commander in the V Corps during the Civil War. The regimental major was Alexander Chambers, who had commanded a division in the XVII Corps during the war. The regiment garrisoned Fort Rice (Headquarters and Companies B, E, F, G and H), Fort Sully (Company A), Fort Buford (Company D) and Fort Berthold (Company D) in the Dakota Territory. Company I and Company K would not be organized until late 1866; they arrived in the Dakota Territory in May 1867. Constructing the forts was very difficult and the various companies, as well as the civilians who were contracted to bring the wood needed to construct the fort, were often attacked by Indians. Lieutenant Oskaloosa M. Smith, 22nd U.S. Infantry, recorded, "The Indian attacks upon the camp occurred almost daily during the summer and fall."[19] Logs used in the construction of the forts were often transported many miles and were under guard from the army as protection from the Sioux.

The soldiers lived in tents until late in the winter of 1867, when the forts were finally completed. "There was deep snow before they moved into their quarters and they got in none too soon at Stevenson and Totten, as a severe snowstorm came upon them, lasting three or four days; the wind was fierce and the weather extremely cold."[20] Mail delivery was often inconsistent and arrived about every ten days along the Missouri River and about once a month at the more remote forts. In the winter, sled dogs were used to deliver the mail, and those people chosen to deliver the mail were also subject to Indian attacks and often killed. While David Stanley was used to the hardships of the Civil War, he was handed what appeared to be equally hazardous duty along the western frontier. The hazards of frontier service were recorded by Lieutenant Oskaloosa M. Smith: "In the beautiful spring of 1868, after a hard winter, a party of soldiers left Totten with the mail for Stevenson, in high spirits, anticipating an enjoyable trip and a meeting with friends at the distant post. About midway between the two posts the party was attacked by a large number of Sioux Indians and every man killed. A rescuing party found their bodies stripped of clothing and mutilated."[21]

In 1870 Brigadier General Thomas L. Crittenden, Stanley's old compatriot from the Army of the Cumberland, arrived in the Dakota Territory to relieve Stanley of the responsibility of Fort Rice, and Stanley moved to Fort Sully. Fort Sully had been constructed in 1863 under the orders of Major General Alfred Sully. It was constructed about four miles southeast of present day Pierre, South Dakota, and was used as a garrison for efforts of the army to deal with the Native American issues of the time. The original fort was abandoned in 1866, when Stanley assumed command, because of the low and wet location. Stanley constructed the "new" Fort Sully about 23 miles northwest of the old fort. Situated on the east bank of the Missouri River, it sat on the high ground referred to as the third terrace.

The new Fort Sully, constructed of cottonwood logs, was the home of the 22nd U.S. Infantry from 1866 to 1873. The soldiers' barracks consisted of two long buildings, while the officers' quarters included nine detached frame houses. The fort also included two cottages, guardhouses at the end of each barracks, quartermasters supply houses, a commissary store house and a hospital. In 1870, the 22nd U.S. Infantry was required to patrol a smaller geographic area. Fort Sully became the headquarters of the regiment and garrisoned Companies, A, E, F, and H. Stanley lived at Fort Sully and Lieutenant Colonel Otis lived at Fort Randall with Companies B, C, D, and G. Company I and Company K were garrisoned at Crow Creek Indian Agency and the Lower Brulé Agency.[22]

Stanley's time in the Dakota Territory was a daily vigilance against the Plains Indians and had its own share of depredation. Although the duty was one of some danger, overall it was a predictable life. For several years, Stanley's life was one without major happenings until the Northern Pacific Railroad made an important decision about the potential route of a railroad. That decision was one which concluded it might be profitable to build a railroad directly through Sioux Indian Territory.

Despite the adversarial conditions between the United States government and the Native Americans of the Dakota Territory, Stanley developed a great respect for the indigenous population. He frequently interacted with the chiefs of the various tribes and worked to improve relations between the two groups. He was outspoken against the action taken in 1870 which resulted in the massacre of the Piegan Blackfeet Indians. Lieutenant General Phil Sheridan had endorsed an expedition commanded by Major Eugene Baker in which the U.S. Army attacked an unsuspecting village, killing 173 men, women and children as part of a policy to subdue Native Americans. Stanley and others vehemently denounced the actions supported by his old friend Sheridan.[23] In fact, Stanley had taken a different and more successful approach in dealing with the Native American tribes. He had worked in cooperation with local missionaries to gain the trust and respect of the local tribes. In a letter written July 12, 1868, he mentioned the success of Catholic missionary Father Pierre-Jean De Smet in securing a peace treaty: "Whatever may be the result of the treaty ... we can never forget nor shall we ever cease to admire, the disinterested devotion of the Reverend Father De Smet." Stanley recorded the efforts to reach a peace treaty which would "preserve some habitations of these savage children of the desert, to whose spiritual and temporal welfare he has consecrated a long life of labor and solitude." This religious outlook revealed much about Stanley's personal objectives and offers a sense of what he considered his role in the Dakota Territory.[24]

Of the policy of militarily attacking the Piegan tribe, Stanley wrote, "I am ashamed [any] longer to appear in the presence of the chiefs of the different tribes of Sioux."[25] From

Stanley's point of view he had labored to work to gain an effective peace with the Indians, and the policy under Sheridan undermined his moral and practical peace efforts and credibility with the tribes.

Stanley was asked later in life to identify his principal Indian victory. He replied simply, "My principal Indian victory was keeping the peace. I commanded for years at Fort Dakota and never had an uprising.... When I took command I sent for the Indians and said, 'I propose to treat you right. If anything goes wrong, come to me and tell me, and I will see that you have justice, but if you attempt to kick up any disturbance, I will lick you and you know me that I can do it. My wife was a very practical sympathetic woman, she was and did what she could to make them comfortable and we never had the slightest trouble in all the years we were there."[26]

THE YELLOWSTONE EXPEDITIONS 1871–1873

The relationship with the Indians deteriorated further during 1871–1873 due to United States and commercial policies of the time. In 1869 the Northern Pacific Railroad decided to build a second transcontinental railroad which would go directly through the Lakota Indians' hunting ground. The decision was made almost immediately after the Fort Laramie Treaty of 1868 was signed which set aside land for use by the Lakota Indians, including the Yellowstone Basin. As a result, the Lakota Indians threatened to resist any efforts to intrude upon their lands. Regardless of this threat, by 1871 the Northern Pacific Railroad had surveyed from Duluth to Bismarck from the east and from Bozeman to Tacoma from the west. No survey had been made in the Yellowstone country until 1871, when three survey teams were sent to find a suitable route for the railroad.[27]

Survey expeditions were conducted in three consecutive years, 1871, 1872, and 1873. David Stanley was not directly involved during the first year except in his capacity of providing field preparations and troops for the march. On September 8, 1871, Thomas Crittenden, David Stanley and Thomas L. Rosser, head engineer of the survey expedition, met for dinner at Fort Rice to discuss the expedition. The officer assigned to the protection of the survey party, Major Joseph N.G. Whistler, was not present for the discussion.

Whistler's command consisted of Companies A, C, H and I of the 22nd Infantry and Companies D and H of the 17th Infantry. The military support for the expedition also included Indian scouts and 104 wagons. The expedition left Fort Rice on September 9 and returned on October 16, traveling over 600 miles.[28] Whistler's command was unsatisfactory and was described as problematic; "[B]efore their mid–October return he misdirected the column at least nine times, causing a minimum of 55 extra miles marched and three days. Whether his problems were caused by alcohol, stubbornness, inability to use a compass, bad maps, or combination of factors, the end result was badly frayed nerves, especially for those on foot."[29]

David Stanley's fourth surviving daughter, Blanche Huntington Stanley, was born on May 14, 1871, just prior to the surveying expedition. The Stanley family was very popular and became part of the social life in the Dakota Territory, such as it was. One of the riverboats going up and down the Missouri River was named the *Josephine* after the oldest Stanley daughter. In 1872, both Anna and David Stanley worked with the local missionaries to improve the educational opportunities for Native Americans near Fort Sully. Anna Stanley wrote to the *New York Evangelist* about her disappointment that no Christian missionaries saw the need to live in the area of Fort Sully and work to improve the conditions of the Indians. Finally, a missionary, the Reverend T.L. Riggs, who had grown up among the Dakotas, arrived to work to improve education and living conditions. Anna noted that two log buildings, whose construction was aided by David Stanley's influence, were added to the existing facilities and sixty children were educated in 1872. A local missionary noted the efforts of Anna Maria Stanley, writing he had found a "good and true Christian" friend in Anna and others at the fort.[30] Father De Smet wrote several letters to Stanley and others at Fort Sully and he always offered his best wishes to Anna Stanley. In a letter to Major J.C. O'Connor written on March 24, 1873, De Smet wrote of the "worthy General Stanley."[31]

Perhaps because of the poor leadership exhibited by Whistler in 1871, David Stanley decided to lead the 1872 expedition himself. The Sioux were expected to be a more difficult than in 1871, when the expedition was unmolested. Stanley wrote a letter to the head of the survey team, Thomas Rosser, about the risk: "I want to come up and see you ... I had a long talk with Spotted Eagle.... [He said] he would destroy the road and attack any party that tried to build it.... I tried to make him understand the fatal consequences. He said he did not care, 'it was life or death and he would fight it out.'"[32]

Stanley was certainly a better choice to lead the expedition than had been Whistler. "The veteran Stanley was skilled, conservative, handled troops well under pressure, understood the Sioux, and was loyal to Sheridan—traits difficult to put together," according to

Spotted Eagle (left, with Heavy Gun, center, and Robert Calf Robe) told Stanley, "It was life or death and he would fight it out" (Library of Congress).

historian, M. John Lubtekin. The army needed someone this experienced and secure in command to march into the land of the Sioux with a group of surveyors. The 1872 expedition consisted of infantry—Companies D, F and G of the 22nd Infantry, Companies A, B, C, F, H and K of the 8th Infantry and Companies A and F of the 17th Infantry. Stanley's request for cavalry was denied. Stanley's brother-in-law, Doctor J.P. Wright, was also included in the expedition as the chief medical officer.[33]

Indeed, the Plains Indians were to play a more important role in 1872. The first attack from them occurred on the evening of August 14. The surveyors grabbed their rifles and fired into the darkness, killing one of the expedition's mules. Stanley, having little confidence in the fighting ability of the surveyors, collected their rifles and insisted the role of his infantry was to protect the survey party; the surveyor's duties were to survey. It was also noted the initial attack remedied any concerns about stragglers thereafter.[34] Stanley's column skirmished with Sioux led by Gall and on August 18 an informal meeting, of sorts, occurred when Gall came to the river and laid down his weapons. The interpreter introduced Stanley to Chief Gall. In response, Stanley laid down his pistol and proposed a meeting on a sandbar in the middle of the river. Gall refused the meeting and, instead, demanded to know what the soldiers were doing on Sioux land. Stanley explained, the surveying expedition and Gall inquired what he himself would be paid. Historian Francis Robertson explained the results of this answer: "Gall then threatened to call all the bands to give the soldiers a 'big fight.' During the discussion, Stanley noticed several of Gall's braves concealing themselves on the opposite bank and thought it time to prepare for action. As soon as he began to step away, the Sioux opened fire." The fire was brisk between the two groups but no casualties were reported and the Sioux moved off.[35]

Stanley's initial goal was to escort his survey team and meet with a second team of surveyors; but he discovered the second survey party had run into trouble with Indians also and returned northward. Eugene Baker's expedition was attacked at Pryor's Fork on August 14 by several hundred Sioux. Upon learning this, Stanley abandoned any further attempt to reach the meeting place and began a return march to Fort Rice.[36]

Stanley began his march back to the east and skirmished again with the Sioux at O'Fallon's Creek on August 21 and 22. He reached Fort Rice on October 15 after marching over 1,000 miles during the summer. The return march was not without its hazards. As the column got closer to Fort Rice and the overall risks were lower, Stanley allowed various parts of the column to

Chief Gall (Library of Congress).

return ahead of the main column. Major Robert Crofton led 125 men of the 17th U.S. Infantry back to Fort Rice on October 2; but unknown to Crofton, he was been stalked by 100 Hunkpapas. While Crofton's infantry camped, Lieutenant Eban Crosby walked a little too far from camp and was captured and killed by the Indians on October 5.[37] On October 4, Stanley's cook, Stephen Harris, was also killed while he was hunting. The body of Harris and the body of his white dog were found side-by-side in a ravine in a pile of spent rifle cartridges. Also, Lieutenant Louis D. Adair of Stanley's 22nd Infantry was hunting and was mortally wounded. Adair, the cousin of President Ulysses Grant's wife, died early the next morning.[38]

Again Stanley's old nemesis, alcohol, reared its head during the march. While the extent of the drinking is not recorded, Thomas Rosser wrote in his diary, "[Stanley] shows signs of going on a spree." It wasn't until October 11 Rosser recorded, "The old man is on a spree."[39] At that point, the expedition was all but over. There is no record of Stanley's inability to lead the expedition. A member of the expedition, Nibsey Swipes, the pseudonym of a non-commissioned officer who wrote for the *Sioux City Daily Journal,* penned on September 12, "'I will here state ... that a better commander than General Stanley for an expedition like this, it is difficult to find. He is cool and collected when any danger threatens and is particularly attentive to the comfort of his men.... He is a good soldier and never puts his men to any unnecessary trouble ... [and] knows and is up to all the tricks of the Indians."[40] This certainly does not reflect a soldier concerned about the leadership ability of his colonel who had just marched through a thousand miles of hostile Indian Territory. Stanley waited until the expedition was over before he allowed himself to start drinking.

While on this expedition, Stanley was favored with the birth of his only son, David Sheridan Stanley, who was destined also to serve his country in the U.S. Army. (Tragically, Thomas Rosser had been informed his infant son had died on August 20 while he labored on the survey expedition.) David Sheridan Stanley, born on September 9, 1872, was named after Stanley's close friend Phil Sheridan.

1873 YELLOWSTONE EXPEDITION

In 1873, Colonel David Stanley was called upon to continue the surveying expeditions which began in 1871 in conjunction with the Northern Pacific Railroad. The expedition began at Fort Rice, about twenty miles south of present-day Bismarck. The Northern Pacific Railroad surveyors were again led by Thomas L. Rosser, a Confederate cavalry general of the Civil War. The expedition was planned to take about two months.

David Stanley was actively engaged in the preparation of the expedition. Charles Larned, a lieutenant in the 7th Cavalry, wrote in a letter in May 1873, "Gen. Stanley is here and has been unreserved in his conversation about it."[41] Stanley planned to take up the expedition from the point the 1872 expedition terminated. The expedition would be composed of two detachments—one moving on a northerly route and another on a more southerly route. The survey was anticipated to be over by October. This time Stanley was granted cavalry to assist in the expedition, but the addition of cavalry was not without its own difficulties when George A. Custer was chosen to lead the cavalry. Larned also noted in his letter a foreboding of the some of the difficulties of the expedition when he wrote of George A. Custer: "He is making himself utterly detested by every line officer of the command, with the exception of one [or] two toadies, by his selfish, capricious, arbitrary, and unjust conduct."[42]

The expedition included ten companies of the 7th Cavalry commanded by Lieutenant Colonel Custer; ten companies of the 8th and 9th U.S. Infantry commanded by Stanley's old IV Corps division commander, Luther P. Bradley; three companies of the 17th Infantry and one company of the 6th U S Infantry commanded by Major Robert Crofton; five companies of the 22nd Infantry commanded by Captain Carlos Dickey; members of the 27th Indian Scouts, commanded by 2nd Lieutenant D. H. Brush; one company of the 22nd U.S. Infantry serving as pioneers; and two artillery squads with two 3-inch Rodman cannon. The supply train consisted of 275 wagons and ambulances and 353 civilians. In addition, there were a total of 2,321 horses and mules. This expedition began on June 20, 1873, with 79 officers and 1,451 soldiers. Four days prior to the main column's leaving Fort Rice, a smaller advance column departed. The smaller column was made up of four companies of the 8th Infantry and 25 men of the 7th Cavalry. In addition, one company of the 6th Infantry from Fort Abraham Lincoln had been assigned escort duty for the engineering party.[43]

Almost immediately Custer and Stanley were at cross purposes. Custer began by arrogantly attempting to commandeer a river boat but the captain of the boat, and a friend of Stanley, left Custer standing on the edge of the Missouri River. As a result of this incident, G.R. Norris, a scout for the expedition, explained Stanley sent an officer to arrest Custer, which never was accomplished. Norris noted, "Custer seemed to me to be generally unpopular; that is I rarely heard him spoken well of. Stanley, on the other hand, always appeared to be a gentleman of rare qualities, one who never forgot to treat a civilian as a man—something many officers were little disposed to do."[44] Custer had been acting badly as he approached the beginning of the expedition and Stanley had been warned by General Alfred Terry to expect trouble. Likewise, Custer had been warned of Stanley's drinking during the previous expedition and expected trouble from him.

The march began as a very wet one. It rained fourteen of the first seventeen days of the march. Again alcoholism became a problem during this expedition and it was recorded Stanley began drinking during the wet period of June 20–22: "Stanley's drinking can be traced from the June 20–22 thunderstorms. The lack of sleep caused to tempers to flare within days between the infantry ... and cavalry."[45] Stanley wrote to his wife: "Camp 45 miles from Rice, June 26th, 1873.... We have had a hard time on account of storms; it rained every night and four days out of six the first six days we were out. This is the 7th day from Fort Rice and we lie over on account of high water delaying our crossing of Heart River. The winds have been terrible, and the whole prairie has become a swamp. I think now we shall do better as it appears to have cleared up."[46] If Stanley was drinking during this period, he was still functioning well and in true Stanley style, Charles Larned reported he "never waits for anything to turn if there is a chance of turning it up himself."[47]

Because of the friction between Stanley and Custer, the men of the infantry and cavalry were also working at cross purposes. Charles Larned wrote to his mother on July 28 "the cavalry and infantry therefore cordially hate each other."[48] However, Stanley made friends with some of the cavalry when he decided to select Charles Larned's cavalry squadron to serve as his escort. Larned happily wrote, "We shall probably be free of Custer from henceforth."[49] The day-to-day routine of the expedition was tedious, with the soldiers awakened at 3:30 a.m. After breakfasting and harnessing the teams, they were underway by 5:30.

On June 28, the Northern Pacific engineers joined the column. Due to wet, soggy conditions, the columns were able to march only three miles. The expedition was destined to be one of frustration for Stanley as he chaffed at Custer's personality. Stanley wrote his wife: " I have had no trouble with Custer, and will try to avoid having any; but I have seen enough of him to convince me that he is a cold blooded, untruthful and unprincipled man. He is universally despised by all the officers of his regiment excepting his relatives and one or two sycophants. He brought a trader in the field without permission, carries an old negro woman, and cast iron cooking stove, and delays the march often by his extensive packing up in the morning. As I said I will try, but am not sure I can avoid trouble with him."[50] Custer had no higher regard for Stanley in return: "Stanley is acting very badly [and] drinking."[51] Historian M. John Lubetkin suggested Stanley should not be discounted due to the allegation of his drinking: "Unless Barrows' account was fabrication—and he had no motivation to lie— Stanley was sober and exercised effective leadership"[52] The Barrows mentioned was Samuel Barrows, who wrote a series of articles for the *New York Tribune,* an important national newspaper. Two sides of Stanley emerge during this expedition: one was an experienced calm commander and the other was a man who struggled with alcohol.

When Stanley's column reached the Little Missouri River, the river was overflowing. He found the approach to it treacherous due to the high water, but also because of quicksand. Stanley, rather ingeniously, found a way around the sand issue. He put his 700 head of cattle and cavalry on the sands and marched them back and forth until the sand was firm enough to walk on. Custer was unhappy about the task assigned his cavalry by Stanley: "Custer fumed, fretted and voiced protests, but Stanley shouted him down. This was a commander used to the hardships of the trail and never awed by any. So, Custer, whether he liked it or not, passed a test he rather would have avoided."[53]

Stanley's column marched through the Badlands and reached the Yellowstone River on July 13. Prior to reaching the Yellowstone, the situation between Stanley and Custer exploded. Stanley had gone through a series of repeated orders to Custer to leave a stove which was delaying the march. Custer ignored the orders. The final straw came when Stanley became angry with Custer over the loan of an army horse to a civilian surveyor. Stanley ordered Custer to his tent under arrest and made him ride at the rear of the column. After a day's punishment, Stanley relented after Thomas Rosser interceded on behalf of Custer, but the incident gained national notoriety. Upon reaching the Yellowstone River, Stanley constructed a fort and placed his supplies with one company of the 17th Infantry and two companies of the 7th Cavalry while the remainder of the expedition continued. After a sixty-mile march— forty miles of which were in total absence of water—through the Badlands, the column reached the Yellowstone again, near the mouth of the Powder River. Then the expedition moved westward along the Yellowstone River.

Stanley's column reached a place to cross the Yellowstone about fifteen miles north of the town of Glendive on July 31. It was after reaching this section of the Yellowstone River that definitive evidence exists of Stanley's being truly under the influence of alcohol to such an extent as to make him ineffective. Lieutenant Charles Larned of the expedition recorded, "'Stanley is under the whiskey curse and gets on periodical tears of two and three days duration during which he manages to disgrace himself and insult everyone who happens to displease him.'"[54] Northern Pacific Engineer Thomas Rosser also recorded Stanley's drinking in his journal on Sunday, July 21, when he wrote, "Stanley very drunk and I fear Custer will arrest him and assume command." Rosser wrote again the next day: "Stanley very drunk."[55]

It is not known what caused the drinking binge on this expedition, but it is important to note that during the latter part of the expedition Stanley received word his son was ill and other children were dying of disease at the fort. Stanley most certainly recalled the news Rosser had received during the 1872 expedition of his own son's death. Stanley's daughter Alice had died at an early age in 1867 while he was garrisoned in the Dakota Territory. Finally, G.R. Norris recalled that Stanley "hardly drew a sober breath from the time the expedition started till a point was reached where the town of Glendive stands today."[56] A point which is of particular interest is that Stanley ordered all the whiskey in the expedition to be poured out over Custer's protests, and this was another point of contention between Stanley and Custer. It was reported some of the soldiers drank from the wagon tracks after the whiskey was poured out. Certainly various sides of Stanley's personality were evident during the expedition. The expeditions of 1872 and 1873 are confirmed incidents where Stanley can be proven to have been under the influence of alcohol while on duty.

During the march, another side of Stanley was also evident as the column advanced deeper into the mountains. Indian burial grounds were encountered and Stanley issued orders against desecration of the sites. He had lived long enough in the western territories to have developed a great respect for the indigenous population.

After crossing the Yellowstone River, the column moved along the western bank and on August 4 a detachment of the 7th Cavalry was attacked. Killed were a veterinarian, a sutler and one of Custer's troopers. The cavalry was some miles ahead of the infantry column. In mid-afternoon Stanley became aware of the battle and ordered the remainder of the cavalry to the rescue. The attack increased Stanley's vigilance and he increased efforts to keep the Indians away from the column and surveyors. Sitting Bull, aware of Custer's camp about four miles west of Stanley's infantry, called on various Indian tribes to join him in attacking Custer on the morning of August 11.

Custer was told by one of his scouts about the impending attacks the evening before, but Custer brushed aside the information, stating he did not believe the Indians would return. However, the cavalry was again attacked, by an estimated 800 Indians, on August 11 opposite the mouth of the Big Horn River. Lieutenant Charles Braden, 7th Cavalry, was severely wounded and Lieutenant H.H. Ketchum, 22nd Infantry, adjutant-general of the expedition, had his horse killed beneath him. Quick action on the part of Stanley and Custer prevented a disaster along the Yellowstone. The aggressive action taken by Stanley's infantry, along with Custer's counterattack, caused the Indians to retreat, and the expedition continued. With the survey complete, the march back to Fort Rice began. The expedition completed its task and returned to Fort Lincoln on September 22 after marching 1,200 miles.[57]

After years of active service, the expedition of 1873 was the last war Stanley would experience for several years. He was ordered to Fort Wayne at Detroit, Michigan, beginning in July 1874, and he remained there until September 28, 1876. The various companies of the 22nd Infantry served at Fort Wayne, at Madison Barracks in Sacket's Harbor, New York; Fort Porter, Buffalo, New York; Fort Brady, Sault Ste. Marie; and Fort Mackinac, Fort Gratiot, Michigan. It was universally accepted by the men of the regiment that the new posts were better locations than the frontier in the Dakota Territory. After the Battle of the Little Big Horn, the 22nd Infantry moved west but David Stanley did not accompany the regiment. He then served as superintendent of General Recruiting Service in New York City until October 1, 1878, and commanded Fort Porter, New York, from October 1878 to April 1879.[58]

Postwar Disagreement Over the Battle of Franklin

Like many generals and others of the Civil War era, Stanley became embroiled in the struggle to record the true events during the war, and this struggle continued long after the final shots had been fired. David Stanley became part of two very public arguments. The first involved Stanley's role at the Battle of Franklin and the second involved a longtime feud with William B. Hazen.

The first issue of the Battle of Franklin centered around the various versions of the events of the battle. David Stanley fought to defend his actions during the battle because of comments and lack of recognition from several individuals. To a small extent he sparred with Emerson Opdycke and Thomas Wood, and in an more serious and long-term verbal and written feud with Jacob D. Cox, who commanded a division in the XXIII Corps and later was elected governor of Ohio. Stanley felt Emerson Opdycke was negligent in acknowledging Stanley's arrival and contribution on the battlefield. General Thomas Wood also chose not to deem Stanley's actions noteworthy. Both of these men were bitterly despised by Stanley as a result. In the case of Opdycke, Stanley felt that some reciprocity of acknowledgment should have been forthcoming because Stanley had been highly complimentary of Opdycke's action at Franklin and because Stanley had played a major part in Opdycke's promotion to the rank of general. Stanley even wrote to President Andrew Johnson urging Opdycke's retention in the regular army after the war was over.

The arguments continued for years over this matter. John Schofield wrote his understanding of the battle in a letter to Jacob Cox in 1881; he tried to insure he did not become personally entangled in this controversy: "It was I who decided that a battle must be fought at Franklin and indicated the position upon which our troops should be formed. It was you who posted the troops and directed their preparation for battle. It was you and Stanley and your officers and men who fought the battle and who in due preparation deserve the credit for the brilliant victory which was granted."[59]

Stanley and Jacob Cox carried their feud into *Century* magazine and history books of various authorship. The major issue between Cox and Stanley was the question of who commanded the Union forces on the defensive line during the battle. These arguments seem petty and beneath the principle characters involved by today's light. Emerson Opdycke claimed the credit for repulsing the Confederate attack at the Battle of Franklin, although several other regiments outside his command were important in the repulse of the attack. Cox claimed credit for the success at Franklin because he was the ranking Union officer on the battlefield and prepared the defenses at Franklin while Stanley and Schofield were at headquarters. Stanley rode directly to the sound of the guns, only to have his horse killed under him, and then he was shot in the neck while rallying the troops. This battle of words continued in the late 1880s and, finally, effectively ended when in 1893 Stanley was awarded only one of three Medals of Honor for bravery at the Battle of Franklin. It is interesting that during this period no one moved to exonerate George Wagner, whose division's collapse caused the crisis. Stanley was Wagner's commanding officer; Cox, by his own words, was responsible for the placement of all the Union regiments before the battle; and Opdycke, a subordinate of Wagner, disobeyed a direct order to remain in advance of the defenses of Franklin.

This should have been the end of the matter, but this was a battle that would not end.

The awarding of the Medal of Honor to Stanley must have been too much for Jacob Cox, who authored a book, *The Battle of Franklin,* published in 1897 in which he described his version of the battle. Stanley also continued his version of the Battle of Franklin in a newspaper article, "Battle of Franklin, Gen. Cox's Recent Account of It Vigorously Handled by Gen. Stanley." Stanley ended the article with an aggressive attack on Cox's character when he wrote, "The point of meeting [between Stanley and Cox at the battle] was at least one or two hundred yards behind that brigade. I was surely coming toward the battle, Cox was just as surely going away from danger."[60]

Stanley certainly had more than enough reasons to take on Cox, but perhaps one was Cox's attack on George Thomas' handling of the Nashville Campaign. On March 12, 1870, an anonymous letter appeared in the *New York Tribune* signed by "One Who Fought at Nashville." The letter exposed a suspended order placing Schofield in command prior to the Battle of Nashville and claimed that Schofield, and not Thomas, was responsible for the success of the campaign.[61] Many in the United States Army were supporters of Thomas, and Stanley was one of those. Thomas died within two weeks of this letter's publication. It was later discovered the author was Jacob D. Cox.

While this was not the only case of generals refighting the Civil War, it was certainly one example which carried on for years. Stanley, Opdycke and Cox all played major roles in the Battle of Franklin and deserve credit and blame for the various aspects of the conduct of actions during the battle. It is important to note the friendship of Cox and Opdycke with James A. Garfield, whom Stanley disliked. It is unknown if Stanley's dislike for Garfield intensified over time or whether the postwar feuds made his distaste for Garfield increase. Another of Garfield's friends was William B. Hazen, the center of Stanley's second postwar feud.

The William B. Hazen Feud

The origins of the feud between David Stanley and William Hazen are really unknown but the dislike between the two generals reportedly began during the Civil War. In a very convoluted chain of events, two professional soldiers, David Stanley and William Hazen, latched on to one another in the 1870s and nearly destroyed their careers and reputations along the way. Certainly, both Stanley and Hazen were delving into the political side of military life throughout this affair. George A. Custer and Philip Sheridan were both enemies of Hazen for his outspoken position on the handling of affairs in the West. Hazen had testified against secretary of war William Belknap during his impeachment and was collaborating with James A. Garfield, Stanley's old nemesis, and Washington McLean to improve Hazen's position in the army. It was Hazen's use of his political influence in this regard that caused Stanley to escalate his attacks on Hazen's reputation.

William Babcock Hazen was two years junior to Stanley and had graduated from West Point in 1855. He progressed from command of the 41st Ohio Infantry to command of the 2nd Division of the XV Corps. Late in the war, he commanded the XV Corps. He, like Stanley, served in various western commands after the war, but he was also disliked by his commander Phillip Sheridan, who was a friend of Stanley.

Secretary of war William Worth Belknap also became entangled with Hazen. Neither

Belknap nor Sheridan liked Hazen, and Stanley was a friend of both these men. In contrast, Hazen was a friend of Emerson Opdycke, Jacob D. Cox, Thomas Woods, and James A. Garfield—all enemies of Stanley. To complicate things even further, George Custer also disliked Hazen, and Custer was a favorite of Sheridan.

In 1876, Belknap was impeached and Hazen volunteered to testified against him during the proceedings. The vote fell short of removing Belknap, who was livid with Hazen, and Belknap requested Hazen be court-martialed for conduct unbecoming an officer. But the head of the army, William Sherman, refused. Because Belknap could not reach Hazen through official channels, he formed an alliance with David Stanley and together they developed a strategy to deal with Hazen.[62]

In 1877 Hazen was appointed military attaché in Vienna, Austria, and remained abroad until late 1878. It was the influence of Garfield and McLean which secured the Vienna assignment for Hazen. In an attempt to prevent Hazen from accepting the European assignment, Stanley preferred charges that Hazen had perjured himself during the Belknap impeachment. President Rutherford Hayes read the charges and to his satisfaction concluded it would be best to have Hazen in Europe.[63] The Hazen-Stanley feud had been going on for years. A biographer of Philip Sheridan, Paul Andrew Hutton, wrote, "Stanley hounded Hazen with accusations of cowardice and of deserting his men in that battle [Shiloh]. He later tacked on charges Hazen had falsely claimed the capture of certain cannons on Missionary Ridge in 1863.... [Sheridan wrote] 'I do not see much in their quarrel.... The investigation of it will result in exposition of the personal habits of both, and I beg that the Army will be saved from the burden of what will, or what may be developed.'"[64]

Stanley hounded William B. Hazen "with accusations of cowardice and of deserting his men in that battle" (Library of Congress).

Sherman had tried to reconcile Stanley and Hazen and was unsuccessful; but he refused to allow their conflict to become public. When Sheridan failed to convene a court-martial, Stanley took the story to the newspapers and a dual court-martial was set. "The *St. Paul Pioneer Press,* hostile to Hazen because of his literary war against the Northern Pacific Railroad, gave early support to the assault. William Belknap, associated with a law firm in Iowa, aided in the dissemination of Stanley's various printed allegations." Stanley, supported by a group of Hazen's enemies, pressed forward with his charges against Hazen. As a result, Stanley was finally charged with conduct unbecoming an officer and was scheduled for a court-martial.[65]

The genius from Stanley's point was the charges against him would, in fact, hold Hazen up to the scrutiny of the nation and the press. Stanley felt he had adequate support from key witnesses to testify on his behalf to prove Hazen a coward; however, such tactics were not without risk. If Stanley was convicted, he would be seen as a slanderous, petty, and jealous aggressor.

David Stanley faced charges and numerous specifications, but the trial focused on Stanley's allegations that Hazen was guilty of cowardice at the Battle of Shiloh; guilty of causing a monument to be built on the site of the Battle of Stones River where his forces were not located; intentionally kept himself out of danger during the Battle of Pickett's Mill; falsely claimed the capture of artillery at the Battle of Missionary Ridge; and, finally, provided false testimony during the impeachment of William W. Belknap. The chief evidence to be used against Stanley was a letter he wrote to Hazen in Vienna: "I have seen the decision of the President upon the charges I preferred against you, that the service would not be conserved by convening a general court martial to try you at this time. I am not disappointed. You know just as well as I do that your trial could have only resulted in your conviction, and you already stand convicted before those who heard you testify. I now give you fair warning that I am fully informed of your disgraceful conduct at Shiloh, and when proper occasion offers will use the information to stop your career of imposture."[66]

Two courts-martial were initially planned, one to try Hazen based on Stanley's charges and the other to try Stanley for conduct unbecoming an officer. David Stanley had many supporters, among them Captain John Gregory Bourke, aid to George Crook. Bourke was serving in the West at the time of the trial. He had served under Stanley at the Battle of Stone's River and that wrote the trial began on April 7: "This was a result of a long and bitter quarrel between the two generals named, dating back as long ago as the Battle of Shiloh, in 1862. Without knowing anything of the merits of the case, my sympathies are entirely with Stanley."[67] Sheridan appeared at the first court-martial and testified against Hazen, as did Alexander McCook, Thomas Wood, and Dr. Robert Murray.

In a letter written to the court on May 2, 1879, Stanley, noted for his quick and relentless ability to criticize, explained his history with Hazen. He wrote that his "official" relations began with Hazen in July 1864 when Stanley gained command of the IV Corps. He wrote that Thomas Wood, commanding the Third Division, "could only get him [Hazen] on his picket line by shaming him—that is going first himself." Upon discovering this type of behavior, Stanley noted he began to look into Hazen's performance during the war. Presumably, this was the beginning of the dislike between the two officers. Stanley also went to the true heart of the matter, for him, in the letter. He sarcastically recalled he met Hazen in the fall of 1872 after a hard summer's duty. Hazen was just returning from his "annual trip to Washington to help run the government." These lines hold the cause of the public battle from Stanley's point of view. In Stanley's mind, here was another underperforming officer being promoted through political machinations which had nothing to do with merit.[68] Garfield supported Hazen in the upcoming trial. It should be noted this episode in Stanley's life, not actions taken in 1863, may have been the cause for his extreme dislike for Garfield, who was a very good friend of Hazen and played an important role in securing a significant promotion for him through his political influence.

Stanley's trial was held and he was given a mild slap on the wrist and convicted of conduct to the prejudice of good order and military discipline. The formal charges were withdrawn against Hazen and the *New York Times* reported "Hazen Trial Prevented by Statute of Limitations" and the matter officially ended. But Hazen felt he had been tried during Stanley's court-martial where only Stanley's allegations were made public.[69] Historian Robert Kroeker wrote of the trial: "The trial had been characterized throughout by personal denunciations and vicious acrimony. Many of Hazen's fellow officers in the Civil War rose up in judgment against him as old battles were refought and petty disputes revived. Colonel Hazen's aggressive and outspoken manner and his criticism of the so-called 'bummer' element in the army, had made him unpopular in certain military quarters. Unfortunately the trial brought into the open much harbored ill will on both sides and left scars that could never be healed."[70]

Perhaps one of the most detrimental points about Stanley was a letter he wrote to Hazen in March 1873 in which Stanley "acknowledged then that I was fully in the wrong in ever having criticized you, and fully resolved to do no more. All I told you was told me, and I am ready now to state to you who told me, and mostly when and where they told me. So, please, don't attribute the authenticity of any part of the matter to me."[71]

Sherman effectively ended the dispute. Hazen was not satisfied and brought a civil suit for libel against Stanley. Stanley had effectively tried Hazen during his trial and Hazen was livid because he wanted his day in court to prove his innocence. Ever the fighter, Stanley responded to questions about the libel suit in the *New York Times* on June 12, 1878: "[Hazen] ... will never be awarded one cent of damages.... He [Stanley] believes Gen. Hazen begins the suit merely for buncombe, and to cover up his anticipated defeat in the recent court-martial. But it will not accomplish its object, nor prove very troublesome to Gen. Stanley. The record of the recent court-martial will be introduced as evidence to save calling many witnesses. Gen. Stanley, however, expects to produce additional proof of Hazen's cowardice and misconduct."[72] Certainly, Stanley's response was full of confidence and fight; but fortunately, the suit was dropped. Sherman, angered at Hazen, wrote that if he persisted in continuing the quarrel, "he [would] regret it to the last day of his life."[73] With this final threat, Hazen dropped his libel suit.

William Hazen's wife, Mildred, wrote in a small memoir about two incidents also reflecting poorly on Stanley. In 1872, Mildred and William B. Hazen were on the steamboat *Muier* and, according to her, Stanley was drunk; once he had sobered he apologized to Mrs. Hazen for being inebriated in her presence. According to Mrs. Hazen, he went on to say "he was poor and weighed down by having to support a large family of children, and Hazen was rich, had married a rich girl and had only one child, and he hated him—for the superfluous family it was somewhat idle to dislike my husband—the episode ended with Stanley also apologizing to General Hazen and promising to guard his tongue thereafter. All of which he did not do."[74] Mrs. Hazen also recounted an incident, presumably the one which resulted in the letter of apology, where William Hazen had dinner with Thomas Crittenden and David Stanley. Mrs. Hazen referred to Stanley as being a beast while Hazen, in her opinion, was "being rather sweet-tempered."[75] It is also important to note Mildred Hazen not only disliked Stanley but also held William T. Sherman in low regard. She wrote of Sherman: "He was as sharp as a briar and intolerant of comment—would not brook suggestion and was overbearing—and he made love to every woman who would like to him. I did not like him—In all his talk he never gave anybody else any credit—he had planned and fought and conquered single-handed and alone."[76]

Mildred Hazen asserted David Stanley stated he was poor and burdened with numerous children. Stanley was known for a wry wit, and perhaps his sarcastic humor played a part in the conversation between him and Mrs. Hazen. In fact, Stanley had very talented daughters and a son who would follow in his footsteps. Stanley's daughter Anna Huntington enrolled in the Buffalo Female Academy while he was stationed in New York; she graduated with honors in 1882. Her "artistic ability became apparent and eventually led to her attending the Philadelphia Academy of Fine arts where she studied under several of the leading painters of the time."[77] The biographer of Anna Stanley described a much different family life than the one described by Mildred Hazen. Nagel wrote, "David and Anna Maria Stanley provided a warm and loving environment for their children. Theirs was a close-knit family. They valued education and encouraged individual accomplishment and cultural enlightenment. They also instilled an abiding belief in God."[78]

The sensational trial ended and the newspapers across the nation reported the results. Many newspapers reported David Stanley was censured for the good of the service. The censure required him not to "bring charges, writing letters and adopting courses which he has taken during the past few years in order to expose and humiliate Gen. Hazen."[79] The newspapers also recorded Stanley had made his case: "The private opinion of all the war department officers seems to be that Stanley has sustained his charges against Hazen at least to a very great extent, and that he has in no way dishonored himself in bringing charges against Gen. Hazen."[80]

The *Daily Globe* reported upon Hazen's death some of the background of the two generals and how Hazen was regarded by some of his peers: "Ridicule of the signal service and Gen. Hazen has been the universal delight of West Pointers for years. It grew partly out of prejudice against Hazen, diligently increased by his enemies, who used his blunders to his disadvantage. His fatal folly at Shiloh in losing his brigade and then sitting down quietly and taking his breakfast on a gunboat could have been forgiven. When Gen. Stanley emptied his wine glass in Hazen's face at Gen. Sturgis' table at Ft. Mead, and he took the insult meekly, Hazen's name simply became a byword for cowardice throughout the army." The newspaper also recorded of Hazen despite his reputation, "Still he was a man of great ability and courage."[81]

Ultimately, Hazen's long-time friend James A. Garfield, through his influence with President Hayes, obtained Hazen's appointment as chief signal officer and promotion to the rank of brigadier general. In 1885, the controversial Hazen was again involved in another public disagreement when he was court-martialed for criticizing secretary of war Robert Lincoln and, ultimately, was lightly admonished by the president.[82]

Stanley Goes to Texas

In 1879, Stanley assumed command of the Military District of North Texas. When the 22nd U.S. Infantry returned to the Dakota Territory in 1876, Stanley left the regiment with Colonel Elwell Otis in command. When the 22nd U.S. Infantry moved to Fort McKavett in Texas in 1879, Stanley again served as colonel for the regiment. While in Texas, Stanley was involved in various activities including maintaining the peace with the Indians and keeping unscrupulous land speculators away from Oklahoma.

Fort McKavett was a good posting and was located in an area which overlooked the San Saba River. The fort had been established as a supply depot and also as a base to deal with hostilities with the Comanche Indians in the area. By the time of Stanley's arrival, most of the hostilities were over. During 1880–1882, Stanley commanded the District of the Nueces at Fort Clark, Texas. In 1882 and 1883 he commanded the district of New Mexico and in late 1883 he commanded a regiment at Fort Lewis, Colorado. From 1880 to 1883, Stanley's efforts were directed at maintaining the peace from raids, primarily from across the Mexican border and some from within the United States, and ensuring the Indians remained on the reservations.

On March 24, 1884, the good and loyal servant of the United States David S. Stanley was promoted to the rank of brigadier general in the U.S. States Army in command of the Department of Texas. He was greatly liked in Texas and his appointment was gratefully received as recorded in the *Fort Worth Gazette*: "His appointment now gives great and general satisfaction to the army people, and is hailed with joy all over the western frontier, where this courteous and faithful officer and true gentleman has had his merits recognized as sensibly as could have been in any other section of the country."[83] Stanley's appointment to the command was accompanied by letters almost too numerous to record. Among the most notable endorsement was a letter signed by the members of the legislature from the state of Texas. A similar letter was sent from the legislature of the state of Ohio. Even more interesting was a letter from Jacob Cox, Stanley's old nemesis regarding the battle at Franklin, Tennessee, who unreservedly endorsed Stanley's promotion.[84]

Throughout Stanley's time as commander of the Department of Texas and thereafter, he assumed the role of trusted commander and statesman. He often was called upon to give speeches and he returned to West Point in 1885 to offer the commencement address.

West Point Graduation Address

On June 13, 1885, David Stanley returned to his beginnings. He must have felt at peace as he returned to the place which was the start of his military career. Much had happened since he arrived at West Point so many years ago and now arrived as a brigadier general in the United States Army.

In his address to the graduates in 1885, Stanley delivered a long speech and one which revealed much about him: "After four years of study and military exercise, you have reached a goal worked for, wished for, longed for; sometimes, perhaps, despaired of; and you now pass from tutelage to that independence and freedom of life, compatible with the profession of arms, and the articles of war." In true Stanley form, he promised not to belabor his speech with rhetoric or "high philosophy." He spoke of the role of the army in the advance of the progress of the country and he referred to the contribution of George Washington and the early leaders in establishing and supporting the United States Military Academy at West Point. Stanley reminded the graduates of the contributions previous graduates had made in the past in the military and also in the political arena.[85]

He defended the military academy from those who disparaged the institution: "Fortunately for the academy and the country, our presidents, their war ministers, and boards of visitors, have not accepted the erroneous theory that military science can be imbibed by intuition, but on the contrary, they have held that some previous education is necessary to qualify a man to exercise the art of war, and that mental, more than physical, qualities of man determine the contest." Stanley further stated the fundamental principle of any lasting institution was one where the citizens felt a duty to defend it.[86] Then he went on to give his personal formula for success: "Obey orders; be studious in habit, and mark your duties with fidelity; observe strictly the articles of war; owe no man—live according to your means; and be not drinkers, or gamblers. Do exactly as you will promise in your oath of office,—that is to say, obey the orders of the President of the United States, and the orders of the officers appointed over you." Stanley also said, "Learn something every day.... Read not as a mere matter of amusement but to learn something."[87]

He gave detailed examples of his intent in each item of personal advice and again demonstrated his religious nature by referring to Saint Paul as a soldier of the cross and quoting him: "'Be instant in season, out of season; reprove, entreat, rebuke with all patience and doctrine. Be thou vigilant: labor in all things; fulfill thy ministry. Be sober.' So that, as he has said, you may say, at that solemn hour, which will surely come: 'I have fought a good fight; I have finished my course; I have kept the faith. For the rest, there is laid up for me a crown of justice, which the Lord, the just judge, will render to me at that day.'"[88]

The Department of Texas

Stanley demonstrated his leadership during his first year in command of the Department of Texas by advocating better rations for the soldiers and lighter clothing, by seeking better schools for the posts, and by interceding on behalf of the legendary Seminole Negro-Indian Scouts at Fort Clark. The Seminole Negro-Indian Scouts had provided exemplary service to the United States during the Texas-Indian Wars. When the hostilities with the Native Americans were over, the United States felt they had no need for this group nor did they provide any land for them to settle. David Stanley wrote in his 1884 annual report to his superiors: "I beg the attention of my superiors. These negroes, perfect Indians by raising, have been gradually gathered into our service during the past thirteen years—forty enlisted men, representing about two hundred souls almost wholly dependent for support upon the pay of the scouts.... These scouts have rendered good service in assisting to free the Texas frontier of Indians and other marauders, and I recommend that means be taken to find a home for them."[89]

One of David Stanley's biggest concerns while commanding the Department of Texas was the border area separating the United States and Mexico, which was inhabited by cattle producers. Raids across the border, south and north, provided the major area of conflict. The citizens in the area felt that without the military presence anarchy would result. In 1886, Stanley interceded to prevent a riot which occurred after certain municipal officers were elected in Laredo. Because the election was contested and because both Mexicans and Americans had interest in the election, ferry boats of Mexicans, supporting their U.S. residing friends and families, were loaded on the boats and they arrived on United States soil. The 8th U.S. Cavalry from Fort McIntosh disarmed both factions.[90]

Also in 1886, Stanley's command in Texas received the recently captured Geronimo. Geronimo, an Apache chief, had surrendered to U.S. government authorities in 1883 and agreed to live on the San Carlos Reservation. In May 1885, he and group of his followers led by Nana, Nachez and himself fled to the Sierra Madre Mountains in Mexico and were pursued by the U.S. Army. On September 4, 1886, Geronimo and his band surrendered again and were transferred to San Antonio, where they were detained for six weeks before being relocated to Florida. Stanley's command received the group on September 10. Captain Henry Ware Lawton received much credit in the capture of Geronimo and his band, and he accompanied the group of Apaches to San Antonio. Both Stanley and Lawton tried to reassure the local civilians that with the capture of Geronimo the Indian campaigns were virtually at an end.[91]

While in Texas in 1887, Stanley enjoyed his family life. His daughter Anna had continued to advance in her artistic abilities and decided to further develop her skills by studying and painting in Paris. Stanley's wife, Anna Maria, accompanied her daughter to Paris to establish living arrangements and then returned to Texas. Anna studied with several famous artists—Gustave Boulanger, Jules LeFevre and J. Robert Fleury. She later went to the Netherlands where some of her most accomplished works were produced.[92]

Meanwhile in Texas, the United States and Mexican relations continued to be strained and in 1889 David Stanley recorded that United States farmers were diverting much of the water from the Rio Grande for their farms to the detriment of their Mexican neighbors. This was very troublesome during the drought years. Stanley recommended this situation be remedied by the State Department. In addition, smuggling continued to be problem along the border.[93] Also, Mexican bandits raided across the border and caused havoc on the Texas side. An example of such a raid occurred in April 1891 when a ranch was attacked near Poulo, Texas, and the rancher and his son were killed during the attack. David Stanley sent a company of his legendary Seminole-Negro Scouts to pursue the bandits.[94]

When Stanley was not chasing bandits, he hosted several ceremonial events. One was the visit of President Benjamin Harrison on a trip to Galveston. As the commander of the Military District of Texas, General Stanley and his wife traveled with the presidential party to insure there were no problems during the visit.[95] Also while in Texas, he enjoyed hunting and fishing, which proved to be life-long pleasures for him.

Also in 1891, Stanley became involved in a very public court-martial of Captain Henry "Harry" Wessels, Jr, for conduct unbecoming to an officer and insubordination, during which very blunt remarks were exchanged. The issue arose when the 3rd U.S. Cavalry was ordered to prepare to embark on an expedition to deal with another uprising of the Sioux Indians. While Wessels' company was preparing for the expedition, he requested a leave of absence, but David Stanley refused his request, citing the importance of the mission. Wessels decided to make the request to Stanley's superior at the War Department and stated in this request that "Gen. Stanley was a drunkard and incompetent to manage a military company." The affair made national news, and newspapers across the country carried the story.[96] Wessels was a fighter and challenged the court-marital. Interestingly, the court-martial was quietly dissolved due to the president's not signing the order for it. Wessels was "severely reprimanded" by the president for his actions during this affair.[97] Wessels' career was not harmed by the incident and he had a successful military career and retired with the rank of brigadier general.

Mexican revolutionaries used the United States as a place to organize their forces and then move into Mexico, much to the unhappiness of the Mexican government. Just prior to David Stanley's retirement he was challenged by events of the Garza Revolution of 1891–1893. While living in Texas, Catarino Garza issued a proclamation to the citizens of Mexico that he intended to lead a revolution in Mexico because of various violations of freedoms of the people of Mexico. The Military Department of Texas and David Stanley became involved when on September 16, 1891, Captain E.L. Randall wired, "I have received information that at six o'clock last night C.E. Garza crossed into Mexico went 14 miles below here with over 50 armed men, his object to attempt a revolution." For the next six months the U.S. Army and the Mexican army tried in vain to capture him and his band.[98]

Property Rights Issues

Part of the command responsibility of the Department of Texas was the oversight of U.S. government property, and David Stanley became involved in two very public legal incidents involving the possession of military property. The first incident, in 1888, involved the arrest of David Stanley and Captain David Rumbough, who would later marry Stanley's daughter and who was serving as his aide. This incident was widely publicized in newspapers across the country. The *Buffalo Express* recorded this: "Trouble in Texas, Brig-Gen. Stanley Under Arrest at Austin" and the *New York Times* noted, "Gen. Stanley Arrested: He Calmly Submits and Texan Sheriff Refuses to Lock Him Up."[99] This event humorously recorded Stanley's sense of theater, as his actions were designed to demonstrate a point regarding government property.

The Stanley family with friends in front of their home, the commanding general's quarters at Fort Sam Houston, 1886. Seated from left are Stanley daughters Anna and Lil (Sarah Elizabeth), Maj. Joseph Wright (Anna Maria Wright Stanley's brother), Gen. Stanley, Mrs. Stanley (Anna Maria Wright), and another Stanley daughter, Josephine. Standing in the background from left are Lt. O.M. Smith and Lt. David Rumbough, holding the horse upon which sits Blanche Stanley. David Sheridan Stanley is on the horse to the right (Martin Callahan).

The arrests were the culmination of events regarding the ownership of property and reflected the problems of being involved in local politics. The board of school trustees in Austin developed a plan to obtain a block of property—an old, vacant fort, owned by the United States government—for the location of a schoolhouse. Texas congressmen successfully and legally provided the donation of the property and the secretary of war signed a deed for the transfer of the ownership to the city of Austin. Unfortunately, the Austin mayor, Joseph Nalle, preferred to have the military occupy the property in question rather than a school. So Mayor Nalle and the city refused the deed, voting 12–2 against accepting the property. During this time of confusion when the government gave up its ownership and the city of Austin declined to accept the deed, J.M. Snyder, moved onto the land and claimed "squatter sovereignty." At the request of the school board, Stanley and Rumbough went to the property and were immediately met with a constable who had a warrant for their arrest for "alleged attempt to commit assault on Snyder." Stanley and Rumbough were arrested and taken to court, which bound them under $500 bond to keep the peace. Both Stanley and Rumbough refused to pay the bond and insisted they be incarcerated. The local sheriff, understanding the local political situation, refused to put them in jail. Stanley and Rumbough were caught in some local political maneuvering and the issue was finally resolved through the intervention of Texas attorney general James "Big Jim" Hogg. Hogg determined the school district had the right to accept the property without consent of the city council and the school was built on the property in question. By all accounts, Stanley was aware of the local bickering and humorously, but stubbornly, played his part.[100]

In the second incident regarding government property, David Stanley again represented the U.S. Army and this case would reach the U.S. Supreme Court. This time the land in question was located in San Antonio. Mary and J.A. Schwalby brought suit against David Stanley and three other defendants on February 23, 1889, because the army possessed land of which they claimed one-third ownership. The United States argued it was an innocent purchaser of the land in 1875 and it had made substantial and permanent improvements. The Schwalbys claimed ownership of the entire property due to their one-third ownership. Ultimately, the case was ruled in favor of David Stanley's actions on behalf of the United States Army.[101]

Yet another incident occurred in El Paso in 1891 when a sheriff forced an eviction of a group of Stanley's soldiers from a plot of land in the center of the city. The order was made by a district court, but David Stanley soon arrived and reclaimed the property by dispatching a large troop of soldiers under the command of Major Hinton. Stanley was satisfied to allow the courts to handle the disagreements, but he was not going to be evicted from United States property by local politicians.[102]

Retirement

David Stanley remained in San Antonio, Texas, until June 1, 1892, when he retired from service after 40 years. He was retired as a full major general, based on his brevetted rank, in appreciation of his numerous contributions to his country, although his official rank in the United States Army was that of brigadier general. On March 29, 1893, Stanley finally gained recognition for his actions at the Battle of Franklin when he was awarded the Medal of Honor: "At a critical moment rode to the front of one of his brigades, reestablished its lines, and gallantly led it in a successful assault." A lifetime of service was finally being rewarded, but the realities of life are ever present. On April 23, 1895, David Stanley's beloved wife died at the age of 65. Anna Stanley had been suffering from a long illness and died at Johns Hopkins Hospital. David Stanley was traveling in Switzerland when his wife relapsed and arrived at her bedside just prior to her death. Anna Maria Wright Stanley was a true army officer's wife, valiantly supporting her family through the many years of campaigning with her husband.[103]

Next, David Stanley was appointed governor of the Soldier's Home in Washington and served there from September 1893 until April 1898. While in charge of the Soldier's Home he strove to make it an enjoyable place to live. He hosted various social events and orchestrated performances for the old soldiers.[104] He even included his family in some of the performances. In 1896, *A Mouse Trap* was performed at the Soldier's Home, followed by *A Leap Year Tragedy*. Miss Blanche Stanley starred in the second play and "was most enthusiastically received by the audience."[105] After leaving this position, Stanley moved to the Army and Navy Club in Washington. He then spent much of his retirement traveling. In his later life he took a trip to the Holy Land and returned with numerous anecdotes of his journey. He died on March 13, 1902, in Washington and was buried in the Soldiers' Home cemetery. David Stanley had suffered from Bright's disease for several years and he died of chronic interstitial nephritis, a kidney disorder.

Conclusion

*I loved and esteemed him, most sincerely,
as a noble soldier, a cultured gentlemen,
a true friend and devoted Christian.*

Summary of David S. Stanley's Military Career

When David Stanley was recommended for retirement from the Unites States Army while holding the rank of brigadier general, a list of the engagements in which he was involved was attached to the recommendation and included the following (the engagements which are bolded resulted in a brevetted promotion for gallant and meritorious service):

Near Arbuckle, Indian Territory	February 27, 1861
Forsyth, Missouri	June 27, 1861
Dug Springs, Missouri	August 31, 1861
Wilson's Creek, Missouri	August 10, 1861
New Madrid, Missouri	March 13, 1862
Island No. 10, Mississippi River	April 7, 1862
Farmington, Mississippi	May 28, 1862
Siege of Corinth, Mississippi	April 22 to May 30, 1862
Iuka, Mississippi	September 19, 1862
Corinth, Mississippi	October 3–4, 1862
Franklin, Tennessee	December 15, 1862
Stones River, Tennessee	**December 31, 1862—January 4, 1863**
Bradyville, Tennessee	February 13, 1863
Snow Hill, Tennessee	March 10 and 30, 1863
Franklin, Tennessee	April 11, 1863
Middleton, Tennessee	May 22, 1863
Shelbyville, Tennessee	June 27, 1863
Elk River, Tennessee	July 2, 1863
Alpine, Georgia	September 9, 1983
Resaca, Georgia	**May 15, 1864**

Cassville, Georgia	May 17, 19, 1864
Dallas, Georgia	May 25, 28, 1864
Pine Mountain, Georgia	May 28 to June 20, 1864
Kennesaw Mountain, Georgia	June 20 to July 2, 1864
Ruff's Station, Georgia	**July 4, 1864**
Peach Tree Creek, Georgia	July 19, 21, 1864
Siege of Atlanta	July 22 to September 2, 1864
Lovejoy's Station, Georgia	September 2, 1864
Near Nashville, Tennessee	November 24, 29, 1864
Spring Hill, Tennessee	November 28, 1864
Franklin, Tennessee	**November 30, 1864**
Powder River and minor skirmishes	August 18, 1872[1]

In many ways, it is easy to summarize David Stanley's career. He was ever brave, professional, gentlemanly, intelligent, diligent to duty, mindful of the needs of his men, respectful of his fellow man and a true patriot. Stanley was a professional soldier who was a traditionalist in his methods. He firmly believed in the methodology of war and approached engagements with a firm knowledge of what to expect on the battlefield.

Stanley was described as cool and calm when he led his men into battle. His intimate knowledge of how infantry, artillery, and cavalry worked together was one of his greatest gifts. Certainly this knowledge served him well as he withstood an attack on May 28, 1862, in the siege of Corinth, during the Battle of Resaca, and during the amazing defense at the Battle of Spring Hill. But he was also prone to ferocity in the midst of battle. The charge during the Battle of Stones River when Stanley stood in his stirrups with saber over his head rallying his troopers is a good example of this. Also, during the counterattack at the Battle of Corinth when Stanley was walking amidst his men serving to align the ranks before sending them into battle is another example of his intensity. Finally, during the Battle of Franklin he nearly paid the ultimate sacrifice working to rally his troops.

During Stanley's career, he routinely faced death and was nearly killed many times. These incidents include a near fatal encounter with a Cheyenne Indian when J.E.B. Stuart was wounded protecting him; when Stanley's horse was killed under him at Forsyth, Missouri; during his famous cavalry charge at Stones River; at Rocky Face when he was forced to seek cover; with Howard during the Atlanta Campaign; when he was wounded in the groin

David Stanley in Texas (U.S. Army Heritage and Education Center).

at Jonesboro; and when he was shot in the neck at Franklin. David Stanley was relentlessly courageous and never failed to ride to the sound of the guns.

Stanley was a soldier's general. There are numerous examples where the rank and file expressed their gratitude to him. He was referred to as "Our Stanley" by his men, and one of his greatest assets was his care for the men who served under him. He strove to give his men a chance to win rather than needlessly sacrificing them for glory, as his professionalism prevented him from doing that. He realized well-cared-for men would fight when called upon; and he knew in almost all cases, he would be called to fight another day. Keeping his men alive was the key to fighting another day. On numerous occasions, he was referred to as a true gentleman and as being calm in all circumstances. He was also noted as a man who felt all men to be equal, and that even the lowest private was worthy of respect and consideration.

Despite, or perhaps because of, his love for his men, he was a sound disciplinarian; but he was not extreme. He tried to teach them the lot of a soldier was hard work and poor conditions. He also taught them that the path to shame and anarchy began when discipline was absent. He was not beyond bringing men to court-martial if they failed to follow orders.

Stanley was a plainspoken individual who had little respect for manipulative or political individuals. This was demonstrated in his attack on William Hazen and his dislike for James Garfield and Robert Mitchell. He felt men should be measured on their ability and not on their influence, although he grew to understand this aspect of the military. He shunned rhetoric and believed actions spoke for the individual. He also had a grand sense of humor and a wry wit. All his life he was respected by his peers as being truthful, forthright, and a sincere man of honor.

But he was not without fault. By some accounts, he was very conservative and traditional in his methods during the war. Certainly, arguments could be made regarding pettiness or vindictiveness in the grudges he carried after the war. Perhaps the most serious charge against Stanley is the bitterness and overcritical nature which came through in his memoirs, which were published in 1917. The decision apparently was made to publish the memoirs as they were written. A great disservice to David Stanley was the handling of this process despite the editorial efforts of his son-in-law Willard Holbrook. In regard to the criticisms found in Stanley's memoirs, his son-in-law General Holbrook was also concerned and asked General James H. Wilson what he thought about publishing the memoirs unedited. Wilson replied, "Gen. Stanley was not the man to write a statement like that, without being convinced about the truth of it." Perhaps all memoirs should be written as Stanley wrote his.[2]

The publication of the memoirs caused some to conclude Stanley to be a critical and bitter man. The David Stanley who wrote the letter to William Rosecrans immediately after the Battle of Chickamauga was not the same man who penned memoirs stating Rosecrans had no knowledge of how to use cavalry. The historical Stanley, the man of the moment, was a sincere, plainspoken man trying to protect his country and his men with his knowledge and experience to the best of his ability.

Certainly, the whole issue of the alcohol continues to be a question about his career. There is a likelihood David Stanley was an alcoholic, at least in the 1870s. There is a great deal of innuendo about his alcohol consumption, but not a lot of facts to support the allegation. Somewhere in his career alcohol became a problem, but it difficult to say when this happened. The facts show he was accused, probably falsely, of being drunk during the Battle of Corinth, and he vehemently denied this allegation as he sought the source in order to stop the rumor. He was accused of alcoholism by Charles Dana after the Battle of Chickamauga, but, again, this claim cannot be substantiated. Stanley could have been drinking heavily after he returned to Chattanooga following his illness. He was in a situation where Alexander McCook, Thomas Crittenden, and his mentor William Rosecrans had all been relieved of command. He was besieged in Chattanooga and he probably knew he was next in line to be demoted. Excessive drinking might have been likely in this scenario. There are no other mentions of excessive alcohol use by Stanley until he was moved to the Dakota Territory in the 1870s. There can be no doubt of his alcohol problem during the Yellowstone Expedition and there are numerous accounts of his drinking. However, there are very few confirmed historical accounts of excessive drinking in other periods of his life, although there were some disparaging remarks made about him by some of his enemies. Accounts of Stanley's drinking revealed him to be an unpleasant person while under the influence of alcohol, but always apologetic after a bout of drinking.

There can be no doubt David Stanley liked to drink but it is important to consider this problem in context of his career. It is very hard to find an example when he drank to the detriment of his job at the time. There are no examples where he was drunk and the job was not done properly. Even during the Yellowstone Expedition, when Custer was isolated and under attack, Stanley's quick action was instrumental in rescuing the cavalry.

Finally, it is important to consider the conditions of Stanley's military life. He was assigned to the dangerous and isolated frontier after completing West Point. Then he spent four years in the Civil War, during which he was nearly killed numerous times. He was next assigned to the frontier in Texas and South Dakota. After a time in New York, he went back to the frontier. Danger, isolation, and boredom were his constant companions for forty years. In Stanley's defense, he always tried to restrict alcohol use by those under his command and he made a point during his speech at West Point to emphasize the need to stay sober. He was clearly a man who struggled with this problem, understanding the danger but sometimes falling under alcohol's control.

Stanley was an intelligent, religious man who valued his family and sought a balance between these values and his military life. He was blessed with a loving wife who understood the way of the military, and his love of the military was obvious from the legacy of his children and grandchildren who made the military their life. Only children who dearly loved their father and mother, and their life, would have chosen to continue in this heritage. In Stanley's personal life and family life he acknowledged a supreme power, and those religious values guided him through some of the most terrible times imaginable. He dedicated his life to his country and to the United States Army. He spent four long years in the Civil War and many, many years living on the western frontier. He left a legacy of which he could be proud.

David Stanley's Family Legacy

David and Anna Stanley's influence continued to live long after their deaths as their children flourished and produced one of the longest lines of military officers in the United States. The couple had seven children, and only five children survived to adulthood. But what a legacy. Two of Stanley's daughters, Blanche and Anna, were accomplished painters. Anna was an Impressionist artist, studying at the Buffalo Female Academy during her high school years, and later at the Pennsylvania Academy of the Fine Arts, headed by the famous Thomas Eakins. Blanche also attended the Buffalo Female Academy and continued to study in preparation for her art. Both sisters traveled to Paris to continue their art studies.

Anna Huntington Stanley "broke the mold of a typical Army daughter, when her talents and determination drove her into the art world that was not at all part of the Stanley makeup at that time. After her time at the Pennsylvania Academy she got permission from her family to join the artists studying in Paris at the Julian Academy—at the time the only recognized Paris art school that admitted women! Her work was chosen to hang in the Paris Salon and she joined other artists who went to Holland to paint during their summer vacations from the Academy."[3]

Anna was deeply involved in her art and exhibited widely in the United States prior to her marriage. She married Willard Ames Holbrook in 1896. While Anna maintained a studio in San Antonio, Holbrook was a career soldier. He had been appointed to the United States Military Academy in 1881. He served in the cavalry and ultimately was promoted to the rank of major general. In 1891 Holbrook served as aide-de-camp to David Stanley in Texas, becoming the first chief of cavalry. Although Anna did not know Holbrook while he served as aide to Stanley, it is likely he became acquainted with her as the family read Anna's letters she wrote while in Europe. Holbrook and Anna did not formally meet until David Sheridan Stanley graduated from West Point. The two would have two sons, Willard Ames Holbrook, Jr., born at Fort Grant in Arizona in May 1898, and David Stanley Holbrook (known as Stanley), born at Angel Island, San Francisco, in April 1900. Anna Stanley Holbrook died in the arms of her husband on February 25, 1907, of pneumonia while the family was assigned to the Pennsylvania Military College in Chester, Pennsylvania. Willard married Anna's sister Josephine a few years later. Josephine died on January 15, 1927, and was interred in Washington, D.C.[4]

Anna Huntington Stanley, Dordrecht, the Netherlands, 1888 (United States Military Academy Special Collections and Archives).

David Stanley with his grandson Willard Ames Holbrook, Jr., Washington, D.C., 1898 (United States Military Academy Library, Special Collections and Archive).

Unfortunately Anna and Willard's son Lieutenant David Stanley Holbrook, known as "Stanley" or "Stan," died in Manila, Philippine Islands, on March 28, 1926. He was serving in the 26th U.S. Cavalry when he was shot and killed by a revolver he was handling. Stanley Holbrook was a very popular officer and was considered one of the best polo players in the Philippines.[5]

Anna's other son, Willard Ames Holbrook, Jr., nicknamed "Hunk," graduated from the United States Military Academy in 1918. Hunk Holbrook had an outstanding military career and served in the 10th Cavalry after graduation, Eleventh Armored Division and Twelfth Armored Division in World War II. Holbrook most notably served as Combat Command "A" Commander, taking the surrender of Linz, Austria, personally. He married Helen Herr, daughter of General John R. Herr, and the couple had three children. Joanne Stanley Holbrook, who would later marry George Patton IV, Willard Ames Holbrook III and Marian Herr Holbrook were children of this marriage. Marian married Lieutenant Colonel Richard Word Roberson. Willard Holbrook III, West Point class 1955, retired as a colonel after thirty years of service.

Blanche Stanley continued her life as an artist and lived in several places during her life, including Massachusetts, Pennsylvania and Paris. She died on January 19, 1951, at the age of 80 and was interred in the U.S. Soldier's and Airmen's Home National Cemetery in Washington, D.C.

Sarah E. "Lily" Stanley married David Jacob Rumbough in 1885. David Rumbough was also a graduate of the United States Military Academy. A native of Virginia, he was appointed to West Point in 1876. After graduation he served with the 3rd U.S. Artillery and rose to the rank of colonel. He died in December 1912. Sarah E. Stanley Rumbough survived her husband and died in May 1952. The Rumboughs' two sons, David Sheridan and Stanley Maddox, also attended West Point and served in the U.S. Army. In addition, a daughter, Sarah Huntington Rumbough, married William Whitehead West, who was a United States Military Academy graduate, class of 1905.

Sarah Rumbough wrote the story of her life in the army, *The Regular Army O!*, in which she recounted her life in the Stanley family and later with David Rumbough. She described an exciting and loving time in the army with her family and her husband and at the end of the work she wrote, "I would not give up my Army life for all the riches in Araby. I have had a wonderful time and 'the caissons go rolling along.'"[6]

David Sheridan Stanley, David and Anna Stanley's only son, continued in the footsteps of his father, attending the United States Military Academy, class of 1895. He served in the Spanish American War and also World War I. Assigned to infantry duty he gained recognition for his outstanding work as a quartermaster, where he reached the rank of colonel. David married Jane Fordyce in Arkansas in 1888. The couple had three children: Jane, Samuel and David Sloane Stanley, Jr. David Sloane Stanley, Jr. was also a graduate of the United States Military Academy, class of 1924. However, he did not remain in the army, but resigned in 1924 and attended the Massachusetts Institute of Technology and earned a degree in industrial biology.

The legacy of the descendants of David Stanley who attended the United States Military Academy and their subsequent military service is remarkable. It remains one of the strongest military lineages at West Point.

The Descendants of David S. Stanley at the United States Military Academy[7]

Son	David Sheridan Stanley
Grandson	Stanley Maddox Rumbough
Grandson	David Sheridan Rumbough
Grandson	Willard Ames Holbrook, Jr.
Grandson	David Stanley Holbrook
Grandson	David Sloane Stanley
Great-grandson	William Whitehead West 3d
Great-grandson	Thomas Quinton Donaldson 4th
Great-grandson	John Willson Donaldson
Great-grandson	David Huntington Rumbough
Great-grandson	Willard Ames Holbrook 3d

Final Remarks

In 1885, David Stanley addressed the graduating class of the United States Military Academy at West Point. Much of his philosophy about life and the military were summarized in the speech: "It is one of the fundamental principles of government that every citizen is bound to defend it when the necessity arises: and this principle applies much more strongly to you, whom the country had educated. I beseech you to obey orders; observe strictly the articles of war; owe no man,—live according to your means; and be not drinkers or gamblers.... Learn something every day.... Read not as a matter of amusement, but to learn, and as a matter of duty and habit. Follow the advice of Carlyle, to read into the very essence and core of books.... As a true guide to service in the army of your country, I beg you, in the words of the illustrious Soldier of the Cross, St. Paul, to 'be instant in season, out of season; reprove, entreat, rebuke with patience and doctrine.... Be thou vigilant; labor in all things; ... fulfill thy ministry. Be sober,' so that, as he has said, you may say at that solemn hour, which will surely come: 'I have fought the good fight; I have finished my course; I have kept the faith. For the rest, there is up for me a crown of justice, which the Lord, the just judge, will render to me at that day.'"[8]

The Very Reverend John Ireland, archbishop of St. Paul, Minnesota, wrote of David Stanley: "I loved and esteemed him, most sincerely, as a noble soldier, a cultured gentlemen, a true friend and devoted Christian. He may have had a few frailties! But, how small they were when seen together with his great qualities of mind and heart!"[9] Thomas MacCurdy Vincent also wrote of him: "Stanley did not hate any man! He did, however, hate the evil in the man, as he hated evil in himself; and he condemned both alike."[10] And, finally, James Edward Kelly had this to say about David Stanley: "He is one of the purest men I ever met; from my first acquaintance with him until now, I have never heard a coarse word cross his lips.... He was deeply religious, and bowed his head in prayer."[11]

Chapter Notes

Preface

1. R.W. Johnson, "Recollections of Distinguished Generals of the Civil War," *National Tribune*, August 15, 1895, p. 1.
2. M. John Lubetkin, *Jay Cooke's Gamble* (Norman: University of Oklahoma Press, 2006), 297.
3. Joseph Vale, *Minty and the Cavalry: A History of Cavalry Campaigns in the Western Armies* (Harrisburg, PA: Edwin K. Myers, 1886), xxxi.

Chapter 1

1. Israel P. Warren, *The Stanley Families of America: As Descended from John, Timothy, and Thomas Stanley of Hartford, Conn.* (Portland, ME: B. Thurston, 1887), 316.
2. David Stanley, *An American General: The Memoirs of David Sloan Stanley*, ed. Samuel W. Fordyce IV (Santa Barbara, CA: Narrative, 2004), 42.
3. Ibid., 44.
4. Ibid.
5. Ibid., 49.
6. Ibid., 49–50.
7. Ibid., 50.
8. Philip Sheridan, *Personal Memoirs of Philip H. Sheridan, General United States Army*, vol. 1 (New York: D. Appleton, 1902), 8–9.
9. *Official Register of the Officers and Cadets of the U.S. Military Academy* (West Point, NY: U.S. Military Academy, June 1852), 7.
10. Stanley, *An American General*, 61.
11. J.J.B. Wright, Letter, April 25, 1853, David Stanley Personnel Records ACP 000183, National Archives Microfiche 1, 001–04–01, Washington, D.C.
12. William H. Hammond, Letter, May 15, 1855, David Stanley Personnel Records, ACP 000183, National Archives Microfiche 1, 001–04–03, Washington, D.C.
13. David S. Stanley, August 4 entry, *David Stanley Diary, United States 2nd Dragoons of a March from Fort Smith, Arkansas, to San Diego, California, Made in 1853*, Martin Lalor Crimmins Papers, Briscoe Center for American History, University of Texas at Austin, Texas.
14. Ibid., August 7 entry.
15. William H. Hammond, Letters, May 15, 1855 and September 10, 1855; Leander Firestone, Letter, October 18, 1855, David Stanley Personnel Records, ACP 000183, National Archives Microfiche 1, 001–04–03, 001–05–001, 001–05–005, Washington, D.C.
16. David Stanley, "A Trip from Jefferson Barracks, Missouri (1856) to Fort Randall," David Stanley Folder, United States Military Academy, Special Collections, West Point, New York, 3.
17. Stanley, *An American General*, 93.
18. Ibid., 98.
19. Eli Long, Diary, July 29, 1857, United States Army Heritage and Education Center, Eli Long Papers, 1855–1892, Carlisle, Pennsylvania.
20. Samuel Stanley, "General David Stanley, Frontier Soldier," *The Real West*, 152, no. 20 (July 1977), 20.
21. Stanley, *An American General*, 113.
22. Ibid., 113.
23. David Stanley, *Personal Memoirs of Major-General D.S. Stanley, USA* (Cambridge: Harvard University Press, 1917), 54.
24. E.D. Townsend, *The War of the Rebellion: A Compilation of the Official Records of the Union and Confederate Armies* (hereafter designated as *Official Records*), Series I, Volume 1 (Washington, D.C.: U.S. Government Printing Office, 1880–1901), 667.
25. John Van Duesen Du Bois, "The Civil War Journal and Letters of Col. John Van Duesen Du Bois, ed. Jared C. Lobdell, *Missouri Historical Review* 61 (July 1966), 446.
26. W.H. Woodson, *History of Clay County, Missouri* (Indianapolis and Topeka: Historical, 1920), 126.
27. Stanley, *An American General*, 121.
28. William Parrish, *History of Missouri, 1860–1875*, vol. 3 (Columbia: University of Missouri Press, 1997), 4.
29. Wiley Britton, *The Civil War on the Border* (New York: G.P. Putnam, 1890), 1.
30. Parrish, *History of Missouri, 1860–1875*, p. 12.
31. Ibid., 22.
32. Floyd A. Showmaker, *A History of Missouri and Missourians* (Columbia, MO: Walter Ridgeway, 1922), 155–156.
33. William Garrett Piston and Richard W. Hatcher III, *Wilson's Creek: The Second Battle of the Civil War and the Men Who Fought It* (Chapel Hill: University of North Carolina Press, 2000), 45.
34. Ibid., 70.
35. Ibid., 125.
36. Ibid., 128.
37. Ibid.
38. Frank Moore, ed., *The Rebellion Record*, vol. 2 (New York: G.P. Putnam, 1862), 438–439.
39. Elmo Ingenthron, *Borderland Rebellion: A History of the Civil War on the Missouri-Arkansas Border*, ed. Kathleen Van Buskirk (Branson, MO): Ozark Mountaineer, 1980), 65.
40. William Riley Brooksher, *Bloody Hill: The Civil War Battle of Wilson's Creek* (Washington, D.C.: Brassey's, 1995), 136.
41. Stanley, *An American General*, 122.

42. David Stanley, Correspondence, March 11, 1863, Union General Papers, Record Group 94, Entry 159, Box 28, National Archives, Washington, D.C.
43. Piston, *Wilson's Creek*, 129.
44. Moore, *The Rebellion Record*, 439.
45. Brooksher, *Bloody Hill*, 137.
46. Thomas W. Sweeny, *Official Records*, Series 1, Volume 3, 44.
47. Piston, *Wilson's Creek*, 139.
48. Moore, *The Rebellion Record*, 469.
49. Frederick Steele, *Official Records*, Series 1, Volume 3, pp. 49–50.
50. Piston, *Wilson's Creek*, 140.
51. James Rains, *Official Records*, Series 1, Volume 3, p. 51.
52. James McIntosh, *Official Records*, Series 1, Volume 3, pp. 51–52.
53. Moore, *The Rebellion Record*, 469.
54. E.F. Ware, *The Lyon Campaign in Missouri* (Topeka, KS: Crane, 1907) (reprinted by Press of Camp Pope Bookshop, Iowa City, IA, 1991), 275.
55. Ingenthron, *Borderland Rebellion*, 79.
56. Piston, *Wilson's Creek*, 141.
57. Nathaniel Lyon, *Official Records*, Series 1, Volume 3, p. 47.
58. Piston, *Wilson's Creek*, 175.
59. Edwin Bearss, *The Battle of Wilson's Creek* (Bozeman: George Washington Carver Birthplace District Association, 1975), 136.
60. John C. Frémont, *Official Records*, Series 1, Volume 3, p. 54.
61. Stanley, *An American General*, 124.
62. John Dubois, James Totten, Frederick Steele, Gordon Granger, Florence Coryrn, *Official Records*, Series 1, Volume 3, p. 98.
63. Stanley, *An American General*, 61.

Chapter 2

1. Jay Carlton Mullen, "Pope's New Madrid and Island Number 10 Campaigns," *Missouri Historical Review* 59 (April 1965), 325–343.
2. Ibid., 328.
3. William G. Bek, "The Civil War Diary of John T. Buegel, Union Soldier," *Missouri Historical Review* 40 (April 1946), 315.
4. Carl Sandberg, *Abraham Lincoln: The War Years*, vol. 1 (New York: Harcourt, Brace, 1939), 340.
5. Ibid., 343.
6. Ibid.
7. John McElroy, *The Struggle for Missouri* (Washington, D.C.: National Tribune Co., 1909), 221–222.
8. David Stanley, *An American General: The Memoirs of David Sloan Stanley*, ed. Samuel W. Fordyce IV (Santa Barbara, CA: Narrative, 2004), 125.
9. Ibid.
10. Ibid., 127.
11. David S. Stanley, Letter, October 15, 1861, David Stanley Personnel File ACP 000183, Nation Archives, Washington, D.C., Microfiche: 0001-06-003.
12. David S. Stanley et al., "Trial of Ebenezer Magoffin, Accused of Murder and Violation of Parole," *Official Records*, Series 2, Volume 1, pp. 292–374.
13. Speed Butler, *Official Records*, Series 1, Volume 8, p. 589.
14. Stanley, *An American General*, 130.
15. Ibid., 131.
16. Ibid.
17. A.B. Gray, *Official Records*, Series 1, Volume 3, p. 705.
18. John Pope, *Official Records*, Series 1, Volume 8, p. 79.
19. Ibid., p. 80.
20. Ibid.
21. Ibid.
22. Larry J. Daniel and Lynn N. Bock, *Island No. 10: Struggle for the Mississippi Valley* (Tuscaloosa: University of Alabama Press, 1996), 56.
23. Charles Schuyler Hamilton, *Official Records*, Series 1, Volume 8, p. 102.
24. Mullen, "Pope's New Madrid and Island Number 10 Campaigns," 331.
25. Ibid., 332.
26. David Stanley, *Official Records*, Series 1, Volume 8, 98.
27. Ibid.
28. W.H. Worthington, *Official Records*, Series 1, Volume 8, p. 106.
29. John Pope, *Official Records*, Series 1, Volume 8, p. 82.
30. David S. Stanley, After Action Report, March 15, 1862, Stanley, Wright, West Papers, United States Army Heritage and Education Center, Carlisle, Pennsylvania, Box 1 1862–1863 Folder, David S. Stanley Family Papers.
31. Stanley, *An American General*, 131.
32. John Groesbeck, *Official Records*, Series 1, Volume 8, p. 99.
33. Mullen, "Pope's New Madrid and Island Number 10 Campaigns," 333
34. John Pope, *Official Records*, Series 1, Volume 8, pp. 83–84.
35. David Stanley, *Official Records*, Series 1, Volume 8, p. 98.
36. David Dixon Porter, *The Naval History of the Civil War* (London: General, 1998), 161.
37. Bern Anderson, *By Sea and By River: The Naval History of the Civil War* (New York: Da Capo, 1962), 105–106.
38. David Stanley, *Official Records*, Series 1, Volume 8, p. 98.
39. Charles H. Smith, *The History of Fuller's Ohio Brigade, 1861–1865: Its Great March with Roster, Portraits, Battle Maps and Biographies* (Cleveland: J.A. Wyatt, 1909), 436.
40. John Pope, *Official Records*, Series 1, Volume 8, 670.
41. Ibid.
42. Ibid., 675.
43. Thomas Scott, *Official Records*, Series 1, Volume 8, p. 676.
44. Clement Evans, ed., *Confederate Military History*, vol. 3 (Atlanta: Confederate, 1899), 3–32.
45. Stanley, *An American General*, 133.
46. John Groesbeck, *Official Records*, Series 1, Volume 8, pp. 99–100.
47. John Pope, *Official Records*, Series 1, Volume 8, p. 90.
48. Stanley, *An American General*, 134.

Chapter 3

1. Peter Cozzens and Robert Girardi, *The Military Memoirs of General John Pope* (Chapel Hill: University of North Carolina Press, 1998), 61.
2. William Stewart, Letter, April 11, 1862, William S., Papers, 1861–1864, (C2991), Western Historical Manuscript Collection, Columbia, University of Missouri/State Historical Society of Missouri.
3. Edwin Stanton, *Official Records*, Series 1, Volume 8, p. 678.
4. Stacy Allen, "Corinth, Mississippi: Crossroads of the Western Confederacy," *Blue and Gray* (2007), 21–22.
5. Thomas Scott, *Official Records*, Series 1, Volume 10, Part 2, p. 116.
6. Speed Butler, *Official Records*, Series 1, Volume 10, Part 2, p. 122.
7. Alden Carter, *Brother to the Eagle: The Civil War Journal of Sgt. Ambrose Armitage, 8th Wisconsin Infantry* (United States, Booklocker, 2006), 85.
8. David Stanley, *Official Records*, Series 1, Volume 10, Part 1, p. 798.
9. W.L. Elliott, *Official Records*, Series 1, Volume 10, Part 1, pp. 798–99.
10. Pope, John. *Official Records*, Series 1, Volume 10, Part 2, pp. 142–143.
11. Oscar Jackson, *The Colonel's Diary* (Sharon, PA: Private Publication, David Jackson, 1922), 57–58.
12. David Stanley, *An American General: The Memoirs of David Sloan*

Stanley, ed. Samuel W. Fordyce IV (Santa Barbara, CA: Narrative, 2004), 138.

13. Thomas Scott, *Official Records*, Series 1, Volume 10, Part 2, p. 172.

14. John Pope, *Official Records*, Series 1, Volume 10, Part 2, p. 173.

15. John Loomis, *Official Records*, Series 1, Volume 10, Part 1, p. 805.

16. Ibid., 806.

17. Ibid.

18. Daniel Ruggles, *Official Records*, Series 1, Volume 10, Part 1, p. 809.

19. John Pope, *Official Records*, Series 1, Vol. 10, Part 2, p. 173.

20. John Loomis, *Official Records*, Series 1, Volume 10, Part 1, p. 806.

21. Ibid.

22. Ibid.

23. Ibid.

24. Ibid.

25. John Pope, *Official Records*, Series 1, Volume 10, Part 2, p. 176.

26. William Stewart, May, 20, 1862.

27. Daniel Ruggles, *Official Records*, Series 1, Volume 10, Part 1, p. 811.

28. John Pope, *Official Records*, Series 1, Volume 10, Part 2, p. 176.

29. David Stanley, *Official Records*, Series 1, Volume 10, Part 1, p. 721.

30. James Edward Kelly, *Generals in Bronze: Interviewing the Commanders of the Civil War*, ed. William B. Styple (Kearney, NJ: Bell Grove, 2005), 185.

31. Allen, "Corinth, Mississippi: Crossroads of the Western Confederacy," 24.

32. John Pope, *Official Records*, Series 1, Volume 10, Part 2, p. 177.

33. Ibid., 198–99.

34. Henry Halleck, *Official Records*, Series 1, Volume 10, Part 2, p. 197.

35. Abraham Lincoln, *Official Records*, Series 1, Volume 10, Part 1, p. 667.

36. David Stanley, *Official Records*, Series 1, Volume. 10, Part 1, pp. 722–23.

37. Ibid.

38. David Stanley, *Personal Memoirs of Major-General D.S. Stanley, USA* (Cambridge: Harvard University Press, 1917), 99.

39. David S. Stanley, After Action Report, June 5, 1862, Stanley, Wright West Papers, United States Army Heritage and Education Center, Carlisle, Pennsylvania, Box 1 1862–1863 Folder, David S. Stanley Family Papers.

40. Timothy B. Smith, *Corinth 1862: Siege, Battle, Occupation* (Lawrence: University Press of Kansas, 2012), 78.

41. Duncan McCall, *Three Years in the Service: Record of the Doings of the 11th Reg. Missouri* (Springfield, MO: Johnson & Bradford, 1864), 9.

42. Henry Halleck, *Official Records*, Series 1, Volume 10, Part 1, p. 668.

43. David Stanley, *Official Records*, Series 1, Volume 10, Part 1, p. 723.

44. Stanley, *An American General*, 140.

45. Ibid., 139.

46. John W. Fuller, "Our Kirby Smith," in *Sketches of War History, 1861–1865: Papers Read Before the Ohio Commandery of the Military Order of the Loyal Legion of the United States, 1886–1888*, vol. 2 (Cincinnati: Robert Clarke, 1888), 169–170.

47. Pope, *Memoirs*, 103.

48. Henry Cist, *The Army of the Cumberland* (New York: Charles Scribner's, 1882), 172–173.

49. Stanley, *An American General*, 140.

50. Ibid.

Chapter 4

1. William S. Rosecrans, William S. Rosecrans Papers, Undated Letter, Box 59, Folder 54, University of California, Los Angeles.

2. Thomas M. Vincent, "David Sloane Stanley," *The Thirty-fourth Annual Reunion of the Association of Graduates of the United States Military Academy at West Point, New York* (Saginaw, MI: Seeman and Peters, 1903), 62.

3. David Stanley, *An American General: The Memoirs of David Sloan Stanley*, ed. Samuel W. Fordyce IV (Santa Barbara, CA: Narrative, 2004), 141.

4. Jack Welsh, *Medical Histories of Union Generals* (Kent, OH: Kent State University Press, 1996), 261.

5. Jacob C. Cohen, Letter, August 1, 1862, to the *Jewish Messenger*, Jewish-American History Documentation Foundation, Lathrup Village, Michigan.

6. Peter Cozzens, *The Darkest Days of the War: The Battles of Iuka and Corinth* (Chapel Hill: University of North Carolina Press, 1997), 37.

7. Ibid., 43

8. Sterling Price, *Official Records*, Series 1, Volume 17, Part 1, p. 120.

9. Bragg, Braxton, *Official Records*, Series 1, Volume 17, Part 2, p. 676.

10. Cozzens, *The Darkest Days of the War*, 50.

11. William Stewart, *William S., Papers, 1861–1864* (C2991), Letter, September 9, 1862, Western Historical Manuscript Collection, Columbia, University of Missouri/State Historical Society of Missouri.

12. Dennis W. Belcher, "Joe Mower's Jackass Cavalry," in *North and South* 13 (November, 2011), 52–61.

13. Cozzens, *The Darkest Days of the War*, 62.

14. W.H. Gilliard, "The Battle of Iuka" *National Tribune*, June 26, 1902, p. 3.

15. Charles H. Smith, *The History of Fuller's Ohio Brigade, 1861–1865: Its Great March with Roster, Portraits, Battle Maps and Biographies* (Cleveland: J.A. Wyatt, 1909), 396.

16. Cozzens, *The Darkest Days of the War*, 92.

17. William Lamers, *The Edge of Glory: A Biography of General William S. Rosecrans, U.S.A.* (New York: Harcourt, Brace & World, 1961), 111.

18. Cozzens, *The Darkest Days of the War*, 111.

19. Andrew Weber, *Official Records*, Series 1, Volume 17, Part 1, p. 88.

20. Ibid.

21. Ibid.

22. Ibid.

23. Wayne Calhoun Temple, "A Chaplain in the 11th Missouri Infantry," *Lincoln Herald* 64 (Summer 1962) (Harrowgate, TN: Lincoln Memorial University Press, 1962), 81–88.

24. David Stanley, *Official Records*, Series 1 Volume 17, Part 1, p. 82.

25. Seven Dossman, *Campaign for Corinth: Blood in Mississippi* (Abilene: McWhitney Foundation, 2006), 79.

26. Lyman Pierce, *History of the 2nd Iowa Cavalry* (Burlington, IA: Hawkeye, 1865), 32–33.

27. Edward Ord, *Official Records*, Series 1, Volume 17, Part 1, p. 119.

28. Stewart, Letter, September 23, 1862.

29. Stanley, *An American General*, 142.

30. William Rosecrans, *Official Records*, Series 1, Volume 17, Part 1, p. 66.

31. Ibid., 76.

32. Ibid., 76–77.

33. Charles Schuyler Hamilton, *Official Records*, Series 1, Volume 17, Part 1, p. 92.

34. Stanley, *An American General*, 142.

35. Cloyd Bryner, *Bugle Echoes: The Story of the Illinois 47th* (Springfield, IL: Phillips, 1905), 53.

36. David Stanley, *Official Records*, Series 1, Volume 17, Part 1, p. 81.

37. David Power Conyngham Papers (CON), "Soldiers of the Cross," University of Notre Dame Archives (UNDA), Notre Dame, Indiana, 26–27.

38. Ibid., 27.

39. Ibid., 28.

40. Ibid., 29.

Chapter 5

1. Peter Cozzens, *The Darkest Days of the War: The Battles of Iuka and Corinth* (Chapel Hill: University of North Carolina Press, 1997), 137.
2. William Rosecrans, *Battles and Leaders of the Civil War*, vol. 2 (New York: Century, 1887), 741.
3. Ibid., 743.
4. Cozzens, *The Darkest Days of the War*, 327–328.
5. David Stanley, Letter to Rosecrans, September 30, 1862, Rosecrans Papers, Box 7 Folder 66, University of California, Los Angeles.
6. Cozzens, *The Darkest Days of the War*, 326–327.
7. Cloyd Bryner, *Bugle Echoes: The History of the Illinois 47th* (Springfield, IL: Phillips, 1905), 57.
8. Cozzens, *The Darkest Days of the War*, 158
9. Ibid., 166.
10. Bryner, *Bugle Echoes*, 58.
11. H.G. Kennett, *Official Records*, Series 1, Volume 17, Part 2, p. 257.
12. David Stanley, *Official Records*, Series 1, Volume 17, Part 1, p. 179.
13. Duncan McCall, *Three Years in the Service: Record of the Doings of the 11th Reg. Missouri* (Springfield, MO: Johnson & Bradford, 1864), 12.
14. Cozzens, *The Darkest Days of the War*, 210.
15. Bryner, *Bugle Echoes*, 58.
16. David Stanley, *Official Records*, Series 1, Volume 17, Part 1, p. 181.
17. David Stanley, *An American General: The Memoirs of David Sloan Stanley*, ed. Samuel W. Fordyce IV (Santa Barbara, CA: Narrative, 2004), 144.
18. Steven Dossman, *Campaign for Corinth: Blood in Mississippi* (Abilene: McWhitney Foundation, 2006), 105.
19. Rosecrans, *Official Records*, Series 1, Volume 17, Part 1, p. 161.
20. Ibid., 168–169.
21. Stanley, *An American General*, 144.
22. Andrew Weber, *Official Records*, Series 1, Volume 17, Part 1, p. 202.
23. Stanley, *An American General*, 144.
24. McCall, *Three Years in the Service*, 12–13.
25. Williams Lamers, *The Edge of Glory* (New York: Harcourt, Brace & World, 1961), 149.
26. Stacy Allen, "Corinth, Mississippi: Crossroads of the Western Confederacy," *Blue and Gray* (2007), 54.
27. Stanley, *Official Records*, Series 1, Volume 17, Part 1, p. 180.
28. McCall, *Three Years in the Service*, 13.
29. Cozzens, *The Darkest Days of the War*, 256.
30. Weber, *Official Records*, Series 1, Volume 17, Part 1, p. 202.
31. Oscar Jackson, *The Colonel's Diary* (Sharon, PA: Private Publication, David Jackson, 1922), 71.
32. Stanley, *An American General*, 145.
33. Dabney Maury, *Official Records*, Series 1, Volume 17, Part 1, p. 394.
34. John W. Fuller, *Our Kirby Smith* (Cincinnati: H.C. Sherick, 1887), 16.
35. John Sprague, *Official Records*, Series 1, Volume 17, Part 1, p. 192.
36. Charles H. Smith, *The History of Fuller's Ohio Brigade, 1861–1865: Its Great March with Roster, Portraits Battle Maps and Biographies* (Cleveland: J.A. Wyatt, 1909), 89.
37. Stanley, *Official Records*, Series 1, Volume 17, Part 1, p. 181.
38. Fuller, *Our Kirby Smith*, 17–18.
39. Wager Swayne, *Official Records*, Series 1, Volume 17, Part 1, p. 191.
40. Jackson, *The Colonel's Diary*, 83.
41. Sprague, *Official Records*, Series 1, Volume 17, Part 1, p. 192.
42. Fuller, *Official Records*, Series 1, Volume 17, Part 1, p. 187.
43. Cozzens, *The Darkest Days of the War*, 264.
44. Frank T Gilmore, Letter, May 22, 1897, David Stanley Folder, United States Military Academy, Special Collections, West Point, New York.
45. James McNeal, "The 11th MO.'s Part: Comrade McNeal Endeavors to Show Where the Credit Should Be Given as to the Fighting at Robinett," *National Tribune*, June 29, 1899.
46. Anonymous, "Corinth: What One Comrade Knows About Battery Robinett," *National Tribune*, March 15, 1894.
47. Joseph Mower, *Official Records*, Series 1, Volume 17, Part 1, p. 198.
48. Rosecrans, *Battles and Leaders of the Civil War*, 752.
49. Sterling Price, *Official Records*, Series 1, Volume 17, Part 1, p. 388.
50. Stanley, *An American General*, 146–147.
51. Rosecrans, *Official Records*, Series 1, Volume 17, Part 1, p. 172.
52. Newton Preston, William Chapman Civil War Pension Record, Letter, October 15, 1862, National Archives, Washington, D.C.
53. Fuller, *Our Kirby Smith*, 19.
54. Stanley, *An American General*, 146.
55. Ibid., 147.
56. D.S. Stanley, Communication, October 5, 1862, Rosecrans Papers Box 7, Folder 94.
57. D.S. Stanley Communication, October 5, 1862, Rosecrans Papers Box 7, Folder 95.
58. Lamers, *The Edge of Glory*, 161.
59. D.S. Stanley, Communication, October 6, 1862, Rosecrans Papers Box 7, Folder 110.
60. Cozzens, *The Darkest Days of the War*, 210.
61. D.S. Stanley, Letter, October 22, 1862, Union General Papers: Record Group 94, Entry 159, Box 28, National Archives.
62. Joseph Vale, *Minty and the Cavalry: A History of Cavalry Campaigns in the Western Armies* (Harrisburg, PA: Edwin K. Myers, 1886), xvii.

Chapter 6

1. Jacob C. Cohen, Letter, November 9, 1862, to the *Jewish Messenger*, Jewish-American History Documentation Foundation, Lathrup Village, Michigan.
2. George McClellan, *Official Records*, Series 1, Volume 7, p. 931.
3. David Stanley, *Personal Memoirs of Major-General D.S. Stanley, USA* (Cambridge: Harvard University Press, 1917), 116.
4. David S. Stanley, Letter to the Second Division, November 12, 1862, Stanley, Wright West Papers, United States Army Heritage and Education Center, Carlisle, Pennsylvania, Box 1, 1862–1863 Folder, David S. Stanley Family Papers.
5. Charles H. Smith, *The History of Fuller's Ohio Brigade, 1861–1865: Its Great March with Roster, Portraits, Battle Maps and Biographies* (Cleveland: J.A. Wyatt, 1909), 319.
6. William Rosecrans, *Official Records*, Series 1, Volume 20, Part 2, p. 5.
7. William Rosecrans, *Official Records*, Series 1, Volume 20, Part 2, p. 27.
8. Arthur C. Ducat, *Official Records*, Series 1, Volume 20, Part 2, p. 12.
9. A.A. Stevens, *Official Records*, Series 1, Volume 20, Part 2, p. 13.
10. *New York Times*, "The Federal Courier's Tale," November 3, 1862.
11. J.B. Anderson, *Official Records*, Series 1, Volume 20, Part 2, p. 14.
12. Alexander McCook, *Official Records*, Series 1, Volume 20, Part 2, p. 15.
13. Arthur Ducat, *Official Records*, Series 1, Volume 20, Part 2, p. 15.
14. Thomas Crittenden, *Official Records*, Series 1, Volume 20, Part 2, pp. 18–19.
15. Arthur Ducat, *Official Records*, Series 1, Volume 20, Part 2, p. 19.

16. Speed F. Fry, *Official Records,* Series 1, Volume 20, Part 2, p. 21.
17. Arthur Ducat, *Official Records,* Series 1, Volume 20, Part 2, p. 21.
18. Ibid., 23.
19. Thomas Crittenden, *Official Records,* Series 1, Volume 20, Part 2, p. 28.
20. William Rosecrans, *Official Records,* Series 1, Volume 20, Part 2, p. 31.
21. Ibid.
22. Ulysses Grant, Special Order No. 15, Union Generals Records, National Archives, Washington, D.C., November 11, 1862.
23. George Thomas, *Official Records,* Series 1, Volume 20, Part 2, p. 39.
24. William Rosecrans, *Official Records,* Series 1, Volume 20, Part 2, p. 45.
25. George Thomas, *Official Records,* Series 1, Volume 20, Part 2, pp. 45–46.
26. Ibid., 56
27. Arthur C. Ducat, *Official Records,* Series 1, Volume 20, Part 2, p. 66.
28. J.P. Garesche, *Official Records,* Series 1, Volume 20, Part 2, p. 94.
29. Society of the Army of the Cumberland, *Twenty-seventh Reunion* (Cincinnati OH: Robert Clark, 1898), 149–150.
30. David Stanley, *An American General: The Memoirs of David Sloan Stanley,* ed. Samuel W. Fordyce IV (Santa Barbara, CA: Narrative, 2004), 150
31. John Beatty, *The Citizen Soldier: The Memoirs of a Civil War Volunteer* (Lincoln: University of Nebraska Press, 1998), 235.
32. W.L. Curry, *Four Years in the Saddle: History of the First Regiment Ohio Volunteer Cavalry* (Columbus, OH: Champlin, 1898), 82.
33. Thomas Edison, *John Hunt Morgan and His Raiders* (Lexington: University Press of Kentucky, 1985), 65.
34. William Rosecrans, *Official Records,* Series 1, Volume 20, Part 2, p. 182.
35. D.S. Stanley, Letter, December 24, 1862, Simon Gratz Collection H250A, Pennsylvania Historical Society, Philadelphia, Pennsylvania.
36. David Stanley, *Official Records,* Series 1, Volume 20, Part 1, p. 617.
37. Gilbert Kniffin, "The Battle of Stone's River," in *Battles and Leaders of the Civil War,* vol. 3 (New York: Century, 1884, 1888), 61.
38. N.H. Davis, *Official Records,* Series 1, Volume 20, Part 2, p. 346.
39. Ibid., 348.
40. Ibid., 346.
41. Ibid., 347.
42. Stanley, *An American General,* 151.
43. Lewis Zahm, *Official Records,* Series 1, Volume 20, Part 1, p. 633.
44. Ibid.
45. Ibid., 635.
46. Ibid., 636.
47. Robert Minty, *Official Records,* Series 1, Volume 20, Part 1, p. 623.
48. N.M. Newell, *Official Records,* Series 1, Volume 20, Part 1, p. 622.
49. Peter Cozzens, *No Better Place to Die* (Urbana: University of Illinois Press, 1991), 58–59.
50. Robert Minty, *Official Records,* Series 1, Volume 20, Part 1, p. 624.
51. Alexander McCook, *Official Records,* Series 1, Volume 20, Part 1, p. 253.
52. Robert Klein, *Official Records,* Series 1, Volume 20, Part 1, p. 646.
53. Ibid., 646–647.
54. Charles Kirk, "The Fifteenth Pennsylvania (Anderson) Cavalry at Stone River," in *History of the Fifteenth Pennsylvania Volunteer Cavalry,* ed. J.C. Reiff (Philadelphia, PA: Society of the Fifteenth Pennsylvania Cavalry,1906), 83.
55. David Stanley, *Official Records,* Series 1, Volume 20, Part 1, p. 618.
56. Stanley, *An American General*,152.
57. Alexander McCook, *Official Records,* Series 1, Volume 20, Part 1, p. 256.
58. Stanley, *An American General,* 152.
59. Edwin C. Bearss, "Cavalry Operations: Battle of Stones River," Stones River National Park, Technical Information Center, Murfreesboro, TN, 1959, p. 59.
60. Stanley, *An American General,* 153.
61. Lewis Zahm, *Official Records,* Series 1, Volume 20, Part 1, p. 637.
62. David Stanley, *Official Records,* Series 1, Volume 20, Part 1, p. 618.
63. Lewis Zahm, *Official Records,* Series 1, Volume 20, Part 1, p. 637.
64. Bearss, *Cavalry Operations,* 65.
65. Robert Klein, *Official Records,* Series 1, Volume 20, Part 1, p. 647.
66. Elmer Otis, *Official Records,* Series 1, Volume 20, Part 1, p. 649.
67. Lewis Zahm, *Official Records,* Series 1, Volume 20, Part 1, p. 637.
68. W.L. Curry, 838–4.
69. Lewis Zahm, *Official Records,* Series 1, Volume 20, Part 1, p. 637.
70. J.W. Paramore, *Official Records,* Series 1, Volume 20, Part 1, p. 643.
71. Ibid.
72. John Kennett, *Official Records,* Series 1, Volume 20, Part 1, p. 621.
73. Ibid.
74. Ibid.
75. E.H. Murray, *Official Records,* Series 1, Volume 20, Part 1, pp. 627–628.
76. Ibid.
77. John Wynkoop, *Official Records,* Series 1, Volume 20, Part 1, pp. 631–632.
78. Stanley, *An American General,* 153.
79. Charles Kirk, *History of the Fifteenth Pennsylvania Volunteer Cavalry,* 93.
80. Robert Minty, *Official Records,* Series 1, Volume 20, Part 1, p. 624.
81. Stanley, *An American General,* 153.
82. David Stanley, *Official Records,* Series 1, Volume 20, Part 1, p. 618.
83. Robert Minty, *Official Records,* Series 1, Volume 20, Part 1, p. 624.
84. Charles Kirk, *History of the Fifteenth Pennsylvania Volunteer Cavalry,* 93.
85. Robert Minty, *Official Records,* Series 1, Volume 20, Part 1, pp. 624–625.
86. Robert Minty, "The Saber Brigade," *National Tribune,* August 11, 1892.
87. Ibid.
88. Eugene Bronson Collection, Letter, January 22, 1863, Kalamazoo College, Kalamazoo, Michigan.
89. John Wharton, *Official Records,* Series 1, Volume 20, Part 1, p. 968.
90. William Lamers, *The Edge of Glory: A Biography of General William S. Rosecrans, U.S.A.* (New York: Harcourt, Brace & World, 1961), 235.
91. Stanley, *An American General,* 154.
92. Lamers, *The Edge of Glory,* 235.
93. Lewis Zahm, *Official Records,* Series 1, Volume 20, Part 1, pp. 637–638.
94. Ibid., 634.
95. Ibid.
96. David Stanley, *Official Records,* Series 1, Volume 20, Part 1, p. 618.
97. Lewis Zahm, *Official Records,* Series 1, Volume 20, Part 1, p. 638.
98. Robert Minty, *Official Records,* Series 1, Volume 20, Part 1, p. 623.
99. Alexander McCook, *Official Records,* Series 1, Volume 20, Part 1, p. 258.
100. William Rosecrans, *Official Records,* Series 1, Volume 20, Part 1, p. 198.
101. Stanley, *An American General,* 155
102. T.F. Dornblaser, *Sabre Strokes of the Pennsylvania Dragoons in the War of 1861–1865, Interspersed with Personal Reminiscence* (Philadelphia: Lutheran Publication Society, 1884), 109.
103. Stanley, *An American General,* 154.

104. William D. Bickham, *Rosecrans' Campaign with the Fourteenth Army Corps of the Army of the Cumberland* (Cincinnati: Moore Wilstach, Keys, 1863), 80

105. Thomas M. Vincent, "David Sloane Stanley," in *The Thirty-fourth Annual Reunion of the Association of the Graduates of the United States Military Academy at West Point, New York* (Saginaw, MI: Seeman and Peters, Printers and Binders, 1903), 54.

Chapter 7

1. William Rosecrans, *Official Records,* Series 1, Volume 20, Part 2, p. 328.

2. Sunderland, Glenn W., *Lightning at Hoover's Gap* (New York: Thomas Yoseloff, 1969), 23–26.

3. *Official Records,* Series 1, Volume 20, Part 2, p. 345.

4. A. C. Sands et al., Letter to Abraham Lincoln, December 1, 1862, David Stanley Personnel File ACP 000183, National Archives, Washington, D.C., 001-06-08.

5. Joseph Vale, *Minty and the Cavalry: A History of Cavalry Campaigns in the Western Armies* (Harrisburg, PA: Edwin K. Myers, Printer and Binder, 1886), 182.

6. Daniel Prickitt, *3rd Ohio Cavalry,* February 24, 1863 diary entry, ed. Col. E. D. Stoltz (Edwin Stoltz: Archbold, Ohio,1988)

7. Larry J. Daniel, *Days of Glory: The Army of the Cumberland, 1861–1865* (Baton Rouge: Louisiana State University Press, 2006), 228.

8. John T. Palmer, *A Conscientious Turncoat: The Story of John M. Palmer, 1817–1900* (New Haven: Yale University Press, 1941), 100.

9. Robert J. Dalessandro, *Major General William S. Rosecrans and the Transformation of the Staff of the Army of the Cumberland: A Case Study,* Strategy Research Project, U.S. Army War College, Carlisle Barracks, Pennsylvania, 2002, 8.

10. Henry Albert Potter, March 17, 1863, Letter from Henry Albert Potter, MS 91-480 Henry Albert Potter Collection, Accession Box 461 Folder 2, Archives of Michigan, Historical Society of Michigan, Lansing.

11. Palmer, *A Conscientious Turncoat,* 103.

12. Gordon Granger, *Official Records,* Series 1, Volume 23, Part 1, p. 224.

13. David Stanley, *Official Records,* Series 1, Volume 23, Part 2, p. 226.

14. David Stanley, *Official Records,* Series 1, Volume 23, Part 2, p. 229–231.

15. Lewis Hanback, Letter, April 11, 1863, Hanback Collection—A H233, Filson Historical Society, Louisville, Kentucky.

16. Potter, Letter, April 14, 1863.

17. Gordon Granger, *Official Records,* Series 1, Volume 23, Part 1, p. 227.

18. Earnest East, "Lincoln's Russian General," *Journal of the Illinois State Historical Society* 52, no. 1 (1959), 106–122.

19. Don Carlos Buell, *Official Records,* Series 1, Volume 16, Part 2, p. 71.

20. David Stanley, *Official Records,* Series 1, Volume 23, Part 2, p. 334–335.

21. Ibid.

22. David Stanley, *Official Records,* Series 1, Volume 23, Part 2, p. 335.

23. David Stanley, *An American General: The Memoirs of David Sloan Stanley,* ed. Samuel W. Fordyce IV (Santa Barbara, CA: Narrative, 2004), 153.

24. Ibid., 158–159.

25. William H. Sinclair, *Official Records,* Series 1, Volume 23, Part 2, p. 568.

26. Stanley, *An American General,* 159.

27. Nadine Turchin, "'A Monotony Full of Sadness': The Diary of Nadine Turchin, May, 1863-April, 1864," ed. Mary Ellen McElligott, *Journal of the Illinois State Historical Society* 70 (1977), 27–89.

28. Stanley, *An American General,* 156.

29. Potter, Letter, May 26, 1863.

30. Prickitt Diary, May 23, 1863.

31. James A. Garfield, *Official Records,* Series 1, Volume 23, Part 2, p. 420.

32. Williams Lamers, *The Edge of Glory: A Biography of General William S. Rosecrans, U.S.A.* (New York: Harcourt, Brace & World, 1961), 270–1.

33. D.S. Stanley, Letter, June 9, 1863, Rosecrans Papers Box 8 Folder 73, University of California, Los Angeles.

34. *Official Records,* Series 1, Volume 23, Part 2, p. 418.

35. James Edward Kelly, "Two Noted Federal Cavalry Leaders," *United States Army Recruiting News* 21, no. 1 (1939).

36. Stanley, *An American General,* 162.

37. William Rosecrans, *Official Records,* Series 1, Volume 23, Part 1, pp. 404–405.

38. David Stanley, *Official Records,* Series 1, Volume 23, Part 1, p. 538.

39. Stanley, *An American General,* 164

40. Vale, *Minty and the Cavalry,* 174–175.

41. David Stanley, *Official Records,* Series 1, Volume 23, Part 1, p. 539.

42. Michael Bradley, *Tullahoma: The 1863 Campaign for the Control of Middle Tennessee* (Shippensburg, PA: White Mane, 1999), 76.

43. David Stanley, *Official Records,* Series 1, Volume 23, Part 2, pp. 540–541.

44. Ibid.

45. Bradley, *Tullahoma,* 79.

46. Stephen Z. Starr, *The Union Cavalry in the Civil War, Volume 3: The War in the West, 1861–1865* (Baton Rouge: Louisiana State University Press, 1985), 246.

47. Quoted in Starr, *The Union Cavalry.*

48. Starr, *The Union Cavalry in the Civil War,* 246–247.

49. David Stanley, *Official Records,* Series 1, Volume 23, Part 1, p. 540.

50. C. Goddard, *Official Records,* Series 1, Volume 23, Part 2, p. 472.

51. William Rosecrans, *Official Records,* Series 1, Volume 23, Part 1, p. 407–408.

52. Stanley, *An American General,* 166.

53. Richard J. Brewer, "The Tullahoma Campaign: Operational Insights," master's thesis, U.S. Army Command and General Staff College, Leavenworth, KS (1978), 142.

54. Stanley, *Official Records,* Series 1, Volume 23, Part 1, pp. 540–541.

55. John Turchin, *Official Records,* Series 1, Volume 23, Part 1, p. 554.

56. William Rosecrans, *Official Records,* Series 1, Volume 23, Part 1, p. 409.

57. Brady, *Tullahoma,* 93–94.

58. Starr, *The Union Cavalry in the Civil War,* 237.

59. James A. Garfield, *Official Records,* Series 1 Volume 23, Number 2, p. 465.

60. Thomas M. Vincent, "David Sloane Stanley," *The Thirty-fourth Annual Reunion of the Association of the Graduates of the United States Military Academy at West Point, New York* (Saginaw, MI: Seeman and Peters, 1903), 57.

61. James Connolly, *Three Years in the Army of the Cumberland,* ed. Paul Angle (Bloomington: Indiana University Press, 1959), 98.

62. Robert J. Dalessandro, "Morale in the Army of the Cumberland During the Tullahoma and Chickamauga Campaigns" (master's thesis, U.S. Army Command and General Staff College, Leavenworth, KS, 1980), 74.

63. Theodore Clarke Smith, *The Life and Letters of James Abram Garfield,* vol. 1 (New Haven, CT: Archon, 1968), 308.

Chapter 8

1. William Rosecrans, *Official Records,* Series 1, Volume 23, Part 2, p. 515.
2. Ibid., 519.
3. James A. Garfield, *Official Records,* Series 1, Volume 23, Part 2, p. 527.
4. David Stanley, *Official Records,* Series 1, Volume 23, Part 2, p. 548.
5. David Stanley, *An American General: The Memoirs of David Sloan Stanley,* ed. Samuel W. Fordyce IV (Santa Barbara, CA: Narrative, 2004), 167–168.
6. John Beatty, *The Citizen Soldier: The Memoirs of a Civil War Volunteer* (Lincoln: University of Nebraska Press, 1998), 303.
7. Mary Jane Chadwick, *Incidents of the War: The Civil War Journal of Mary Jane Chadwick,* Nancy Rohr, ed. (Huntsville: SilverThread, 2005), 110.
8. *Chicago Times,* "The War In Tennessee, an Expedition into the Enemy's Country," August 4, 1863.
9. *Nashville Daily Press,* "Court-Martialed," July 16, 1863.
10. *Chicago Times,* "An Expedition into the Enemy's Country," July 22, 1863
11. David Stanley, *Official Records,* Series 1, Volume 23, Part 2, p. 549.
12. William Sinclair, *Official Records,* Series 1, Volume 23, Part 2, p. 568.
13. Vale, Joseph, *Minty and the Cavalry: A History of Cavalry Campaigns in the Western Armies* (Harrisburg, PA: Edwin K. Myers, 1886), 196
14. James Edwin Love, Letter, August 6, 1863, James Edwin Love Papers (1859–1865) ARC A0940, Missouri Historical Society, St. Louis.
15. Mary Jane Chadwick, *Incidents of the War,* 180.
16. C. Goddard, *Official Records,* Series 1, Volume 30, Part 3, pp. 35–38.
17. Ibid., 37.
18. Edward McCook, *Official Records,* Series 1, Volume 30, Part 3, p. 43.
19. Horatio Van Cleve, *Official Records,* Series 1, Volume 30, Part 3, p. 92.
20. William Rosecrans, *Official Records,* Series 1, Volume 30, Part 3, pp. 98–99.
21. Gordon Granger, *Official Records,* Series 1, Volume 30, Part 3, p. 105.
22. Horatio Van Cleve, *Official Records,* Series 1, Volume 30, Part 3, p. 166.
23. Eli Long, *Official Records,* Series 1, Volume 30, Part 3, p. 206.
24. Robert Minty, *Official Records,* Series 1, Volume 30, Part 3, p. 237.
25. *Official Records,* Series 1, Volume 30, Part 3, pp. 274–275.
26. Edwin Stanton, *Official Records,* Series 1, Volume 30, Part 3, pp. 229–230.
27. *Milwaukee Journal,* "Eccentric Brother of Famous Editor," November 27, 1897, p. 11.
28. Alexander McCook, *Official Records,* Series 1, Volume 30, Part 3, p. 326.
29. David Stanley, *Official Records,* Series 1, Volume 30, Part 3, p. 331.
30. Robert Mitchell, *Official Records,* Series 1, Volume 30, Part 3, p. 332.
31. Beatty, *The Citizen Soldier: The Memoirs of a Civil War Volunteer,* 309.
32. Alexander McCook, *Official Records,* Series 1, Volume 30, Part 3, p. 332.
33. Ibid., 345.
34. Ibid., 346.
35. David Stanley, *Official Records,* Series 1, Volume 30, Part 3, p. 353.
36. Ibid., 353–354.
37. William B. Hazen, *Official Records,* Series 1, Volume 30, Part 3, p. 371.
38. David Stanley, *Official Records,* Series 1, Volume 30, Part 3, p. 374.
39. Ibid., 374.
40. Edward McCook, *Official Records,* Series 1, Volume 30, Part 3, p. 375.
41. Ibid., 376.
42. James A. Garfield, *Official Records,* Series 1, Volume 30, Part 3, p. 374.
43. W.H. Sinclair, *Official Records,* Series 1, Volume 30, Part 3, p. 375.
44. Edward McCook, *Official Records,* Series 1, Volume 30, Part 3, p. 376.
45. James Garfield, *Official Records,* Series 1, Volume 30, Part 3, p. 397.
46. Paul Shelton, "The Blame Game: Federal Intelligence Operations During the Chickamauga Campaign" (master's thesis, U.S. Army Command and General Staff College, Fort Leavenworth, KS, 2000), 87.
47. James Garfield, *Official Records,* Series 1, Volume 30, Part 3, p. 412.
48. David Stanley, *Official Records,* Series 1, Volume 30, Part 3, pp. 431–432.
49. William Rosecrans, *Official Records,* Series 1, Volume 30, Part 3, p. 432.
50. Ibid., 468.
51. David Stanley, *Official Records,* Series 1, Volume 30, Part 3, p. 468.
52. Williams Lamers, *The Edge of Glory: A Biography of General William S. Rosecrans, U.S.A.* (New York: Harcourt, Brace & World, 1961), 303.
53. Lamers, *The Edge of Glory,* 307.
54. Beatty, *The Citizen Soldier,* 257.
55. George Crook, *General George Crook: His Biography* (Norman: University of Oklahoma Press, 1960), 104.
56. William Sinclair, *Official Records,* Series 1, Volume 30, Part 3, pp. 469–470.
57. David Stanley, *Official Records,* Series 1, Volume 30, Part 1, p. 889.
58. Alexander McCook, *Official Records,* Series 1, Volume 30, Part 3, pp. 541–542.
59. J.P. Drouillard, *Official Records,* Series 1, Volume 30, Part 3, p. 511.
60. Alexander McCook, *Official Records,* Series 1, Volume 30, Part 3, pp. 551–552.
61. Frank Bond, *Official Records,* Series 1, Volume 30, Part 3, p. 588.
62. Robert D. Richardson, "Rosecrans' Staff at Chickamauga: The Significance of Major General William S. Rosecrans' Staff on the Outcome of the Chickamauga Campaign" (master's thesis, Command and General Staff College, Fort Leavenworth, Kansas, 1989), 135.
63. David Stanley, *Official Records,* Series 1, Volume 30, Part 3, p. 637.
64. Larry J. Daniel, *Days of Glory: The Army of the Cumberland, 1861–1865* (Baton Rouge: Louisiana State University Press, 2006), 305.
65. David Stanley, *Official Records,* Series 1, Volume 30, Part 3, p. 653.
66. Robert Mitchell, *Official Records,* Series 1, Volume 30, Part 3, p. 653.
67. William Rosecrans, *Official Records,* Series 1, Volume 30, Part 4, pp. 249–250.
68. Robert J. Dalessandro, "Major General William S. Rosecrans and the Transformation of the Staff of the Army of the Cumberland: A Case Study," Strategy Research Project (U.S. Army War College, Carlisle Barracks, Pennsylvania, 2002), 6.
69. Robert Mitchell, *Official Records,* Series 1, Volume 30, Part 4, p. 371.
70. Henry Cist, *Official Records,* Series 1, Volume 30, Part 4, p. 444.
71. Robert Mitchell, *Official Records,* Series 1, Volume 30, Part 4, p. 462.
72. Joseph Hooker, *Official Records,* Series 1, Volume 30, Part 4, pp. 466–467.
73. William McMichael, *Official Records,* Series 1, Volume 31, Part 3, p. 126.
74. David Stanley, *An American General,* 171.
75. Benson Bobrick, *Master of War: The Life of George H. Thomas* (New York: Simon and Schuster, 2009), 38.

76. David Stanley, Union General Papers, Communication, November 20, 1863, Record Group 94, Entry 159, Box 28, D. Stanley, National Archives, Washington, D.C.
77. Charles Dana, *Official Records,* Series 1, Volume 31, Part 2, p. 63.
78. Charles Dana, *Official Records,* Series 1, Volume 30, Part 1, p. 220.
79. David Stanley, *An American General,* 172.
80. Ibid.
81. Peter Cozzens, *This Terrible Sound* (Urbana: University of Illinois Press, 1992), 13.
82. Ibid., 80.
83. Ibid.
84. Peter Cozzens, *The Shipwreck of Their Hopes* (Urbana: University of Illinois Press, 1994), 52.
85. Society of the Army of the Cumberland, "Burial of General Rosecrans, Arlington National Cemetery" (Cincinnati: Robert Clarke, 1903), 90.
86. David Power Conyngham Papers (CON), "Soldiers of the Cross," University of Notre Dame Archives (UNDA), Notre Dame, IN, 46.
87. David S. Stanley, William S. Rosecrans Papers, Rosecrans, Letter written to William Rosecrans, September 26, 1863 Box 8, Folder 132, University of California, Los Angeles.
88. Peter Cozzens, *This Terrible Sound,* 64.
89. *Twenty-Ninth Annual Reunion of the Association of the Graduates of the United States Military Academy,* June 9, 1898, pp. 70–71.
90. Robert D. Richardson, "Rosecrans' Staff at Chickamauga: The Significance of Major General William S. Rosecrans' Staff on the Outcome of the Chickamauga Campaign" (master's thesis, Command and General Staff College, Fort Leavenworth, Kansas, 1989), 183.
91. James A. Garfield, *Official Records,* Series 1, Volume 30, Part 3, p. 322.
92. David Stanley, Union General Papers, Surgeon's Certificate, September 21, 1863.
93. Robert Mitchell, *Official Records,* Series 1, Volume 30, Part 3, p. 653.
94. George Crook, *General George Crook: His Biography,* 106–107.
95. Stephen Z. Starr, *The Union Cavalry in the Civil War,* vol. 3, *The War in the West, 1861–1865* (Baton Rouge: Louisiana State University Press, 1985), 263.
96. William Rosecrans, *Official Records,* Series 1, Volume 30, Part 1, p. 52.
97. John Londa, "The Role of Union Cavalry During the Chickamauga Campaign" (master's thesis, Fort Leavenworth, Kansas, 1991), 118, 123
98. William Rosecrans, *Official Records,* Series 1, Volume 30, Part 1, pp. 79–80.

Chapter 9

1. David Stanley, *An American General: The Memoirs of David Sloan Stanley,* ed. Samuel W. Fordyce IV (Santa Barbara, CA: Narrative, 2004), 172.
2. Stanley, *An American General,* 173.
3. *Official Records,* Series 1, Volume 32, Part 2, pp. 283–284.
4. David Stanley, *Official Records,* Series 1, Volume 32, Part 2, p. 375.
5. George Thomas, *Official Records,* Series 1, Volume 32, Part 2, p. 395.
6. William Sherman, *Official Records,* Series 1, Volume 32, Part 3, 171.
7. Larry J. Daniel, *Days of Glory: The Army of the Cumberland, 1861–1865* (Baton Rouge: Louisiana State University Press, 2006), 386.
8. Oliver O. Howard, *The Autobiography of Oliver Otis Howard* (New York: Baker & Taylor, 1907), 504.
9. Ibid., 506.
10. David Stanley, *Official Records,* Series 1, Volume 38, Part 1, p. 220.
11. Howard, *The Autobiography of Oliver Otis Howard,* 506.
12. Chesley Mosman, *The Rough Side of War: The Civil War Journal of Chesley A. Mosman,* ed. Arnold Gates (New York: Basin., 1987), 196–197.
13. David Stanley, *Official Records,* Series 1 Volume 38, Part 1, p. 220.
14. Stanley, *An American General,* 176.
15. Albert Castel, *Decision in the West: The Atlanta Campaign of 1864* (Lawrence: University Press of Kansas, 192), 164.
16. Ibid.
17. David Stanley, *Official Records,* Series 1, Volume 38, Part 1, p. 221.
18. Castel, *Decision in the West,* 165.
19. John N. Beach, *History of the Fortieth Ohio Volunteer Infantry* (London, OH: Shepherd & Craig, 1884), 68.
20. Castel, *Decision in the West,* 165–166.
21. David Stanley, *Official Records,* Series 1, Volume 38, Part 4, p. 178.
22. Stanley, *An American General,* 176.
23. Howard, *The Autobiography of Oliver Otis Howard,* 510.
24. Ibid.
25. Ibid., 513–5.
26. Daniels, *Days of Glory: The Army of the Cumberland,* 399.
27. David Stanley, *Official Records,* Series 1, Volume 38, Part 1, p. 221.
28. Stanley, *An American General,* 176.
29. David Stanley, *Official Records,* Series 1 Volume 38, Number 1, p. 222, May 3-July 26, 1864.
30. Chesley D. Bailey Papers (1863–1864) Diary, May 19, 1864, Bailey Papers, Mss. A B155, Filson Historical Society, Louisville, Kentucky.
31. Castle, *Decision in the West,* 202.
32. Daniel, *Days of Glory: The Army of the Cumberland,* 402.
33. Stanley, *An American General,* 179.
34. Stanley, *Official Records,* Series 1, Volume 38, Part 1, p. 223.
35. Stanley, *An American General,* 180.
36. Howard, *The Autobiography of Oliver Otis Howard,* 563.
37. David Stanley, *Personal Memoirs of Major-General D.S. Stanley, USA* (Cambridge: Harvard University Press, 1917), 172.
38. David Stanley, *Official Records,* Series 1 Volume 38, Number 1, p. 223.
39. Bailey, Diary entry, June 19, 1864.
40. Lewis W. Day, *Story of the One Hundred and First Ohio Infantry* (Cleveland: W. M. Bayne, 1894), 225.
41. David Stanley, *Official Records,* Series 1, Volume 38, Part 1, p. 224.
42. G.W. Herr, *Nine Campaigns in Nine States* (San Francisco: Bancroft, 1890), 226.
43. Lewis Hanback, Letter, June 24, 1864, Hanback Collection, Mss A H233, Filson Historical Society, Louisville, Kentucky.
44. Alexis Cope, *The Fifteenth Ohio Volunteers and Its Campaigns, 1861–1865* (Columbus OH: Alexis Cope, 1961), 505.
45. Stanley, *An American General,* 181.
46. David Stanley, *Official Records,* Series 1, Volume 38, Part 1, p. 224.
47. Ibid.
48. Stanley, *An American General,* 181.
49. John Thomas Smith, *A History of the Thirty-first Regiment of Indiana Volunteer Infantry in the War of the Rebellion* (Cincinnati: Western Methodist, 1900), 109.
50. David Stanley, *Official Records,* Series 1, Volume 38, Part 1, p. 226.
51. Ibid., 225.
52. Ibid., 226.
53. Mosman, *The Rough Side of War: The Civil War Journal of Chesley A. Mosman,* 246.

54. David Stanley, *Official Records*, Series 1, Volume 38, Part 1, p. 226.
55. Jay Caldwell Butler, *Letters Home*, arranged by Watson Hubbard Butler (Binghamton, NY: privately published, 1930), 137.
56. Glenn V. Longacre and John E. Haas, eds., *To Battle for God and the Right: The Civil War; Letterbooks of Emerson Opdycke* (Urbana: University of Illinois Press, 2003), 203.
57. William T. Sherman, *Memoirs of William T. Sherman*, Vol. 2 (New York: D. Appleton, 1904), 85.
58. Donald Allendorf, *Long Road to Liberty: The Odyssey of a German Regiment in the Yankee Army; The 15th Missouri Volunteer Infantry* (Kent, OH: Kent State University Press, 2006), 211–212.
59. Mosman, *The Rough Side of War: The Civil War Journal of Chesley A. Mosman*, 254.
60. Herr, *Nine Campaigns in Nine States*, 275.
61. Charles A. Partridge, *History of the Ninety-sixth Regiment Illinois Volunteer Infantry* (Chicago: Brown, Pettibone, 1887), 664.
62. David Stanley, *Official Records*, Series 1, Volume 38, Part 1, p. 213.
63. Castel, *Decision in the West*, 497.
64. Ibid., 499.
65. Stanley, *An American General*, 185.
66. David Stanley, *Official Records*, Series 1, Volume 38, Part 1, p. 214.
67. Ibid.
68. Ibid.
69. Ibid., 215.
70. Ibid., 216.
71. Castel, *Decision in the West*, 531.
72. John A. Palmer, *The Personal Recollections of John M. Palmer: The Story of an Earnest Life* (Cincinnati: Robert Clarke, 1901), 201–221.
73. William Sherman, *Official Records*, Series 1, Volume 38, Part 5, p. 734.
74. John Schofield, *Forty-Six Years in the Army* (New York: Century, 1897), 156–157.
75. Stanley, *An American General*, 186–187.
76. Ibid., 186.
77. Castel, *Decision in the West*, 570.
78. William Sherman, *Official Records*, Series 1, Volume 38, Part 4, pp. 507–508.
79. Sherman, *Memoirs of William T. Sherman*, 108.
80. Castel, *Decision in the West*, 520.
81. James L. McDonough and James Pickett Jones, *War So Terrible: Sherman and Atlanta* (New York: W.W. Norton, 1987), 306.

Chapter 10

1. David Stanley, *An American General: The Memoirs of David Sloan Stanley*, ed. Samuel W. Fordyce IV (Santa Barbara, CA: Narrative, 2004), 191.
2. George Thomas, *Official Records*, Series 1, Volume 39, Part 1, p. 585.
3. David Stanley, *Official Records*, Series 1, Volume 39, Part 1, p. 907.
4. Chesley Mosman, *The Rough Side of War : The Civil War Journal of Chesley A. Mosman*, ed. Arnold Gates (New York: Basin, 1987), 292–3.
5. Charles W. Wills, *Army Life of an Illinois Soldier* (Washington, D.C.: Globe, 1905), 312.
6. David Stanley, *Official Records*, Series 1, Volume 39, Part 1, p. 908.
7. Stanley, *An American General*, 193.
8. Mosman, *The Rough Side of War*, 300.
9. George Thomas, *Official Records*, Series 1, Volume 39, Part 1, p. 589.
10. Southard Hoffman, *Official Records*, Series 1, Volume 39, Part 3, p. 638.
11. Ulysses Grant, *Official Records*, Series 1, Volume 39, Part 2, p. 684.
12. David Stanley, *Official Records*, Series 1, Volume 45, Part 1, p. 960.
13. Hatch, Edward, *Official Records*, Series 1, Volume 39, Part 1, p. 687.
14. Stanley, *An American General*, 197.
15. N.a., *Official Records*, Series 1, Volume 45, Part 1, pp. 1197–1198.
16. John Schofield, *Official Records*, Series 1, Volume 45, Part 1, p. 1000.
17. David Stanley, *Official Records*, Series 1, Volume 45, Part 1, p. 112.
18. Stanley, *An American General*, 194
19. David Stanley, *Official Records*, Series 1, Volume 45, Part 1, p. 113.
20. John Schofield, *Official Records*, Series 1, Volume 45, Part 1, p. 1141.
21. David Stanley, *Official Records*, Series 1, Volume 45, Part 1, p. 113.
22. David S. Stanley, *Address of General Stanley: Reunion of the Society of the Army of the Cumberland, Twenty-sixth Reunion* (Cincinnati: Robert Clarke, 1897), 53.
23. David Stanley, *Official Records*, Series 1, Volume 45, Part 1, p. 114.
24. Ibid.
25. William J. Twining, *Official Records*, Series 1, Volume 45, Part 1, p. 1138.
26. John Schofield, *Forty-Six Years in the Army* (New York: Century, 1897), 217.
27. David Stanley, *Official Records*, Series 1, Volume 45, Part 1, pp. 114–115.
28. Wiley Sword, *The Confederacy's Last Hurrah: Spring Hill, Franklin and Nashville* (Lawrence: University Press of Kansas, 1993), 151.
29. David Stanley, *Official Records*, Series 1, Volume 45, Part 1, p. 115.
30. Wilbur Hinman, *The Story of the Sherman Brigade* (Published by the Author, 1897), 667.
31. Sword, 152.
32. Stanley, *An American General*,199
33. John Schofield, *Official Records*, Series 1, Volume 45, Part 1, p. 1171.
34. Sword, 167.
35. Ibid.
36. Ibid., 170–172.
37. J.S. Fullerton, *Official Records*, Series 1, Volume 45, Part 1, p. 1174.
38. Sword, 175.
39. Ibid., 176.
40. Stanley, *An American General*, 201.
41. Sword, 189.
42. Joseph Conrad, *Official Records*, Series 1, Volume 45, Part 1, p. 271.
43. John Shellenberger, *The Battle of Franklin, Tennessee, November 30, 1864: A Statement of the Erroneous Claims Made by General Schofield, and an Exposition of the Blunder Which Opened the Battle* (Cleveland: Arthur H. Clark, 1916), 37–38.
44. Ibid., 40.
45. William Sumner Dodge, *A Waif of the War; or, The History of the Seventy-fifth Illinois Infantry* (Chicago: Church and Goodman, 1866), 187.
46. James L. McDonough and Thomas L Connelly, *Five Tragic Hours: The Battle of Franklin* (Knoxville: University of Tennessee Press, 1983), 105.
47. David Stanley, *Official Records*, Series 1, Volume 45, Part 1, pp. 115–116.
48. James Edward Kelly, *Generals in Bronze: Interviewing the Commanders of the Civil War*, ed. William B. Styple (Kearney, NJ: Bell Grove, 2005), 188.
49. Shellenberger, *The Battle of Franklin*, 39–40.
50. L.G. Bennett and William M. Haigh, *History of the Thirty-sixth Regiment Illinois Volunteers During the War of the Rebellion* (Aurora, IL: Knickerbocker & Hodder, 1876), 652.
51. David Stanley, *Official Records*, Series 1, Volume 45, Part 1, p. 117.
52. Stanley F. Horn, *The Decisive Battle of Nashville* (Baton Rouge: Louisiana State University Press, 1957), 32.
53. John Schofield, *Official Records*, Series 1, Volume 45, Part 1, p. 343.
54. George Thomas *Official Records*, Series 1, Volume 45, Part 2, p. 441.
55. Jack Welsh, *Medical Histories of*

Union Generals (Kent, OH: Kent State University Press, 1996), 317–318.

56. Glenn V. Longacre and John E. Haas, eds., *To Battle for God and the Right: The Civil War; Letterbooks of Emerson Opdycke* (Urbana: University of Illinois Press, 2003), 250.

57. Benson Bobrick, *Master of War: The Life of General George H. Thomas* (New York: Simon & Schuster, 2009), 287–288.

58. N.a., *Official Records*, Series 1, Volume 45, Part 1, p. 645.

59. David Stanley, Letter to Nathan Kimball, January 15, 1867, Kimball Mss., Lilly Library, Indiana University, Bloomington.

60. David Stanley, Letter to President Andrew Johnson, May 13, 1865, Opdycke Mss. Ohio Historical Society, Columbus, Ohio.

61. Journal of the IV Corps, *Official Records*, Series 1, Volume 45, Part 1, p. 150.

62. Jacob Cox, *Official Records*, Series 1, Volume 45, Part 1, p. 354.

63. David Power Conyngham Papers (CON), "Soldiers Of The Cross," University of Notre Dame Archives (UNDA), Notre Dame, 49.

64. Kelly, Ibid., 188–189.

Chapter 11

1. Mary Jane Chadwick, *Incidents of the War: The Civil War Journal of Mary Jane Chadwick*, ed. Nancy Rohr (Huntsville: SilverThread, 2005), 242, 261.

2. Ibid., 279.

3. William Sinclair, *Official Records*, Series 1, Volume 69, Part 2, pp. 343–344.

4. David Stanley, *An American General: The Memoirs of David Sloan Stanley*, ed. Samuel W. Fordyce IV (Santa Barbara, CA: Narrative, 2004), 211

5. Isaac Henry Clay Royse, *History of the 115th Regiment Illinois Volunteer Infantry* (Terre Haute: Isaac Royse, 1900), 251.

6. H.O. Harden, *History of the 90th Ohio Volunteer Infantry of the Great Rebellion in the United States, 1861 to 1865* (Stoutsville: Press of Fairfield-Pickaway News, 1902), 158.

7. *Nashville Daily Union*, "The 4th Army Corps," June 9, 1865, p. 3.

8. William Sinclair, *Official Records*, Series 1, Volume 48, Part 2, p. 1062.

9. J. Schuyler Crosby, *Official Records*, Series 1, Volume 48, Part 2, p. 1094.

10. Alexis Cope, *The Fifteenth Ohio Volunteers and Its Campaigns, 1861–1865* (Columbus Ohio, Alexis Cope, 1961), 786.

11. David S. Stanley, *Official Records*, Series 1 Volume 48, Part 2, p. 1168.

12. Phil Sheridan, *Official Records*, Series 1 Volume 48, Part 2, p. 1087.

13. David Stanley, *Personal Memoirs of Major-General D.S. Stanley, USA* (Cambridge: Harvard University Press, 1917), 228.

14. Fred S. Perrine, "Uncle Sam's Camel Corps," ed. Lansing Bloom and Paul Walter, Historical Society of New Mexico at the Museum Press, Santa Fe, NM, *New Mexico Historical Review*, no. 4 (October 1926), 434–444.

15. Charles Ramsdell, "Presidential Reconstruction in Texas," *Quarterly of the Texas State Historical Association* 14 (April 1908), 277–317, 288.

16. Wilbur Hinman, *The Story of the Sherman Brigade* (Published by the Author, 1897), 762.

17. M. John Lubetkin, *Jay Cooke's Gamble* (Norman: University of Oklahoma Press, 2006), 118.

18. Anna M. Stanley, Letter to her children, July 9–14, 1870, Stanley, Wright West Papers, United States Army Heritage and Education Center, Box 3, David S. Stanley Family Papers, Carlisle, Pennsylvania.

19. Oskaloosa M. Smith, *Twenty-second Regiment of Infantry,* ed. Theo F. Rodenbough and William Haskin, U.S. Army (New York: Maynard, Merrill, 1896), 681

20. Smith, 682.

21. Ibid.

22. Oskaloosa M. Smith, *History of the Twenty-second United States Infantry* (Governor's Island, New York: Regimental, 1922), 3.

23. *Nashville Union and American*, "Philanthropy and Assassination," March 15, 1870, p. 2.

24. Hiram Chittenden and Alfred Richardson, *Life, Letters and Travels of Father Pierre-Jean De Smet, S.J., 1801–1873* (New York: Francis P. Harper, 1905), 1587.

25. *Nashville Union and American*, "Philanthropy and Assassination," March 15, 1870, p. 2.

26. James Edward Kelly, *Generals in Bronze: Interviewing the Commanders of the Civil War*, ed. William B. Styple (Kearney, NJ: Bell Grove, 2005), 192.

27. John M. Lubetkin, "The Forgotten Yellowstone Surveying Expeditions of 1871: W. Milnor Roberts and the Northern Pacific Railroad in Montana," *Montana* 52 (Winter 2002), 32–47.

28. Smith, *History of the Twenty-second United States Infantry*, 4.

29. Lubetkin, *Jay Cooke's Gamble*, 98.

30. *Mary and I: Forty Years with the Sioux*, ed. Stephen R. Riggs (Boston: Congregational Sunday School and Publishing Society, 1887), 326–328.

31. Hiram Chittenden and Alfred Richardson, *Life, Letters and Travels of Father Pierre-Jean De Smet*, 1547.

32. Lubetkin, *Jay Cooke's Gamble*, 115.

33. Ibid, 118.

34. Ibid.

35. Francis Robertson, "'We Are Going to Have a Big Sioux War': Colonel David S. Stanley's Yellowstone Expedition, 1872," *Montana* 34, no.4 (Autumn 1984), 2–15.

36. Lubetkin, *Jay Cooke's Gamble*, 123.

37. Oskaloosa M. Smith, *Twenty-second Regiment of Infantry*, 684.

38. Lubetkin, *Jay Cooke's Gamble*, 148.

39. Ibid., 158.

40. Ibid., 153.

41. Charles Larned, Letter, May 24, 1873, Charles Larned Diary and Letters, United States Military Academy Special Collections, West Point, New York.

42. Ibid.

43. David S. Stanley, *Report on the Yellowstone Expedition of 1873* (Washington: Government Printing Office, 1874), 3.

44. *Rapelje Advocate*, "Norris one of the Few Survivors of Stanley's Expedition on Yellowstone in 1873; Five Wagon Loads of Booze Poured Out," May 16 1921.

45. Lubetkin, *Jay Cooke's Gamble*, 189.

46. David Stanley, *Personal Memoirs of Major-General D.S. Stanley, USA*, 238.

47. Lubetkin, *Jay Cooke's Gamble*, 190.

48. Larned, Letter July 28, 1873.

49. Larned June 25, 1873.

50. David Stanley, *Personal Memoirs of Major-General D.S. Stanle,y USA*, 239.

51. Marguerite Merington, *The Custer Story: The Life and Times of George A. Custer and His Wife Elizabeth* (Lincoln: University of Nebraska Press, 1950), 251.

52. Lubetkin, *Jay Cooke's Gamble*, 192.

53. Samuel Stanley, "General David Stanley, Frontier Soldier," Stanley File, United States Military Academy Special Collections, West Point, New York, 62.

54. Larned, Letter, July 28, 1873.

55. Rosser, Thomas, "1873 Diary of Thomas L. Rosser," vol. 4, Accession Number 1171-d-e Box 2, University of Virginia, Charlottesville, Virginia.

56. *Rapelje Advocate*, "Norris One of the Few Survivors of Stanley's Expedition on Yellowstone in 1873; Five Wagon Loads of Booze Poured Out," May 16 1921.

57. Lubetkin, *Jay Cooke's Gamble*, 194.
58. Oskaloosa M. Smith, *Twenty-second Regiment of Infantry*, 685.
59. John M. Schofield, Letter, December 5, 1881, Stanley File, United States Military Academy, West Point, New York.
60. *New York Sun,* October 24, 1897, "The Battle of Franklin, Gen. Cox, Recent Account of It Vigorously Handled by Gen. Stanley,"Clayman C. Myers Papers, 1824–1930, Undated Manuscript Number 47003542, U.S. Army Education and Heritage Center, Carlisle, Pennsylvania.
61. Benson Bobrick, *Master of War: The Life of General George H. Thomas* (New York: Simon & Schuster, 2009), 329.
62. Marvin E. Kroeker, *Great Plains Command: William B. Hazen in the Frontier West* (Norman: University of Oklahoma Press, 1976), 153–4.
63. Edward S. Cooper, *William Babcock Hazen: The Best Hated Man* (Madison, Teaneck, NJ: Farleigh Dickinson University Press, 2005), 264.
64. Paul Andrew Hutton, *Phil Sheridan and His Army* (Norman: University of Oklahoma Press ,1985), 148.
65. Marvin E. Kroeker, *Great Plains Command*, 155.
66. Congressional Record, Forty-Seventh Congress, Second Session, Appendix to the Congressional Record, Volume XIV, Part III (Washington: U.S. Government Printing Office, 1882), 61.
67. John G. Bourke, *The Diary of John Gregory Bourke*, vol. 3, ed. Charles M. Robinson III (Denton: University of North Texas Press, 2007), 816.
68. *New York Times,* "Arguing for a Verdict," May 3, 1879.
69. *New York Times,* "The Stanley-Hazen Quarrel: Hazen's Trial Prevented by Statute of Limitations," June 18, 1879.
70. Kroeker, *Great Plains Command*, 160–161.
71. *New York Tribune,* "Gen Hazen Vindicated," May 2, 1879, p. 5.
72. *New York Times,* "The Hazen-Stanley Fight: Gen. Stanley Sued for Libel," June 12, 1879.
73. Edward S. Cooper, *William Babcock Hazen,* p. 277.
74. Edward S. Cooper, *William Babcock Hazen,* p. 218.
75. Mildred Hazen, "Memoir," Rutherford Hayes Presidential Library, 126.
76. Ibid., 102–103.
77. Anne Sullivan, "Anna Huntington Stanley," Holbrook Collection, United States Military Academy Special Collections, March 28, 1975.
78. Olivia Nagel, "Anna Huntington Stanley," Personal Communication, January 2013.
79. *Daily Globe,* "Gen. Stanley to be Censured," May 19, 1879, p. 1.
80. *Bismarck Tribune,* "Personal and Political," May 24, 1879, p. 2.
81. *Daily Globe,* "The Ruthless Reaper," January 17, 1887, p. 1.
82. James A. Garfield, *The Diary of James A. Garfield, 1872–1874,* vol. 2, ed. Harry James Brown and Frederick D. Williams (Michigan State University Press, 1967), 33.
83. *Fort Worth Gazette,* "General Stanley's Appointment Giving Satisfaction," March 27, 1884, p. 2.
84. Jacob D. Cox, Letter, February 1, 1884, to the Secretary of War, Stanley Personnel Files, National Archives, Washington, D.C.
85. David S. Stanley, Graduation Address at West Point Military Academy, Stanley File- 006-06-010, United States Military Academy Special Collections, West Point, New York, June 13, 1885.
86. Ibid.
87. Ibid.
88. Ibid.
89. David S. Stanley, *Annual Report of the Secretary of War for the Year 1884,* Report of Brigadier-General Stanley (Washington: Government Printing Office. 1884), 125.
90. David S. Stanley, *Annual Report of the Secretary of War for the Year 1886,* Report of Brigadier-General Stanley (Washington: Government Printing Office, 1884), xx.
91. *Fort Worth Daily Gazette,* "Geronimo at San Antonio," September 11, 1886, p. 1.
92. Anne Sullivan, "Anna Huntington Stanley," Holbrook Collection, United States Military Academy Special Collections, March 28, 1975.
93. David S. Stanley, *Annual Report of the Secretary of War for the Year 1890,* Report of Brigadier-General Stanley, (Washington: Government Printing Office, 1890), 184
94. *North Platte Tribune,* "A Raid by Mexican Bandits," April 8, 1891, p. 1.
95. *Rock Island Daily Argus,* "Texas Is Cordial," April 20, 1891, p. 4.
96. *Sunday Herald and Weekly National Intelligencer,* "Army Officer to Be Court Martialed," February 15, 1891, p. 8.
97. *Sun,* "Reprimanded by the President," March 21, 1891, p. 7.
98. "The Garza Revolution, 1891–1893," Records of the U.S. Army Continental Commands, Department of Texas (LexisNexis, Reed Elsevier, Inc. PIN 103935, 2009), 1.
99. *New York Times,* "Gen. Stanley Arrested: He Calmly Submits and Texan Sheriff Refuses to Lock Him Up," December 25, 1888; *Buffalo Express,* "Trouble in Texas, Brig-Gen. Stanley Under Arrest at Austin," December 27, 1888.
100. "Stanley Arrested," Palm School Folder, Austin History Center, Austin Texas.
101. *St. Paul Globe,* "Court Called Down: Lessons Read to Texas Jurists by the Supreme Bench," March 24, 1896, p. 5.
102. *Fort Worth Gazette,* "The City of El Paso Sets Up a Claim Against Uncle Sam," October 16, 1891, p. 4.
103. *Evening Star,* "Death of Mrs. Stanley," April 24, 1895, p. 8; *National Tribune,* "Gen. Stanley's Wife Dead," May 2, 1895, p. 5.
104. *National Tribune,* "The Crown of Life," July 9, 1908, p. 5.
105. *Evening Star,* "Amusements," January 30, 1896.

Conclusion

1. Report 1245, "Gen. David S. Stanley," *Reports of the House of Representatives,* 52nd Congress, 1st Session (Washington: U.S. Government Printing Office, 1892), 1–3.
2. James Edward Kelly, *Generals in Bronze: Interviewing the Commanders of the Civil War,* ed. William B. Styple (Kearney, NJ: Bell Grove y, 2005), 275.
3. Joanne Patton, "Anna Huntington Stanley," Personal Communication, October 2013.
4. Anne Sullivan, "Anna Huntington Stanley," March 28, 1975, Holbrook Collection, United States Military Academy Special Collections, West Point, New York.
5. *Strait Times,* "U.S. Officer's Suicide-Tragedy of General's Son at Manila," April 22, 1926.
6. Sarah Rumbough, *The Regular Army O!* Rumbough Collection, United States Military Academy, Special Collections, West Point, New York, 1939.
7. 2010 Register of Cadets and Former Cadets Booklet (West Point: United States Military Academy, 2011), 3.
8. Thomas MacCurdy Vincent, "David Sloane Stanley," *Thirty-fourth Annual Reunion of the Association of the Graduates of the United States Military Academy* (Saginaw, MI: Seeman and Peters, 1903), 61.
9. Ibid., 63.
10. Ibid., 67.
11. James Edward Kelly, "Two Noted Federal Cavalry Leaders," *United States Army Recruiting News* 21, no. 1 (1939), 3.

Bibliography

Primary Sources

Austin History Center, Palm School Folder, Austin Texas.

Bailey, Chesley D. Diary, Bailey (1863–1864). Filson Historical Society, Louisville, Kentucky, Mss. A B155, May 19, 1864.

Beatty, John. *The Citizen Soldier: The Memoirs of a Civil War Volunteer.* Lincoln: University of Nebraska Press, 1998.

Bek, William G. "The Civil War Diary of John T. Buegel, Union Soldier." *Missouri Historical Review* 40 (April 1946).

Bourke, John G. *The Diary of John Gregory Bourke.* Vol. 3. Edited by Charles M. Robinson III. Denton: University of North Texas Press, 2007.

Bronson, Eugene. Collection, Special Collections, Kalamazoo College, Michigan.

Butler, Jay Caldwell. *Letters Home.* Arranged by Watson Hubbard Butler. Binghamton, NY: privately published, 1930.

Carter, Alden. *Brother to the Eagle: The Civil War Journal of Sgt. Ambrose Armitage, 8th Wisconsin Infantry.* United States: Booklocker, 2006.

Chadwick, Mary Jane. *Incidents of the War: The Civil War Journal of Mary Jane Chadwick.* Edited by Nancy Rohr. Huntsville: SilverThread, 2005.

Chapman, William. Civil War Pension Record. National Archives, Washington, D.C.

Chittenden, Hiram, and Alfred Richardson. *Life, Letters and Travels of Father Pierre-Jean De Smet, S.J., 1801–1873.* New York: Francis P. Harper, 1905.

Cohen, Jacob C. Civil War Letter Collection. Jewish-American History Documentation Foundation, Lathrup Village, Michigan.

Conyngham, David Power. Papers (CON). "Soldiers of the Cross." University of Notre Dame Archives (UNDA), South Bend, Indiana.

Dewey, Mildred McLean Hazen. "Memoirs." GA 52, Rutherford Hayes Presidential Library, Fremont, Ohio.

Du Bois, John Van Duesen. "The Civil War Journal and Letters of Col. John Van Duesen Du Bois." Edited by Jared C. Lobdell. *Missouri Historical Review* 61 (July 1966), 446.

Eleventh Missouri Infantry Order Book. National Archives, Washington, D.C.

Garfield, James A. *The Diary of James A. Garfield, 1872–1874.* Vol. 2. Edited by Harry James Brown and Frederick D. Williams. East Lansing: Michigan State University Press, 1967.

Gratz, Simon. Simon Gratz Collection, H250A. Pennsylvania Historical Society, Philadelphia, Pennsylvania.

Hanback, Lewis. 1839–1897, 1862–1865 Letters. A H233, Filson Historical Society, Louisville, Kentucky.

Holbrook Family Collection (Helen Hoyle Herr Holbrook and Willard Ames Holbrook, Jr., Collection). Papers, 1828–1980. Special Collections, United States Military Academy, West Point, New York.

Jackson, Oscar. *The Colonel's Diary.* Edited by David Jackson. Sharon, PA, 1922.

Kimball, Nathan. Papers (1828–1908). Kimball Mss. Lilly Library, Indiana University, Bloomington, Indiana.

Larned, Charles. Letters and Diary. United States Military Academy, Special Collections, West Point, New York.

Long, Eli. *Diary.* Eli Long Papers, 1855–1892, United States Army Heritage and Education Center Carlisle, Pennsylvania.

Longacre, Glenn V., and John E. Haas, eds. *To Battle for God and the Right: The Civil War; Letterbooks of Emerson Opdycke.* Urbana: University of Illinois Press, 2003.

Love, James Edwin. Papers (1859–1865). ARC A0940, Missouri Historical Society, St. Louis.

Mosman, Chesley. *The Rough Side of War: The Civil War Journal of Chesley A. Mosman.* Edited by Arnold Gates. New York: Basin, 1987.

Myers, Clayman C. Papers, 1824–1930. Manuscript Number 47003542, United States Army Heritage and Education Center, Carlisle, Pennsylvania.

Opdycke, Emerson. Papers Mss. (microform), 1811–1913; Opdycke, Emerson, 1830–1884. Ohio Historical Society, Columbus, Ohio.

Opdycke, Emerson. *To Battle for God and the Right: The Civil*

War Letterbooks of Emerson Opdycke, Ed. Longacre, Glenn V. and John E. Haas. Urbana: University of Illinois Press, 2003.

Potter, Henry Albert. MS 91-480, Henry Albert Potter Collection, Accession Box 461 Folder 2, Archives of Michigan, Michigan Historical Society, Lansing.

Prickitt, Daniel (3rd Ohio Cavalry). *Diary*. Edited by Col. E.D. Stoltz. Archbold, OH: Edwin Stoltz, 1988.

Richards, Henry. *Letters of Captain Henry Richards of the Ninety-third Ohio Infantry*. Cincinnati: Wrightson, 1883.

Rosecrans, William S. Papers, 1810-1920. Collection 66, University of California, Los Angeles, Library, Department of Special Collections.

Rosser, Thomas. 1873 Diary of Thomas L. Rosser. Vol. 4, Accession Number 1171, General Thomas L. Rosser and Rosser Family Papers, 1774-1983, Special Collections, University of Virginia, Charlottesville.

Smith, Theodore Clarke. *The Life and Letters of James Abram Garfield*. Vol. 1. New Haven, CT: Archon, 1968.

Stanley, David. Folder, United States Military Academy, Special Collections, West Point, New York.

Stanley, David. Papers, 1828-1902. University of Wyoming American Heritage Center, Laramie.

Stanley, David. Personnel Records. ACP 000183, Microfiche, National Archives Washington, D.C.

Stanley, David. Union General Papers. Record Group 94, Entry 159, Box 28, National Archives, Washington, D.C.

Stanley, David S. *David Stanley Diary, United States 2nd Dragoons of a March from Fort Smith, Arkansas, to San Diego, California, Made in 1853*. Martin Lalor Crimmins Papers, Briscoe Center for American History, University of Texas at Austin.

Stanley, David Sloane. Memoirs and Related Papers. Accession number 3466, Minnesota Historical Society, St. Paul.

Stanley David. West—Stanley—Wright Family Papers. Folder, David S. Stanley Family, United States Army Heritage and Education Center, Carlisle, Pennsylvania.

Stewart, William. Papers, 1861-1864. C2991, Western Historical Manuscript Collection, University of Missouri/State Historical Society of Missouri, Columbia.

Temple, Wayne Calhoun. "A Chaplain in the 11th Missouri Infantry." *Lincoln Herald* 64 (Summer 1962), 81-88. Harrowgate, TN: Lincoln Memorial University Press, 1962.

Turchin, Nadine. "'A Monotony Full of Sadness': The Diary of Nadine Turchin, May, 1863-April, 1864." Edited by Mary Ellen McElligott. *Journal of the Illinois State Historical Society* 70 (1977), 27-89.

Wills, Charles W. *Army Life of an Illinois Soldier*. Washington, D.C.: Globe, 1905.

Regimental Histories

Allendorf, Donald. *Long Road to Liberty: The Odyssey of a German Regiment in the Yankee Army; The 15th Missouri Volunteer Infantry*. Kent, OH: Kent State University Press, 2006.

Annals of the Fifty-seventh Regiment Indiana Volunteers, Dayton, OH: W.J. Shuey, 1868.

Barnes, James A., James R. Carnahan and Thomas H.B. McCain. *The Eighty-sixth Regiment Indiana Volunteer Infantry*. Crawfordsville, IN: Journal, 1895.

Bailey, Chester. *The Mansfield Men in the Seventh Pennsylvania Cavalry, Eighth Regiment*. Mansfield, PA: Published by Author, 1986.

Beach, John N. *History of the Fortieth Ohio Volunteer Infantry*. London, OH: Shepherd & Craig, 1884.

Beaudot, William J.K. *The 24h Wisconsin Infantry in the Civil War: The Biography of a Regiment*. Mechanicsburg: Stackpole, 2003.

Belcher, Dennis W. *The History of the Eleventh Missouri Infantry in the Civil War*. Jefferson, NC: McFarland, 2011.

Bennett, L.G., and William M. Haigh. *History of the Thirty-Sixth Regiment Illinois Volunteers During the War of the Rebellion*. Aurora, IL: Knickerbocker & Hodder, 1987.

Bryner, Cloyd. *Bugle Echoes: The Story of the Illinois 47th*. Springfield, IL: Phillips, 1905.

Clark, Charles T. *Opdycke's Tigers, 125 O.V.I.: A History of the Regiment and of the Campaigns and Battles of the Army of the Cumberland*. Columbus, OH: Spahr & Glenn, 1895.

Cope, Alexis. *The Fifteenth Ohio Volunteers and Its Campaigns, 1861-1865*. Columbus OH: Alexis Cope, 1961.

Curry, W.L. *Four Years in the Saddle: History of the First Regiment Ohio Volunteer Cavalry*. Columbus, OH: Champlin, 1898.

Day, Lewis W. *Story of the One Hundred and First Ohio Infantry*. Cleveland: W.M. Bayne, 1894.

Dodge, William Sumner. *The Waif of the War; or, History of the Seventy-fifth Illinois Infantry*. Chicago: Church and Goodman, 1866.

Dornblaser, T.F. *Sabre Strokes of the Pennsylvania Dragoons in the War of 1861-1865, Interspersed with Personal Reminiscences*. Philadelphia: Lutheran Publication Society, 1884.

Harden, H.O. *History of the 90th Ohio volunteer Infantry in the War of the Great Rebellion in the United States, 1861 to 1865*. Stoutsville, OH: Fairfield-Pickaway News, 1902.

Hinman, Wilbur. *The Story of the Sherman Brigade: Sixty-fourth Ohio Veteran Volunteer Infantry, Sixty-fifth Ohio Veteran Volunteer Infantry, Sixth Battery Ohio Veteran Volunteer Artillery, McLaughlin's Squadron Ohio Veteran Volunteer Cavalry*. Alliance, OH: Published by Author, 1897.

History of the Seventy-ninth Regiment, Indiana Volunteer Infantry. Indianapolis: Hollenbeck, 1899.

Kelly, Welden. *A Historical Sketch of Company E, 26th Ohio Infantry*. Osborne, MO, 1909.

Kimberly, Robert, and Ephraim Holloway. *The Forty-first Ohio Veteran Volunteer Infantry in the War of the Rebellion, 1861-1865*. Cleveland: W.R. Smellie, 1897.

Kirk, Charles. "The Fifteenth Pennsylvania (Anderson) Cavalry at Stone River." In *History of the Fifteenth Pennsylvania Volunteer Cavalry*. Edited by J.C. Reiff.

Philadelphia, Pennsylvania: Society of the Fifteenth Pennsylvania Cavalry, 1906

Lathrop, D. *History of the Fifty-ninth Regiment Illinois Volunteers.* Indianapolis: Hall & Hutchison, 1865.

Lewis, G.W. *The Campaigns of the 124th Regiments Ohio Volunteer Infantry.* Akron: Werner, nd.

McCall, Duncan. *Three Years in the Service: Record of the Doings of the 11th Reg. Missouri.* Springfield, MO: Johnson & Bradford, 1864.

Morris, George W. *History of the Eighty-first Regiment of Indiana Volunteer Infantry.* Louisville: Franklin, 1901.

Newlin, W.H. *History of the Seventy-third Regiment of Illinois Infantry Volunteers.* 1890.

Partridge, Charles A. *History of the Ninety-sixth Regiment, Illinois Volunteer Infantry.* Chicago: Brown, Pettibone, 1887.

Pierce, Lyman. *History of the 2nd Iowa Cavalry.* Burlington, IA: Hawkeye, 1865.

Reunion of the 9th Indiana Veterans Volunteer Infantry Association: Including Annual Reunions and Proceedings 9 Through 18, 1892–1904. Chicago: Barlow-Sinclair, 1892.

Royse, Isaac Henry Clay. *History of the 115th Regiment Illinois Volunteer Infantry.* Terre Haute: Published by Author, 1900.

Seventy-Seventh Pennsylvania at Shiloh: History of the Regiment. Harrisburg: Harrisburg, 1905.

Smith, Charles H. *The History of Fuller's Ohio Brigade, 1861–1865: Its Great March, with Roster, Portraits, Battle Maps and Biographies.* Cleveland: J.A. Wyatt, 1909.

Smith, John Thomas. *A History of the Thirty-first Regiment of Indiana Volunteer Infantry in the War of the Rebellion.* Cincinnati: Western Methodist, 1900.

Smith, Oskaloosa M. *History of the Twenty-second United States Infantry.* Governor's Island, New York: Regimental Press, 1922.

___. *Twenty-second Regiment of Infantry.* Edited by Theo F. Rodenbough and William Haskin. New York: Maynard, Merrill, 1896.

Vale, Joseph. *Minty and the Cavalry: A History of Cavalry Campaigns in the Western Armies.* Harrisburg, PA: Edwin K. Myers, 1886.

Williams, John Melvin. *The Eagle Regiment: 8th Wis. Inf'ty Vols.* Belleville, WI: Recorder, 1890.

Woodruff, George, H. *Fifteen Years Ago: Of the Patriotism of Will County.* Joliet: Joliet Republican, 1876.

Official Documents

Congressional Record, Forty-Seventh Congress, Second Session, Appendix to the Congressional Record, Volume XIV, Part III. Washington: U.S. Government Printing Office, 1882.

House of Representatives. Committee on Military Affairs. 52nd Congress, 1st Session. Report 1245, "Gen. David S. Stanley." In *The Reports of Committees of the House of Representatives.* Washington: U.S. Government Printing Office, 1892.

Stanley, David S. *Annual Report of the Secretary of War for the Year 1884.* Report of Brigadier-General Stanley. Washington: U.S. Government Printing Office, 1884.

___. *Annual Report of the Secretary of War for the Year 1886.* Report of Brigadier-General Stanley. Washington: U.S. Government Printing Office, 1886.

___. *Annual Report of the Secretary of War for the Year 1890.* Report of Brigadier-General Stanley. Washington: U.S. Government Printing Office, 1890.

___. *Report on the Yellowstone Expedition of 1873.* Washington: U.S. Government Printing Office, 1874.

United States War Department. *The War of the Rebellion: A Compilation of the Official Records of the Union and Confederate Armies.* Series I, Volume 1. Washington, D.C.: U.S. Government Printing Office, 1880–1901.

Journal Articles

Allen, Stacy. "Corinth, Mississippi Crossroads of the Western Confederacy," *Blue and Gray* (2007), 21–22.

Bek, William G. "The Civil War Diary of John T. Buegel, Union Soldier." *Missouri Historical Review* 40 (April 1946), 315.

Belcher, Dennis W. "Joe Mower's Jackass Cavalry." *North and South* 13 (November 2011), 52–61.

Du Bois, John Van Duesen. "The Civil War Journal and Letters of Col. John Van Duesen Du Bois." Edited by Jared C. Lobdell. *Missouri Historical Review* 61 (July 1966), 446.

East, Earnest. "Lincoln's Russian General." *Journal of the Illinois State Historical Society* 52, no. 1 (1959), 106–122.

Kelly, James Edward. "Two Noted Federal Cavalry Leaders." *United States Army Recruiting News* 21, no. 1 (1939), 2–19.

Lubetkin, M. John. "The Forgotten Yellowstone Surveying Expeditions of 1871: W. Milnor Roberts and the Northern Pacific Railroad in Montana." *Montana* 52 (Winter 2002), 32–47.

Mullen, Jay Carlton. "Pope's New Madrid and Island Number 10 Campaigns." *Missouri Historical Review* 59 (April 1965), 325–343.

Perrine, Fred S. "Uncle Sam's Camel Corps." *New Mexico Historical Review*, no. 4 (October 1926), 434–444. Edited by Lansing Bloom and Paul Walter. Historical Society of New Mexico at the Museum Press, Santa Fe.

Ramsdell, Charles. "Presidential Reconstruction in Texas." *Quarterly of the Texas State Historical Association* 14 (April 1908), 277–317.

Robertson, Francis. 'We Are Going to Have a Big Sioux War': Colonel David S. Stanley's Yellowstone Expedition, 1872." *Montana* 34, no. 4 (Autumn 1984), 2–15.

Stanley, Samuel. "General David Stanley, Frontier Soldier." *The Real West* 152, no. 20 (July 1977).

Newspapers

Bismarck Tribune
Buffalo Express
Chicago Times
Daily Globe (St. Paul, MN)
Evening Star (Washington, D.C.)
Fort Worth Gazette
Milwaukee Journal

Nashville Daily Press
Nashville Union and American
National Tribune (Washington, D.C.)
New York Sun
New York Times
North Platte Tribune
Rapelje Advocate (Rapelje, MT)
Rock Island Daily Argus
St. Paul Globe
Straits Times (Singapore)
Sun (New York)
Sunday Herald and Weekly National Intelligencer (Washington, D.C.)

Other Sources

Anderson, Bern. *By Sea and By River: The Naval History of the Civil War*. New York: Da Capo, 1962.

Bearss, Edwin C. *The Battle of Wilson's Creek*. Bozeman: George Washington Carver Birthplace District Association, 1975.

___. "Cavalry Operations: Battle of Stones River." Stones River National Park, Technical Information Center, 1959.

Bickham, William D. *Rosecrans' Campaign with the Fourteenth Army Corps of the Army of the Cumberland*. Cincinnati: Moore, Wilstach, Keys, 1863.

Bobrick, Benson. *Master of War: The Life of George H. Thomas*. New York: Simon and Schuster, 2009.

Bradley, Michael. *Tullahoma: The 1863 Campaign for the Control of Middle Tennessee*. Shippensburg, PA: White Mane, 1999.

Brewer, Richard J. "The Tullahoma Campaign: Operational Insights." Master's thesis, U.S. Army Command and General Staff College, Leavenworth, KS, 1978.

Britton, Wiley. *The Civil War on the Border*. New York: G.P. Putnam, 1890.

Brooksher, William Riley. *Bloody Hill: The Civil War Battle of Wilson's Creek*. Washington, D.C.: Brassey's, 1995.

Castel, Albert. *Decision in the West: The Atlanta Campaign of 1864*. Lawrence: University Press of Kansas, 1992.

Cist, Henry. *The Army of the Cumberland*. New York: Charles Scribner's Son, 1882.

Connolly, James. *Three Years in the Army of the Cumberland*. Edited by Paul Angle. Bloomington: Indiana University Press, 1959.

Cooper, Edward S. *William Babcock Hazen: The Best Hated Man*. Madison, NJ: Farleigh Dickinson University Press, 2005.

Cozzens, Peter. *The Darkest Days of the War: The Battles of Iuka and Corinth*. Chapel Hill: University of North Carolina Press, 1997.

___. *No Better Place to Die*. Urbana: University of Illinois Press, 1991.

___. *The Shipwreck of Their Hopes*. Urbana: University of Illinois Press, 1994.

___. *This Terrible Sound*. Urbana: University of Illinois Press, 1992.

Cozzens, Peter, and Robert Girardi. *The Military Memoirs of General John Pope*. Chapel Hill: University of North Carolina Press, 1998.

Crook, George. *General George Crook: His Biography*. Norman: University of Oklahoma Press, 1960.

Dalessandro, Robert J. *Major General William S. Rosecrans and the Transformation of the Staff of the Army of the Cumberland: A Case Study*. Strategy Research Project. U.S. Army War College, Carlisle Barracks, Pennsylvania, 2002.

___. "Morale in the Army of the Cumberland During the Tullahoma and Chickamauga Campaigns." Master's thesis, U.S. Army Command and General Staff College, Leavenworth, KS, 1980.

Daniel, Larry J. *Days of Glory: The Army of the Cumberland, 1861–1865*. Baton Rouge: Louisiana State University Press, 2006.

Daniel, Larry J., and Lynn N. Bock. *Island No. 10: Struggle for the Mississippi Valley*. Tuscaloosa: University of Alabama Press, 1996.

Dossman, Steven. *Campaign for Corinth: Blood in Mississippi*. Abilene: McWhitney Foundation Press, 2006.

Edison, Thomas. *John Hunt Morgan and His Raiders*. Lexington: University Press of Kentucky, 1985.

Evans, Clement, ed. *Confederate Military History*. Vol. 3. Atlanta: Confederate, 1899.

Fuller, John W. "Our Kirby Smith." In *Sketches of War History, 1861–1865: Papers Read Before the Ohio Commandery of the Military Order of the Loyal Legion of the United States, 1886–1888*. Vol. 2. Cincinnati: Robert Clarke, 1888.

Garza Revolution, 1891–1893. Records of the U.S. Army Continental Commands, Department of Texas. LexisNexis, Reed Elsevier, Inc., PIN 103935 (2009).

Herr, G.W. *Nine Campaigns in Nine States*. San Francisco: Bancroft, 1890.

Horn, Stanley F. *The Decisive Battle of Nashville*. Baton Rouge: Louisiana State University Press, 1957.

Howard, Oliver O. *The Autobiography of Oliver Otis Howard*. New York: Baker & Taylor, 1907.

Hutton, Paul Andrew. *Phil Sheridan and His Army*. Norman: University of Oklahoma Press, 1985.

Ingenthron, Elmo. *Borderland Rebellion: A History of the Civil War on the Missouri-Arkansas Border*. Edited by Kathleen Van Buskirk. Branson, MO: Ozark Mountaineer, 1980.

Kelly, James Edward. *Generals in Bronze: Interviewing the Commanders of the Civil War*. Edited by William B. Styple. Kearney, NJ: Bell Grove, 2005.

Kniffin, Gilbert. "The Battle of Stone's [sic] River." In *Battles and Leaders of the Civil War*. Vol. 3. New York: Century, 1888.

Kroeker, Marvin E. *Great Plains Command: William B. Hazen in the Frontier West*. Norman: University of Oklahoma Press, 1976.

Lamers, William. *The Edge of Glory: A Biography of General William S. Rosecrans, U.S.A.* New York: Harcourt, Brace & World, 1961.

Londa, John. "The Role of Union Cavalry During the Chickamauga Campaign." Master's thesis, U.S. Army Command and General Staff College, Leavenworth, KS, 1980.

Lubetkin, M. John. *Jay Cooke's Gamble*. Norman: University of Oklahoma Press, 2006.

McDonough, James L., and James Pickett Jones. *War So Terrible: Sherman and Atlanta*. New York: W.W. Norton, 1987.

McDonough, James L., and Thomas L Connelly. *Five Tragic Hours: The Battle of Franklin*. Knoxville: University of Tennessee Press, 1983.

McElroy, John. *The Struggle for Mis-*

souri. Washington, D.C.: National Tribune, 1909.

Merington, Marguerite. *The Custer Story: The Life and Times of George A. Custer and His Wife Elizabeth*. Lincoln: University of Nebraska Press, 1950.

Moore, Frank, ed. *The Rebellion Record*. Vol. 2. New York: G.P. Putnam, 1862.

Nagel, Olivia. "Anna Huntington Stanley." Personal Communication, January 2013.

Palmer, John A. *The Personal Recollections of John M. Palmer: The Story of an Earnest Life*. Cincinnati: Robert Clarke, 1901.

Palmer, John T. *A Conscientious Turncoat: The Story of John M. Palmer, 1817–1900*. New Haven: Yale University Press, 1941.

Parrish, William. *History of Missouri, 1860–1875*. Vol. 3. Columbia: University of Missouri Press, 1997.

Piston, William Garrett, and Richard W. Hatcher III. *Wilson's Creek: The Second Battle of the Civil War and the Men Who Fought It*. Chapel Hill: University of North Carolina Press, 2000.

Porter, David Dixon. *The Naval History of the Civil War*. London: General, 1998.

Richardson, Robert D. "Rosecrans' Staff at Chickamauga: The Significance of Major General William S. Rosecrans' Staff on the Outcome of the Chickamauga Campaign." Master's thesis, Command and General Staff College, Fort Leavenworth, Kansas, 1989.

Riggs, Stephen R., eds. *Mary and I: Forty Years with the Sioux*. Boston: Congregational Sunday School and Publishing Society, 1887.

Rosecrans, William. "The Battle of Corinth." In *Battles and Leaders of the Civil War*. Vol. 2. New York: Century, 1887.

Rumbough, Sarah. *The Regular Army O!* Rumbough Collection, United States Military Academy, Special Collections, West Point, New York, 1939.

Sandberg, Carl. *Abraham Lincoln: The War Years*. Vol. 1. New York: Harcourt, Brace, 1939.

Schofield, John. *Forty-Six Years in the Army*. New York: Century, 1897.

Shellenberger, John. *The Battle of Franklin, Tennessee, November 30, 1864: A Statement of the Erroneous Claims Made by General Schofield, and an Exposition of the Blunder Which Opened the Battle*. Cleveland: Arthur H. Clark, 1916.

Shelton, Paul. "The Blame Game: Federal Intelligence Operations During the Chickamauga Campaign." Master's thesis, U.S. Army Command and General Staff College, Fort Leavenworth, KS, 2000.

Sheridan, Philip. *Personal Memoirs of Philip H. Sheridan, General, United States Army*. Vol. 1. New York: D. Appleton, 1902.

Sherman, William T. *Memoirs of William T. Sherman*. Vol. 2. New York: D. Appleton, 1904.

Shoemaker, Floyd A. *A History of Missouri and Missourians*. Columbia, MO: Walter Ridgeway, 1922.

Smith, Timothy B. *Corinth, 1862: Siege, Battle, Occupation*. Lawrence: University Press of Kansas, 2012.

Society of the Army of the Cumberland. "Burial of General Rosecrans, Arlington National Cemetery." Cincinnati: Robert Clarke, 1903.

Society of the Army of the Cumberland. *Twenty-seventh Reunion*. Cincinnati: Robert Clark, 1898.

Stanley, David S. *Address of General Stanley, Reunion of the Society of the Army of the Cumberland: Twenty-sixth Reunion*. Cincinnati: Robert Clarke, 1897.

___. *An American General: The Memoirs of David Sloan Stanley*. Edited by Samuel W. Fordyce IV. Santa Barbara, CA: Narrative, 2004.

___. Graduation Address at West Point Military Academy. Stanley File, United States Military Academy Special Collections, West Point, New York, June 13, 1885.

___. *Personal Memoirs of Major-General D.S. Stanley, USA*. Cambridge: Harvard University Press, 1917.

Starr, Stephen Z. *The Union Cavalry in the Civil War*. Vol. 3, *The War in the West, 1861–1865*. Baton Rouge: Louisiana State University Press, 1985.

Sunderland, Glenn W. *Lightning at Hoover's Gap*. New York: Thomas Yoseloff, 1969.

Sword, Wiley. *The Confederacy's Last Hurrah: Spring Hill, Franklin and Nashville*. Lawrence: University Press of Kansas, 1993.

The Twenty-Ninth Annual Reunion of the Association of the Graduates of the United States Military Academy, June 9, 1898.

2010 Register of Cadets and Former Cadets. West Point: United States Military Academy, 2011.

U.S. Military Academy. *Official Register of the Officers and Cadets of the U.S. Military Academy*. West Point, NY: U.S. Military Academy, June 1852.

Vincent, Thomas M. "David Sloane Stanley." *The Thirty-fourth Annual Reunion of the Association of the Graduates of the United States Military Academy at West Point, New York*. Saginaw, MI: Seeman and Peters, 1903.

Ware, Eugene F. *The Lyon Campaign in Missouri*. Topeka: Crane, 1907. Reprinted by the Press of Camp Pope Bookshop, Iowa City, 1991.

Warren, Israel P. *The Stanley Families of America: As Descended from John, Timothy, and Thomas Stanley of Hartford, Conn*. Portland, ME: B. Thurston, 1887.

Welsh, Jack. *Medical Histories of Union Generals*. Kent, OH: Kent State University Press, 1996.

Woodson, W.H. *History of Clay County Missouri*. Indianapolis: Historical, 1920.

Index

Numbers in ***bold italics*** indicate pages with photographs.

Adair, Lt. Louis 227
Alabama units: 7th Cavalry 135; 37th Infantry 70; 42nd Infantry 84; 51st Cavalry 109; Ketchum's Artillery Battery 54
Allison, Robert 58
Anderson, Dick 12
Anderson, George B. 10
Anderson, George "Tige" 12
Anderson, James Patton 53
Anderson, Robert 105
Anderson Cavalry 93, 98–99, 103–104, 106, 110, 111, 117–118, 120–122; mutiny 104–106; *see also* 15th Pennsylvania Cavalry
Arkansas units: 1st Infantry 54; 15th Infantry 84; 23rd Infantry 84
Armstrong, Frank 65–67, 76, 199
Ashby, Henry 113
Atchison, David 13
Atlanta, siege of 184–187

Bailey, Chesley 179, 181
Baker, Eugene 223, 226
Baldridge, Samuel 71
Baldwin, Philemon 108, 110
Battery Lothrop 81
Battery Phillips 80–81
Battery Robinett(e) 80, 81–87, 90
Battery Tanrath 81
Battery Williams 80–81, 84
Beach, John 176
Beatty, John 99, 143, 150–151, 156, 162, 167
Beatty, Samuel ***194***, 201–202
Beauregard, Pierre G.T. 36, 40, 46–47, 49–51, 56, 58–60, 64
Beauregard Line 76
Belknap, William Worth 232–234
Bennett, Lyman 213
Bickham, William 122
Blair, Frank 18

Boonville, Battle of 19
Bourke, John Gregory 234
Bradley, Luther ***194***, 200, 203, 205–207, 210, 228
Bragg, Braxton 52, 56, 64–65, 75–76, 93, 102–104, 107, 119, 121, 129, 132–134, 138–140, 142, 145, 148–150, 152, 154–159, 163, 166, 172
Breckenridge, John 18, 65
Bridge Creek, engagement 57–58
Britton's Lane 65
Bryner, Cloyd 77, 79
Buell, Don Carlos 46–47, 50–51, 55–57, 61, 64–66, 75, 89, 92–93, 104–105, 130
Buford, Abraham ***102***, 119–120
Burke, Joe 111

Calhoun, Patrick 12
Campbell, Archibald 133, 137, 146, 148
Canby, Edward 220–221
Carlin, William 58
Carlisle Barracks, Pennsylvania 11, 14
Carr, Eugene 15
Carthage, Battle of 19
Casey, Thomas 10
Cassville, Battle of 178–180
Century magazine article 231
Chadwick, Mary Jane 143, 145
Cheyenne Indians 13, 244
Cincinnati Commercial Newspaper 122
Cist, Henry 60, 160
Clark, Temple 54
Cleburne, Patrick 208, 211, 214; at Atlanta 187; at Bridge Creek 57–58; at Spring Hill 205
Cliffe, Daniel 209, 211
Cobbert, Sarah 15, 63
Cohen, Jacob 63, 92

Comanche Indians 13–14, 237
Condit, Lieutenant 114
Confederate Units: 1st Cavalry Regiment 112
Conrad, Joseph 187, 200, 210–212, 220–221
Cooke, Philip St. George 11, 13
Cope, Alexis 220
Corinth: advance upon 46–55; Battle of 81–89; defenses 64; May 28 engagement 57–58; siege 55–60
Cosby, George 10
courier service 66, 94, 96, 116, 125, 136, 154, 157–158, 175
courts martial 130, 143–144, 187, 239, 234–236, 239, 245
Cox, Jacob 180, 189, 199, 201, 206, 207, ***209***–210, 212–213, 215–216, 231–233, 237
Cox, John 112
Crittenden, Thomas L. 93–97, 102, 104, 106, 108–109, 119, 134, 139, 145–146, 148, 153, 156–159, 162, 223–224, 235, 246
Crook, George 10, 13, ***144***–146, 149–151, 155–158, 160–163, 167, 234
Crosby, Eban 227
Cruft, Charles 169–170, 174–176, 179
Curry, W.L. 99
Curtis, Samuel 9–10
Custer, George 227–230, 232–233, 246

Dana, Charles 149, ***161***–164
Davidson, Henry B. 10, 44
Davidson, John W. 90
Davies, Thomas 58–59, 76–81, 83, 88–89
Davis, Jefferson C. 58, 61, 145

267

Index

Davis, Mathew 10
Davis, N.H. 104–105, 145, 171, 173–174, 181, 183, 189, 191, 193–195
Dees, A.W. 48–49, 56–57, 98
De Smet, Father Pierre-Jean 223, 225
Dibrell, George 145–146
Dilger, Hubert 183
discipline 2, 21, 29, 37, 40, 43, 44, 63, 88, 93, 99, 105, 106, 124, 129–130, 143–144, 146, 162, 168, 172, 197, 234, 245
Dodge, Grenville 129
Dodge, William 212
Dornblaser, T.F. 122
Ducat, Arthur 95–96, 98
Ducatel's Orleans Guard 52
Dug Springs 24–27, 29, 243
Dumont, Ebenezer 100

Eagle Brigade 48, 51, 81, 87, 90
Elliott, Washington L. 43, 49, 160, *194*
Emory, William 16–17
Erdmann, Adolphus 186–187

Farmington, Mississippi 49–50; engagement 51–55
Farrish, James 116
Field, Charles 12
Firestone, Leander 8–9, 12, 159
Fordyce, Jane 249
Forrest, Nathan B. 2–3, 93–94, 97, 99, 102–103, 122, 128–129, 137-*138*, 139, 141, 146, 153, 155, 157, 163, 196–198, 202–203
Forsyth Expedition 21–24
Fort Arbuckle 15, 243
Fort Bankhead 38, 41
Fort Chadbourne 12
Fort Cobb 15
Fort Donelson 36–37
Fort Henry 36–37
Fort Kearney 14
Fort Leavenworth 13–14, 16–17, 19, 21
Fort Pillow 30–31, 36, 45–46, 60
Fort Rice 221–224, 226–228, 230
Fort Riley 14–15
Fort Smith 11–12, 15–16, 29, 63
Fort Sully 222–225
Fort Taylor 30
Fort Thompson 38, 44
Fort Washita 7, 16, 23, 29
Franklin: Battle of 208–216; engagement 127–130
Frémont, John C. 19, 21, 28, 30–34
Fry, Speed 95
Fuller, John 48, 60, 68, 81, 83-*86*, 88, 93

Gall, Chief *226*
Gantt, Edward 44
Garber, Hezekiah 10
Garesche, Julius 100, 111
Garfield, James A. 5, *125*–126, 129–132, 140–143, 150–154, 156–160, 162–164, 167, 232–234, 236, 245
Garza Revolution 239–240
Georgia units: 2nd Cavalry 135, 152; 3rd Cavalry 152; 4th Cavalry 135, 152; 54th Infantry 184
Geronimo 238–239
Gibson, William 112
Gilliard, William 67
Govan, Daniel 205
Granger, Gordon 33, 38, 43, 48, 59, 128-*129*, 134–138, 140–142, 144–146, 160, 162–163, 169–171, 217
Granger, R.S. 197
Grant, Ulysses 36, 46–47, 59–60, 62–68, 71–75, 80, 87–88, 93, 96–97, 102, 132–133, 149, 172, 194, 198, 214–215, 218, 227
Gray, Asa 36
Green, Martin 79, 83
Groesbeck, John 33, 39–40, 43–44, 48–50
Grose, William 169–170, 177, 179–180, 184–186, 189, 191, 200, 202
gunboats, Union: USS *Benton* 41; USS *Carondelet* 41, 43; USS *Cincinnati* 41; USS *Mound City* 41; USS *Pittsburg* 41, 43; USS *St. Louis* 41

Halleck, Henry 14, 33–34, 37, 40, 42, 46-*47*, 49–51, 55–56, 58–61, 63–64, 80, 92–94, 96, 98–99, 103, 153, 155, 198
Halleck Line 76
Hamilton, Charles Schuyler 33, 37–38, 40–43, 47, 49, 56, 58, 60, 65, 67–70, 72–73, 77–78, 80–81, 83, 85, 88–89
Hanback, Lewis 128, 183
Hardee, William 3, 12, 30–31, 56, 60, 75, 104, 110, 134, 178–181, 188, 191, 193–195
Harker, Charles 96, 162, 183
Harlan, John 101
Harney, William Selby 12–13, 18, 28
Harney-Price Agreement 18
Harris, Stephen 227
Hartsville 95–98; Battle of 100
Hascall, Milo 10
Hatch, Edward 68, 199
Haugh, William 213
Hazen, Mildred 235–236
Hazen, William 152, 180, 231–236, *233*, 245
Hazen-Stanley feud 232–236
Hébert, Louis 70–71, 76, 83
"hell hole" 181

Herr, Helen 249
Herr, John 249
Herr, Washington 182
Hinton, Richard 55
Hodgson's Battery 52; *see also* Louisiana units
Holbrook, David Stanley 247
Holbrook, Joanne Stanley 249
Holbrook, Marian Herr 249
Holbrook, Willard Ames 247
Holbrook, Willard Ames, Jr. 247
Holbrook, Willard, III 249
Holloway, Edmunds 17
Hood, John Bell 6, 75, 172, 175, 177–180, 184, 187–189, 196–199, 201–203, 205–211, 213–214
Hooker, Joseph 133, 160, 162–163, 177–178, 180
Howard, Oliver O. *171*–175, 177–178, 180–181, 184–185, 187–189, 191–192, 194
Hoxton's Tennessee Artillery 52, 54
Hurlbut, Stephen 87

Illinois units: 2nd Artillery 41; 21st Infantry 58, 170, 200, 220; 22nd Infantry 54; 26th Infantry 48, 51, 53–54, 68, 70, 79, 81; 27th Infantry 41, 54, 128; 36th Infantry 200, 213; 38th Infantry 58, 170, 200; 40th Infantry 176; 42nd 54, 59, 200; 44th Infantry 200; 47th Infantry 48, 51, 53–54, 68, 70, 73, 77, 79, 81, 90; 51st Infantry 54–55, 200, 205; 59th Infantry 170, 173, 182, 185, 187, 197, 200; 73rd Infantry 200; 74th Infantry 212; 74th/88th Infantry 200; 75th Infantry 170, 200; 79th Infantry 200; 80th Infantry 170, 200; 84th Infantry 170, 200, 220; 89th Infantry 200; 96th Infantry 170, 173, 187, 200; 98th Infantry 124; 100th Infantry 200; 103rd Infantry 197; 115th Infantry 170, 200, 220; 123rd Infantry 124; Bridge's Battery 201; Chicago Board of Trade (Stokes) Battery 133, 149
Independence, Missouri, skirmish at 17
Indiana units: 2nd Cavalry 103, 122, 133, 148, 152; 2nd Infantry 119; 3rd Cavalry 103–104, 110, 112–113, 121, 128, 131, 133, 136, 148–149; 4th Cavalry 133, 148, 152; 5th Artillery 170, 175, 181; 9th Infantry 170, 185, 200; 17th Infantry 124; 29th Infantry 170; 30th Infantry 170, 200; 31st Infantry 170, 176, 183, 200; 32nd Infantry 169; 35th Infantry 170, 182, 200; 36th Infantry 170, 182, 200; 39th

Index

Infantry (mounted) 131, 133, 142; 40th Infantry 200; 51st Infantry 200; 57th Infantry 200; 72nd Infantry 124; 77th Infantry 220; 79th Infantry 200; 81st Infantry 170, 176, 200; 84th Infantry 170, 173, 200; 86th Infantry 200
Iowa units: 1st Infantry 25, 27, 29; 2nd Artillery 48, 57, 68; 2nd Cavalry 43, 49, 53–54; 5th Cavalry 133, 135, 149; 5th Infantry 70, 73
Ireland, John 62, 250
Island Number 10 35, 36, 39–44, 46, 121, 205, 243; advance upon 37–38
Iuka 62, 75, 80, 96, 165; battle 68–74, 76, 88–89, 92–93, 121, 243; capture of Union depot 66–67
Iverson, Alfred 15

Jackson, Claiborne Fox 18–19
Jackson, Oscar 50, 84
Jefferson Barracks, St. Louis 12
Jewish Messenger 63
Johnson, Richard 6, 111–113, 145, 180
Johnston, Albert Sydney 12, 46, 75
Johnston, Joseph 132, 172, 174–175, 178–180, 184, 195–196
Jonesboro 3, 196–198, 215, 245; Battle of 188–192; controversies 192–195
Jordan, Thomas 126, 133

Kansas slavery issues 7, 13, 16
Kansas units: 1st Infantry 21; 2nd Infantry 21–22, 27; 8th Infantry 145, 201
Kellogg, Lyman 10
Kelly, James Edward 216, 250
Kelly, Lt. M.J. 27
Kennesaw Mountain, Battle of 181–183, 244
Kennett, John 94–98, 103–104, 108, 115–116, 121–122, 130
Kentucky units: 1st Artillery 201, 212; 1st Infantry 170, 212; 2nd Cavalry 101, 133; 2nd Infantry 170; 3rd Cavalry 103, 109, 111, 116–118, 121–122; 4th Cavalry 128, 133, 148; 5th Cavalry 133, 142, 148; 6th Cavalry 133, 148, 149; 6th Infantry 172; 7th Cavalry 133, 149; 8th Infantry 170; 9th Infantry 179, 181; 17th Infantry 201; 21st Infantry 170, 200; 23rd Infantry 200; 28th Infantry 200
Kilpatrick, Hugh Judson 187
Kimball, Nathan 186, 189, 191–192, *194*–195, 199, 202–203, 205–207, 215, 220

Klein, Robert 103, 110, 112–113, 115, 121, 128, 133, 149
Kniflin, G.C. 173

Lahm, Samuel 9
Lane, James H. 32
Lane, James Q. 200, 202–203, 205, 210–212
Larned, Charles 227–229
Lee, Fitzhugh 15
Lee, Robert E. 59, 75–76, 172, 217–218
Lee, Stephen Dill 188
Lexington, Battle of 28, 31–32, 63
Lincoln, Abraham 15, 17–18, 31, 33, 56, 59, 125, 130, 171
Little, Henry 66
Lomax, Lunsford 13, 15, 23
Long, Eli 13, 126, 130–131, 133, 139, 149
Loomis, John 48, *51*–55
Louisiana units: 4th Infantry 49; 11th Infantry 53; 13th Infantry 49, 54; 16th Infantry 53; 17th Infantry 49; 18th Infantry 54; 19th Infantry 54; 20th Infantry 49, 54; 25th Infantry 49, 53; Hodgson's Battery 52; Orleans Guard 54
Love, Hiram 49
Love, James 145
Lovejoy's Station Battle of 191–192, 196, 244
Lovell, Mansfield 76, 78, 81, 83
Lowrey, Mark 205
Lowry, Elsie Ann 8
Lyon, Nathaniel 18–19, 21–22, 24–25, 27

Mackall, William 43–44
Magoffin, Ebenezer trial 33
Marmaduke, John 19
Marshall, Louis 34
Martin, William T. 136–137, 150–151, 154–155
Maurice, T.D. 48, 57
Maury, Dabney 66, 71, 75, 83–84
McArthur, John 78, 88–89, 214
McCall, Duncan 58, 79, 81, 83
McClellan, George B. 13–14, 59, 72
McClernand, John 64
McCook, Alexander 10, 60, 93–96, 104, 106–107, 109–112, 114–115, 117, 119, 134–135, 142, 145, 148, 150–*151*, 154–156, 158, 160, 162–163, 171, 234, 246
McCook, Daniel 183
McCook, Edward 133, *146*, 148–153, 155, 157–159, 166, 177
McCown, John 36, 40, 43, 111
McCullough, Benjamin 19
McDowell, Samuel 183
McIntosh, James 15, 25–26
McKean, Thomas 76–78, 80, 89

McPherson, James 89, 172–173, 179, 185, 192
Mexican War 9
Michigan units: 1st Artillery 48; 2nd Cavalry 108, 133, 148; 3rd Artillery 56, 68–69, 98; 3rd Cavalry 69, 108; 4th Cavalry 103–104, 108–109, 111, 117–119, 121–122, 127–129, 132–133, 135–136, 149; 7th Cavalry 99; 7th Infantry 98; 14th Infantry 54
Milliken, Minor 103, 114
Minnesota: 1st Artillery 78; 5th Infantry 57, 62, 81, 83
Minty, Robert 102–104, *108*–109, 111, 116–118, 120–122, 126, 130–131, 133, 135–137, 139, 145–146, 148–150, 152–154, 157–158, 166–167
Mississippi units: 3rd Infantry 31; 21st Infantry 78; 35th Infantry 84; 36th Infantry 53, 70; 37th Infantry 54, 70; Falkner's 1st Rangers 68–69
Missouri Home Guard 22
Missouri Presidential Election 1860 17–18
Missouri State Guard 19, 21–25, 27–28, 30, 33
Missouri units: 1st Artillery 54, 68, 78; 3rd Infantry 79; 11th Infantry 46, 48, 51–52, 54, 56–57, 63, 66–68, 70–73, 79, 81, 83–88, 90; 15th Infantry 186–187, 200; 21st Infantry 78; 26th Infantry 70, 73; Faris's Artillery 70; Hescock's 53; Light Backof's 28
Mitchell, Robert 22, 105, 130, 132–136, 139, 144–146, 149–*150*, 151, 156, 158–163, 165–167, 245
Moore, Absalom 100
Moore, David 112
Moore, Jesse 169–170, 200
Moore, John 78, 84
Morgan, James D. 105
Morgan, John Hunt 93–103, *100*, 124, 217; Christmas raid 101
Mosman, Chesley 173, 185, 187, 197
Mower, Joseph 39, *52*, 54, 56, 63, 67–68, 70–71, 73, 79, 81, 83, 87, 91
Murphy, Robert 48, 63, 66–67, 74
Murray, Eli 103, 115–116, 121

Negley, James 97, 104, 157, 162
Nelson, William 50, 61
New Hope Church, Battle of 180–181
New Madrid, siege 38–41
Newell, Nathaniel 103, 109, 128, 133, 149

Newton, John 172–174, 178, 181, 183–187, 189, 191, 193, 195–196
Norris, G.N. 228, 230
Northern Pacific Railroad 223–224, 227–229, 233
Noyes, Edward F. 40, 56

Ohio units: 1st Artillery 103, 109, 116–117, 133, 149, 183, 201; 1st Cavalry 99, 103, 107, 112, 114–116, 120, 133, 143, 149; 2nd Infantry 10; 3rd Cavalry 94, 103–104, 107, 112, 114–116, 120, 122, 126, 128, 131–133, 149; 3rd Infantry 9; 4th Cavalry 94, 97, 103, 107, 114–115, 120, 128, 131, 133, 148–149; 6th Artillery 201, 207, 212; 10th Cavalry 133, 149; 10th Infantry 111; 11th Artillery 70; 13th Infantry 201; 15th Infantry 201, 220; 18th Artillery 136; 19th Infantry 201; 20th Artillery 201; 24th Infantry 170; 26th Infantry 200; 27th Infantry 33, 40, 48, 50, 63, 68, 81, 84, 86, 90, 92; 39th Infantry 33, 40, 44, 48, 56, 59, 68, 81, 84; 40th Infantry 128, 170, 182, 184, 200; 41st Infantry 200, 232; 43rd Infantry 33, 38, 40, 42, 48, 60, 68, 81, 84–85, 88; 45th Infantry 200; 49th Infantry 201; 51st Infantry 170, 200; 63rd Infantry 33, 40, 48, 50, 68, 81, 84–86, 92; 64th Infantry 200; 65th Infantry 200, 221; 71st Infantry 201; 90th Infantry 170, 200, 220; 93rd Infantry 201; 97th Infantry 200; 99th Infantry 170, 182, 184; 101st Infantry 101, 176, 182, 200; 124th Infantry 201; 125th Infantry 200
"Old Abe" eagle 48, 80
Oliver, John 77–78
Opdycke, Emerson 186, *194*, 200, 202–203, 207, 209–210, 212–*213*, 214–216, 231–233
Ord, Edward 67–72, 74, 88
Otis, Elmer 96, 103, 113, 121–122, 130

Paine, Eleazer Arthur 34, 41–43, 47, 49, 53–54, 58–59
Palmer, John 33, 37, *43*, 48, 52–55, 60, 104, 109, 116, 126–127, 135, 145, 188, 192
Panabaker, William E. 48
Paramore, J.W. 115, 126
Patton, George IV 249
Pea Ridge, Battle of 16, 46, 64, 75
Pegram, John *101*–102, 157
Pennsylvania units: 7th Cavalry 103, 109, 111, 116–119, 121–122, 133, 136–137, 144, 149; 9th Cavalry 133, 137, 148; 15th Cavalry

98–99, 103, 104, 110, 118, 120, 125–126, 128, 131, 145, 158; mutiny 104–106 (*see also* Anderson Cavalry); 77th Infantry 170, 200, 220; Independent Artillery Battery 183; Pennsylvania Light Artillery 201
Phifer, C.W. 79, 84
Pickett's Mill, Battle of 180–181, 234
Pillow, Gideon 30–31, 36, 45
Pine Mountain, advance on 180–181, 197, 244
Pleasanton, Alfred 12
Plummer, Joseph 34, 41–43, 48, 51, 54, 58; death 63
Polk, Leonidas 36; death 181
Pope, John 12, 33, **34**–52, 54–61
Potter, Henry Albert 127, 129, 132
Preston, Newton 88
Price, Sterling 18–19, 21, 24, 27–28, 30–32, 48, 52, *64*, 198; at Corinth 75–76, 81, 83–84, 87–88; at Iuka 63–73
Prickitt, Daniel 126, 132
Prime, Frederick 76
Prince, W.E. 17
property rights 240–241
Pulaski 197–198; defense of 199

Rains, James 24–27
Reiff, Americus 24
Resaca 172–173, 181, 187, 197, 205; Battle of 174–178, 243–244
Reynolds, J.J. 124, 138
Riggs, T.L. 225
Roberson, Richard Word 249
Rocky Face Ridge and Buzzard's Roost 173–174, 197
Rogers, William 86–87
Rome raid 152–154
Rosecrans, William S. 2, 5, 62, 64–67, 75, **80**, 87–90, 92, 94–100, 102–105, 111, 120–122, 124, 127, 129–134, 142–143, 159–160, 162–168, 245–245; advance on Chattanooga 145–146, 148–158; assumes command of the Army of the Cumberland 93; assumes command of the Army of the Mississippi 59; Battle of Corinth 78–83; Battle of Iuka 68–74; Battle of Stones River 115–117, 119; evaluation of cavalry at Chickamauga 168; siege of Corinth 58–60; Tullahoma Campaign 134–141
Rosecrans Line 64, 76
Rosengarten, Adolph 103, 110, 121
Ross, Frederick 217
Ross, Lawrence 207
Rosser, Thomas 224–225, 227, 229–230
Rousseau, Lovell 104, 107, 196
Royse, Isaac 220

Ruff, Charles 11
Ruff's Mill, Battle of 184
Ruggles, Daniel 52–53, 55
Rumbough, David Jacob 249
Rumbough, David Sheridan 249
Rumbough, Sarah Huntington 249
Rumbough, Stanley Maddox 249

Sanborn, John 68–70
Schofield, John 172–173, 179, **186**, 188–189, 191–193, 196–199, 201–203, 205–206, 208–216, 231–232
Scott, Joseph 90
Scott, Thomas 42, 47, 50, 55
Scott, William 114
Scott, Winfield 33
Shelbyville, engagement 133–138
Sheridan, Philip 10, 131–132, 153, 169, 221, 223–225, 227, 232–234
Sherman, Thomas 59
Sherman, William T. 3, 64, 104, 132, 171–174, 178, 180–**188**, 192–196, 198, 215, 221, 233, 235
Shiloh, Battle of 46, 74, 93, 233–234, 236
Sigel, Franz 19, 27–29
Simonson, Peter 170, 173–177, 181, 183
Sioux 12–13, 222–223, 225–227, 239
slaves 2, 15–16, 45, 63, 142–143
Slocum, Henry 10, 188
Smith, A.J. 198, 208
Smith, G.W. 10
Smith, J.L. Kirby 33, 38, 60, 84, 88
Smith, Kirby 65
Smith, Oskaloosa 222, **240**
Solaski, George 21–23
Solomon Fork 13
South Carolina units: 10th Infantry 110; 19th Infantry 110
Spoor, N.T. 48–49, 51, 53, 57; *see also* Iowa units, 2nd Artillery
Spotted Eagle **225**
Sprague, John 48, 85–86
Spring Hill, Battle of 201–208
Stanley, Alice May 222
Stanley, Anna Huntington 171, **247**
Stanley, Anna Maria Wright 10–12, 14–15, 29, 132, 172, 217, **219**, 222, 224–225, 236, 239; death 242
Stanley, Blanche Huntington 224, **240**, 242, 247, 249
Stanley, David Sheridan 227, **240**, 249
Stanley, David Sloan: allegations 89–90; appraisal of Nathaniel Lyon 28; Bridge Creek engagement 57–58; charge at Dug Springs 24–27; charge at Stones River 116–118; command of IV Corps 185; conflict with Custer

229–230; Corinth, Battle of *83*, 78–90; Corinth siege *45*–61; discipline 12–13; early Life 8–10; Emory's expedition 16–17; family legacy 246–250; farewell to cavalry 160–161; Franklin, Battle of 208–216; grandparents 9; illness 11–12, *154*–160; Independence skirmish 17; Jonesboro 188–195; letter to Rosecrans 164; marriage 14; Medal of Honor 3, 215, 231–232, 241; medical education 8–9; message to division Army of the Mississippi 92–93; military career summary 243–244; Pott's fracture 33; promotion to brigadier general *32*–33, 236; recruiting service 231; religion 8, 12; religious conversion 62; retirement 241–242; Rome raid 152–154; slaves 15; Solomon's Fork 13–*14*; Spring Hill 201–208; U.S. Military Academy address 237–240; U.S. Military Academy education 10–12; wounded at Franklin 216
Stanley, David Sloane, Jr. 249
Stanley, Florence Elizabeth 15
Stanley, James Bartholomew 8
Stanley, Jane 249
Stanley, John Bratton 8
Stanley, John Calvin 8
Stanley, Jonathan 8
Stanley, Josephine Huntington 15, 222, 224, *240*, 247
Stanley, Mary Ann 8
Stanley, Samuel 249
Stanley, Sarah Peterson 8
Stanley, William Clinton 8
Stanton, Edwin 42, 46, 96, 98, 124, 129, 149, 163
Steedman, James 128, 196, 217
Steele, Frederick *24*–25
Stevenson, Carter 175–176
Stewart, Alexander P. 36, 175
Stewart, William 46, 66, 72
Stewart's Creek 109, 111, 116
Stones River, Battle of 111–119
Streight, Abel 129–130, 141, 166, 200, 202
Stuart, J.E.B. 13
Sturgis, Samuel 12, 16, 19, *21*, 29, 32, 236
Sullivan, Jeremiah 70
Sumner, E.V. 13–15
Swayne, Wager 84–85
Sweeny, Thomas *22*–24, 175

Tennessee units: 1st (1st East Tennessee) Cavalry 118, 121, 133, 135, 148; 2nd Cavalry 113; 2nd (2nd East Tennessee) Cavalry 103–104, 107, 114–115, 119–121, 128, 133, 148; 3rd Cavalry 120; 4th Infantry 107; 5th Cavalry 152; 5th (1st Middle Tennessee) Cavalry 117, 103–104, 111, 119, 121, 128, 133, 136, 145–146, 149; 24th Infantry 58; 38th Infantry 54; Davis' Tennessee Battalion 107; Hoxton's Battery 54; White's Battery 112
Texas units: 2nd Infantry 54, 84, 86; 6th Cavalry 84; 8th Cavalry 112; 9th Cavalry 84
Thomas, George 46–47, 93, 97–98, 101, 104, 106–107, 119, 132, 134–135, 139–140, 145, 151, 157–163, 171–172, 174, 182–183, 185–188, 191–192, 194–199, 201, 206, 208, 212–215, 220, 232
Thompson, M. Jeff 30–31, 38
Thrall, W.R. 50
Thrush, William A . 79
Tidball, John 12
Townsend, E.D. 16
Trapier, James H. 52
Trecy (Tracy), Jeremiah 62, 74, 164, 216
Trudeau, James 36
Tullahoma, advance on and capture 134–140
Tunnel Hill 172–173
Turchin, John 130–134, 139–140, 144, 167
Tyler, Daniel 49–50, 57

United States Military Academy (West Point) 1, 5, 7, 9–10, 16, 29, 33–34, 50, 62, 84, 192–194, 247, 249, 250; address 237–239
United States units: 1st Cavalry 7, 11–13, 15–16, 21–23, 28, 44, 105; 1st Infantry 39, 67; 2nd Artillery 48, 68; 2nd Cavalry 75; 2nd Dragoons 11–13; 3rd Artillery 249; 3rd Cavalry 239; 4th Artillery 13; 4th Cavalry 54, 74, 96, 103, 113–114, 121–122, 128, 131, 136, 164; 6th Infantry 13, 228; 7th Cavalry 228; 7th Infantry 11; 8th Cavalry 238; 8th Infantry 12, 17, 228, 238; 9th Infantry 228; 10th Cavalry 249; 17th Infantry 224, 227–228; 22nd Infantry 221–224, 227–228, 236; 26th Cavalry 249

Van Cleve, Horatio 95, 104, 145–146, 148–149
Van Deusen, John 21
Van Dorn, Earl 15, 47, 52, 55–56, 63–65, 67–68, 71–72, 75, *76*–81, 87–89, 128–129
Villepigue, John Bordenave 77
Vincent, Thomas MacCurdy 250

Wagner, George 126, 191, 200, *202*–203, 205, 207, 209–216, 231
Walke, Henry 43
Ward, Frank 110, 121
Waters, Lewis H. 170, 220
Watkins, Jennie 217
Watkins, Louis 133, 142, 148, 157–158
Weber, Andrew 67, 70, 81, 84
Wessels, Henry 239
West, William Whitehead 249
Wharton, John *102*, 107, 111–112, 114, 116, 118–119, 136, 154–155
Wheeler, Joseph 2, 93, 97, 99–*100*, 102, 104, 108–109, 111, 117–122, 136–138, 150–151, 153, 155, 157, 166
Whipple's Topographical Expedition 11–12
Whistler, Joseph N.G. 224
Whitaker, Walter 172, 175–176, 179, 182, 184, 200, 202
Wilder, John 124–125, 127, 138–141, 145, 148, 152, 154, 166
Williams, Alpheus 177–178
Willich, August 110, 112, 169
Wills, Charles 197
Wilson, James H. 202, 245
Wilson's Creek, Battle of 27–31, 63, 130, 243
Wisconsin units: 1st Cavalry 133, 148; 5th Artillery 116; 8th Infantry 48, 51–54, 57, 63, 68, 70, 74, 78–81, 89, 91; 16th Infantry 78; 24th Infantry 200
Wood, Samuel 22, 27
Wood, Thomas J. 60, 95–96, 104, 126, 145, 162, 172–174, 179–180, 182, 185–186, 191, *194*–195, 200, 202–203, 205–209, 213–216, 220, 231, 233–234
Wood, T.K. 32
Worthington, William 38
Wright, Anna Maria *see* Stanley, Anna Maria
Wright, Eliza 12
Wright, John Jefferson Burr 10, *11*, 14
Wynkoop, John 103, 116, 121

Yellowstone Expeditions 224–231

Zahm, Lewis 94–96, 102–104, 106–108, 110–117, 119–122, 130